D1726391

Stravinsky, God, and Time

Consciousness, Literature and the Arts

VOLUME 59

The titles published in this series are listed at *brlll.com/cla*

Stravinsky, God, and Time

By

Helen Sills

BRILL

LEIDEN | BOSTON

Cover illustration: Lisa Gifford – www.lisagifforddesign.com

Library of Congress Cataloging-in-Publication Data

Names: Sills, Helen, author.
Title: Stravinsky, God, and time / by Helen Sills.
Description: Leiden ; Boston : Brill, 2022. | Series: Consciousness,
    literature and the arts, 1573-2193 ; volume 59 | Includes bibliographical
    references and index.
Identifiers: LCCN 2022022265 (print) | LCCN 2022022266 (ebook) |
    ISBN 9789004518247 (hardback) | ISBN 9789004518537 (ebook)
Subjects: LCSH: Stravinsky, Igor, 1882-1971–Criticism and interpretation. |
    Stravinsky, Igor, 1882-1971–Religion. | Music–20th century–History and
    criticism. | Sacred music–20th century–History and criticism. | Time in music.
Classification: LCC ML410.S932 S56 2022 (print) | LCC ML410.S932 (ebook) |
    DDC 780.92–dc23/eng/20220510
LC record available at https://lccn.loc.gov/2022022265
LC ebook record available at https://lccn.loc.gov/2022022266

Typeface for the Latin, Greek, and Cyrillic scripts: "Brill". See and download: brill.com/brill-typeface.

ISSN 1573-2193
ISBN 978-90-04-51824-7 (hardback)
ISBN 978-90-04-51853-7 (e-book)

Printed by Printforce, the Netherlands

For Peter

Contents

Acknowledgements

Over the many years that this book has been taking shape I have been fortunate to enjoy the interest and expertise of many close friends and colleagues. Their support has been invaluable as I have explored a different perspective on the music of Stravinsky. In the early days, Natalia Dissanayake undertook to translate Arthur Lourié's substantial article on the music of Stravinsky in *Versty,* and shared many valuable insights into Russian life and language that arose in connection with Russian spirituality. Keiko Miyakita was immensely conscientious in translating the finely-nuanced Japanese poems of Stravinsky's *Three Japanese Lyrics,* and similarly provided much Japanese background. I was also fortunate to find Mary Worthington, who translated the chapter contents of Nesmelov's *The Science of Man*, and Professor Raymond Chapman, who provided valuable information about the poems that Stravinsky set in *Cantata.* I stand in admiration of the dedication to detailed and painstaking research that has characterised all these friends on my behalf.

As I delved deeper into the question of time in music, particularly in Stravinsky's music, I chanced upon an article in *The Times' Higher Education Supplement* about Julius T. Fraser, the charismatic founder of The International Society for the Study of Time. I was subsequently accepted as a member of the Society in 1995. The scope and understanding of Julius' knowledge as a polymath was inspirational, but he also had the gift of relating to every time-smith in the Society as a companion on a shared journey. I have benefited enormously from his personal affirmation, and feel honoured to have known Julius and his wife Jane as friends. I also wish to thank many other members of the Society for their unwavering support and advice over the years, particularly Dr Claudia Clausius, Dr Steven Ostovich and Dr Carol Fischer.

In the final stages of shaping this book I have owed an enormous debt of gratitude to Dr Katharina Clausius and Paul Trepte for reading the draft text and making a wealth of constructive suggestions for improving it on many levels. My grateful thanks also go to my long-standing friends Dr Diana Bickley and Jonathan Burton for their scrupulously thorough reading of many of the chapters, and their immensely helpful comments in improving their style and consistency. I have been fortunate to find Christine Gwyther-Scott and benefit from her expertise and patience in reproducing all the musical examples. Finally, I couldn't have completed my task without the support of my husband Peter, to whom I dedicate this book. He has been a perpetual source of encouragement, my chief theological adviser, and a tower of strength in times of technological challenge.

Helen Sills

Tables and Illustrations

Tables

Illustrations

Notes on Previously Published Material

Zvezdoliki (*Le Roi des Etoiles*), *Chant Dissident,* and *Les Noces,* are published by Chester Music, and the musical extracts are reprinted by permission of Hal Leonard Europe Ltd.

All the other scores of Stravinsky's music referred to are published by Boosey and Hawkes, and reproduced by permission of Boosey and Hawkes Music Publishers Ltd.

Musical examples from 'Bell' by Percival Price: *The New Grove Dictionary of Music and Musicians*, published by Oxford Publishing Limited, are reproduced with permission of the Licensor through PLSclear.

Examples of znamenny chant from 'Le Chant Eccléstiastique Russe' by Jacques Handschin: *Acta Musicologica* XXIV, 1952: 3, 16 are reproduced by permission of Bärenreiter-Verlag Karl Votterie CmbH & Co. KG.

The original versions of *Petrushka* (1911) and *Symphonies of Wind Instruments* (1920) are held in the Boosey & Hawkes archive.

Earlier versions of material presented in Chapters 3, 4 and 5 were published in 'Stravinsky and Time' in *A Laboratory of Spring*, eds. Witold Wachowski, Przemyslaw Nowakowski, Monika Wludzik. Avant: The Journal of the Philosophical-Interdisciplinary Vanguard/Trends in Interdisciplinary Studies, Special Issue, IV/3, 2013: Centre for Philosophical Research, Warsaw. 173–203.

An earlier version of material presented in Chapter 4 was published in 'Emergent Temporalities in Stravinsky's *Le Sacre du Printemps*' in *Kronoscope* 12/2, eds. Remy Lestienne & Yves Abrioux. Brill Publishing, 2012. 257–269

An earlier version of material presented in Chapter 5 was published in 'Time, Trace and Movement in Stravinsky's *Three Japanese Lyrics*' in *Time and Trace: Multidisciplinary Investigations of Temporality*, The Study of Time vol. 15, eds. Sabine Gross & Steve Ostovich. Brill Publishing, 2016. 61–82.

Prologue

Readers of the primary sources of information about Stravinsky – his letters, articles, autobiography, lectures on the poetics of music, conversations with Robert Craft and the posthumous collection of pictures and documents of his life[1] – will be familiar with the many ways in which Stravinsky expressed his deep Christian faith in relation to his music and his many other interests. Like his contemporary Schoenberg, Stravinsky worked with a very real sense of the close relation between the spiritual dimension of his life and his creativity. Unlike Schoenberg, Stravinsky's spirituality was linked with the question of time, the ontological time of being and becoming, and music's function as a purely temporal art. He believed that music's sole aim was to establish an order in things and co-ordinate the listener with time.[2] Yet exploration of the spiritual and temporal aspects of Stravinsky's life and works is still rare in the Stravinsky literature; their connections with his music, which I believe to be vitally important to an appreciation of its unity, have been sadly neglected in favour of theoretical analysis.[3] This study contributes a new perspective on Stravinsky's legacy and challenges the current view of his music as composed of 'discontinuities'.

Stravinsky spoke often, and openly, of the things that were of supreme importance to him; his recorded remarks express a deep Christian faith, and a concern for music as a temporal art, that was corroborated unreservedly by his son Theodore.[4] Details of the dates of his sketches, commissions and performances are readily available elsewhere, but this study looks more deeply into Stravinsky's expressions of faith as recorded in the primary sources and takes them seriously, so that another aspect of his strong musical personality emerges.

Crucially, this study pursues a new direction in Stravinsky studies by relating his spirituality to his music from a Christian understanding. My analyses of his spiritual works are based on Stravinsky's wish to restore time in music

---

1   Stravinsky, Vera & Craft, Robert, 1979. With respect to the *Conversation* books Robert Craft confirms that Stravinsky did write them, and that 'most of the language, with its more foreign than English vocabulary, was his'. Robert Craft states that his contribution lay in their 'presentation'. Op. cit., 439.
2   Stravinsky, Igor. 1975, 54.
3   Stephen Walsh writes of the connection between Stravinsky and Jacques Maritain, but from the perspective of aesthetics: see Walsh, Stephen. 2002, especially 431–4.
4   Stravinsky, Theodore. 1953.

as expressed in his *Autobiography, Poetics of Music,* and in the rich body of information collected by Robert Craft. It also takes into account the important influence of less well-known writings by the Church Fathers, Bishops Nicholas of Cusa and Jacques-Bénigne Bossuet, and the philosopher Victor Ivanovitch Nesmelov, that Stravinsky read throughout his life. These writings hardly feature in contemporary accounts of Stravinsky's sources of inspiration. The picture of Stravinsky's creative development that emerges from his wide range of reading, for example, has a consistently spiritual-temporal theme and differs widely from that with which we are currently familiar. His religious nature is constantly affirmed by the testimony of those who knew or understood him intimately: the writer and patron of the arts, Pierre Souvtchinsky, Stravinsky's musical assistants Arthur Lourié and Robert Craft, and the philosophers Jacques Maritain and Gisèle Brelet. Above all, his faith and musical mission is revealed in the subjects and constructive methods of the works themselves.

Spirituality, in today's parlance, has come to mean different things to different people. In this study, the term spirituality is used in its widest sense:

> Our spirituality is the core of our being; it is what shapes the whole of our life, our whole way of being in the world. Spirituality is not just a religious thing confined to 'spiritual' people. To be human is to have a spirit, the animating, life-giving part of our being connecting our beliefs and our behaviour, our character and our motivations. Our spirituality is the way our spirit expresses itself.[5]

This study proposes that the way in which Stravinsky's spirituality expresses itself, and the innovative means by which he embodies time in music, have great relevance and value for the listening public generally, not just for those who have a religious faith or an interest in religious matters.

It is evident from the primary sources that Stravinsky had a remarkable memory for the sights and sounds of the Russia that he knew in his early years, and that his rootedness in Russian Orthodox culture was an important part of his spirituality. This study therefore begins by taking a brief look at some of the spiritual influences that began to emerge in his compositional 'voice' immediately after the death of his teacher, Rimsky-Korsakov, in 1908. Firstly, asymmetrical musical 'patterning' in the native forms of Russian folk song and liturgical chant was directed towards the creation of different qualities of time. The term 'patterning' in this context describes the constant variation of a small

---

5   Sills, Peter. 2020, 8.

group of largely step-wise pitches which characterised these native forms, and the expansion and contraction of these variations in asymmetric phrases. In folk singing, musical patterning and the all-important matter of tempo was an expression of the spirit that varied according to the location and context; in the liturgy, the patterning of the chant reflected a spiritual response to the text, and shaped the temporal form of the psalm by its variable densities. The time qualities created in folk song and church chant were enriched by a play upon resonant sonorities; Stravinsky absorbed their techniques of matching musical contours to haunting vowel sounds, and of using the minor seventh above the tonic found in the harmonic series, the natural order of sound, for its open, spatial quality.

Secondly, these native forms and the rites of passage of everyday life were ordered by the spiritual quality of *apatheia*, an ancient concept of the Russian Orthodox faith that comes from the teachings of the Church Fathers. *Apatheia* is the right ordering of the emotions in order to perceive the essence of things, their inner being and becoming, and the objective beauty of ontological time. Ontological time is the time world unique to each being or created thing, its own *umwelt*.

My analyses of Stravinsky's spiritual works are based on the following qualities of time:

Ontological time: the continuous, indivisible time world (*umwelt*) of being becoming that is unique to every created thing from the cosmos to a beetle. A memorable example of ontological time may be found in the bride's song that opens *Les Noces*: it does not express emotions but plays with the natural structure of sound, to reach beyond emotion to an underlying reality. Ontological time is objective and uniquely embodied in music through tempo, rhythm, and rates of rhythmic and harmonic change that are authentic to the expression of being.

Lived time (la durée réelle): the ontological time world of one's own being and becoming as an indivisible, continuous experience.

Psychological time: the sense of time passing quickly or slowly, influenced by personal emotions, events, memories, etc.

Musical time: the sense of time created by the materials and formal organisation of music according to the composer's intention.

Gestural time: the rhythmic manners of being becoming that may be simultaneously 'lived through' by the listener, as in ballet and mime.

Performance time (le temps d'espace): the measurable length of a piece of music in clock-time.

Stravinsky's keen perception of being, and its becoming in time and space in terms of rhythmic movement, was nurtured in his early years by his frequent attendance at the Mariinsky Theatre in St Petersburg, where he could enter the worlds of the operatic characters and identify with the movements of the ballet dancers. Besides absorbing this rich culture, Stravinsky read much spiritual literature, and enjoyed the company of friends who were engaged in the contemporary renaissance of Russian culture, particularly its folk song, rituals and liturgical chant. These musical forms were expressions of the Russian spirit in sound and time, specific terms that Stravinsky later used in describing the speculative action of music in his *Poetics of Music*.[6] In this study themes arising from the expression of the Russian spirit in sound and time are explored as a vital part of Stravinsky's 'Russian-ness'.

With Stravinsky's arrival in Paris and rapid rise to fame through the presentations of the Ballets Russes from 1910, the colourful features of Russian life and its native music suddenly became part of the contemporary explosion of interest in time as a relative, multi-level concept. This study briefly recalls some examples of these wider scientific, artistic, and spiritual enquiries in order to show the topical nature of Stravinsky's innovative time-creating techniques, and the timeliness of his appearance in Western culture. Stravinsky had many interests, particularly those that had a bearing upon musical construction; uncovering the contribution of these sources of inspiration to his music has involved delving into a wide range of subjects from ancient Japanese poetry to the mathematics of Poincaré. The different constructive methods of these areas inspired Stravinsky to find musical analogies and they provide a broad, interdisciplinary body of evidence that testifies to the one over-riding concern of his creative life: that of unifying varied qualities of ontological time into an autonomous musical form to allow a glimpse of a reality beyond the physical. In pursuit of his aim, Stravinsky's extensive reading, from the philosophy of Victor Nesmelov to the depth psychology of Anton Ehrenzweig, points to his deep interest in the workings of human consciousness and the effects of music upon the listener. For this reason I include some reports on neuroscience research which make interesting connections with Stravinsky's musical patterning and contrasting layers of rhythm and timbre, and also promote the understanding of artistic creativity from a scientific point of view. Stravinsky's perception of being and becoming as rhythmic, the relation of the living patterns of being to the natural generation of patterns in the brain, and the appeal of his music to the processing preferences of each hemisphere at the higher brain frequencies, are all, I would suggest, important areas for future research.

---

6   Stravinsky, Igor. 1947, 27.

Stravinsky saw his spiritual-musical vocation as the construction of a unified temporal form with close relationships of pitch, rhythm and time qualities. His early style and innovative techniques advanced rapidly, running many steps ahead of his critics. For this reason, rather than select certain key topics and examples for discussion, I have chosen a simple chronological approach that focuses on the rapid development from one spiritual work to the next. These works have been selected for their spiritual subject, or for their new way of creating depth of time and timelessness, or for their new formal shape. This process has helped to show the progress of his methods and the various influences upon them more clearly, and, most importantly, to show the sources of their unity. Stravinsky's techniques developed rapidly from Act I of *Le Rossignol* (*1908*), in which time worlds are differentiated by tonality, timbre and musical style, to *Requiem Canticles* (*1966*), in which complex time-creating techniques evoke spiritual qualities with the greatest economy.

The spiritualities of Stravinsky, Schoenberg and Webern are compared, not only to affirm Stravinsky's continuing search for increasingly close relationships and temporal unity in his later works, but also to throw further light on Stravinsky's adoption of serialism and the incorporation of his music into the Western mainstream.

The figure numbers given throughout the text refer to the rehearsal figures in Stravinsky's published scores. I have adapted some of the musical examples taken from the printed scores, without altering their substance, in order to illustrate points made in the text more simply. But this study of Stravinsky's spiritual works does not aim to involve the reader in looking at the score references, so much as to guide the listener to 'hear through' recordings or performances to experience Stravinsky's patterning of ontological time. There is a haunting resonance in many of his spiritual works which strives to escape the human boundaries of time and space.

CHAPTER 1

The Stravinsky Legacy?

It is characteristic of great artists that appreciation of their radical insights and techniques continues to develop long after their lifetime, as the understanding of their historical context and aesthetic criteria become part of a recognised cultural development. The major works of Igor Stravinsky would appear to be a good example of this process, for fifty years or so after his death the precise nature of his legacy is still unclear. His works continue to be described in terms of fragmented and discontinuous segments and passages of stasis, yet Stravinsky himself spoke of his works as unified objects that are the products of rhythm and motion. Although his works are felt to have some quality of unity, it remains a unity that is elusive and indefinable.

Assessing Stravinsky's legacy over the years of the 20th century, Jonathan Cross remarks upon the growing sense of Stravinsky's far-reaching influence on the development of music, and lists the 'modernist' traits with which he worked, among others, as fragmentation, discontinuity, primitivism, eclecticism, pluralism and oppositions, orientalism, objectivity, static, ritualistic characteristics and repetition.[1] Despite detailed documentation of Stravinsky's life and views by Robert Craft, extensive examination of Stravinsky's Russian background by Richard Taruskin, exhaustive analysis of his rhythms and pitch collections by Allen Forte, Claudio Spies, Pieter van den Toorn and many other distinguished scholars, and the application of such analytical tools as Schenkerian analysis, serial techniques and set theory, there still seems to be no general consensus as to the source of unity in Stravinsky's major works. Analysis of his music ranges from Richard Taruskin's 'splinteredness' and stasis, and Jonathan Kramer's discontinuous moments, to Elliot Carter's view that Stravinsky's neo-classical music, especially, holds together 'in new and telling ways' and that Stravinsky achieves a 'unified fragmentation' from his eclectic musical materials.[2] It seems to be generally felt that Stravinsky focuses on 'the moment' as an independent event. I would contend that Stravinsky's music as it has come to be understood as a 'synthesising balance' between discontinuities,

---

1 Cross, Jonathan. 1998. 7–8, 9–10.
2 Op. cit., 8, 14.

© KONINKLIJKE BRILL NV, LEIDEN, 2022 | DOI:10.1163/9789004518537_003

though generating a plethora of modernist styles, is not what Stravinsky intended, and that it is time for this view of his music to be reconsidered.[3]

This study not only affirms the unity of each of Stravinsky's major works, but also the unity of his life's work, as arising from his understanding of time in music and his Christian spirituality. In the twenty-first century, the idea of time as existing 'somewhere' like the measurable dimensions of space, still persists, added to which, modes of time experience in music have become a source of confusion. In particular, the understanding of ontological time as a spiritual quality has declined as the culture of the West has become increasingly secular. For example, Roger Shattuck has observed that 'the time Stravinsky tells is not any time we ever lived until he composed it', but sees Stravinsky's 'simple distinction' between ontological time and psychological time as misleadingly implying 'some kind of universal time beating beneath all experience for all to touch, particularly music, which is clearly not the case'.[4] Jonathan Kramer lists ontological time as Stravinsky's term for 'absolute time', but defines this as 'objective time that is shared by most people in a given society and by physical processes', also defining absolute time as both 'real time', and 'normal time'.[5] Jonathan Cross defines ontological time as 'real or clock-time' and suggests that Stravinsky creates a new kind of 'musical time', a 'virtual time' (that he defines as Bergson's *durée réelle*) and also a non-directed 'timeless-ness'.[6] Cross describes the rhythmic innovations of *The Rite of Spring* as replacing development by recurrence and becoming by being, and Richard Taruskin sums up Stravinsky's legacy as 'a music not of process but of state, deriving its coherence and its momentum from the calculated interplay of "immobile" uniformities and abrupt discontinuities'.[7]

Stravinsky spoke of music as a form of speculation in terms of sound and time, carefully distinguishing between the different kinds of time that music may embody.[8] He emphasises that he engages with 'real time', by which he meant ontological time, the time of being. Being expresses itself in ontological time by the manner in which it becomes, and every being that develops into

---

3 Taruskin writes of *Le Sacre*: 'Its methods of construction and continuity-by-means-of-discontinuity were to become normal and normative to generations of younger musicians'. Taruskin, Richard. 1996. vol 1, 965.
4 Shattuck, Roger. 1963, 257.
5 Kramer, Jonathan. 1988, glossary, 452–4.
6 Cross, Jonathan. 1998, 82–3.
7 Op. cit., 85.
8 Stravinsky, Igor. 1947, 30–31.

a unified entity does so within its own *umwelt*, or temporal world.[9] Hence the range of temporal qualities that may be created in music is seemingly infinite, from a dynamic linear passage that promotes a keen sense of 'clock-time' to variable densities that create remote or elusive temporal qualities. Contrary to modern technological parlance, Stravinsky's 'real time' is that of being becoming in its own time, and he clearly distinguished it from clock-time, psychological time and the time of musical performance. Stravinsky unifies the time qualities of being and becoming into a temporal form, juxtaposing rhythmic layers horizontally and sections vertically to shape not only the pace of the structure's linear momentum but also its qualities of depth. In this way his juxtapositions are able to reflect the changing temporal qualities of a narrative, a ritual, or a spiritual experience, and create unified temporal forms that are truly innovative.

The analyses that follow are not concerned with patterns of tension and release, or the proportions of sections in minutes and seconds, but set out to show Stravinsky's embodiment of ontological time in music.[10] To have incorporated a full account of Stravinsky's harmonic movement, the changes of pitch collection that are already well-documented, would have made this book unwieldy. Stravinsky's harmonic vocabulary, though complex in itself, is indeed sometimes static and repetitive, but Stravinsky describes these passages of 'stasis' as 'a contradiction to development'.[11] Often constructed with layers of differing rhythmic complexity, they play an important part in changing the sense of time from momentum in clock-time to one of a greater temporal depth. These different qualities of time and movement not only create time in music but also vary the depth and density of its form.

Stravinsky's patterning of ontological time has its ultimate source in his personal spirituality and deep quality of 'Russian-ness'. The restoration of music as a temporal art was an important part of Stravinsky's early spiritual response to God, to whom he felt accountable for his musical gifts. Inheriting the musical

---

9   See Macquarrie, John. 1977, 358–9. Theologians hold that Being, as it becomes in Time, is both expressive and unitive. Being needs time in which to expand and express itself, just as a human being needs time to realise selfhood. But Being is not only expressive but unitive, just as a self is not a mere series of 'nows' but a stable unity that gathers up the flow of instants into a whole. John Macquarrie makes the important observation that *time is in Being*, rather than Being in time.

10   At the end of his life, Stravinsky remarked: 'But then the present has already begun to make me giddy – that discovery at Cambridge, for instance, showing that in certain insects the sense of time is encoded in two or three cells. (So, then, time is ontological?)'. Stravinsky, Igor & Craft, Robert. 1972, 112.

11   Stravinsky, Igor & Craft, Robert. 1979, 27–28.

tradition of Mussorgsky and Glinka who sought to recover the living intonations of folk music, his radical treatment of ontological time owed a great deal to the way in which the spirituality of the Russian people was expressed in the liturgical chant of the Russian Orthodox Church and in Russian folk song. He possessed a peculiarly Russian awareness of being that also strongly manifested itself in the philosophies of Berdyaev, Shestov and Rozanov, and in the novels of Dostoevsky, whom he much admired. He inherited a natural awareness of the temporal aspects of life that had been born of great hardship in Russia, and that had been nurtured through the centuries by the intensity of the Christian faith that had taken root there.[12]

The turn of the 20th century was a time of intense enquiry into the nature of time. Rapid advances in scientific research were matched by developments in philosophy and psychology that revealed time-consciousness as having qualitatively differing aspects. In particular, the publication of Henri Bergson's *Essai sur les données immédiates de la conscience* (Time and Free Will, 1889) had made an enormous impact. In this and following works, Bergson distinguished the measurable Newtonian time of scientific enquiry and social calendars (*temps espace*) from the personal, inner experience of a flowing, irreversible succession of phenomena that come together to give a sense of a continuous 'lived time', *temps vécu,* or *durée réelle.* He described the sense of 'lived time', that sense of pure consciousness uniting habit, volition and memory and the source of creative energy, as accessed, not by the analysing intellect, but solely through the integrating function of intuition.[13] He defined this sense of duration as qualitative, not quantitative, and as a unified, continuous process of change experienced as pure mobility. Experience affirms that both kinds of temporal experience defined by Bergson, Newtonian time and 'lived time', have their own functional domains and practical applications.

---

12   Byzantine liturgical influence began with the evangelising missions of SS Cyril and Methodius to the southern Slavs in the mid-ninth century. Russia's conversion to Christianity during the reign of Vladimir (980–1015 CE) was inspired by the worship held in the Basilica of St Sophia in Constantinople. Chroniclers report that Vladimir's emissaries returned saying that they did not know whether they were in heaven or earth, such was the beauty of the worship there. In the Oriental world, Sophia (Wisdom) was an intermediary between the divine and human worlds, and could designate Christ, the Holy Spirit, the Mother of God, or the Church.

13   Bergson, Henri. 1911. Bergson describes intuition as 'giving access to the living reality which the intellect has broken up and made static, and by the sympathetic communication which it establishes between us and the rest of the living ... introduces us into life's own domain, which is reciprocal interpenetration, endlessly continued creation'. *Creative Evolution,* 186–7 in Macquarrie, John. 1981, 170–1.

Bergson also speculated on the nature of time embodied in works of art, noting how these experiences, close to *durée réelle* in nature, differed from those of ordinary life.[14] Stravinsky and the philosopher Pierre Souvtchinsky extended these ideas to the question of time in music, distinguishing between music that reflects the composer's personal psychological flux, and music that evolves parallel to the process of ontological time, embracing and penetrating it. The ontological time of a musical form, like Bergson's sense of *durée réelle,* is also experienced as pure mobility, but it is only embody-able in art and accessible to the sense of intuition when empty of all personal psychological influences and all expressions of individuality and self-centredness. It is the state entered into by icon painters who clear their minds of all subjective influences. Stravinsky understood the restoration of music as a temporal art to require an ordering of musical elements analogous to that of Bergson's architectural motifs that 'oscillate in such a way as to absorb the spectator's attention and subsume it into a dynamic yet self-contained state outside the consciousness of one's own personality'.[15] The objective patterning of all the temporal aspects of musical units induces 'dynamic calm', in contrast to what Stravinsky saw as the vagaries of psychological time.

Stravinsky's search for the means of greater musical unity is supported by the similarity of his views to those of the philosopher Jacques Maritain, a pupil of Bergson.[16] As Maritain worked on the proposition that art may achieve a transcendent quality, Stravinsky, also 'moved by a spiritual impulse', sought unity as a musical analogy of 'the One that precedes the Many'.[17] He believed that 'harmonised varieties', as an ordering of the 'Many', would enable communion between people, and between people and the Supreme Being.[18] Stravinsky's temporal forms are a vital expression of his Christian faith, a relationship that is affirmed by their religious subjects and understanding of spiritual growth. His deep commitment to his faith is the constant source of energy that runs through his life's work; his renewal of music as a temporal

---

14   Stravinsky, Igor. 1947, 30–31. Pierre Souvtchinsky had been a friend of Stravinsky's younger brother Goury in St Petersburg before the Revolution. Souvtchinsky was a political activist, involved in the Eurasian movement, and a scholar of znamenny chant, publishing articles on it in *Melos*. He reconnected with Igor Stravinsky in Berlin in 1922 and enjoyed a close friendship with him in the 1930s. Stravinsky was of the opinion that Souvtchinsky, whose ideas on music and time were so similar to his own, was the only man capable of dealing with his archive after his death. Allen, Edwin in Pasler, (ed.). 1986, 329.

15   Bergson, Henri. 1889, 19.

16   See Chapter 11 for a comparison of their views.

17   Stravinsky, Igor. 1947, 32.

18   Op. cit., 140–142.

art from *Le Rossignol* to *Requiem Canticles* is a continuous response to a power beyond himself.

Stravinsky's current legacy has largely grown out of the influence that his early style was seen to have on his contemporaries. The 'shock factor' of *The Rite of Spring* with its clear-cut sections, abundance of ostinati and irregularly repeating rhythmic cells naturally made an enormous impact, but as Stravinsky had no pupils, and until his *Autobiography* in 1936 had published only short articles on *The Rite of Spring* and the *Octet,* it is possible that its innovative features were interpreted in terms of 'clock-time', and its events heard as discontinuous events in musical space. *The Rite* initiated modernist movements that explored the potential of polyrhythms, polytonality, and discontinuous blocks of material to liberate the spatial dimensions of music. This spatialisation continued Charles Ives' earlier experiments with simultaneous musics in *From the Steeples and the Mountains* (1901) and *Three Places in New England* (1914). The three instrumental groups of Ives' *The Unanswered Question* (1908) are even located separately to reinforce the effect of spatial distance created by the contrasting timbres of the strings, flutes and trumpet.

The consensus of scholarly opinion, as summed up by Paul Griffiths, sees two French composers, Edgard Varèse and Olivier Messiaen, as among the first inheritors of Stravinsky's rhythmic layers and 'disjunct' blocks. Edgard Varèse's *Intégrales, Amériques* and *Ionisation* explore the organisation of spatial relationships in sound, unfolding objective, geometric patterns that are Cubist in conception. Fascinated by experimental sonorities and discordant sounds, including those of everyday life produced by non-musical objects, Varèse's use of instrumental colour and contrasting dynamics delineated the interactions of sound masses and planes that penetrate or repulse each other, or do not blend. His crystalline forms split musical ideas into sound shapes that differed in direction and speed, and freely juxtaposed their different types of movement both horizontally and vertically. Stravinsky, who knew of Varèse as a pioneer in the 1920s, and also knew his *Déserts* in the 1950s, described him as 'a prophet of spatial music'.[19] The advent of electronic research centres and *'musique concrète'* in the early 1950s enabled Varèse to pursue his spatial organisation of sounds further with a mix of natural and electronic sounds. Stravinsky thought that some of the electronically realised sounds did seem to come from a distance and as though from the ends of spirals, presence and distance being apparent structural factors in the composition.

---

19   Stravinsky, Igor & Craft, Robert. 1982, 110–111.

Olivier Messiaen was also influenced by the presenting features of Stravinsky's early works: as an original and complex thinker, he explores tone colour, including the manipulation of overtones, polymodality (including archaic scales and plainsong-like melodies), polyrhythms, the practices of exotic cultures and a love of ritual, as well as Stravinsky's block structures. He extends Stravinsky's play of regular and irregular metres by devising additive, symmetrical and non-reversible rhythmic cells, superimposed in diminished and augmented forms to build a rhythmic language of his own based on both Western and Eastern sources.[20] He too, superimposes differentiated layers, but unlike Stravinsky's living variations of density, they are made up of disparate musical genres from around the world, highly systematised rhythmic permutations, *personnages rythmiques*, or bird song. Messiaen's approach to musical time differed from that of Stravinsky: at the macro-level of the unified work, he juxtaposes blocks of material and makes large-scale repetitions that negate the sense of narrative progress, and tend to expand the sense of time into infinity. Deeply religious like Stravinsky, Messiaen often turned to scripture and the liturgy of the Roman Catholic Church, expressing his mystical faith in works that seem to have no beginning or end but which, through their slow tempi and metrical freedom, invite the listener to lose all sense of time in deep contemplation. Works such as *L'Ascension* (1933) and the *Quartet for the End of Time* (1941) do not embody ontological time so much as portray a static absorption in the meaning of sacred images.

The second generation of composers after Stravinsky – strong musical innovators such as Stockhausen, Boulez and Cage – experimented with other ways of spatialising music, introducing the elements of chance and electronic sound, tapes, aleatory techniques, group compositions, improvisation, total serialism, percussion music, I-Ching and neo-dadaism. Those composers of the post-war years who did pick up the challenge of time in music largely experimented with the layering of simultaneous polyrhythms, creating ingenious rhythmic and durational techniques that were systematic in nature. Various measures of linear time were pitted against each other at different tempo markings and brought into relationship as individual segments of duration: Elliott Carter's *First String Quartet* (1951) superimposes four themes that have their own rhythmic, intervallic and metric identity, and correlates overlapping pulses in its outer movements to give the impression of varying rates of flux and character. Stockhausen's *Gruppen* (1955–7) superimposes different tempos in spatially separated forces; Ligeti juxtaposes repeated, independent phrases of different

---

20   See Messiaen, Olivier. 1939, 1944.

length in his *Second String Quartet* (1968), while Carter's *Double Concerto for Piano and Harpsichord* (1961) superimposes metres in a complex structure that Stravinsky described as 'an effective example of an interlocking of tempos by a held-over beat pattern'. An acceleration for the piano is superimposed on a ritardando for the harpsichord and orchestra to clarify the final drama between these two spatially separated forces. Stravinsky, who in his 'long slow climb' up the 1950s had transformed serial techniques to embody greater dynamism and flexibility, described this work as 'a masterpiece'.[21] He also admired Boulez's *Le Marteau sans maître* (1954), though he said that he did not always feel the sense of movement or location in time in Boulez's Structures or in 'those fascinating score-plans by Stockhausen, which often seemed to him like essence of the static'.[22] Stravinsky's rhythmic innovations, particularly those in *The Rite of Spring,* had elevated rhythm as the premier element, but his imitators, as he himself put it, 'imitated not so much my music as my person in my music'.[23] Rather than creating a dynamic passage through qualities of time, modernists of the mid-20th century tended to continue the manipulation of *temps espace* – the clock-time of past, present and future.

Stravinsky's non-retrogradable rhythmic cells that had their origin in the spontaneously irregular rhythms of Russian folk song lost their original spiritual expression as the patterning of ontological time, to become material for systematic rhythmic schemes, *per se*. Stravinsky's play of regular and irregular metres to articulate ontological time became simply a novel way of disrupting linear periodicity in clock-time. Stravinsky's irregular metres, often conflicted by accents, that pattern a single chord and emphasise forward momentum, are contrasted with combinations of ostinati that vary the depth of time quality and shape the temporal form. But in the absence of harmonic progression and rhythmic development, Stravinsky's ostinati and their juxtapositions are currently heard as areas of stasis in clock-time.

This spatialisation has led to rather vague descriptions of some contemporary music as articulating 'new kinds of musical time'. Amongst these new 'directions' in time, 'processive' and 'non-processive' musical time appear to refer to linear or non-linear qualities of movement, while 'vertical time' is created by simultaneous musical layers that lack phrasing, temporal articulations, and tonal consistency, and offer a single present stretched out into an

---

21 Stravinsky, Igor & Craft, Robert. 1982, 99–101. But Stravinsky added that 'analysis as little explains a masterpiece or calls it into being as an ontological proof explains or causes the existence of God'. Ibid, 101.

22 Op. cit., 127.

23 Stravinsky, Igor & Craft, Robert. 1981, *Memories & Commentaries,* 123.

enormous duration, a potentially infinite 'now'.[24] By contrast, some imitators of Stravinsky's layering of materials have created complex polyrhythmic constructions for analysis by the intellect, rather than a passage through qualities of time that builds a particular experience.

The distinction between spatially-conceived and temporally-conceived musical forms may be illustrated by the interesting 'rough' parallels that Jonathan Kramer draws between many imaginative modernist forms and the temporal levels of Julius T. Fraser's hierarchical theory of Time.[25] Fraser identifies six organisational levels of temporality in Nature, that make up a nested hierarchy. According to his theory, time has evolved along a scale of qualitative changes, such as an increase in the degree of freedom or unpredictability at each new level, and remains an open-ended process in which earlier temporalities are not replaced but subsumed by later ones. As each higher level of temporality arises from a lower level, some of the same processes and structures are retained amongst those of the new level. Each new level, bridged by short transitional phases which soon fall away, is characterised by level-specific processes and determines a qualitatively different temporality. As each new level of increased complexity brings new freedoms, a richer language is required to define it. Fraser proposes that just as space does not expand into a pre-existing space, time does not evolve within a pre-existing expanse of time, but rather, is created as an aspect of the increasing complexity that characterises evolution.[26]

The first three levels are not time-less, but now-less: there is no 'flow' of time in the physical world and now has no meaning. The first level, the world of electro-magnetic radiation, is a world of atemporality, of absolute chaos in which there is a total absence of causation. Kramer compares this to 'vertical time' in which all musical events are simultaneous and unchanging. The most primitive form of time appears in Fraser's second level, prototemporality, the time of atomic and nuclear particle-waves. Kramer draws a musical parallel with the probabilistic nature of moment form, in which there is no fundamental linearity between arbitrary self-contained events. Fraser's third

---

24   Kramer, Jonathan. 1988, 55.

25   The Hungarian natural scientist and polymath J.T. Fraser (1923–2010) has formulated a theory of time that suggests that time had its genesis at the birth of the universe and has been evolving through the expanding consciousness of sentient beings ever since. He founded The International Society for the Study of Time in 1966. His books include *The Genesis and Evolution of Time, Time, Conflict and Human Values,* and *Of Time, Passion and Knowledge,* and he was the founder editor of the Society's interdisciplinary journal *Kronoscope.*

26   Fraser, Julius T. 1999, 38.

level, eotemporality, is the time, 't', of physics, the astronomical time of galax-
ies and the oldest form of continuous time. It has no present moment, as the
physical world has only chance simultaneities, but its events are countable and
orderable, forming a pure succession without a preferred direction. Kramer
compares this to multiply-directed musical forms in which cause and effect are
indistinguishable and there is no significant temporal direction, describing it
as a multi-dimensional vector field.

In the next three temporal levels, 'now' begins to acquire meaning. The
fourth level, biotemporality, is the time world of living organisms, including
human biological functions, that distinguishes past, present and future, but
has limited temporal horizons and a species-specific organic present. The
connection between biotemporal events is driven by necessity, and is directed
toward short-term concrete goals that preserve the organism's life. Kramer
compares this to non-directed linearity in music, represented graphically by a
meandering line. The fifth level, nootemporality, is the temporal world of the
mature human mind in its waking state. It is characterised by open temporal boundaries and a mental present, a 'now', that has continuously changing
temporal boundaries and cognitive content. Events in the nootemporal world
are connected by long-term intentionality toward both concrete and symbolic
goals and an interest in the continued integrity of the self. Kramer compares
this to directed linearity in music.

Following the 'now' of the organic present and the mental present, Fraser's
sixth level is the 'now' of sociotemporality: the social present. He acknowl-
edges the difficulty here of distinguishing this level of temporality from that
of his fifth level, the noetic level, as it requires its own language of meanings
derived from collective experience; but he does define it in temporal terms, as
the social consensus necessary for the survival of a society, the ethical rules
guiding society in view of its history and future goals.[27] Kramer does not offer
a musical parallel, but Stravinsky, in seeking to restore music's temporal role
and establish communion between people and between humankind and the
'Supreme Being', strives to achieve his own vision of 'sociotemporality' that
is rooted in the Christian hope of bringing about the Kingdom of Heaven
on earth.

This very brief resumé of Kramer's comparisons between modernism's conception of temporalities and Fraser's evolutionary levels of time demonstrates
how far modernist composers have experimented with our familiar experience

---

27   Op. cit., 37–38. Fraser's hierarchical theory of time may be found in *Time, Conflict, and
      Human Values,* 26–43.

of time as linear, by introducing discontinuities, negating relationships or ordering events in diverse spatial directions, as occurred in earlier evolutionary levels of temporal organisation. But where modernism has experimented with linearity and non-linearity, Stravinsky has continued the direction of time's evolution by juxtaposing qualities of ontological time as layers and sections of differing degrees of regularity and irregularity. It has resulted in the contrast between linearity and depth at a new level of temporal organisation and complexity.

Stravinsky made a very clear distinction between music conceived in terms of musical spaces and music conceived in terms of time qualities, observing that 'A time series may very well postulate a new parable about time, but that is not the same thing as a time experience, which for me is a dynamic passage through time ...' Stravinsky rejected the spatial concept of a vector employed by the 'Zen generation', as 'a metaphor in no way analogous to a musical experience', emphasising that music is a temporal art.[28] Far from wishing to free music to be a vehicle of imaginative spatial designs, discontinuities or elements of chance, Stravinsky's temporal forms frequently recreate the qualities of time implicit in a religious ritual or spiritual journey. From *Symphony of Psalms* (1930) onwards, this spiritual journey is made explicit, and the predominant themes of his works become repentance, faith and self-sacrifice.

Stravinsky's true legacy is revealed in considering aspects of his personality, spirituality and musical inheritance as a whole. By the time the philosopher Gisèle Brelet wrote extensively on Stravinsky's importance in the 1940s, the view of Stravinsky's music as regressive in seeking to reconstruct and reanimate classical forms had begun to consolidate so that, since then, the influence of Stravinsky's spirituality upon his creativity has remained comparatively unexplored in the Stravinsky literature.

Stravinsky's skill at representing differing time worlds in music is first evident in *Le Rossignol* (1908), and rapidly gained momentum until its potential overwhelmed him in the writing of *The Rite of Spring* (1913). But in 1914 the French philosopher Jacques Maritain published *La Philosophie Bergsonienne*. A pupil of Henri Bergson, he offered a critique of his teacher's theories of being and becoming, free will, and the concept of a heterogeneous duration. In this and his following book, *Art et Scolastique*, published in 1920, Maritain set out his ideas on the unity of an art work, and on the artist as a craftsman, *homo faber*. Based on the scholastic teaching of St Thomas Aquinas, Maritain's

---

28   Stravinsky, Igor & Craft, Robert. 1982, 127. At that time, the 'Zen generation' described
        those who practised meditation in order to live 'in the moment' as a remedy for stress.

philosophy was concerned with the creation of a higher, spiritual level in art to enable access to a Divine reality. It is in *Art et Scolastique* that Maritain voiced his important insight about the dimension of time, an insight that was central to Stravinsky's creative purpose.[29] Published in Paris as Stravinsky was working there with the Ballets Russes, *La Philosophie Bersonienne* proved timely for Stravinsky's stylistic development: just as Maritain was working to moderate Bergson's philosophy by a greater input of the intellect, Stravinsky was moving towards a greater formal structuring of time qualities. Stravinsky embraced Maritain's philosophical ideas, and in 1924, announced that the formal unity of his works would now be based on making an 'object' that 'shines' with perfect relationships.

Although rebelling as a teenager against the Church as an institution, Stravinsky had been aware from early childhood that he had a personal relationship with God as the Author of his musical gifts. In 1939–40 he set out his spiritual beliefs in the closing words of his lectures on the poetics of music, revealing his vision of music as a means of communion and spiritual insight. In the last years of his life, in the works from *Cantata* (*1952*) to *Requiem Canticles* (*1966*), the relationships within his temporal forms were further strengthened by his adoption of serial techniques.

1 'Time' for a New Legacy?

How has the understanding of Stravinsky's works as fragmented and discontinuous been sustained for so long? Some answers may perhaps be found in the cultural circumstances of the first half of the 20th century. Stravinsky's success in constructing different qualities of time in music was initially very rapid, and, because he was endlessly curious about new ideas, he frequently changed his musical style. There is a striking contrast, for example, between the language of Stravinsky's article of 1913 on *The Rite of Spring* and his article on the *Octet* just ten or so years later. In *The Rite,* which he described as 'a vast abstraction', he wished to express the growth of power in nature renewing itself: the Prelude to *The Rite* embodies the great fear that weighs upon every sensitive spirit before the power of being, *'la chose en soi'*, that can grow and develop indefinitely.[30] By contrast, he announced that his *Octet* was a musical 'object',

---

29 See Chapter 7.
30 Stravinsky, Igor. 1913 in Lesure, Francois. 1980, 13–15. Stravinsky described *The Rite of Spring* as an 'act of faith'.

based on objective elements that constituted the impelling force of the composition and determined its form.

As I have suggested, the rhythmic innovations of *The Rite of Spring* were
largely interpreted by those he influenced as events in musical space rather
than in ontological time. As Stravinsky changed style, composers such as
Messiaen and Varèse, Stockhausen and Boulez continued to interpret and
develop Stravinsky's innovative use of rhythmic cells and block structures in
their own ways, initiating further modernist trends.

In the 1920s, as Stravinsky moved away from his early 'Russian' style to seek
new ways of creating temporalities in music, and as criticism of his work as
backward-looking grew, so did the influence of Schoenberg's 12-tone system.
Schoenberg's aim, which he furthered chiefly through his own compositions
and those of his pupils Alban Berg and Anton Webern, was to ensure the
dominance of the Austro-German musical tradition for the next one hundred
years. By the 1940s it may have been that the impact of Schoenberg's new 12-
tone system, which was more straightforward to analyse and apply, was simply too great for Stravinsky's exploration of time qualities in music to be fully
appreciated.

Not until Stravinsky's *Autobiography,* first published in 1936 when he had
become associated with the neo-classical style and was beginning to be seen
as the antithesis of Schoenberg, did Stravinsky speak of the principle guiding his work. He saw music as given to us with the sole purpose of establish-
ing an order in things and co-ordinating humankind and time. For this, the
indispensable and single requirement was construction.[31] This passage in his
Autobiography reassures us that, far from being composed of fragmented sections and frequent passages of stasis, his musical constructions are designed to
co-ordinate the listener with a coherent and unified temporal journey.

A few years later, support for Stravinsky's insights into sound and time
came from the Russian émigré philosopher, Pierre Souvtchinsky, who in 1939
published an article, *La Notion du Temps et la Musique.*[32] Souvtchinsky had
known Stravinsky through his brother Goury since he was a boy, and from
around 1925 Stravinsky and Souvtchinsky had been members of the same
Russian émigré community in Paris. Souvtchinsky's article also drew attention to the difference between ontological time and the flux characteristic of

---

31   Stravinsky, Igor. 1975, 54. Stravinsky's autobiography *Chroniques de ma Vie* was ghost-
        written in French by his trusted friend Walter Nouvel but there is no reason to doubt the
        validity of Stravinsky's opinion here.

32   Souvtchinsky, Pierre. 1939; *numéro consacré a Igor Stravinsky.* 312, (72). Stravinsky recom-
        mended this article to C. A. Cingria for publication.

a composer's personal, psychological time. In 1943 Gisèle Brelet was inspired by Souvtchinsky's article to write *Le temps musical* (1949), a book which Stravinsky recommended to Robert Craft as 'important' and which he kept in his personal collection.

Stravinsky elaborated on his particular understanding of music's temporal nature in the second of the six lectures given at Harvard University between 1939–40, later published as *Poetics of Music*. He states that he cannot better Pierre Souvtchinsky's definition of musical creation 'as an innate complex of intuitions and possibilities based primarily upon an exclusively musical experiencing of time – *chronos* – of which the musical work merely gives us the functional realisation'.[33] In this lecture, Stravinsky describes the distinction between ontological time and psychological time as 'of capital importance'. The 'real time' of which Stravinsky speaks is not the clock-time of current technological language, but ontological time that is discernible only in the absence of psychological time, the continuous, indivisible time from which all ego-driven subjective thoughts and feelings have been excluded. Fluid and infinitely variable, it is the time quality, for example, that is patterned by the articulations of plainsong to create 'other than clock-time' qualities. Hearing Stravinsky's music as discontinuous blocks in musical space or his sections as proportions in clock-time does not lead to the type of temporal journey that Stravinsky intended his listeners to experience.[34]

Stravinsky's aims regarding time in music were only revealed to the public in the late 1930s and 1940s when Europe was occupied with the mounting tensions and conflicts of the Second World War. At this time, when Stravinsky was also regarded as going against the spirit of the times, his expressed aim of co-ordinating man [*sic*] and time, and his spiritual insights about sound, time and construction, seem to have remained largely unexplored.[35] Stravinsky's sudden adoption of serialism in the early 1950s introduced a further distraction from the important matter of time in music, as the study of his works then became more focused upon the analysis of rhythm and pitch.

---

33   Stravinsky, I. 1947, 30.

34   See, for example, Kramer, Jonathan D. In Pasler, ed., 1986, 194.

35   The philosopher Gisèle Brelet being a notable exception. Poulenc also understood Stravinsky, writing to him from Paris on December 28th, 1945: 'At any rate be assured that I am one of those for whom you carry the light. You must have heard talk of the polemics surrounding your recent works. Allow me to say that I find it beautiful to be as misunderstood at age sixty as at age thirty'. Craft, Robert, ed. 1985, 212.

At a time when the neo-classical opera, *The Rake's Progress* (1948–51), tended to confirm that Stravinsky's style had run aground, the philosopher Theodor W. Adorno published his *Philosophy of Modern Music* (1949). Massively influential for many years after, the book was highly critical of Stravinsky. It articulated the fundamental antithesis that Adorno perceived between Schoenberg's style – of which he approved – as developmental and progressive and embodying a principle of 'identity in non-identity', and that of Stravinsky – of which he did not approve – as non-developmental and reactionary and as displaying an infantile pseudo-primitivism. In Adorno's view, Schoenberg's 12-tone method was at least dialectical, allowing a dynamic development of music in time, whereas he heard the 'near' repetitions of Stravinsky's music as robbing music of all subjective expression in favour of the collective, and presenting a negation of forward development and a static ideal. Adorno dismissed Stravinsky's neo-classicism and 'borrowing' of past styles as formally meaningless, saw his objective use of myth and ritual in Freudian terms as arising from fear, criticised his 'fetish' of rhythm as 'cut off from musical content', hearing 'only fluctuations of something always constant and totally static ... in which the irregularity of recurrence replaces the new'.[36] He experienced Stravinsky's works as the 'time-less products of a time-based art', but heard his 'endless repetitions' as bowing to the order of time only to suggest obsessively that time had stopped.[37] Apparently not appreciating Stravinsky's patterning of ontological time by momentum and depth, he added greatly to the contemporary misunderstanding of Stravinsky's innovative organisation of rhythm and movement.

The unity of Stravinsky's spiritual works owes a great deal to the spiritual ethos of the Russian Orthodox Church, a rich source that nourished Stravinsky throughout his life. Variation of pace and depth in the Russian Orthodox liturgy is designed to lift the worshipper out of 'clock-time' to experience ontological time and a foretaste of the 'new time' of heaven. This experience has a crucial bearing on an important distinction that is only just beginning to be made between music in time, where events are arranged spatially according to the emotions or imagination of the composer, and the contrary, time in music, in which ontological time is varied by the construction of the music itself.

The subjects of Stravinsky's 'spiritual' works embody the rhythmic manners and temporalities of fairy tales, folk festivals, classical myths, religious texts

---

36   Adorno,Theodor, W. 1973, 154–5.

37   Op. cit., 152–3.

and rituals. Stravinsky borrows rhythmic manners from many sources, not only the rhythmic articulations of Russian Church chant and folk music, but also the rhythmic techniques of poetry, the visual arts and mathematics.

Stravinsky's early fascination with mechanical instruments such as the player-piano, probably arose from his interest in reproducing the inexorable regularity, objectivity, and clarity with which they articulate musical patterns. Stravinsky's temporal constructions exclude opportunities for subjective interpretation, but the objective interplay of time qualities (for example, in *Symphonies of Wind Instruments* and *Symphony of Psalms*) achieves a beauty that many have found to have a spiritual quality.

Since the publication of Stravinsky's conversations with Robert Craft, there has been a renewed interest in a phenomenological approach to music, with books such as Thomas Clifton's *Music as Heard,* Jonathan Kramer's *Music in Time* and Christopher Hasty's *Metre as Rhythm,* and articles on the relativity of time in music as a function of information processing and memory.[38] There has also been a move towards a multi-disciplinary examination of artistic creativity, including a desire to bridge the worlds of art and science, and science and religion. These movements have been contemporary with the development of technology that is able to record brain activity with increasing clarity and definition. Recent advances in neuroscience have increased the understanding of how the brain constructs a sense of time and its infinite variety of qualities, and are thereby contributing to a re-assessment of Stravinsky's work.

The closing words of Poetics of *Music* that describe musical unity and the echo of its resonance that is caught by the soul, present a rare insight into the depth of Stravinsky's faith and musical purpose. Although he frequently referred to his faith in relation to composing, he discussed his deepest spiritual beliefs with only a few very close friends. Those who worked with Stravinsky and knew him well – Diaghilev, Arthur Lourié, Robert Craft – knew him to be a deeply religious man, yet the religious beliefs behind the aesthetic views that he expressed in articles and books, and most importantly gave rise to the works themselves, are seldom discussed.[39] The following analyses of Stravinsky's 'spiritual' works also look briefly at the theological and artistic issues that they

---

38   See, for example, Orlov, Henry F. 1979/65, 368; also Lochhead, Judy, & Stambaugh, Joan, in
      Smith, F. Joseph. 1989.

39   Robert Craft criticises Mikhail Druskin's book *Igor Stravinsky: His Life, Works, and Views*
      for its failure to transcend his Marxist orientation, 'surely a necessity in attempting to
      understand a composer for whom religious beliefs are at the core of both life and work'.
      Craft, Robert. 1992, 33.

raise, together with findings in neuroscience that shed light on aspects of his creative style. Contrary to his legacy as currently perceived, this preliminary study of the temporal aspects of Stravinsky's 'spiritual' works affirms that the construction of unified temporal forms was the principal and most profound aim of his creative life.

CHAPTER 2

Being and Time: A Nightingale Sings …

Stravinsky's rapid development as a composer arose largely from a unique and fortuitous blend of circumstances: not only was he born into a musical family with a personality in which the spiritual and the artistic were intrinsically bound together, but he was also born at a time that saw a renaissance of Russia's hitherto neglected artistic and spiritual inheritance. He was uniquely placed to redirect the development of music's style and substance away from what have been perceived as the Romantic excesses of the late 19th century.

1 Stravinsky's Spirituality …

In his conversations with Robert Craft, Stravinsky speaks openly of his faith in God and of the intrinsic connection between his spirituality and his creativity.[1] Aware since early childhood of a power greater than himself, by whom he believed he had been made 'the custodian of musical aptitudes',[2] he had always prayed to God for the strength to use his talents, seeing absolutely no reason to become puffed-up with pride over something that he had received.[3] His pledge to be worthy of his 'musical aptitudes' began a lifelong personal relationship with God that determined the spiritual subjects of many of his major works and their objective presentation. Like the great Christian contemplatives, Stravinsky's response was to 'wait' upon God for 'gifts', but he wrestled with every musical idea that he received, and worked on it exhaustively until it proved 'good', confessing that all he was able to do was to surrender himself to the experiment being conducted in and by him.[4] Although Stravinsky's relationship with his Creator was a deep and integral part of his personality,

---

1   Robert Craft, who described himself as 'not religious', transcribed or reported many of Stravinsky's revelations regarding his spiritual life, but the authenticity and consistency of their Christian themes and values testifies to their validity.
2   Op. cit., 125. Stravinsky recognised the same connection in the work of Krenek, observing that Krenek 'is profoundly religious, which goes nicely with the composer side'. Stravinsky, Igor & Craft, Robert. 1982, 103.
3   Stravinsky writing to his biographer, Domenico di Paoli, 1933. Stravinsky, Vera & Craft, Robert. 1979, 23. Conversely: 'Why do they blame me for my music?' Stravinsky would rage. 'Why don't they blame God? He gave me my gifts!' Op. cit., 633, n. 65.
4   Stravinsky, Vera & Craft, Robert. 1979, 196.

he described waiting for his God-given initial ideas as 'anguish'.[5] At the end of his life, he spoke of the lifelong sense of accountability to God that had sustained him.

As with many people of strong faith, Stravinsky perceived Creation as having intrinsic meaning. His need to compose went hand in hand with a gift for observation: he felt a compulsion to seek things out, 'like a pig snouting truffles', and the humblest thing around him could be of note.[6] In the working out of an accidental find, any obstacle would stimulate his creativity, and he found inspiration and pleasure in striving to realise its potential. Like the theologians of pure love in the Middle Ages he spoke of this in spiritual terms, as 'rising spirally' by the reciprocal action of love and understanding. He held the Christian view that meaning may be found in even the most commonplace things of life, a view in direct contrast to that of Buddhists and Stoics who regard the material world as a burden to be overcome, or to be transcended, by ascetic discipline.

This combination of spiritual and musical gifts heightened Stravinsky's awareness of being and becoming.[7] He was sensitive to the rhythmic movements that revealed the unique 'being' and essence of things. In this, Stravinsky seems to have inherited a strong dramatic sense from his father, an opera singer renowned for his portrayal of character.[8] Stravinsky asserted that he liked to perform, and felt that, just as his father was renowned for his dramatic talent as much as for his voice, so acting was an element in his own make-up.[9] Boris Asaf'yev remarked upon this quality in Stravinsky's music after hearing *The Soldier's Tale* and wrote: 'It is not the inner subjective experiences of people that fascinate him but the styles in which the people display themselves. Stravinsky's music embodies the motive forces of life and the rhythms that give life its organisation'.[10]

---

5   Horgan, Paul. 1972, 184.

6   Stravinsky, Igor. 1947, 54–55.

7   Stravinsky uses the terms 'rhythmic manners' and 'musical manners' in connection with the music of *Oedipus Rex* meaning the essence of the musical act: 'the manner of saying and the thing said are, for me, the same'. Stravinsky, Igor & Craft, Robert. 1982, 26, 28.

8   Fyador Stravinsky was the leading bass soloist at the Mariinsky Theatre in St Petersburg for some 25 years. He was renowned for his dramatic interpretations of some 66 roles, including Leporello, Sparafucile, Pistol, Kaspar, and many others in operas by Bellini, Donizetti, Verdi and Wagner. Stravinsky,Vera & Craft, Robert. 1979, 42. Photograph 3 in Theodore Stravinsky's Family Album, 1975, shows Fyador Stravinsky in the part of Makagonenko in Rimsky-Korsakov's *La Nuit de Mai.*

9   Craft, Robert. 1972, 28.

10   Asaf'yev, Boris. 1929, 160.

As with those who undertake the monastic life, Stravinsky's awareness of the created world as God-given heightened his sense of 'now' – of living in the present moment; he came to feel that to compose was to be awake.[11] His spirituality differed significantly from that of Debussy, for example, who lived in a world of the imagination that was set in motion by something suggested to him by his intimate surroundings rather than by outside influences.[12] Debussy wanted music to have a freedom that was not limited to a more or less exact representation of Nature, but was, rather, an expression of 'the mysterious affinity between Nature and the Imagination'. Debussy did not worship 'according to the established rites', but had made the mysteries of nature his religion, before which he was seized with an incomparable emotion and a sense of prayer: his introspective delight in the evocative notes of an Egyptian shepherd's flute, or the intricate and delicate counterpoint of traditional Javanese music, were worth much more to him than any 'documents of real life'.[13] In striking contrast to Stravinsky, Debussy believed that music was an art form to which people came to seek oblivion: 'Art is the most beautiful deception of all!' he wrote, 'Let us not disillusion anyone by bringing too much reality into the dream'.[14] He advised Stravinsky to 'Remain unique! ... Being too influenced by one's milieu spoils an artist; in the end he becomes nothing but the expression of his milieu'.[15]

Stravinsky likened the act of composing to being caught up in the stream of a primordial force, and being led by that instinct for form without which nothing can exist; he saw creativity as the natural function of the soul.[16] He gave full weight and meaning to the transformative nature of this creative force by comparing it to the movement of the Holy Spirit. In response to Nicodemus' question about being 'born again to new life', Jesus had compared the movement of the Holy Spirit to that of the wind: 'Spiritus ubi vult spirat', the Spirit blows where it will.[17] Stravinsky emphasised the word WILL, for he believed that in musical composition as in the spiritual life, 'the principle of speculative volition is a fact'. Debussy had described the prime essence of music as mystery,

---

11 Stravinsky remarked to a reporter: 'I live in the present. St Augustine wrote a masterpiece about that'. Interview, 1938: Stravinsky, Vera & Craft, Robert. 1979, 643, n.16.
12 'Debussy Talks of his Music'. 29th August, 1908. Lesure, François. 1977, 232.
13 Debussy, April 1902. 'Why I wrote Pelléas': Op. cit., 74.
14 Debussy. October 1902. 'The Orientation of Music'. Musica. Op. cit., 85.
15 Debussy. 'Conversation with M. Croche'. La Revue Blanche, July, 1901, Op. cit., 47.
16 Stravinsky, Igor. 1947, 48.
17 Jesus' encounter with Nicodemus is recorded in St John, ch. 3, v. 8.

but for Stravinsky composing was a religious experience, 'a matter of balance and calculation through which the breath of the speculative spirit blows'.[18]

Stravinsky's friends remarked upon the *élan vital* of his own being and personality. The Swiss novelist C. F. Ramuz, whom Stravinsky engaged to translate Russian texts into French for *L'Histoire du Soldat*, remarked that Stravinsky possessed 'une certaine qualité de déléctation, où tout l'être est interessé', a love of life and a quality of delight in all living things which involved his whole being. He noticed that Stravinsky had the power to invest the humblest things with a sacramental quality by his enjoyment of them.[19] Tamara Karsavina, the first Firebird and also the first Ballerina in *Petrushka*, who lived at one time in an apartment on the floor above Stravinsky, recalled the primeval spontaneity of the sharp, incisive, reiterated movements of his head and hands while talking of music; the composer and writer Nicholas Nabokov was struck by the parallel between his physical gesture and the inner gesture of his music, his peculiarly elastic walk and abrupt stops in conversation, accompanied by a broad sarcastic grin. Ludmilla Pitöeff, the first to perform the Princess in *The Soldier's Tale*, watched Stravinsky as he played the piano and percussion parts and was reminded of a devil in a Byzantine icon, 'so red, so black, so resonant'. She observed that 'his curiosity was so great that he awakened that quality in all those around him and led them into unknown kingdoms'.[20] His physical vitality did not wane in later life. In 1956, Robert Craft observed that Stravinsky's physical appetites and body gestures were apparent 'long before the mind comes out of hiding', and that his unlimited capacity for abstract thought 'is never dissociated from physical instinct'.[21]

The conductor Ernest Ansermet, who had become a close friend in 1911, was one of the first to remark upon Stravinsky's spiritual gift of embodying being and becoming in music, and to attribute it to Stravinsky's constructive use of tonality and timbre. He later wrote:

> To this perceptive intuition, he testifies constantly in his life. One must have visited a zoological garden with him as I often did, to know all the significance that he attaches to the physiognomy and behaviour of an

---

18   Op. cit., 50.
19   Ramuz, Charles. F. 1929, 24–26.
20   Stravinsky, Vera & Craft, Robert. 1979, 167.
21   Craft, Robert. 1972, 60. After Stravinsky's bout of pneumonia in March 1970, his doctor remarked that he had never seen such inner vitality and life force, such alertness, powers of observation and acuteness of the critical faculties – for he could formulate the subtlest distinctions – and his inner physical elasticity was no less amazing. Op. cit., 377.

animal, and this significance always bears on a certain modality of being. The physiognomy and behaviour of people speak to him in the same way. And it is *his lively intuition for the transcendent significance of the perceptible* that he applies to tonal structures, and not only to tonal structures but to different musical timbres – whence the important role of timbre in his music.[22]

Stravinsky's son Theodore described the relationship between his father's creativity and his Christian faith as 'unequivocally religious, that is, metaphysical and ontological, not sentimental or intellectual'. He affirmed that praying and adoring were 'functions of his father's deepest self',[23] and that his unshakeable belief in the objective Truth of his works did not merely defend his 'ego', but the values on which his work was founded. 'He had', Theodore wrote, 'the intransigence of the believer'.[24] Theodore believed that his father's religious nature 'helps to reveal the ultimate essence of his art, even to those to whom spiritual questions have become foreign or chimerical'.[25] Theodore's book about the essential nature of Stravinsky's music was the first that entirely satisfied his father, who wrote to him 'But I like your book not because it's an apologia ... but above all because your apologia has an entirely solid basis, both ethically and aesthetically'.[26]

Stravinsky had been baptised by a prelate of the Russian Orthodox Church in Oranienbaum.[27] Although Stravinsky did not think that his parents were believers, nevertheless the family observed the fasts and feasts of the church calendar strictly, and as a child Stravinsky was required to attend holy services and to read the Bible.[28] As a teenager of fourteen or fifteen he began to criticise the Orthodox Church and rebel against organised religion, although he retained the sense of a personal relationship with God.[29] He recalled, for example, that he was profoundly moved by the annual Epiphany ceremony at the River Neva, during which Tsar Alexander III 'baptised' a large silver cross on a

---

22   Ansermet, Ernest. April 1964 (my italics).

23   Stravinsky, Theodore. 1953, 18–19.

24   Op. cit., 36.

25   Op. cit., 19.

26   Quoted in Stephen Walsh. 2007, 238–9.

27   A few days later, he was ceremoniously joined to the Russian Church in the Nikolsky Cathedral in St Petersburg, by full immersion.

28   Stravinsky, Igor & Craft, Robert. 1981, *Expositions and Developments*, 72–75.

29   From the time of his baptism Stravinsky wore a small gold cross and silver roundel of the Virgin, which were buried with him. Craft, Robert. 1972, 326.

chain.[30] His spirituality was not shared by his teacher Rimsky-Korsakov whose rational mentality was robustly described by Stravinsky as 'almost bourgeois atheism', and closed to any religious or metaphysical idea. Rimsky-Korsakov had no interest in the relation of art to religion, and summarily dismissed the possibility of life after death.[31]

Amongst Stravinsky's wider intellectual circle in St Petersburg that included painters, young scientists, scholars and enlightened amateurs, he gained spiritual support from two friends in particular, Valentin Serov and Stepan Mitusov. Valentin Serov, born in 1865 and one of the most talented Russian painters of the time, was a founder of the early Russian Impressionist School. Serov's masterly portraits, including those of Nicolai Rimsky-Korsakov and Tamara Karsavina, were ahead of their time, being admired and respected for the way in which they captured the 'being' of their subject, and for their depiction of spontaneous movement, particularly in his portraits of children. Serov was a member of the Mir Iskusstva (World of Art) movement that had been formed in 1898 by a group of students, including Alexandre Benois and Léon Bakst, to fight what they saw as the current positivistic trend and the anti-aesthetic nature of contemporary art. Sergei Diaghilev was the first chief editor of Mir Iskusstva's magazine, and after 1909, Diaghilev gradually involved those connected with the movement in productions of the Ballets Russes. Serov was one of the first to believe in and encourage Stravinsky's vocation as a composer, and continued to champion Stravinsky's work in the early years.

Stepan Mitusov, who met Stravinsky at Rimsky-Korsakov's weekly Wednesday meetings, became a kind of literary and theatrical tutor to him. He took a keen interest in all the latest artistic movements in Europe and introduced Stravinsky to the 'Evenings of Contemporary Music' concert series in St Petersburg. It was Mitusov whom Stravinsky chose to co-author the libretto for *Le Rossignol*.[32]

While at St Petersburg University (1901–5), Stravinsky was interested in the theoretical and abstract questions of criminal law and legal philosophy, and read mostly Russian literature and literature of other countries in translation, such as novels by Dostoevsky and Gorky, Strindberg and Ibsen, and philosophers of Being such as Berdyaev, Shestov and Rozanov. In later life Stravinsky re-read and quoted constantly from the works of Rozanov, liking to compare his style and ideas with those of Gogol and Dostoevsky.[33] Strongly influenced

30   Stravinsky, Igor & Craft, Robert, 1981, *Expositions and Developments*, 74–5.
31   Stravinsky, Igor & Craft, Robert. 1981, *Memories and Commentaries*, 55.
32   Stravinsky, Igor & Craft, Robert. 1981. *Expositions and Developments*, 20–27.
33   Nabokov, Nicholas. 'Christmas with Stravinsky' in Corle, Edwin, ed. 1969, 152.

by Kierkegaard, whom Stravinsky regarded highly, philosophers of Being affirmed a transcendent reality, most of them maintaining that God's transcendence and incarnation remained essentially inexplicable and paradoxical; as God was held to be qualitatively different from and discontinuous with our earthly existence, a radical decision of faith was called for. Berdyaev and Bulgakov, appropriating the ideas of Eastern Christianity, affirmed that a personal relationship with God was possible because of an intrinsic God-like element within humankind. Berdyaev held that the human race can play a real, creative part in transforming the material world, a view that was typical of much of these philosophers' optimistic thinking.

In 1897, Victor Ivanovitch Nesmelov (1863–1920), Professor of Philosophy at Kazan Theological Academy, published *The Science of Man*, two volumes based on his work concerning the correlation of positive science and revealed religion.[34] In tune with the spirit of the age, this work proved popular, with a second edition in 1902; Stravinsky owned the third edition of 1905.[35] *The Science of Man* raised many of the serious questions which occupied Stravinsky as he strove to be worthy of his pledge to God: the structure of consciousness and thought; the separation of the subjective and objective; the relation of personal psychology to faith and knowledge; the conflict of individuality and free will; and the evolution of religious consciousness. The book had a crucial bearing on what Stravinsky saw as music's role in bridging the physical world of phenomena and the transcendent world of faith, and also in expressing that sense of continuity between earth and heaven that is an important tenet of the Russian Orthodox faith. The many annotations that Stravinsky made in his copy of Nesmelov's book reveal that he was seeking to understand the role of consciousness and thought in artistic creativity and the nature of human perception. He was soon to find direction for his thinking in the neo-Thomist philosophy of Jacques Maritain, and his interest in these questions was lifelong: during the material and spiritual difficulties of the 1940s, and even in his last years, Nesmelov's book remained at his bedside.[36]

Nesmelov begins *The Science of Man* by discussing consciousness as the universal expression of the human spirit and its links with thought, the ways in which the world of ideas and concepts is organised, and the development of

34 The chapter contents of Nesmelov's book *The Science of Man* are given in Appendix 1.

35 In 1937, towards the end of her life, Stravinsky's first wife Catherine asked her husband to bring her a book by Nesmelov – probably *The Dogmatic System of St Gregory of Nyssa* (1887). Robert Craft, ed. 1982, 17.

36 Robert Craft observed that to judge from Stravinsky's extensive annotation of this book, Nesmelov exerted a major influence on the composer's thought. Ibid.

life. He proceeds to questions of knowledge, perception and faith, necessity and free will, individuality, the existence of God and the purpose of mankind. As a research fellow at the Kazan Academy during the late 1880s Nesmelov's approach to the philosophical problem of knowledge was highly critical. He had dismissed all formerly established forms of philosophy as delusion and was also strongly averse to metaphysics. Influenced by his teacher, Snegirev, he came to believe that the only reliable knowledge came from the findings of empirical science, but that this knowledge was only to be discovered in the realm of physical phenomena since scientific findings were unable to access the transcendent reality that is the realm of faith. Nesmelov thought it important, however, for science and faith to be brought together in an ultimate synthesis.

Like Kant, Nesmelov pointed to the fundamental paradox between the findings of knowledge which is limited to phenomena, and faith which is concerned with the realm of absolute reality. In place of Kant's 'practical reason' to enable access to a transcendent reality beyond the phenomenal world, Nesmelov proposed 'immediate insight'. Faith is both 'immediate insight' into reality and the position reached as the result of scientific argument. He suggests that self-awareness, which both reveals our dual nature as part of the material world and as imperishable substance, also enables consciousness of the Divine in ourselves: humankind is a living image of the Divine Creator, in that His nature is reflected in our own being.

The Science of Man was Nesmelov's response to the positivist ideas that were current in the last decades of the 19th century. His book aims to answer the question of doubt by making a philosophical critique of religion and looking at the psychological aspects of religious scepticism. Above all, he seeks to demonstrate the credibility of Christian revelation by rational and scientific arguments, and to correlate empirical science with 'revealed religion', the means by which God reveals knowledge of Himself.[37] Nesmelov belonged to a generation in Russia that sought to defend Christianity with a mixture of arguments from empirical science, ethics and common sense.

Stravinsky and his first wife, Catherine Nossenko, shared a deep interest in the spiritual questions of life and the teaching of the Russian Orthodox Church. Their reading centred on the *Dobrotolyubiye*, the Russian version of the *Philokalia*, which contained the collected wisdom of the Church Fathers from the earliest times.[38] Together with Holy Scripture, the definitions of the

---

37   Nesmelov, Viktor Ivanovitch. 1971. I am indebted to Georges Florovsky for his introductory
       commentary to *The Science of Man*.
38   *Philokalia* means 'the love of the good' or 'the beautiful'.

seven Œcumenical Councils and the liturgical texts, the *Philokalia* makes up the four major sources of spiritual wisdom and tradition in the Eastern Orthodox Church.[39]

Since early Christian contemplatives such as St Dionysus the Areopagite, St Gregory of Nyssa, St Maximus the Confessor and Origen, the spiritual life has been variously described as a journey in three stages.[40] The first stage, purity of heart, is known in the Orthodox Church as the state of *apatheia,* the redirection and transfiguration of human, self-centred passions into an all-consuming love of God and Man. The state of *apatheia* equips the pilgrim for the second stage, which is to grasp the 'being' of created things and their inner principle or logos.[41] The third stage of the spiritual life is union with God.

Some of the beliefs that Stravinsky expressed in his later writings clearly echo the wisdom of the early Fathers. St Isaac, for example, speaks of his attitude of complete trust in waiting upon God for grace and a sign of His presence:

> That heart is pure, which, always presenting to God a formless and imageless memory, is ready to receive nothing but impressions which come from Him, and by which He is wont to desire to become manifest to it.[42]

The Church Fathers, who waited upon God with a 'formless and imageless memory', entered a state of prayer which heightened their perception of

---

39   The Greek *Philokalia* was compiled in the 18th century by Macarius of Corinth and Nicodemus of the Holy Mountain on Mount Athos and published in Venice in 1782. Translated first into Slavonic in 1794 and then into Russian by Bishop Theophan the Recluse, it appeared in a five-volume edition in the 1870s and then a three-volume edition in 1905 as the *Dobrotolyubiye*. In October 1937 Catherine Stravinsky wrote to her husband: 'I'd like to have another volume of the *Dobrotolyubiye,* since I have already reread everything and am rereading everything again'. Craft, Robert, ed. 1982, 17.

40   Dionysus the Areopagite, the first Bishop of Athens in the 1st century is said to have been converted to Christianity by St Paul; St Gregory, born c.335, was Bishop of Nyssa and one of the Cappadocian Fathers; Maximus the Confessor, born c.580 was a Father of the Church, a monk and theologian who was persecuted for teaching that Christ had both a human and divine will. All three are recognised by the Orthodox Church as Saints. Origen, born c.184 was one of the earliest influential and controversial writers. A prolific writer, he founded the Great Library at Caesarea. His main work, *Hexapia,* presents the Old Testament in the original Hebrew with various translations into Greek in adjacent columns, with critical markers. He is not recognised as a Saint by the Orthodox Church.

41   In this second stage, essential being is apprehended in its ontological *umwelt* or time world.

42   Writings from the *Philokalia* 1951, 236, para. 66. This St Isaac, born c.354. was probably the Catholicos of the Armenian Church.

meaning in the created world, and of a divine, changeless reality.[43] Stravinsky 'waited' upon God with a similar attitude, as 'an insect can wait', and remarked that first ideas were very important as they came from God.[44] The quality of *apatheia* bound the spiritual and artistic aspects of Stravinsky's personality into a single seamless whole: the discipline of prayer, of remaining open to God, controlled his everyday life as much as his periods of creativity. In 1930, at a time when he was composing *Symphony of Psalms,* he spoke of the Christian doctrines which were a secret source of inspiration for him, and of the internal discipline which was necessary to produce art 'which was made of itself'.[45]

The wisdom of the early Fathers also underlies Stravinsky's distinction between the emotional and the spiritual, which reaches to the heart of the Christian faith and the religious life. St Simeon the New Theologian, for example, who claimed to experience God directly as 'divine light', writes that 'the only possible beginning to the spiritual life is the diminishing and taming of passions. ... When through the heart's opposition to them, passions are completely subdued, the mind begins to long for God'.[46] St Isaac wrote that 'Passionlessness does not mean not feeling passions, but not accepting them',[47] and St Maximus taught that 'wise love of virtue usually produces passionlessness of will, and not passionlessness of nature. Through this passionlessness of will the mental grace of Divine bliss enters the soul'.[48] This taming of the passions, and hence of the 'imagination', is a fundamental tenet of the Orthodox faith:

> Imagination is one thing, thinking or thought is another ... for thought is the action or production of mind and imagination is the fruit of passion ... therefore no imagination can be admitted in relation to God, for He exceeds all mind.[49]

---

43 See Vanstone, William H. 1983, 103. In the Catholic tradition, this prayerful state is petitioned in the final collect of the service of Compline: 'Be present O merciful God ... so that we who are wearied by the changes and chances of this fleeting world, may repose upon thy eternal changelessness'.

44 Horgan, Paul. 1972, 184.

45 Stravinsky, Vera & Craft, Robert. 1979, 295.

46 Writings from the *Philokalia*, 1951, 160. St Simeon the New Theologian was the Abbot of the Monastery of St Mamas in Constantinople and the last Theologian to be canonised by the Eastern Church.

47 Op. cit., 252.

48 Op. cit., 219.

49 Op. cit., 235.

Stravinsky could only test the authenticity of the 'gifts' he received from God through this process of self-emptying. The teaching of the Fathers was echoed in his important distinction between personality and individuality: 'Personality', he said, 'is almost a divine concept, the quality of being as a gift from God. Individuality is recognised in the world of spirit as a form of refined pride or egoism'.[50] In *Poetics of Music* he spoke plainly of that 'capriciousness of imagination' and of the new age that 'seeks to reduce everything to uniformity in the realm of matter while it tends to shatter all universality in the realm of the spirit in deference to an anarchic individualism'.[51] When referring to the expression of feelings in music, fearing that people regarded his music as 'dry' and lacking in spirit, he drew attention to the distinction made by the Apostle Paul between emotional and spiritual, a distinction, he said, that people continue to ignore after 2,000 years.[52]

The teaching of the Church regarding the quality of *apatheia* and the taming of the passions also, indirectly, formed part of Stravinsky's well-known view of music as essentially powerless, by its very nature, to express anything at all, whether a feeling, an attitude of mind, a psychological mood or a phenomenon of nature, etc.[53] Unlike poetry and art that communicates through the concrete intermediaries of words and paint, music that embodies ontological time gives form, not to the representational, but to the otherwise inexpressible. Stravinsky drew attention to all the feelings, attitudes, moods and phenomena of nature that we had 'unconsciously or by force of habit' come to confuse with the essential being of music.[54] Expression, in his view, had never been an inherent property of music, nor its purpose. The taming of expressivity, or the passions, allows the perception of the inner principles and being of things, as much in music as in the spiritual life.

Music that embodies ontological time, free from psychological influences, has a spiritual expressivity and beauty of its own. It prompted Stravinsky's insistence that his compositions be performed exactly as he had specified. Nadia Boulanger, who took a keen interest in the relation of musical time to

---

50 Le Vingtième, May 27th, 1930, in which Stravinsky linked Expressionism with individuality and Cubism with personality. Stravinsky, Vera & Craft, Robert. 1979, 195.

51 Stravinsky, Igor. 1947, 74.

52 Letter to Gavril Païchadze April 11th, 1946. Craft, Robert, ed. 1982, 18. n.41. Stravinsky may have been thinking of St Paul's letter to the Romans 8. 5–6: 'Those who live on the level of our lower nature have their outlook formed by it, and that spells death; but those who live on the level of the spirit have the spiritual outlook, and that is life and peace'.

53 Stravinsky, Igor. 1975, 53.

54 Ibid, 53–4.

performance, defended Stravinsky's view, often quoting his remark that 'music should not be interpreted but transmitted':

> All that is needed is to play exactly what is written exactly as he wrote it ... It already contains the emotions you are to feel. The expressiveness of the music is ... made by the composer in his score and not added afterwards by the performer.[55]

The word 'religious' did not correspond in Stravinsky's mind to states of 'feeling or sentiment', but to vigorously held 'dogmatic beliefs'.[56] He fought a long battle to dissociate his early music from the preconceived emotional connections, romantic images and analogies which others wanted to attach to it. He liked to quote Fritz Cassirer's definition of art as a discovery of reality, not an imitation of it.[57] It was important that a composition was beyond personal feelings: to appeal to the spirit a musical form had to be autonomous, and free from the influences of a composer's psyche.[58]

Robert Craft has described how Stravinsky used logic formally and relied on it to explain things that have long since been elucidated by psychology: no other contemporary composer, he said, has been so entirely uninfected by 'psychological modes'.[59] Craft observed that Stravinsky's profoundest belief 'was in the divine nature of artistic inspiration', but that this was a constant struggle, for, like St Paul, he knew 'that in me dwelleth no good thing: for to will is present with me ...'[60] Stravinsky drew a stark contrast between Romantic music which is the product of sentiment and imagination, and his own music, which is the product of motion and rhythm.[61] This description of his music remained true over his lifetime: in a note about his *Variations (Aldous Huxley in Memoriam,* 1965), Stravinsky wrote that in the absence of harmonic modulation to delineate the form, 'some of us think that the role of rhythm is larger today than ever before'. In a striking reversal of terms he continued: 'the composer must be certain of building rhythmic unity into variety'.[62]

---

55   Transcript of 'Music of the Week', October 30, 1938, quoted in Jeanice Brooks, 2011, 114.
56   Stravinsky, Igor & Craft. Robert. 1982, 26.
57   Stravinsky, Igor & Craft, Robert. 1981, *Expositions and Developments*, 101–102.
58   Stravinsky, Igor 1975, 175.
59   Craft, Robert. June 1957, 8.
60   Craft, Robert. 1992, 83. See also Paul's Letter to the Romans 7. 2–23.
61   Interview, Paris, June 1928: Stravinsky, Vera & Craft, Robert. 1979, 209.
62   White, Eric W. 1979, 537.

2   ... and Musical Inheritance

In Stravinsky's early years, the liveliest musical circles in St Petersburg were looking not only to the music of the avant-garde but also to Russia's strong native heritage of folk song and liturgical chant.

This process of renaissance gathered pace in 1886 and 1893, when Czar Alexander III sent two expeditions to the northern provinces of Russia where older musical traditions had been kept alive. They brought back folk songs and celebratory rituals which were published in collections by Istomin, Diutch and Liapunov, a pupil of Balakirev. By the turn of the 20th century, phonograph machines were available to record the variations and subtleties of these songs more fully, and reveal their full beauty and purity. Listopadov, for example, issued three sets of *Songs of the Don Cossacks* between 1901 and 1906, and Eugènie Lineff issued two volumes of *Great Russian songs in the People's Harmonisation* in 1905 and 1911. On the death of his father in 1902, Stravinsky had inherited earlier anthologies of folklore that included Sakharov's *Songs of the Russian People* (1838–9), Daniil Kashin's *Russian Folksongs* (1833–34), Alexander Afanasyev's *Russian Folktales* (1873) and *The Slav's Poetic Outlook on Nature* (1865–9).[63] Stravinsky took a keen interest in the melodic intonations of the old songs: in 1904 he made a copy of sixteen Georgian folk songs selected from a Russian anthology of Georgian folklore, and later wrote down the song of a blind moujik at his summer home in Ustilug.[64] He also possessed a phonograph set of Eugènie Lineff's two volumes of *The Peasant Songs of Great Russia,* and wrote to his mother in 1916 asking her to send any others.[65] Stravinsky recalled that he was undoubtedly influenced by the collections of Russian folk music published by Tchaikovsky, Liadov and Rimsky-Korsakov – maybe because his 'powers of fabrication' were able to tap some unconscious 'folk' memory.[66]

Since the mid-17th century and the rule of Czars Alexei and Peter the Great, this rich national heritage had been overlaid by musical influences from the West. It began to be recovered in 1790 with a collection of folk songs by Prach, but their natural intonations and harmonies were misunderstood and badly adapted by early 19th century composers. Only from about 1850 did their true beauty begin to be revealed under the influence of Glinka, Prince Odoyevsky, Stahovich, and the priest, Razumovsky. Tchaikovsky and Prokunin published a collection of authentically treated folk songs in 1872, and Anatoly Liadov,

---

63   Monighetti, T.B. in Levitz, Tamara, ed. 2013, 63.
64   Stravinsky, Theodor. 1975, photograph no. 23.
65   Stravinsky, Vera & Craft, Robert. 1979, 28.
66   Stravinsky, Igor & Craft, Robert. 1981, *Memories and Commentaries,* 97–8.

formerly a pupil of Rimsky-Korsakov, published *Eight Russian Folksongs* in 1905. Stravinsky much admired Mussorgsky's skill in capturing the typical intonations of Russian folk song (*pèssennost*) in his music, and preferred Mussorgsky's 'infinitely more true musical interest and genuine intuition' to the 'perfection of Rimsky-Korsakov's learned arrangements'.[67]

The Russian 'soul' arose from a keen awareness of the temporal aspects of life. Both folk song and the znamenny chant of the Russian Orthodox Church patterned short melodic motifs to create a variety of time qualities, from that of working on the land, to the 'new' time of heaven in church worship.[68] Folk song and znamenny chant explored the temporal aspects of patterning, both their rhythmic articulations of ontological time and the frequency with which melodic variants reoccur. Both the nonsense songs, in which the regularity of the metre is frequently relieved by irregular metres, and the folk laments and church chants, that pattern melodic variants and their articulations, are characterised by the quality of asymmetry. These native forms express the varied time qualities of lived experience through making patterns out of short groups of pitches, and were valued for their naturalness of expression and freedom from academic formality.

Vladimir Stasov (1824–1906), the patriarch of St Petersburg's musical life and an intimate friend of Tolstoy, was a strong champion of Borodin and Mussorgsky. He recognised that they were able to 'hear below the surface' of Russian folk song, catch their characteristic intonations, and give them new life in such works as *Prince Igor* and *Boris Godunov*. Stasov had spoken with Mussorgsky about bringing the naturalness of folk singing to opera choruses. A disciple of Glinka, Stasov had published a monograph on Glinka's use of folk motifs as early as 1846, and since then had worked constantly to promote research into Russia's musical past. In the 1860s he had been especially concerned to preserve Russian national culture from Anton Rubinstein's cosmopolitan ideals. By 1882 Stasov was deploring the fact that the Russian music conservatories had turned out to be purely foreign institutions – German ones – and that within their walls no mention was made of native Russian music at all. Similarly, the Academy of Arts did not mention Russian painters.[69]

---

67   Draft letter of September 4th, 1957. Stravinsky, Vera & Craft, Robert. 1979, 439. These lyrical folk intonations – the quality of *pèssennost* – were most evident in the long drawn-out elegy (*protyojnaia*) of complaint or grief. See the Mother's lament in *Les Noces* at figure 35 and example 26 in Chapter 6.

68   'Znamenny' means chanting by signs. In Byzantine chant, pitch was relative and intervals were shown by signs or neumes.

69   Stasov, Vladimir. *Izbranniye sochineniya*. 2: 537–8, quoted in Richard Taruskin 1996, 25–26.

Stasov was honoured for his work in the 1880s.[70] Boris Asaf'yev recalled that in Stasov's last years, he held frequent soirées at which he would instruct his disciples in the 'cult of *listening*'.[71]

In *The Peasant Songs of Great Russia*, Eugènie Lineff stressed that the spiritual – as opposed to the emotional – quality of Russian folk singing cannot be overestimated, and that 'Everywhere one can see the effort of rescuing from oblivion this truest expression of the spiritual life of the people'.[72] She describes how the Russian peasants 'lived' their songs, and regarded the song as 'a parable of life'.[73] The highest praise that could be bestowed on a singer was that 'his soul is long', meaning that he has a long breath; she records the common saying that 'An ancient song flows like the river with its bends and twists, and the new song runs like a railway'.[74]

Lineff defines three areas of Russian folk singing as of great interest in embodying the living quality of Russian spirituality. Firstly, *podgoloski,* subsidiary parts to the melody, are freely improvised in relation to its harmonic structure to create a spontaneous heterophony, a texture halfway between harmony and counterpoint.[75] Secondly, there is a fine balance between regular and irregular rhythmic groups, and between the 'time' of the words and the 'time' of the music. Rhythmic accents of the verse could be displaced from the accents of the melody, and move from one syllable to another in the same word, or from one word to another in the same verse, to meet the demands of the sense and to avoid monotony. The division of a song into 'bars' was dependent upon the contours of the melody, and where extra syllables were needed to fill out the phrases, exclamations could be added. Thirdly, Lineff remarked that folk singers have a particular understanding of the relation between tempo and the expression of 'being': although the style was initially set by a solo singer, the tempo always reflected the location and activity of the group, and was vital to the integrity of the song's performance.

---

70 Stravinsky remarked that 'all music in Russia stems from him'. Stravinsky, Igor & Craft, Robert. 1979, 58.

71 Olkhovsky, Yuri.1983, 135 (my italics). It seems probable that Stravinsky was among these disciples.

72 Lineff, Eugènie. 1911, Introduction, lxxiv.

73 Lineff, Eugènie. 1905, Introduction, xxvi.

74 Lineff, Eugènie. 1911, Introduction, xxvii.

75 Eugènie Lineff thought that the prevalence of tonic, sub-dominant and dominant harmonies underlying points of emphasis in the improvisations of peasant singers who had no idea of the science of harmony, showed the existence of a natural harmony, and confirmed the theory of higher and lower harmonic tones ... which are heard in every strong, full sound. Lineff, Eugenie. 1911, Introduction, lxii.

Lineff believed that the natural spirituality of the Russian peasants as expressed in their folk singing could revive contemporary 'composed' music, and she closed her second volume of *The Peasant Songs of Great Russia* with this idea.[76] She wrote to Stasov about this matter in 1904 as she sent him a copy of her first volume of songs, and he warmly agreed that opera choruses, with their 'falsity to life', must aim at the truth and naturalness of peasant singing. He referred particularly to the flexibility of this native inheritance, the changes in the number of singers, rhythm, movement and even mood, which are natural to people who live and feel what they sing. She subsequently published his response in the two volumes of her folk songs, keen that the folk song, with its flexible melody, free rhythm and free voice-leading, should be preserved.[77]

Alfred Swan collected and recorded ancient folk songs in Russia as recently as 1936. Like Lineff, he noted some of the songs' common characteristics: tetrachordal groupings wavering between major and minor, a particular uncertainty of tonality arising from the displacement of the tonic, and a fondness for the minor seventh degree of the natural scale. Heterophonic group singing produced much variation in density as secondary parts joined in or fell silent, improvising upon the harmonies as the spirit required. He also recorded much parallel movement of unisons, octaves, thirds, fifths, occasionally fourths, but, it appears, no consecutive sixths or chords in their first inversion.

Russian folk songs were distinguished by a high degree of rhythmic irregularity: 'The mistrust of regular formation is carried so far that … the singer will suddenly insert an odd measure or beat and thereby lift the whole construction high above the ordinary'.[78] Stravinsky inherited this desire to compose 'as purely non-symmetrically as the Incas', a stylistic trait that permeates all his works from the folk melodies of *Petrushka* to the serial patterning of *Requiem Canticles*. This stylistic trait played a large part in his grafting of Russian style onto that of the West as he reinterpreted Baroque dance movements for *Pulcinella*.[79]

Historically, the links between folk song and church chant had always been strong; the art of melodic patterning had characterised both sacred and secular Russian music for the best part of a thousand years. In both forms, the Russian

---

76   Eugènie Lineff reported in the Introduction to Volume 2 that whereas instruments were associated with light-hearted revelry, singing, as the natural expression of the soul, was approached with great seriousness: there was a saying that 'the song is truth'.
77   Op. cit., LXXV.
78   Swan, Alfred J. Oct. 1943, 513–4.
79   Stravinsky, Igor & Craft, Robert. 1979, 20.

'soul' is expressed in a few recurring pitches of largely step-wise movement, with ever-changing pitch centres and melodic and rhythmic emphases.

During an early period of isolation in Russia, Byzantine chant had evolved from ancient Syrian chant and developed into znamenny chant (*znamenny raspev*). It had been modified further in the 12th–14th centuries by Russian folk-singing practices. The eight diatonic echoi of Byzantine chant corresponded in external order and substance to the eight Gregorian modes, although they were differently numbered.[80] Owing to Syrian influence, which distinguished these echoi more by their characteristic melodic patterns than by any particular arrangement of tones and semitones, Byzantine chant and subsequently znamenny chant became in practice the art of formulaic composition: melodic formulæ from a single echos or diatonic collection were woven into the liturgical text. These melodic figurations varied in length from three-note motifs to longer melody types, and were identified with a single echos largely on grounds of their characteristic patterns and mood.[81] Melodic formulæ were often associated with a certain position in the verse structure and in the larger formal design, and all the figurations were subject to transformation by contraction or expansion according to the demands of the text. A skilled singer was able to match these patterns to points of significant spiritual teaching in the text to heighten the experience of 'sacred' time. The text was not solely scriptural but interwoven with reflective theological teaching to guide the faithful.[82]

By the 14th century, in such cultural and religious centres as Moscow and Novgorod, znamenny singers had developed great skill in matching these melodic formulæ to the structure and spiritual sense of the text. From the 15th century a kinship had grown between the melodic formulæ of znamenny

---

80   Both systems have four finals on D, E, F, G and authentic and plagal forms. The four authentic echoi correspond to the Dorian (I), Phrygian (III), Lydian (V) and Mixolydian (VII); the four plagal echoi to the Hypodorian (II), Hypophrygian (IV), Hypolydian (VI), and Hypomixolydian (VIII). 'Byzantinische Musik': *Die Musik in Geschichte un Gegenwart*, vol. 2, 591.

81   Each of the eight echoi (Russian: glassye) is distinguished by the predominant mood of its patterns. The first glas is the most festive and is also used for the most solemn occasions, the second tender and sweet, the sixth, mournful, etc. The number of patterns in each glas varies enormously: there are around ninety in the first and sixth glassye and they even have names. It is always possible to identify the glas from the succession of patterns. Some figurations ('wandering formulæ') are found in more than one *echos*, but are distinguished by slightly varying inflections or differences in melodic intervals. Swan, Alfred, J. 1940 Part II, 375.

82   In Vespers, for example, six or eight psalm verses (usually eight, with ten verses on special days of the year) are interspersed with New Testament hymns that draw parallels with their meanings.

chant that voiced a spiritual response to divine revelation and those of folk song that ritualised the joys and hardships of everyday life. After the mid-17th century Russia was subject to Western musical influences, including that of modern notation upon the five-line stave.

Interest in the ancient musical traditions of the Russian Orthodox Church had begun in the earlier years of the 19th century with the research of Prince Odoyevsky and the priest Razumovsky.[83] Odoyevsky, who spent fifteen years writing *A Manual of the Fundamental Laws of Melody and Harmony adapted principally for the reading of our Old Church Singing,* had constantly drawn Glinka's attention to the beauty of znamenny chant, and together they studied the four volumes of znamenny chant which had been published by the Holy Synod in 1772. The old church style was also studied by Mussorgsky, who wrote that he was 'frequently visiting ... Father Kruptsky. I could, thanks to him, penetrate deeply into the substance of the old church music, both Greek and Roman'.[84] Tchaikovsky fought a court battle, with the aid of his publisher Jurgenson, to break the monopoly of the Imperial Chapel over the use and publication of church music, and for the right to compose his own setting of the liturgy of St John Chrysostom, which he eventually completed in 1878. After this, Tchaikovsky turned to the study of ancient music, writing to Madame von Meck of 'the new path which lies in ... the resurrection of the ancient chant in the proper harmonisation'. Rimsky-Korsakov, who had assisted at the Imperial Chapel from 1883, used later versions of znamenny chant in his *Russian Easter Festival Overture* and in *The Legend of the Invisible City Kitej and the Maiden Fevronya.*[85] Smolensky, the head of the Conservatoire and Synodal School in Moscow, introduced his pupils Rachmaninov and Scriabin to the study of the old neume notation of znamenny chant, and he himself subsequently travelled to the monastery on Mount Athos to work on the Byzantine manuscripts there.

By the turn of the 20th century the St Petersburg and Moscow 'schools' of composers existed in a certain amount of rivalry with respect to the performance of early church music:

---

83   Odoyevsky wrote to I.P. Saharov, a collector of old manuscripts: 'I have analysed it in detail and can construct a whole theory of our ancient melody and harmony quite different from that of the West and very profound ... To interest you further, I have discovered the scale of our folk-songs ...' Swan, Alfred J. 1973, 71.

84   Op. cit., 84.

85   Rimsky-Korsakov's knowledge of Russian national culture was extensive: for example, he writes that the recitative of *Sadko* is not the ordinary language of speech but a sort of stylised epic narrative or chant, the prototype of which can be found in the declamation of the Riabinin bylinas. Rimsky-Korsakov, Nicolai: Chronicle, 353.

Les Muscovites, d'accord en cela avec Glinka, tendaient à appliquer à l'ancienne mélodie ecclésiastique le contrepoint classique du style a cappella, comportant un compromis entre le majeur-mineur et les modes ecclésiastiques: les Pétersbourgeois voulurent plutôt lui appliquer les procédés de cette polyphonie spontanée et originale qui apparait dans la chanson paysanne russe.[86]

[The Muscovites, agreeing with Glinka, tended to apply unaccompanied counterpoint in the classical style to the ancient church melody, allowing a compromise between major and minor and the ecclesiastical modes: the Petersburgers, rather, wanted to apply to it the methods of this spontaneous and original polyphony which was found in the Russian peasant song.]

Among Stravinsky's contemporaries, some highly regarded friends were involved in this research into the ancient forms of chant: particularly Anatoly Liadov, whom Stravinsky described as 'one of the most progressive of the musicians of his generation',[87] and Nicolas Miaskovsky, whom Stravinsky later entrusted with the proof-reading of Part One of *The Rite of Spring*. Around 1909–10 Stravinsky met the Eurasianist writer and publisher Pierre Souvtchinsky, and also Jacques Handschin who taught at the Conservatory of the Imperial Music Society, both of whom were scholars of early Russian church music. Stravinsky's early style was based not so much on the 'borrowing' of specific folk melodies and znamenny chants, though examples may be found,[88] but on the variation of time quality that could be created by their asymmetric, organic patterning of melodic formulæ. Regular patterns were contrasted with irregular patterns that were created by extension or contraction of the phrase: repeating motifs increased density or 'spontaneously' added extra beats to the bar. This spiritually expressive movement through changing qualities of time was an important part of Stravinsky's 'Russian-ness' and of his early musical formation.

---

86   Handschin, Jacques. 1952, 13 Jacques Handschin was a musicologist and organist. In 1933 he published *Igor Stravinsky: Versuch einer Einführung* (*Igor Stravinsky: An Attempt at an Introduction*). Jacques Handschin hoped to translate a book on Stravinsky by Boris Asaf'yev (*nom de plume,* Igor Glebov). Craft, Robert. 1992, 306, 256.

87   Stravinsky, Igor & Craft, Robert. 1981, *Memories and Commentaries*, 63.

88   For example, the second theme in the Russian Dance in *Petrushka* is a song for St John's Eve, June 23rd: White, Eric W. 1979, 199.

3   Temporality in Znamenny Chant

Pierre Souvtchinsky drew attention to the organic patterning of znamenny chant, and to Stravinsky's revival of its principles of articulation as a basic feature of his 'Russian-ness':

> Le plain-chant russe est une forme musicale dans laquelle le développement musical, l'articulation et l'écoulement du temps musical ne font qu'un. Stravinsky – c'est lui le premier qui indirectement ... notamment dans *Les Noces, les Pribaoutki ... le Renard, Oedipus Rex* – et peut-être inconsciemment – a repris et rehaussé par son génie créateur certains principes d'articulation des chants religieux russes ... Le fait démontre une fois de plus à quel point toute l'organisation musicale de Strawinsky, ses concepts et son intuition ont leur origine dans l'élément ontologique de la musique russe et de la musique tout court.[89]

> [Russian plainchant is a musical form in which the musical development, the articulation and flow of musical time are one. Stravinsky – is the first, who indirectly ... notably in Les Noces, Pribaoutki ... Renard, Oedipus Rex – and perhaps unconsciously – has taken up and enhanced certain principles of articulation in Russian religious chants by his creative genius ... The fact shows once more to what point all Stravinsky's musical organisation, his concepts and his intuition, have their origin in the ontological element of Russian music and music as a whole.]

Znamenny chant is the art of patterning melodic formulæ and their asymmetric articulations of time to create the greatest variety. Greater variety may be gained by introducing other melodic formulæ from the same echos, while similarity is promoted by the recurrence of a melodic pattern or its variation to link related spiritual ideas in the text. The close correspondence between znamenny formulæ, their organic variants, and the time qualities of the text can be seen, for example, in the stichera set to melodic formulæ of the fifth echos used at matins on Easter morning (Ex. 1).[90] Rimsky-Korsakov quoted this well-known chant (in a 17th – 18th century Novgorod version) in his *Russian Easter*

---

89   Souvtchinsky, Pierre. 'Un Siècle de Musique Russe' in Brelet, Gisèle. 1947, 20–21.
90   A sticheron is a poetic intercalation between verses of a psalm. This is a modern, reformed version quoted by Jacques Handschin, and reprinted from the Triodion of 1899, published by the Holy Synod: Handschin, Jacques. 1952, (3) 16.

Festival Overture, premièred in St Petersburg in December 1888 and dedicated to Mussorgsky and Borodin: [91]

(Fl. Ob. Clar. Fag.)

In the following setting of Psalm 67 (Ex. 1) phrases (a) and (b) set words from the first verse: 'Let God arise, let his enemies be scattered', after which the first sticheron offers reflections on the arrival of Easter and the liberating qualities of the risen Christ:

EX. 1   Verse 1: Psalm 67 v.1 and sticheron set to znamenny chant of the 5th echos

---

91   The programme note for Rimsky-Korsakov's overture quotes verses from Psalm 68, the story of the women at the tomb on Easter morning (Mark XVI, 1–6) and an unacknowledged doxology about the disappearance of God's enemies 'as smoke', the singing of 'Resurrexit' by angels in heaven and priests on earth in clouds of incense amidst candles and the sound of triumphant bells.

In the first of the phrases marked (c), the immediacy of the the the arrival of Easter is signalled by a sudden drop to the trichord below for 'Today, Holy Easter has come', that reoccurs for 'Christ the Liberator' (line 3). The four phrases marked (d) celebrate aspects of Easter: it is fresh, holy and contains a mystery, it is pure and for the faithful. The two phrases marked (e), the highest in pitch, refer to the honour due to Easter as the event that opens the gates of paradise. The motifs are concise and their patterns of recurrence and cross-referencing are dense and compact as befits their joyful annunciatory purpose.

In telling the story of Easter and in illustrating the dispersal of the wicked 'as smoke is driven away or wax melted before the fire', the second and third verses either greatly extend the patterning of motifs or thin their occurrence, explore more remotely related melodic motifs, or elaborate their figurations into joyful melismas. Ontological time is patterned, not according to the personal emotions of the singer, but as a spiritual response to the text: in each verse the formulæ are varied to unite in small musical forms that differ in weight and density, reflecting the forward momentum or depth of significance in the spiritual teaching. The musical 'weight' of each sung verse is determined not only by the number of cross-referenced patterns it contains but also by the degree of expansion and contraction in its motifs, the number of recurring pitches within its motifs, the frequency with which certain melodic motifs reoccur and the resonance of recurring vowel sounds.

In verse 4 (Ex.2), these verses are followed by a setting of Psalm 117, v. 24: 'This is the day which the Lord hath made; we will rejoice and be glad in it'.[92] Here, the weight and shape of the verse has quite changed. The chant takes up two wider variants from the previous verse, and concentrates on phrases c, d, and e of verse 1 to express the joy of Christ's resurrection. The fifth echos figurations are now much more elaborate, with an extended melisma on the word 'Easter' at phrase (g). After the thinning of recurring patterns and the more remotely related patterns of verse 3, the celebratory patterning of this verse is confined to a narrower range of familiar phrases but the frequency of its patterning is increased.

Souvtchinsky describes the articulations of the syllables of the text as blending with the flow of musical time, where they synthesise in an 'eternal present'.[93] Stravinsky begins his well-known digression on time in his *Autobiography* by describing the same experience but in different words: he suggests that although we have to submit to the passage of time from past to future, music is the sole domain in which we can realise the substance and stability of the present.[94] The spiritual sound world that Stravinsky inherited

---

92   Op. cit., 17–18.
93   Souvtchinsky, Pierre. 1949/6.
94   Stravinsky, Igor. 1975, 54.

EX. 2   Verse 4: Psalm 117 v.24 and sticheron set to znamenny chant of the 5th echos

from Russian chant is skilled at building the substance and stability of the present moment into an 'eternal present'.

The intensity and weight of the patterning in each verse builds a unique temporal form in response to the text. Znamenny chanters developed great skill in creating other-than-clock-time qualities that mirrored the spiritual movements of the liturgy, and some virtuosi chanters became justly famous for their musical interpretations. Znamenny singers sought to penetrate and fill the acoustic with sound, to lift worshippers into a 'new' time.[95] Alfred Swan remarked upon their beauty of form:

> Confined to the narrow compass of the chant, tied down by the exigencies of the text, faithful to the traditional patterns, it was principally in the structure of the canticles that the Russian singers showed their originality ... Each canticle seems to follow its own course, devise its own fanciful shape ... an endless variety of perfectly thought out forms, each a living organism.[96]

There were various forms of church chant and their liturgical use was strictly regulated. Dméstvenny chant, whose style Stravinsky introduced into several of his works, was a highly decorated single line used on festal occasions, particularly on days dedicated to the Lord or the Blessed Virgin Mary.[97] This type of chant patterns a small number of neighbouring pitches with an intensity that almost creates a fluctuating drone, and was often used when addressing prayer to the Trinity or the Virgin Mary.[98] The polyphonic strotchny chant varied in density like the folk song and differed from the polyphony of Western Europe in being more homogeneous in texture. Both znamenny and strotchny chants were used on Sundays and Saints' days. Strotchny chant was embroidered by voices that joined the group to enlarge its substance and texture without altering its character; these added voices could be very dissonant, and they frequently crossed each other. Sometimes a drone (or ison) was added to enlarge the musical space and mark its entry into a new, Divine space.

---

95   The ecclesiastical practice of penetrating the acoustic with sound is reminiscent of a spiritual practice described in *The Cloud of Unknowing*, an anonymous 14th century English mystical treatise. The author insists on the impossibility of knowing God by reason, so that the 'cloud of unknowing' which lies between God and man is pierced not by the intellect but by a 'sharp dart of longing love'. *The Cloud of Unknowing and Other Works*, trans. Clifton Wolters, Penguin 1961, 1978, p. 68.

96   Swan, Alfred J. 1940, 365.

97   Stravinsky evokes the festive dméstvenny chant in *Dissident's Song* (1919), *Oedipus Rex* (1926), *Cantata* (1952) and *Canticum Sacrum* (1955).

98   A 16th century dméstvenny chant *May my prayer rise to Thee* from the Monastery of Suprasi, and a 17th century strotchny chant *Hymn to the Mother of God*, performed by the Russian Patriarchate Choir (dir: Anatoly Grindenko) may be found on HM 90, Opus Production, Paris, 1993.

4 Resonance

Church chant and folk song were both characterised by resonance. Alfred Swan recorded that the melodic formulæ of the monodic znamenny chant were based on a 'scale' of four symmetrical trichords separated by a semitone, each group containing two whole-tone steps. Starting from G (Ex.3), this results in a major third, B♮, in the lower octave and a minor third, B♭, in the upper octave: notated enharmonically as B – A♯ the resonant interval between the two is a major 7th, the dissonant 0–11 interval. The sound world of znamenny chant was divided into four timbral registers, low, sombre, bright and thrice bright:

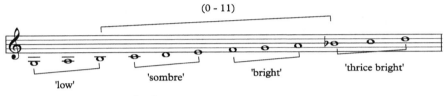

EX. 3   Znamenny trichords

Skilled znamenny chanters were able to improvise around the three types of trichord made on successive degrees of the scale (tone + tone, tone + semitone, semitone + tone), and use the different placement of the semitone to nuance the text.

As the diatonic tonality of Western Europe became increasingly chromatic, Russia was also recovering the beauty of the natural minor scale that gave an open spatial quality to many of its folk songs. It corresponded to the upper eight notes of the znamenny scale (Ex.4), and both of these scales passed through a distinctively resonant part of the harmonic series when sung in just intonation:

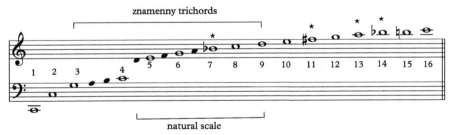

EX. 4   The znamenny scale and the natural scale passing through the harmonic series, which is numbered and written in open notes
Notes marked with an asterisk are distinctly flatter than the modern tuning.

EX. 5   The two orderings of the octatonic scale

EX. 6   The descending octatonic scale derived from the harmonic series

The octatonic scale, which Rimsky-Korsakov claimed to have 'discovered', was also part of this resonant sound world. In its most familiar form the octatonic scale was a perfectly symmetrical eight-note scale of alternating tones and semitones.[99] Its two forms, beginning with either the tone or semitone (Ex.5) may begin on any one of three consecutive semitones as collections I, II, and III before their pitches repeat.

The octatonic scale (Ex. 6) is formed by overlapping the 8th, 7th and 6th degrees of the harmonic series on successive fundamental notes placed at the interval of a minor third.

This resonant three-note 'overtone' figure is found not only in both orderings of the octatonic scale but also in the diatonic scale, so that it can migrate seamlessly between the two pitch collections. In the descending octatonic scale this 'overtone' figure is numbered 025, referring to the numbering of its semitone steps.[100] The octatonic scale has greater resonance than the diatonic

---

99   Much used by the circle of composers around Rimsky-Korsakov, the octatonic scale became known in St Petersburg as the 'Korsakovian' scale. Taruskin, Richard. 1985, 132.

100   'The 0235 tetrachord is the principal melodic fragment of *The Rite*, as it is for the "Russian" period generally ... It may nonetheless be (025/035) incomplete ... lacking either pitch number 2 or 3'. Van den Toorn, Pieter, C. in Pasler, Jann. ed. 1986, 133. The 0235 tetrachord 'may in its referential implications be either octatonic or diatonic. It serves therefore as

scale through the closer relationship of its overtones on each alternate step of the scale. It was used by Rimsky-Korsakov and others to distinguish scenes of magic or fairy tale from those of real life, which were set diatonically.

Through the publication of folk song collections and the involvement of friends in research into liturgical chant, Stravinsky would have absorbed many prominent features of these native forms: the asymmetrical patterning of melodic formulæ and rhythms, their 'living' variations of density and intensity, the resonance of the natural and octatonic scales, and the asymmetric articulation of ontological time. Boris Asaf'yev observed that 'the Russian melos is the living speech of Stravinsky, his native language, and not just material from which he takes quotations'.[101] Nicholas Roerich recalled that Stravinsky believed true music always to have the most simple origin, as it came from the soul: it was always inherent in the people, their folk tunes and dances unveiling a multitude of possibilities.[102]

In his early years, Stravinsky frequently attended rehearsals and performances of Russian opera at the Mariinsky Theatre, where each year from 1836 until 1917 the opera season opened with Glinka's opera *A Life for the Tsar*. It was at a performance of this opera that Glinka's intelligent balance of tone, distinguished and delicate orchestration, choice of instruments and ways of combining them, made a indelible impression on Stravinsky, although he was only nine or ten years old.[103] The opera seasons regularly included works by Mussorgsky, Borodin, Dargomyzhsky, Tchaikovsky and Rimsky-Korsakov; Stravinsky recalled that he must have seen all of Rimsky-Korsakov's operas.[104] But it was probably at the ballet, an important part of Stravinsky's early musical background, that he experienced the pure movement and patterning of ontological time that would influence his future style. Although he was only seven or eight years old and ballet at that time was rigidly conventional, he was excited by a performance of *The Sleeping Beauty*; not only did he know the plot and the music, but he could also identify the dance positions and steps.[105] He

---

a pivot, as the principal connecting link between blocks of octatonic, diatonic, or octatonic/diatonic content'. Op. cit., 139. '... the frequent (025) incomplete articulation of the (0235) tetrachord becomes the connecting link between the tetrachordal and "dominant seventh" [i.e. diatonic] partitionings of the octatonic collection'. Op. cit., 137.

101   Asaf'yev, Boris. 1929, 7.
102   Roerig, Nicholas. In Pasler, ed. 1986, Appendix 2, 322.
103   Stravinsky, Igor. 1975, 6.
104   Stravinsky, Igor & Craft, Robert.1981, *Expositions and Developments*, 62–83. Mussorgsky's *Boris Godunov* (in Rimsky-Korsakov's version), Borodin's *Prince Igor*, Dargomyzhsky's *Russalka* and *The Stone Guest*, and the operas of Tchaikovsky: *Eugene Onegin, The Golden Slippers* and *The Queen of Spades*.
105   Stravinsky, Igor & Craft, Robert. 1981, *Memories and Commentaries*, 31.

empathised with the 'being' of the dancers as they created rhythmic patterns in time and space; recalling the performances of the great ballerina Pavlova, for instance, Stravinsky thought that although the lines of her form and her mobile expression were always beautiful, her dancing was always the same and 'quite devoid of constructive interest'.[106] Musically, Stravinsky liked to contrast dynamic movement and 'gestural time' with temporal depth, notably in *Petrushka*, the second of the *Three Pieces for String Quartet* and *A Narrative*. His juxtapositions of different movement patterns to create a 'new' time quality may well have been fostered by watching the simultaneous movements of different groups of dancers on stage. Entering into and 'living through' the gestural movements of ballet is to experience the patterning of ontological time that builds meaning. This experience had been described by the philosopher Henri Bergson, who had defined a state of consciousness ('intellectual sympathy' or intuition) 'whereby one places oneself within an object in order to coincide with what is unique in it and is consequently inexpressible'.[107] Bergson described this consciousness as a quality of movement and change that is continuous and indivisible, unlike space, that can be measured and 'chopped up'. Bergson gave the example of a melody, in which attention is fixed not on the things that are moving and changing but *on the quality of movement and change itself*.[108] Bergson likened this quality of continuous change to the flow of our inner life, 'which has a variety of qualities, continuity of progress and unity of direction'. It is this flow that constitutes *la durée réelle,* or *la durée vraie.*[109]

Musical life in St Petersburg not only saw the promotion of Russian opera and ballet and a renaissance of interest in Russian folk song and chant, but was also enriched by the founding of the Evenings of Contemporary Music concert series by Pokrovsky, Nouvel and Nurok. This society began to promote the latest French music, including the quartets and songs of Debussy and Ravel and pieces by Dukas and d'Indy. Other performances of Debussy and Ravel, though rare, were organised by Alexander Siloti, a champion of new music: besides bringing Schoenberg to St Petersburg to conduct his symphonic poem *Pelleas und Melisande* (1903), Siloti also promoted Stravinsky's recently composed *Scherzo Fantastique* and *Fireworks*. It was through meeting artists

---

106 Stravinsky, Igor & Craft, Robert. 1981, *Memories and Commentaries*, 32.
107 Bergson, Henri. 1913, 6. Bergson contrasts this penetration by the intuition with analysis by the intellect, which is 'the operation which reduces the object to elements already known ... to elements common to both it and other objects'.
108 Bergson, Henri. 1911, 24–26 (my italics).
109 Bergson, Henri. 1913, 13.

and journalists at these concerts that Stravinsky came into contact with the newest artistic developments in Berlin and Paris.

Stravinsky remembered Siloti's performances of Debussy's *Nocturnes* and *L'Après-midi d'un Faune* as among the major events of his early years.[110] Stravinsky was impressed by Debussy's style, which sought to reinvest melody with the spontaneous improvisatory quality it had lost. Debussy had become fascinated by the haunting intonations of oriental scales and their arabesques, and was inspired by the Impressionist painters who sought to capture the play of light and evoke the transience of the moment as it appeared to the eye. Debussy believed in the power of the ear alone to determine the articulation of sounds and the arrangement of chords, and in the repetition of sounds to be enjoyed simply for their intrinsic beauty. But Stravinsky perceived that Debussy's innovations began to reclaim music from being the expression of a composer's personal emotions, and that it was an important step in providing a way of 'escape', particularly from the Wagnerian style. Stravinsky later acknowledged Debussy as his 'father in music' and the composer to whom he himself and musicians of his generation owed the most.[111] However, he thought that 'even the admirable music of *Pelléas et Mélisande* ... was unable to get us into the open'.[112] Debussy had begun to set music free to be a temporal art, even if it still remained imprisoned by the passive movements associated with visual sensuality.

5   Le Rossignol (1908–14)

Stravinsky's first stage work, *Le Rossignol,* sets Hans Christian Andersen's tale about the power of Love and the beauty of Creation. It employs Rimsky-Korsakov's brilliant orchestral colours and contrasts of pitch collection, but is the first of Stravinsky's works to distinguish the time qualities of its distinctive time worlds by differing types of rhythm and movement.

Andersen's tale is about the importance of greater in-depth listening. It contrasts the song of the real Nightingale with that of the artificial nightingale, over which the real Nightingale ultimately triumphs. In Act 1, Stravinsky conveys the meaning of the story by abutting four different qualities of time in close succession, each with its own melodic style, rhythmic construction, and timbral palette. Stravinsky draws attention to the swift change from one time

---

110   Stravinsky, Igor & Craft Robert. 1981, *Expositions and Developments,* 59.
111   Stravinsky, Vera & Craft, Robert. 1979, 63.
112   Op. cit., 48.

world to the next by juxtaposing them with very little transitional material. Stravinsky wrote to warn his librettist, Mitusov, that the first scene was full of the most vivid contrasts: he had set the Nightingale – the personification of soul and the bosom of nature – in contrast to the gang of semi-farcical Chinese nobility, so that the Nightingale, would stand out in greater relief 'in all the beauty of its intimacy'. He remarked in a post-script that he was in despair at how 'opaque' the word 'soul' had become.[113]

In 1914 Stravinsky told Romain Rolland that he liked to make sudden contrasts in music between the portrayal of one subject and another completely different and unexpected subject.[114] The juxtaposition of different musical materials and styles emphasises the change of movement and time quality between them, but Stravinsky unifies these different time qualities into a temporal form: passage through these time qualities carries a spiritual meaning. Achieving temporal unity was to become a lifelong aim of Stravinsky's style.

Stravinsky's music for Act I shares many of the fine qualities of Andersen's prose: a great economy of style which presents only the essential structural elements, a distancing of the time and place to objectivise the message, and a bold mix of styles to introduce a mood of gentle parody. Stravinsky may have been attracted to the subject of *Le Rossignol* because it was another 'inspired parody of uninspired art':[115] whilst at university he had made musical sketches for the satirical writings of Koz'ma Prutkov. This collection of poems, prose and plays, written anonymously by Aleksej Tolstoy and the Zemcuznikov brothers as though by a petty government official, mocked all that was oppressive and dysfunctional in Russia under Tsar Nicholas I, in the vaudeville spirit of the 1830s.[116] Both Koz'ma Prutkov and Hans Andersen take an objectively

---

113   Walsh, Stephen. 2002, 126. By March 1913, however, these contrasts no longer satisfied him. He wrote to A.A. Sanine: 'The scene ... is well rounded, entirely finished, and stands alone ... As it is, the scene lacks a middle; also there is a conspicuous absence of musical contrast'. Craft, Robert. 1984, 200.

114   Stravinsky, Vera & Craft, Robert, 1979, 131.

115   Monter, Barbara H. 1972, 118–119.

116   Stravinsky re-read *Kozma Prut'kov* in 1914 and decided to postpone *Les Noces* in order to set *The Affinity of all Worldly Powers*, the last piece in the book. This was a mystery play in eleven scenes by Aleksej Zemcuznikov that 'parodies all allegories with a 'higher' meaning and especially ... romantic symbolism à la Faust'. Monter, Barbara. 1972, 42. The subject is the Romantic hero who, obsessed with his own emotions, is oblivious to the changing forces around him that affect his existence. Stravinsky wrote to Alexander Benois about this piece: 'God himself, I do believe, is showing us where we must work ... I think only about this, I dream only of it'. Stravinsky, Vera & Craft, Robert, 1979, 133. Stravinsky's response already reveals, perhaps, a recognition of his role in the 'turning around' of music.

humorous view of life; Stravinsky was again attracted to this spirit of burlesque in setting Pushkin's poem *The Little House at Colomna* in his opera *Mavra* (1922).

The first time world is that of the ancient forest. Stravinsky wondered what Debussy would have made of his 'Mussorgsky-Debussy' beginning.[117] Referring to a passage in Act 3 of *Pelléas et Mélisande* (1902), in which Debussy's repeating patterns create a supermetrical level but negate spatial direction, Thomas Clifton observed that Debussy does not blend one pattern with another, but that each facet simply alternates with others. At this point in Act 3, time is drawn out at the supermetrical level by the slower rate at which events change, and repetition and recurrence are also crucial to the sense of non-direction.[118]

In contrast to Debussy's static patterning, Stravinsky's quaver patterns at ♪ = 92 rise from register to register in a spiral motion. One and two-bar phrases, large changes of pitch, and repeated dyads, create a supermetrical level of change that mirrors the ancient evolution of the forest and its slow patterns of growth: some two-bar phrases are repeated, some move to another pitch centre, some merely alternate two pitches to delay development. The small fluctuations between consonant, bare, and dissonant intervals add to the slow momentum, but rhythmic contrast is minimal. This musical space is enlarged first by a high, rhythmically-differentiated melody for flute (fig. 4) and then by a swaying melody for strings based on repeated dyads against the background resonance of (optional) choral humming (fig. 5).

The second time world, the world of the Fisherman who is waiting longingly for the Nightingale, is set at a tempo of ♪ = 60 (Ex.7): softened by a fluttery figure (not shown), his lyrical three-bar melodic phrases are juxtaposed to a syncopated one-bar ostinato with a suggestion of bitonality that adds resonance (fig. 8 + 4).

The melody patterns the natural scale of D, with the seventh note C♮ bringing the spatial resonance of the harmonic series as the Fisherman waits to hear the beautiful song of the Nightingale.[119] But the low D of the ostinato, the fundamental note of this natural scale, also functions as the dominant of G major, the key of the ostinato accompaniment; this light tonal ambiguity changes the time quality. Each verse of the Fisherman's serene song refers to the 'Breath of God', conveying his spiritual nature and evoking the time at the beginning of the world when the Spirit of God hovered over the waters and created the fish

---

117   Stravinsky, Igor & Craft, Robert. 1981. *Memories and Commentaries*, 132.
118   Clifton, Thomas. 1983, 104.
119   See Chapter 6 for Stravinsky's use of the minor seventh in *Les Noces* for its natural resonance.

EX. 7   Juxtaposition of two tonalities (adapted)

and the birds.[120] A faster-moving section (fig. 10) maintains the deeper time quality of the verse with a close canonic 'echo' of his melody on the 'distant' timbre of the horns (figs. 10, 16), the resonant minor 7th (fig. 11 + 3) and a foretaste of the Nightingale's free-flowing song (fig. 12 + 1 – 2).

The third time world is the transcendent world of beauty represented by the real Nightingale (fig. 18) at the still slower pulse of ♩ = 58. Its song, set to 'Ah', avoids the time qualities introduced by words and their precise meanings.[121] The Nightingale's song is luxuriantly free-flowing, with the largest melodic intervals and widest pitch range so far, and its movement is characterised by the tension of duplets against triplets. Its slow 'other-worldly' quality gathers increasingly luxuriant orchestral textures, tremolo figures and finally a spacious countermelody (fig. 23).[122]

The fourth time world returns abruptly to clock-time at the faster pace of ♩ = 88 as the courtiers come to look for the Nightingale (fig. 25 – 2). Often in a low register, staccato, angular in pitch, and set with sharper timbres, the music lacks the resonance, musical flow, and timbral contrasts of the first three scenes. Only the Cook, who has heard and wondered at the Nightingale's song, recognises something of its heavenly free-flowing harmonies (figs. 27 – 29). The music remains in the here-and-now but accumulates textural density as,

---

120   Genesis 1. 1–2, 20. In Andersen's text, the Fisherman exclaims 'Blessed God, how beautifully it sings!' In Mitusov and Stravinsky's draft text for Act I, the spiritual nature of the Fisherman's time world is emphasised by the refrain 'the Breath of God', which occurs twice in each of the first two verses, and once each in the third and fourth verses that end Acts 2 and 3. The complete text is given in Richard Taruskin: 1996, vol. 1, 466.

121   Later, Stravinsky wished the Nightingale's part to be sung from the orchestra pit: 'The music is more important than the action ...' Craft, Robert. 1972, 318.

122   As the personification of 'soul' the Nightingale later tells the Emperor that he will sing of those who are happy and those who suffer, and the good and the evil that happen around him yet are hidden from him.

in their haste, the courtiers do not listen, and mistake the lowing of a heifer and the croaking of frogs for the song of the Nightingale. The musical style fails to create any musical space, and conveys their single-minded focus on their present purpose.

Stravinsky links the first three time worlds by the fluctuating movement of two alternating pitches (i.e. fig. 1), a figure that is developed in *Petrushka* and *Symphonies of Wind Instruments* and features prominently in his later serial works. In *Le Rossignol* the imminent arrival of the Fisherman and the move from historic time to human time is signposted by fragments of alternating figures at a faster speed ($\bf\downarrow$ = 60); at the arrival of the real Nightingale whose song has transcendent beauty, they quicken to become a tremolo figure. Despite there being very little action, Stravinsky's four discrete temporal cameos unify to convey a parable about being still and *listening*: the music moves forward from the deep historical time of the forest to the human time of the beauty-loving Fisherman, whose longing for the spiritual brings about the appearance of the Nightingale, the symbol of soul and Love. These three time qualities evoke the beauty of the natural world, perhaps embodying something of that 'lost beauty of a realistic fairy-tale world' that Stravinsky remembered from the *Petrushka* shows and elk-drawn sleighs of his childhood.[123] The fourth section contrasts this passage through changing depths of temporality with the clock-time realism of the Emperor's busy courtiers.

Stravinsky explained to Stepan Mitusov that there were almost no leitmotifs. 'In place of this reminder to the audience of what's going on', he wrote, 'my music draws the listener into the mood and style of this or that person or topic. All this applies chiefly to the Nightingale and to nature. With the Chinese it's the contrary.'[124]

Fearing that the later completion of the opera would reveal too great a change of style, and in spite of the fact that Act 1 lacked the appearance of the artificial nightingale, Stravinsky regarded this first act as an autonomous work and either could not, or would not, extend it. In 1912 he announced that Act 1 would be published as a separate piece. Although it was only eighteen minutes long – and in February 1913 the parts were still at the printers – he persuaded the Moscow Free Theatre to perform it.[125]

Act 1 of *Le Rossignol* captures that quality of simple holiness of feeling towards each of God's essents that Stravinsky later recognised in Webern.[126]

123 Stravinsky, Igor & Craft, Robert. *Expositions and Developments*, 33.
124 Walsh, Stephen. 2002, 127.
125 Stravinsky, Igor. 1984, 197. This project collapsed in 1914.
126 Stravinsky, Igor & Craft, Robert. 1981, *Memories and Commentaries*, 103.

The spiritual aspect of Stravinsky's work was enhanced by Diaghilev's subsequent staging of the (complete) opera, in which the singers performed from the orchestra pit; in this way they did not detract from the impact of its contrasting time worlds.

Stravinsky thought that Act I of *Le Rossignol* was eminently suited to being paired with the ballet *Petrushka* on a double bill. Both works create a passage through different levels of temporality, but as with fairy tales, myths and rituals, the meaning of a work does not necessarily emerge from the succession of individual temporal elements but from the way in which those elements are combined and form into a unity. As Stravinsky later pointed out in the closing words of his first lecture on the poetics of music, the true hierarchy of phenomena emerges at a new, metastructural level. Stravinsky's stark contrast between deeper qualities of time and the shallow and the transitory brings out the meaning of Hans Andersen's tale and its affirmation of the beauty of creation and eternal spiritual values. In this it is similar in function to the folk tale, which presents an eternal truth through the juxtaposition of temporal elements that are both familiar and symbolic.[127]

---

127   The early years of the 20th century also saw the growth of a formalist school of anthropologists in Russia who pioneered an interest in the metastructure of myths and folk tales. The work of Vladimir Propp, finally published in Russia in 1928, began to explore how myths and folk tales co-ordinate and explain the present, past and future and create a parable about time. Propp's ideas about the effect of bringing individual elements into relationship and organising them as a succession of temporal events are similar to Stravinsky's ideas for the structure of music. Propp, like Stravinsky with regard to musical form, concluded that the folk tale, like any living thing, can only generate forms that resemble itself: myths and folk tales derive their meaning from the way their elements are combined in relationships. Propp was among the first to compare the mythological matrix with the 'rules' of musical composition, and his ideas were taken up by Claude Lévi-Strauss, who posited that structure has no distinct content: it is content itself, comprehended in a logical organisation conceived as a property of the real. Lévi-Strauss. 1977, 115. Stravinsky made a similar point: the true hierarchy of phenomena, as well as the true hierarchy of relationships, takes on substance and form on a plane entirely apart from that of conventional classifications. Stravinsky, Igor. 1947, 19.

CHAPTER 3

From Now to Eternity

Stravinsky's early works were composed at a time of great interest in the sub-ject of time: its implications for the origin of the universe, the psychological make-up of Man, and the place of religious belief in relation to new scientific theories. In every field, long-held beliefs were being examined and thought experiments carried out into the nature of time, whether defined as a dimen-sion, a relative measurement, or a variable subjective experience. In the early years of the 20th century, as Einstein was formulating a revolutionary theory of relativity and Minkowski the concept of spacetime, Stravinsky was developing the technical means of creating both familiar and unfamiliar time qualities and the concept of temporal form through the special ordering of sound.

Research into the nature of time had gathered pace from the middle of the 19th century and had inspired both scientists and artists. The breakdown in the concept of the mechanical universe had escalated in the latter years of the 19th century after Charles Darwin had demonstrated that the different species are not individual 'kinds' but the result of processes of change over time. Scientists, theologians and public alike had been striving to come to terms with Darwin's ideas as set out in *On the Origin of Species by Means of Natural Selection* (1859), *The Descent of Man* (1871) and *The Power of Movement in Plants* (1880), all of which had raised fundamental questions about creation and evolution. Old absolutes and certainties about the age of the world and the origin of life were being undermined by radical evidence that the diversity of created forms arose from their peculiar adaptation to a particular environment. Darwin's evidence revealed that the difference between humankind and the animals was one of degree, and that time – a very long time – had changed and modified life itself.

Perhaps most unsettling of all, Albert Einstein's paper *On the Electrodynamics of Moving Bodies* (1905) was the first stage of a fundamental revolution in the understanding of our spatial-temporal environment.[1] Until then, time was thought to have an independent existence as a fixed and unchanging medium

---

1 Albert Einstein published the basis of his General Theory of Relativity in 1916, following work on the production and transformation of light and an exploration of Brownian motion. It is now accepted that the movement of a body and the action of a force affects the curvature of space and time, and that in turn the structure of space and time affects the way in which bod-ies move and forces act. Space and time not only affect, but are also affected by, everything that happens in the universe. Hawking, Steven. 1988, 33.

for tracking motion mathematically, and was not thought to be created or influenced by movement. Einstein's paper proposed a new relationship between time and movement, demonstrating that measurements of time in the physical world are malleable and stretch and shrink according to the motion of the observer. It not only sent shock waves through the scientific community and society in general, but also inspired experiments into the relationship of time and movement among artists, writers and musicians. In 1907 the mathematician Hermann Minkowski made the radical proposal that time and space are not separate entities but are intrinsically linked, and suggested that Einstein's Special Theory of Relativity could best be represented geometrically as a four-dimensional space, known thereafter as 'Minkowski spacetime'. The concept of Man as a highly rational being in a clockwork universe, which had come to dominate intellectual life since Isaac Newton's work in the 17th century, was radically challenged by these new ideas; both the origin and structure of physical reality and the nature of the human psyche were undergoing vigorous questioning and experiment.

At the beginning of the 20th century, time was ripe for both scientific and phenomenological investigation. Discoveries were not limited to chronological time: during the 19th century the study of the human psyche and of mental well-being had also made great advances. Sigmund Freud's *On the Interpretation of Dreams* (1900) explored differing levels of time and consciousness, raising new and unsettling questions about human free will and the disruptive influence of unconscious motivations against the mind's defences. The tyranny of the clock had been gradually undermined by a phenomenological approach to time, and awareness of the complexity of temporal experience had been widened by Edmund Husserl's work *On the Phenomenology of the Consciousness of Internal Time*, begun in 1893. He reflected particularly on subjective experiences of time, the activity of the human mind and its 'stream of consciousness' in relation to the temporal features of objects in clock-time. He developed a theory about the awareness of the present moment and the retention and protention of mental thoughts, and made what is perhaps one of the first experiential links between music and time by exploring the role of memory in building successive melodic phrases into a musical form. Like Bergson, he spoke of another level of mental life as 'absolute flux' and considered it to be non-temporal or quasi-temporal and without enduring content. William James devoted a whole chapter to the psychology of time in *Principles of Psychology* (1890), in which he discussed the 'specious present', the transition from simultaneity to succession, the difference between experiences of time in passing and in retrospect, and speculated on the effects of information content. He observed that periods of 'empty' time seem longer when we pay attention to the passage of time itself, whereas the length of a period of time in retrospect depends upon the amount of memories it contains. In James' pragmatic view the fundamental fact about our experience as human beings rooted in temporality is that life is a process of constant change, and that all interpretations of our experience of reality, are, in the end, finite and tentative.

The exploration of many varied temporalities as qualities of both clock-time and duration was also taken up by literary writers. Lewis Carroll's *Alice's Adventures in Wonderland* (1865) and *Through the Looking Glass* (1872) contain many complex allusions to the patterns of the calendar, to clocks and time, and make frequent significant references to the hour of the day. At the other end of the temporal spectrum, the limitless possibilities of time travel were explored by H. G. Wells in books such as *The Time Machine: An Invention* (1895) and *Tales of Space-Time* (1899), which contain interesting early speculations about time as the fourth dimension, a kind of space. But perhaps the most exhaustive con-temporary literary exploration of differing temporalities is found in Thomas Mann's novel, *The Magic Mountain* (1924), founded on the experiences of his wife Katia as she was treated for tuberculosis in a sanatorium in 1913. In this story of a visitor to a sanatorium who intends to stay for three weeks but stays for seven years, Mann explores temporality and timelessness on every level, from clock-time and the times of inner experience to the transitory nature of reality and the myth of the Eternal Return. The novel mirrors its historical period from a sociological point of view, explores varieties of experiential time from many perspectives, and manipulates the reader's experience of time in its literary structure.

Artists followed suit in exploring time. Following Cézanne's radical rep-resentation of three-dimensional form in works exhibited at the Salon d'Au-tomne in Paris between 1904 and 1907, Picasso and Braque had begun to reduce their subjects to geometric outlines, and to combine multiple views of them in fragmented and abstracted forms that the critic Louis Vauxcelles termed *bizarreries cubiques*. At first, Cubism, which developed rapidly after Picasso's *Les Desmoiselles d'Avignon,* broke up objects and figures into planes which were then juxtaposed and superimposed to create a three-dimensional form with a greater spatial context. Paintings such as Braque's *Houses at L'Estaque* (1908), which had initiated the Cubist style, explored space, volume and mass, and broke the tradition of linear perspective in which the illusion of real space was seen from a fixed point in time. The representation of multiple viewpoints soon developed a temporal aspect. Salon Cubists such as Albert Gleizes, Henri le Fauconnier, Robert Delaunay, Fernand Léger and Juan Gris challenged the concept of separate spatial and temporal dimensions. They developed the theory of simultaneity, in which a succession of viewpoints was depicted as if viewed at the same time from many angles, in relative motion, and in multiple times and dimensions. In the spring of 1911, at Salle 41 in the Salon des Indépendants, the Salon Cubists exhibited paintings that sought to capture both the subjective experience of time as a continuum from past to future, and a fluidity of consciousness that recalled Henri Bergson's topical definition of 'duration'.

As the 19th century drew to a close, the philosophy of Henri Bergson as developed in *Time and Free Will* (1889) and *Matter and Memory* (1896) was a particularly influential reaction against scientific and mechanistic thought. Bergson appealed to immediate experience, differentiating two distinct and contrasting qualities of time, chronological time and the sense of duration. He described chronological time as a symbol of space, divisible into a series of consecutive, measurable moments, which enables the intellect to bring stability and order to an otherwise ceaseless flow. Duration, on the other hand, is the continuous progression of past, present and future dissolved into an unbroken flux, and is founded on change. The changes that bring about our becoming as we live and move form our being: our becoming is our 'being'. Bergson saw duration as a dynamic process of sustained becoming that is apprehended through the intuition. He proposed that it is intuition which also reveals the instinctive life force (*élan vital*) that has the creative power to lead us toward spiritual truth and positive action. For Bergson, as for Stravinsky, art was a combination of freedom and necessity, bringing about a dynamic fusion of spirit and material perceptions in which spirit endows matter with its own freedom of movement.

This exploration of time in its many aspects raised questions of mortality and eschatology, and provoked an interest in religion as a natural phenomenon. In the human sciences both Edward Burnett Taylor, first Professor of Anthropology at Oxford in 1889, and Scottish anthropologist James George Frazer, the author of *The Golden Bough* (1890), did much to promote an understanding of religion as part of the evolutionary growth of man from savagery to civilisation. The new and popular study of myth and folklore from all parts of the world suggested a 'progression' in human thought, which might pass from magic to religion and then on to science, newly equipping humanity with rational methods of observation. The discoveries of psychologists also supported a naturalistic view of religion: religious belief was seen to say more about human needs than about the objective existence of God. The psychologist James Leuba maintained that the reason for the existence of religion is not the objective truth of its conceptions but its biological value, while Freud held that religious belief is a flight from reality. It was not until 1912 that Carl Jung broke away from the Freudian view to uphold the separate existence of spirit and its value in the individuation process. Three years before Stravinsky was born, the Roman Catholic Church had met the challenge from the sciences by reaffirming neo-Thomism as the official philosophy of the Church, in the encyclical *Aeternis Patris* (1879). Neo-Thomism seeks a balance between faith and reason, in which reason must provide a firm rational basis for the superstructure of revelation. Correctly applied, reason would eventually lead to assertions in harmony with the Christian creed and be synthesised with Christian faith. In this way the Roman Catholic Church sought to appropriate the spirit of the sciences.

Amidst this maelstrom of enquiry into time and all its dimensions and qualities, Stravinsky, 'refreshed' after the great success of *The Firebird* (1910), returned to the techniques with which he had created the temporal worlds of *Le Rossignol* (Act I, 1908). He no longer wished to write descriptive music: instead, *Petrushka* (1911) would create *resemblances*.[2] Originally conceived as a Konzertstück that parodied the self-absorbed Romantic artist engaged in combat 'to the point of hammer blows' with the orchestra, the ballet became the story of the traditional fairground puppet, Petrushka, a droll, sentimental and shifting character, who was always in a explosion of revolt. Set in the context of the Shrovetide Fair, it provided Stravinsky with the opportunity to compose a work with many temporal levels, from whose contrasts and juxtapositions would come unity and spiritual meaning.

1   Petrushka (1911)

The story is 'located' at a Shrovetide Fair, but its musical dramatisation constructs an objective archetypal event that has five embedded temporal levels. In addition, the linear present is nuanced by the representation of memories and associations, and its various events are distinguished by contrasts of time quality.

At the first and deepest temporal level, the Fair is associated in the collective memory with the coming of spring. Pre-Christian spring rituals gave an account of Creation and called upon the supernatural to break through again and regenerate the natural world. The old was destroyed to make way for the new: in one of the oldest Slavic celebrations, Maslenitsa, a puppet of straw or wood (Iarilo, Chuchilo or Chudo) was destroyed by drowning or burning, symbolising the end of winter. This return to origins gave the hope of rebirth

---

2   Working notes for *The Flood*, 1962 in Stravinsky, Igor & Craft, Robert, 1982, 72 (my italics).

and the renewal of energy and life. In the Orthodox Church, the three-week period of Shrovetide begins on 'Publican and the Pharisee' Sunday, and prepares for the fasting of Great Lent and the Orthodox Pascha. Shrovetide is a time of spiritual renewal during which it is customary to make confession to a priest and to be 'shriven', to be absolved from past sins and given new life. The traditional story of Petrushka, therefore, is set within the remembrance of ancient rituals of repentance, sacrifice and renewal that move from profane chronological time to 'sacred time'.

Until the early 17th century, the one-man marionette or hand puppet theatre was a traditional entertainment given by skomorokhi or wandering minstrels at major religious festivals. Skomorokhi were largely responsible for the unique blend of pagan and Christian beliefs that made up Russian spirituality. In *Petrushka* this ancient temporal level is represented through the traditional characters and events associated with the Shrovetide Fair: the peasant with the dancing bear, the skomorokh strumming his gusli,[3] the early arrival of the volochebniki (the Easter Monday carol singers), the dances of the wetnurses, gypsies, rake vendors and coachmen. The mummers, masked as goats, wild oxen, bears and wolves, represent the pre-Christian pagan origins of the Festival. Stravinsky's *Petrushka*, set in the 1830s, has retained some original features of this entertainment but has also incorporated Stravinsky's own version of the puppet's adventures.

The second temporal level – the immediacy of the present moment and the bustling excitement of the Fair at $\bigJ$ = 138 – is established by the inclusion of well-known popular tunes that some contemporary commentators, like Boris Asaf'yev, considered to be 'musical rubbish'. Vendors, carol singers and old Russian street-cries establish a non-European background tonality with the patterning of octatonic tetrachords and prominent melodic intervals of a fourth. Against this, some events stand out from the general hurly-burly by their differently constructed time qualities. As in a film, attention is directed to the drunken crowd of Easter carol singers, whose confusion of mind is mocked by a canonic rendering of a carol at two pitch centres (figs. 11, 40). Attention is also directed to the Barbary organ and dancer by their mechanical patterning of time at the suddenly slower pace of $\bigJ$ = 88 (figs. 18, 22) and their contrasting portrayal by solo instruments and diatonic harmony.

The third temporal level is the chromatic sound world of the magic trick (*tour de passe-passe*) at $\bigJ$ = 50. It is separated from the clock-time experiences

---

3   The gusli is a kind of horizontal harp or psaltery. It is Russia's oldest instrument.

of the Fair by a drum roll and flute solo (figs. 56, 60) and negates both the sense of here-and-now and forward movement. Stravinsky imitates Debussy's non-directional, non-developing repeated motifs to evoke the Magician's deceiving gestures, his magic illusion and occult suspension of natural laws. Here the melodic shapes are fragmented and contrasts of register and timbre are minimal; the texture is transparent with many muted glissandi and harmonics. In the 1947 version Stravinsky refined this web of sound, emphasising its homogeneous, transparent quality by reducing two harps to one, omitting the rich high register of the bassoons, thinning the lower strings, removing the resonant depth of the bell notes, and replacing the harp and celeste by a piano. The effect is magical, but static and totally lacking in depth, since the Magician 'does not hear the melodies in Petrushka's heart or see the pictures in his soul'.[4]

The change to the fourth time quality, that of psychological separation and alienation (fig. 93) is created within the two-part stage on the stage, and is directed not at the festival crowd but at the audience. The turmoil of Petrushka's inner life is expressed in his impetuous arrival on stage at $\quad$ = 100 and by the irregular, spasmodic gestural movements that follow. The tritone between the harmonic planes of C and F♯ (fig. 95) ensures the maximum possible dissonance of overtones and the interweaving of regular and irregular rhythms, contrasting timbres and dissonant intervals confuse the time quality, further diminishing the memory of the clock-time activities at the Fair. Petrushka's alienation from the other puppets, the Moor and the Ballerina, is suggested by the contrasting regularity of their tempo: the Moor's sinister sense of humour is represented in the slow, step-wise patterning of six low pitches (fig. 125), and the Ballerina's shallow emotions are captured in the simple patterned arpeggios of her melody (fig. 135) and those of her accompaniment (fig. 140). Stravinsky also separates the Moor from the Ballerina in the Valse by juxtaposing the Moor's 2/4 metre at a slower pace against the Ballerina's 3/4 metre and differentiating them in style, register and timbre.

The final change to the fifth time quality reveals the work's allegorical and spiritual aspect. In the religious context of the Shrovetide Fair, Petrushka rebels against his confinement in the shallow artificiality of the Magician's time world and is searching for a life that is real. His double existence is revealed as 'the key to the enigma, a key not possessed by the Magician who believes that he has given him life'.[5]

---

4   Stravinsky, Vera & Craft, Robert. 1979, 200.
5   Op. cit., 67.

As Petrushka lies dying, the time quality deepens and a large musical space is opened (fig. 258): the piccolo, flute and clarinets project their fragmented figures in bright timbres against a three-tiered haze of tremolo harmonics in the strings, separating Petrushka's vivid new experience from the now far-distant activity of the fairground. Four aspects of Petrushka's life are recalled: a nostalgic phrase on the clarinet; a simple, warm solo on the violin; a wistful phrase for bassoon; and a brief figure from his former disturbed state in the low register of the piccolo. These snatches of melody bring remembrances of time past.

As at the end of Act I of *Le Rossignol,* we return abruptly to the contrast of clock-time as the policeman arrives to repetitious and angular music at fast walking speed (fig. 260). Three events of Petrushka's life are heard in quick succession as the Magician also arrives: the magic trick motif, a phrase from Petrushka's first exit from his cell, and the bustle of the fairground far below, now muted and suggested by slowly undulating triplet quavers. The triplet figure is slowed further to duplets a tone higher, enlarging and settling the musical space (fig. 263). Two highly contrasted qualities of movement are jux-taposed to create an unfamiliar hybrid quality of time (Ex.8): Petrushka's out-of-time experience, his new life, is set apart from the distant, muted movement of the Fair by the joyfully interwoven rhythms and bright timbre of two muted trumpets playing a fanfare figure (fig. 265).

Petrushka's final moments form the climax to the hierarchy of temporalities in this work: just as the Shrovetide Festival throws off the old and celebrates the coming of new life on earth, so Petrushka is released from his puppet's body to experience the new, vibrant life of his soul. The arpeggiated figure symbolising his turmoil of spirit (fig. 95) has grown from its original piano

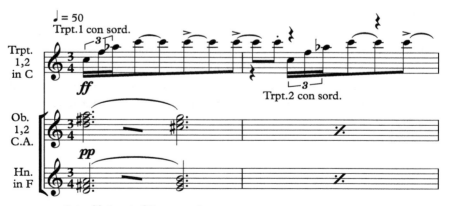

EX. 8   Petrushka's out-of-time experience

statement 'in two keys' (C/F♯) for the soft timbre of two clarinets, to a defiantly unison line for two, then three very loud muted trumpets (figs. 100, 116). Finally it is heard in a triumphant form for two muted trumpets fortissimo in the 'two keys' version (C/F♯ enharmonically, fig. 267 – 2), conveying the transformation of his former state. The final resonant pizzicato tritone asks a question that is left unanswered. Later, Stravinsky remarked 'I was, and am, more proud of these last pages than of anything else in the score'.[6]

Perhaps encouraged by the separation he had achieved between Petrushka's out-of-time experience and the simultaneous clock-time activity of the Fair, Stravinsky embarked on a much more ambitious setting of other-than-clock-time qualities: Konstantin Balmont's poem about an encounter with the 'Star-faced One'.

2   Zvezdoliki (1911)

A great number of spiritual verses preserved among the Old Believers (Raskolniki) are about flight into the desert, since they believed the way to find salvation and eternal life was to move away from the world's temptations.[7] Stravinsky thought the poem obscure as both poetry and mysticism, but as he sought words for their sounds, not their meanings, these words were 'good' for his purpose.[8] The poem itself contains little to suggest a journey, but Stravinsky shapes the poem as a passage through qualities of time and movement, from present turbulence to timelessness and to an evocation of eternity.

Stravinsky later described *Zvezdoliki* as, in one sense, his most 'radical' and difficult composition.[9] Debussy, to whom the work was dedicated, was disconcerted by its musical idiom: after playing the work with Stravinsky as a piano duet, he wrote to tell him that it was probably Plato's harmony of the eternal spheres, being a cantata for planets whose performance on earth would be lost in the abyss.[10]

---

6   Stravinsky, Igor & Craft, Robert. 1981. *Expositions and Developments*, 137.
7   The Old Believers consisted of religious groups protesting against 17th century musical reforms. A poustinia, generally a hut in a lonely, silent place, provides a place in which to enter into 'the desert', a state of mind and heart.
8   Stravinsky, Igor & Craft, Robert, 1981, *Memories and Commentaries*, 83.
9   Stravinsky, Igor & Craft, Robert. 1979, 51.
10   Ibid.

2.1   *Stravinsky and the Old Believers*

Stravinsky's spiritual and psychological type has been described by Pierre Souvtchinsky as a complex combination of two contrasting qualities that is reminiscent of a distinctive type of Russian mentality:

> ... les éléments rationnels et mystiques sont étroitement liés dans la personnalité et l'œuvre de Stravinsky; toutefois, ce phénomène est très évocateur d'un certain type de l'esprit russe ... Cette fusion d'une croyance abstraite, presque inhumaine, tendue vers un monde invisible, avec un fanatisme de réalisation immédiate ... est un trait dominant de la typologie russe, ou le messianisme va de pair avec un génie pratique et réalisateur.[11]

> [... rational and mystical elements are closely bound together in the personality and work of Stravinsky; however, this phenomenon is very evocative of a certain type of Russian spirit ... This fusion of abstract, almost inhuman, belief, reaching out towards an invisible world, with a fanatical desire for immediate realisation ... is a dominant trait of the Russian type, in which messianic calling goes hand in hand with a talent for practical realisation.]

This mentality was particularly characteristic of the Old Believers in Russia, who, vividly aware of both physical sense perceptions and the world of the spirit, strived constantly to bridge these two worlds. Souvtchinsky observed:

> On est porté à croire que, dans la structure de l'esprit russe, l'élément irrationnel et l'émotivité primitive l'emportent sur la raison et sur une spéculation concertée et logique; or, il est fréquent d'y retrouver cette synthèse d'éléments disparates qu'on pourrait nommer un 'rationalisme mystique'. Chez les Vieux-Croyants et chez les différentes sectes les plus extrémistes, on trouve cette illumination mystique, doublée d'un rationalisme tout aussi ardent et exalté; c'est ce qui faisait d'eux des meneurs et des fanatiques religieux, mais aussi des practiciens et des techniciens de la vie.[12]

> [One is led to believe that, in the make-up of the Russian spirit, the element of irrationality and primitive feeling prevail over reason and considered, logical speculation; but, one often discovers there this synthesis

---

11   Souvtchinsky, Pierre. 1946/2, 20–21.
12   Ibid.

of disparate elements that one could call a 'mystical rationalism'. Among the Old Believers and other more extreme sects, one finds this mystical enlightenment, doubled with a rationalism that is just as ardent and exalted; that is what makes them religious leaders and fanatics, but also practitioners and technicians of life.]

Stravinsky himself acknowledged these two sides of his personality; he told a Spanish interviewer, for example, that his religion made him a dualist, and, 'in the search for the beautiful, the fusion of material and spiritual is everything'.[13] Towards the end of his life he described himself as 'a talent with natural traction mated to a mind with too little conception; a mind divided in the attempt to hold up the shattered wall of religious beliefs on the one hand and the scientific analysis wall on the other ...'[14]

Souvtchinsky also perceived a tension in Stravinsky's personality between a need for artistic freedom and the necessity of the given:

Jamais une expérience, une conviction existentielle ne sont transformées avec une telle précision, de telles conséquences dans un esthétique, un art et un métier. Le contact de Strawinsky avec 'tout ce qui n'est pas lui', ne s'établit pas sur le plan de l'homme, et en cela Strawinsky est opposé aussi bien à Moussorgsky qu'à Tchaikowsky ... Il y a pour Strawinsky comme deux mécanismes, deux systèmes de lois qui agissent simultanément, ... il y a deux dialectiques, celle de la liberté et de la necessité, du bas et du haut[15] ... l'existence de Strawinsky est celle d'un sage frénétique, devorant la vie, et en même temps, hanté par cette idée d'ordre sacré qui trace toujours la limite entre ce qui est permis et ce qui s'impose, entre l'imaginaire et le défini, la liberté et la necessité.[16]

[Never has an experience, an existential conviction, been transformed with such precision, with such consequences into an aesthetic, an art and a profession. Stravinsky's contact with 'everything that is not him', is not set up according to the scheme of Man, and in this Stravinsky is as opposed to Mussorgsky as to Tchaikovsky ... There are for Stravinsky two mechanisms, two systems of laws which operate simultaneously, ... there are two dialectics, that of liberty and necessity, from below and from on

13 Stravinsky, Vera & Craft, Robert, 1979, 195.
14 Stravinsky, Igor & Craft, Robert. 1966, 26.
15 Souvtchinsky, Pierre. 1946/2, 22.
16 Op. cit., 31.

high ... Stravinsky's existence is that of a frenetic sage, devouring life, and at the same time haunted by this idea of sacred order which always draws the boundary between what is permitted and what is imposed, between the imaginary and the determined, liberty and necessity.]

Stravinsky's interest in the Old Believers led him to compose two songs Op. 6 to poems by Gorodetsky: *Spring* (The Cloister), and *Song of the Dew* (1907–8) – a sectarian poem of the ancient Khlysts or Russian flagellants – and also *Chant Dissident* (1919). While working on *The Rite of Spring* he orchestrated the final chorus of Mussorgsky's *Khovanshchina,* which is sung by Old Believers who are about to die on a funeral pyre. Later in life he wrote on his piano score of the work that it had been 'composed by Igor Stravinsky after Mussorgsky's own and authentic sectarian themes'.[17] Rimsky-Korsakov had arranged the sectarian theme that he had found amongst Mussorgsky's rough sketches (Ex.9): Stravinsky felt moved to extend it from 25 to 116 bars. Rimsky-Korsakov had preceded the theme with an off-stage trumpet fanfare and a downward chromatic scale.

EX. 9   Final chorus of Old Believers: Mussorgsky's *Khovanshchina* (arr. Rimsky-Korsakov)

The characteristically Russian emphasis upon G♭, the seventh degree of the natural scale, prevents the tonic, A♭, from being a point of rest until the end of the theme.

The Old Believers clung to the original forms of Orthodox worship. The worship of the Greek Orthodox Church had been established in Russia by Grand Prince Vladimir of Kiev in 988CE and had been expressed in Byzantine chant.[18] During the following 200 years, during which the many races that make up the 'Russian' people were isolated under Mongol rule, the chant inevitably

---

17   Stravinsky, Igor & Craft Robert, ed. 1982, 422.
18   Following the work of Preobrazhensky, as part of the Russian 'Renaissance' at the beginning of the 20th century, it is now accepted that the neumes found in the manuscripts of the 11th and 12th centuries are of Byzantine origin.

followed a separate course of development, influenced by folk singing practices and reflecting the extent to which the sacred and the secular were felt to
be one.[19] Znamenny chant, as the 'Russianised' version became known, flourished from the 12th to the 17th centuries, after which Russian music was subject to influences from the West.[20]

During the 16th century, new forms of znamenny chant had appeared from
centres such as Moscow, Kiev and Novgorod, and from individual virtuoso
singer/composers such as Ivan the Terrible, who was especially associated with
the Kazan chant. At this time, too, a taste grew for greater melodic embellishment (*bol'shoy raspev*) which resulted in the many festive melismas of dméstvenny chant, sung only by specially trained singers on feast days, and also the
wider melodic intervals of the 'Great Chant'.[21] In 1665 and 1668 two commissions headed by a monk, Alexander Mesenetz, were charged with the reform
of znamenny chant. They sought to abolish the practice of embellishing the
chant with long coloraturas (*anenaiki*), and to codify the system of red (cinna-
bar) letters invented by Ivan Shaidur, a virtuoso znamenny singer of the famous
Novgorod school, to denote actual pitch. These reforms were in preparation
for the adoption of the Western system of notation on the five-line stave that
eventually prevailed. Several groups, known collectively as the Old Believers,
protested against these proposed reforms, suspecting also that the Orthodox
Church was becoming an instrument of the state. The conflict between the
Church of 'the people' and the official Church was only addressed by an edict
that declared tolerance as late as April 1905, bringing the Old Believers a certain freedom from persecution. At this time, Stravinsky was 23 years old.

Pierre Souvtchinsky has described Russian culture, particularly before the
period of enforced Europeanisation, as 'pleine d'un sens sacré et confessionel,
lourde d'expérience et caracterisée par un humanisme très particulier ...' [*full
of a sense of the sacred and confessional, heavy with experience and characterised by a very particular humanism*].[22] He believed that religious music had

---

19   In 1955 Vladimir Malyshev's expedition to the far north of Russia discovered an anthology
      of 16th century liturgical music including eleven Gospel canticles by Feodor the Christian.
      These were found to be suffused with folk song idioms and a great many more of his own,
      very imaginative patterns, 'that occasionally have an almost pictorial character in con-
      veying the texts of the Gospel stichera'. Brajnikov, M. 'Russian church singing in XII-XVIII
      centuries'. In Alfred J. Swan, 1973, 43.

20   The concept of a 'scale' encompassing the range of each echos (rather than a mode)
      seems to have emerged only at the beginning of the 17th century with notational reforms.

21   Book IV of the *Obikhod*, (Ordinarium), a collection of liturgical chants containing canti-
      cles (in order) from Vespers to the Divine Liturgy, also lists a few examples of dméstvenny
      chant. Stravinsky described *Symphonies of Wind Instruments* as a 'Grand Chant'.

22   Souvtchinsky, Pierre. 1949/6, 79.

always been important in Russia because it expressed 'des incertitudes et le tourment de l'esprit et de la sensibilité russe' [*the uncertainties and torment of spirit in the Russian sensibility*].[23] Plainchant, he observed, had always held a special place in Russia's musical development, since 'L'esprit russe dans sa façon de concevoir le monde et la vie a toujours été théocentrique, a toujours possédé une dialectique tourmentée et vivante de l'absolu'. [*The Russian spirit, in its way of looking at the world and life, has always been theocentric, has always been characterised by a tormented and lively sense of the absolute.*][24]

The 17th century was a time of transition from the old Russian culture. Although the Holy Synod published four books of znamenny chant in 1772 based on manuscripts preserved from the time of Mesenetz's reforms, Russian music in cathedrals, churches and even monasteries gradually absorbed innovative influences from Western Europe, Poland and Ukraine. The ancient traditions were kept alive solely by the Old Believers in the remoter parts of Russia, the Ural mountains and Western Siberia. Seated in a circle, the Old Believers continued to sing from a central elevated songbook written in the old neume notation.[25] It was here too that spiritual verses and bylinas (historical songs), which also bore the imprint of early Byzantine culture, were preserved against incoming alien cultures.

2.2   *Time Qualities in Zvezdoliki*

Example 4 in Chapter Two showed how the trichords of the znamenny 'scale' pass through overtones 2–8 of the harmonic series, filling in the notes in between and drawing on its resonance (Ex. 10).

The opening motif of *Zvezdoliki* (Ex.11), which heads the work as a kind of 'motto', is composed of the 5th, 6th and 7th overtones, E – G – A, on the fundamental note, A. Stravinsky also uses this three-note 'overtone' motif in *Chant Dissident* (1919), a work particularly associated with the Old Believers.[26] At the beginning of *Zvezdoliki* Stravinsky disguises this motif with a different pitch order G – A – E and dense six-part vocal harmonies that progress towards its fundamental note A in the bass of the final chord.

---

23   Op. cit., 94.

24   Op. cit., 82–3.

25   In 1936 in Riga, Alfred Swan heard a choir of Old Believers in the Grebenshchikovska Obshchina community sing the canticle 'Let everything that hath breath praise the Lord'. He described it as a weird type of singing, full of chromatic and even ultra-chromatic steps, and quite unlike anything else they sang. They claimed that it was the dméstvenny chant. Swan, Alfred, J. 1940, 236.

26   See Chapter 7.

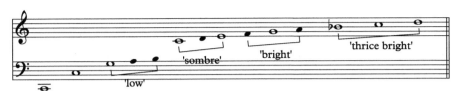

EX. 10   The znamenny 'scale' passing through overtones 2–8 of the harmonic series on C
shown as open notes

MOTTO:

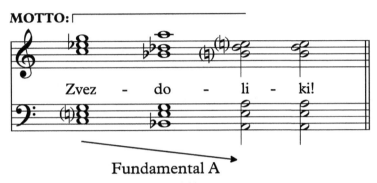

EX. 11   Opening motto of *Zvezdoliki*

After this dense statement in clock-time, the motto – and the time quality – is stretched, and the E♮ drops to E♭ before resolving upwards onto E♮ in
bar 3 to introduce the voices of the pilgrims. The motif is disguised at the
reference to the 'resurrection' of the 'Star-faced One' (fig. 3 + 1 – 2) and is not
revealed in its true form until the crucial question 'Do you keep the Word?'
(fig. 7).

Like the 'Old Believers', Balmont's visionary poem 'reaches out to an invisible world'.[27] The first chord of the motto (Ex. 11) 'sizzles' with an E♮ in the basses
and an E♭ in the tenors, and this resonance continues to deepen the time quality as they chant that 'his face was like the sun', the dazzling chord on 'sun' (fig. 1
+ 1) containing the major third C♯ (as D♭, basses) against the minor third C♮ (tenors). The work is 'located' only as accelerating movement towards Christ ('He
who has been resurrected': fig. 3 + 1 – 2) and as the pilgrims' slow journey into
the desert to seek salvation after their judgement. Although the work narrates
an event in the present, it does not create the quality of clock-time: it *floats*

---

27   Konstantin Balmont was part of the Russian Symbolist movement that reacted against
19th century positivism.

throughout in a time-less domain. Stravinsky achieves this by several means. In the first part of the work (figs. 2 – 7) the pilgrims progress quickly towards Christ, their movement conveyed by a layer of dense homophonic choral movement that is juxtaposed against that of the orchestra. As the orchestral textures and rate of harmonic change increase, the time quality is further deepened by rhythmic tensions of 3 against 2 and 4 against 3, and a directionless, chromatic bass line. This descriptive passage also relies upon the strong, onomatopœic sounds of the words, especially 'r' sounds for the rolling red thunders (fig. 4) in contrast to mellow vowels and choral humming for the golden clusters of stars that burn like candles around Christ (figs. 5–7).

The floating quality is maintained (figs. 7–10) by seven densely-scored statements of the 'Old Believers' motif in a vast musical space of over five octaves. It gives great weight to the chorus' question 'Do you keep the Word?', set dissonantly on F♯ against the static orchestral chord of C. After the proclamation, 'I am the Alpha and the Omega' to two dense orchestral statements in which the bass line descends chromatically to C, the motif is then slowly interwoven by chorus and orchestra (Ex.12). Archaic biblical words announce that the harvest of souls at the end of the age is ready (fig. 9).

EX. 12   'Old Believers' motifs at the harvest of souls

The timelessness of this section arises not only from its slow, stately movement between pauses but also from its rootless succession of 'overtone' motifs. The chord accompanying the first motif for voices (fig. 7) has both the major and minor 3rd of the znamenny scale on C. The motif begins in unison for clarity, but the following orchestral and vocal motifs are set to densely scored octatonic chords (from fig. 8), their successive semitone clashes evoking the dazzling face of the 'Star-faced One' and the radiance with which he is transfigured. The orchestral motifs progress towards their fundamental notes as in the opening motto (figs. 8–10). The cumulative effect is one of free-floating sound worlds.

As the pilgrims move away into the desert on their journey to find salvation (fig. 10) the time quality changes. After the rapid increase in density to the moment of judgement, an elongated motif recalling the opening bars begins to stretch time, suggesting that the journey is very long. The weight of the temporal form slowly diminishes to a light and inconclusive bitonality: in the final bar, an open orchestral chord composed of the harmonic series on C is juxtaposed against the vocal layer in which the tenors' lower B♮ of the znamenny 'scale' on G 'sizzles' radiantly once more against the 6th overtone in the strings, B♭ (as A♯).

CHAPTER 4

A Russian Spring

Stravinsky's contrasting sections, patterned layers and juxtapositions of regular and irregular qualities of movement, draw the listener into the temporal qualities of their different time worlds. The innovative techniques with which Stravinsky had created the temporalities of *Le Rossignol* (Act 1), *Petrushka* and *Zvezdoliki* were remarkable enough, but the question of time *in* music gained sudden, very public, prominence with his construction of *The Rite of Spring*. In this work his patterning of ontological time offered a radically new perspective on the old question: What is Time?

Time has been described by Maurice Merleau-Ponty as 'unfolded or constituted by consciousness'.[1] The human brain is bombarded with a multitude of stimuli at any one moment; some are filtered out by the senses, and some are organised and simplified by our perceptive faculties. As the situation changes, we select those stimuli most important to our needs, with the result that, as Robert Ornstein observed, 'our consciousness changes continually within a day, from sleep and dreaming to the kind of "borderline" state on awakening, from tiredness to excitement, from daydreaming to directed thinking. These "daily" alterations in consciousness are much more extreme than we normally realise'.[2]

In *The Dry Salvages*, T. S. Eliot draws attention to the varied nature of our many familiar, if sometimes elusive, experiences of time. He distinguishes between the time of human 'curiosity' that 'searches past and future' and the 'unattended moment, the moment in and out of time' and also the 'point of intersection of the timeless with time'.[3] Stravinsky creates familiar time qualities but also particularly elusive or profound time qualities of his own devising. How may this process of co-ordination between music and the listener be understood in terms of the physical effects of music upon the brain?

Linear time, 'that dimension to which we cling' as Eliot expresses it, arises from the sense of continuity and duration created by our short- and long-term memory systems and from perceptions of simultaneity and causality. The experience of time as linear brings a strong sense of past, present and future and enables us, among many other things, to acquire knowledge, to learn and

---

1 Merleau-Ponty, Maurice. 1966, 414.
2 Ornstein, Robert. 1986, 62.
3 Eliot, Thomas S. 1968. *The Dry Salvages*, V, 41.

© KONINKLIJKE BRILL NV, LEIDEN, 2022 | DOI:10.1163/9789004518537_006

understand language, to pursue scientific enquiry, and to manage our social timetables. Although many civilisations have existed without the clock as we know it, the precise physical measurement of time has become necessary in our present fast-moving technological society for the functioning of daily life.

Each day, however, we move in and out of linear and non-linear modes of temporal experience, between alert focus on the succession and causes of events and a holistic perception of events as intertwined and mutually influential in 'time-less' relationships. Life in the 21st century has perhaps become more focused on the linear and the here-and-now; Martin Heidegger has described our linear world-time as time 'in which datability and significance' is 'levelled off' and 'covered up' by the way in which we ordinarily understand it, in contrast to time qualities that are 'saturated with significance and structure'.[4] Stravinsky's spiritual works enhance the contrast between linear time and time that is 'saturated with significance', drawing attention to the movements of our time-consciousness.

1   Time as a Mental Construct

The body has many 'clocks', but in the last years of the 20th century it was found that a time-keeping structure in the brain that controls motor function and movement also keeps track of short intervals of time, from seconds to minutes. Cells in the substantia nigra, located in the brain stem, act as a 'metronome', sending a steady stream of pulses to the striatum in the left temporal lobe. These nerve cells not only control movement and the sense of clock-time but also act as a 'gatekeeper', turning the awareness of clock-time intervals on and off. This mechanism creates a fundamental pulse, which, integrated with many other rhythms of the body, underlies the focused sense of clock-time that is essential for our survival in daily life. It allows us to make important temporal judgements, for instance, such as whether we have time to cross the road in front of an oncoming car.[5] When it is 'turned off', it allows experiences of non-linear qualities of time.

Modes of time consciousness, influenced by external circumstances, thoughts, feelings and associated memories, are personally unique. Although the right and left hemispheres of the male and female brain differ in their specialisations, and temporal experience differs from person to person, recent

---

4   Heidegger, Martin. 1978, 474.
5   Meck, Warren. Sept/Oct 1996.

research into the complementary functions of the hemispheres does throw some light on the different types of time consciousness. It is now accepted that 'the extent to which a linear concept of time participates in the ordering of thought is one of the most important differences between the hemispheres'.[6]

Normally both hemispheres receive information simultaneously and co-operate in its processing, but each has a preference for a certain type of information and specialises in a particular type of processing. Each hemisphere is superior to the other in some processing areas and less competent in others.[7] The left hemisphere, with more densely packed neurons, makes faster, more short-range connections and prefers to work in a linear and sequential fashion. It naturally excels in tasks that require a methodical approach, such as the grammatical aspects of language, logic, mathematics, scientific analysis and successive complex physical movements. With regard to music, specialised areas of the left temporal lobe process basic metrical rhythms and their development, and analyse the more dissonant intervals and their overtones. When stimulated by these musical elements, as in the courtiers' scene in Act 1 of *Le Rossignol* and the arrival of the policeman and Magician in *Petrushka,* the left hemisphere constructs a sense of linear clock-time.

The right hemisphere, with less densely packed neurons but more white matter, has a slower processing style but makes a greater number of far-reaching connections across both hemispheres. Its speciality is synthesis. Diffuse and holistic, and more concerned with space than time, the right hemisphere is adept at synthesising multiple inputs simultaneously and is superior at comparing and relating phenomena, especially in relating diverse parts to a whole. It excels in spatial and relational activities, especially artistic activities in which a linear sense of time may be depressed into a background sense of an infinite present. Musically, the right hemisphere has specialised areas for processing melodic contour, prosody, harmonic relations and timbre. Music in which these elements predominate, such as the Nightingale's song and the death of Petrushka, stimulates the right hemisphere to create depths of time and space. With regard to the right hemisphere, Robert Ornstein writes:

---

6   Bogen, Joseph E. 1969. The Other Side of the Brain. In Ornstein, Robert. 1986, 129. See also McGilchrist, Iain. 2009, 27–8 and 32–93 for a fuller account of the differences between the two hemispheres.

7   'This right-left specialisation is most prevalent in right-handed men. It is slightly different in women and left-handers [whose specialisations] … are less consistent; some have reversed specialisation of the hemispheres, but some have mixed specialisation … Women have fewer differences between their hemispheres than do men … At least in very young people, each side does possess the potential for both modes … and in adults … it's just that each side is better than the other at its best talent'. Ornstein, Robert. 1986, 91.

This simultaneous processing is advantageous for 'spatial literacy' – the integration of diffuse inputs – such as orientation in space and movement such as dance – when motor kinesthetic and visual input must be quickly integrated. This mode of information processing, too, would seem to underlie an immediate 'intuitive', rather than a mediated 'intellectual' integration of complex entities.[8]

Changes of sensory input moderate the interaction of the hemispheres across the whole brain and the qualities of time that they construct. As the sense of focused time in the left hemisphere is diminished, the right hemisphere experiences increasing depth of both time and space.[9] Iain McGilchrist writes of this simultaneous process:

> As it is the right hemisphere that gives 'depth' to our sense of time, in the visual realm it is the right hemisphere that gives us the means of appreciating depth in space ... The right hemisphere has a tendency to deal with spatial relations in terms of the degree of distance ... in contrast with the strategy of the left hemisphere, which tends to be more categorical: 'above', 'below' ... There is a parallel here with the sense of time: duration belongs to the right hemisphere, while sequencing ('before', 'after' = 'above', 'below') belongs to the left.[10]

Neuroscience research confirms the view that 'time ... is a measure of our implication with the events of the world as lived-in. The breadth and depth of time have more to do with our relation to events than to any absolute measurement ... a matter of the amount of work required of consciousness to constitute a meaning'.[11] As Stravinsky observed, 'reality is not determined by our consciousness, but the other way around'.[12]

Both hemispheres of the brain search for recurring spatial-temporal patterns in order to make sense of the environment.[13] In music, patterning may be dominated by musical elements that are more specialised for one hemisphere of the brain than the other. Subsequent changes in the musical elements that are dominant moderate the involvement of the hemispheres, while

---

8   Ornstein, Robert. 1986, 130.
9   McGilchrist, Iain. 2009, 77.
10   Ibid.
11   Smith E. J. & White, J. D., eds. 1976, Vol. 2, 84.
12   Stravinsky, Igor & Craft, Robert. 1972, 109.
13   See Chapter 7.

the juxtaposition of rhythmic layers and contrasting sections increases neural activity according to their degree of complexity and compatibility. In *The Rite of Spring*, for example, the combination of compatible, 'low-relief' patterns in homogeneous movement adds to the fullness of texture or intensifies the dynamic quality of linear time, while the juxtaposition of highly contrasted layers that are incompatible rhythmically or melodically creates unfamiliar qualities of time and large musical spaces. The mental task of relating several contrasting patterned layers simultaneously increases neural activity, diminishes attention to the here-and-now, and allows the experience of Eliot's 'unattended moments' or even of timelessness.

These experiences of time as different in quality indicate that time is a mental construct; as Stravinsky remarked, 'time does not pass but only we pass'.[14] Recent neuroscience research on time-consciousness and the brain's natural generation of patterns has begun to explain the temporal effects of Stravinsky's patterned layers and juxtaposed sections. Neurons interpret and classify information and respond to changes in state with different patterns of electrical activity; they also appear to have 'expectations' and 'models' that govern whether these changes cause surprise or not.[15]

The experience of time is malleable: a period of time may seem longer or shorter according to the complexity of its content or lack of it, or because it is pleasurable or – conversely – uncomfortable. If the contents of normal consciousness are artificially restricted, the experience of duration shortens; if a multi-dimensional musical structure is listened to with great attention, the experience of duration lengthens and deepens.[16] As *The Rite of Spring* amply demonstrates, an animated passage through time may be varied not only by the number and complexity of events but also the musical elements that are dominant at any one time, and by juxtapositions of contrasting rhythmic movements. These variations in forward momentum and depth of time shape the work's temporal form and give it flexibility.

2   The Rite of Spring

Music was precipitated into the modern age on the evening of May 29th 1913, when Stravinsky's exploration of time in music reached a dramatic climax. The occasion was the première of his new ballet, *The Rite of Spring*, commissioned

---

14   Stravinsky, Igor & Craft, Robert. 1982, 105.
15   Shaw, Gordon L. 2000, 107–115.
16   Ornstein, Robert. 1986, 136.

by Serge Diaghilev for the fashionably exotic season of the Ballets Russes at
the Théâtre des Champs-Elysées in Paris. The representation of an archaic,
pagan ritual was particularly timely, for issues around movement and change
in time – the nature of creation and evolution, the influence of dreams on
the conscious mind, the relationship between time and motion – were in the
collective unconscious following the revolutionary ideas of Darwin, Freud and
Einstein. Paris was buzzing with rumours about the première and every critic
in Paris was invited to the dress rehearsal the previous day. The uproar provoked by the first performance of *The Rite of Spring* must surely rank amongst
the most talked-about of premières: people sang, whistled, hooted and even
started fights. One hundred years or so after the protests that greeted its first
performance, the music (and the choreography) can still have a powerful effect
upon an audience through their capacity to mesmerise and even to shock.

Stravinsky's vision required an ambitious treatment of time qualities.
Ancient Slavic tribes had known time intuitively, marking the rhythms of
nature and its cycles of return, and taking part in rituals to propitiate the creative power that regenerates and sustains the world. For the choreodrama of
this ballet, in which sage elders seated in a circle watch a young girl dance herself to death, Stravinsky approached Nicholas Roerich, a painter specialising
in pagan subjects. Roerich understood the spiritual dimension of the scenario,
later speaking of 'the rhythm of human striving and the victory of the spirit'
in artistic creation as providing a key to understanding the Supreme Creator.[17]
Stravinsky asked Roerich to represent in his designs for sets and costumes a
number of pictures that showed 'earthly joy' and 'celestial triumph' as understood by the Slavs.[18]

The First Part, *The Kiss of the Earth*, which Stravinsky marked 'day', depicts
the Slavs' closeness to the earth and the intense 'now' of their annual ritual.
On the stage we see the ritual dances and games of young girls, the divining
of the future by a very old woman, a game of abduction, and the arrival of the
oldest and wisest man of the village to imprint a sacred kiss on the earth. The
Second Part, *The Sacrifice*, takes place later that night and builds towards the
ritual offering of a human life. The power of this group ritual evokes a remote
other-worldly experience to ensure the celestial regeneration of the earth as it
was 'in the beginning'.[19] Young virgins dance in circles on the sacred hill and
choose the victim whom they will honour. She will dance herself to death in

---

17   Roerich's address was given in 1930: Pasler, ed. 1986, 68.
18   Stravinsky, Igor. Letter, December 15, 1912 in Stravinsky, Vera & Craft, Robert. 1979, 77.
19   Stravinsky preferred Part One to be called *Kiss of the Earth*, and Part Two *The Exalted
      Sacrifice*. Craft, Robert. 1992, 211–213.

front of elders clad in bearskins, since the ancient Slavs believed the bear to be
Man's ancestor.

The composition of *The Rite* came as a sudden, overwhelming experience, as if it erupted not from conscious technical theories but directly from
Stravinsky's subconscious: 'I heard and I wrote what I heard', he wrote later,
'I am the vessel through which *Le Sacre* passed'.[20] After the journal *Montjoie*
had distorted the language and even the ideas of his article about *Le Sacre,*
Stravinsky made it quite clear that the value of the work lay in its purely musical construction: it existed as a simple musical monument.[21] Stravinsky feared
that *The Rite*, created as a larger abstraction, and no longer appealing to the
spirit of fairy tales, or to human joy or sorrow, would disconcert those who had
shown him 'a special goodwill'.[22]

Stravinsky's representation of the temporalities of the archaic Slavic rite took
the public by storm. The conductor, Pierre Monteux, recalled that the audience
threw everything that they could at the orchestra. Perhaps to the sophisticated
Parisian audience both the music and the choreography appeared to be threat-
eningly unfamiliar and 'primitive'; perhaps it was even felt to be a provocative
comment by the Russians on the decadence of contemporary Western society.
Diaghilev and the Ballets Russes probably intended it to be a proud display
of their current cultural renaissance and the rise of Russian neo-nationalism.

3   Time Qualities in The Rite of Spring

The Rite is 'a single endless dialogue, an inconceivable conversation'.[23] This dialogue comprises four distinct types of time-creating movement that progress
according to a geometrical process, recalling Aquinas' dictum that 'Art imitates
Nature in its way of operating'.[24] In this natural process successive musical
points form a line, compatible lines of movement combine into a strong surface movement, and surface movements are juxtaposed in contrasting layers
to create musical volumes of various sizes.[25] This process of emergent levels of
temporality *was completely new in music.*

---

20   Stravinsky, Igor & Craft, Robert. 1981, *Expositions and Developments*, 147–8.
21   Interview: The Observer, July 3, 1921. In Lesure, François. 1980, 77.
22   Stravinsky, Igor. 1913. In Lesure, François. 1980, 13.
23   Grainger, Roger. 1974, 90–91.
24   *Ars imitatur naturam in sua operatione.* St Thomas Aquinas: *Summa Theologica* I, 1.117. a.1.
25   In this context, a musical volume describes a musical space, not levels of loudness or
      softness.

Although the time qualities of *The Rite of Spring* are juxtaposed in discrete sections with little transitional material, Stravinsky was very proud of his smooth junctures between the different parts of the stage action.[26] The transformation from one time quality to the next is accomplished not only with increased levels of complexity but also by changes in the musical elements that are dominant, as though instinctively aligning with the processing preferences of the brain's left and right hemispheres.

The four types of time-creating movement that make up the growth of *The Rite* may be differentiated simply as A, B, C, D, each movement having its own type of construction and time quality.

Movement Type A is heard only in the Introduction to Part One and is created by the individual, unrelated movements of living creatures, the 'Many', in the here-and-now of clock-time.[27] This Introduction represents 'the awakening of nature, the scratching, gnawing, wiggling of birds and beasts',[28] and 'the terror ... at secret forces ... that can grow and develop infinitely'.[29] Solo wind instruments develop their lines independently of each other with the rhythmic characteristics of their own *umwelt,* or time world. All the individual lines are held discrete by highly contrasting timbres but the textures grow and wane *en masse.* The arrow of time is present but it has no collective, unifying function.

Movement Type B makes its first, dramatic appearance at the beginning of The Augurs of Spring with a sudden, dynamic surface movement, a linear force in which rhythmic and harmonic compatibility are the dominant musical elements. Dynamic surface movement may be composed of one or more rhythmically compatible layers unified by a single pitch collection and pitch centre, but the musical space it creates may vary in width and texture. This homogeneous surface movement brings massive forward propulsion. The weight of movement B is sometimes increased by syncopation, and the sense of here-and-now intensified, by the conflict of off-beat accents with the pulse. Accents marked in the orchestral score, signifying 'jumps' for the dancers (as at the beginning of The Augurs of Spring and in Sacrificial Dance), also counterpoint the metre, introducing an interesting 'hocket' texture.[30]

---

26   Letter from Stravinsky to Roerich 13/26.9.1911 in Stravinsky: *Perepiska s russkimi korrespondentami: Materialy k biografii* 1/ 300. In Järvinen, Hanna. 2013.

27   Stravinsky referred to the pursuit of 'the One' out of 'the Many' as the inevitable problem of ontological enquiry: Stravinsky, Igor. 1947, 140.

28   Stravinsky, Igor & Craft, Robert. 1981. *Expositions and Developments*, 141.

29   Stravinsky, Igor. 1913. In Lesure, François. 1980.

30   Craft, Robert. 1992, 240–247.

Movement Type C begins to emerge from this dynamic linear movement in fragments, just nine bars after the beginning of The Augurs of Spring (fig. 14).
Individual lines and narrow surface movements, now circular in character
and held discrete by contrasting timbres, are juxtaposed at a new level of
organisation to create a three-dimensional musical space. These musical volumes vary in size according to the degree of contrast between their
layers and their rhythmic compatibility: single lines or ostinati that divide
the pulse in simple ratios create slight temporal depth and small musical
spaces by their juxtaposition, while less compatible or even conflicting
surfaces negate the sense of metre and create greater depth of time and
musical space. This fluctuation of depth simulates the variation of human
time-consciousness.

   The sometimes wide-ranging angular pitch activity of movement B
is replaced in movement C by short 'ostinato-style' motifs. The patterned
strata of movement C may be symmetrical or asymmetrical and are held
discrete by contrasts of timbre, though they may also be recessed by texture
and dynamics. The extent to which the sense of present time is diminished
depends on three criteria: the degree to which the strata are synchronised
and compatible in pacing; the degree to which they are rhythmically regular
and harmonically related; and the degree of timbral contrast between them.
The most complex juxtaposition of irregular circular layers in movement
C begins just before Procession of the Sage. An expanded and irregularly
repeating pattern for trombones is juxtaposed with a repeating circular
theme for woodwind and strings (fig. 64), then joined by what will become
an expanded motif for horns (fig. 65 + 2), and finally counterpointed by a
strident motif for trumpets (fig. 70) that completes the large time-negating
musical space.

   The linear momentum in clock-time of surface movement B makes a
great contrast to the time-deepening, space-enlarging processes of movement C, in which the sense of 'now' recedes: time diminishes to the extent
that the right hemisphere is able to relate strata of varied complexity. The
circular movements of the original choreography augment this effect, as in
The Augurs of Spring and Spring Rounds where the movements of the dancers are both synchronised and counterpointed with those of the orchestra.
These circular dance formations originated in the ancient Slavs' imitation of
the cycles of nature to promote a sense of 'sacred' time.

Movement Type D establishes a remote time quality in the Introduction to
Part Two, *The Sacrifice*, for the sacred mystery of nature's regeneration. This
deeper quality of time at a new slow pulse ($\downarrow$ = 48) comes from the juxtaposition of just two layers of movement that are very greatly contrasted in

pacing and timbre: one is rhythmically regular, with the fluctuating movement of two alternating pitches and drifting chromatics, the other is irregular, fragmented and barely audible. Like the two contrasting temporalities
that portray Petrushka's 'ghost' against the fairground, the time quality
created by fragments of a Khorovod melody drawn out in two-bar phrases
with changing metres and timbres is set against the present time quality
of drifting quaver movement. Bringing these two very different qualities of
time and movement into relationship diminishes the present, distances the
work in time and enlarges the musical space. Its other-worldly quality is
enhanced by a very wide pitch range, highly contrasted dynamics, transparent textures, harmonics for stringed instruments and muted wind and
brass tones.

Each of the four movement types has a particular structure:

a)   movement type A = the individual *umwelt* of each line
b)   movement type B = collective rhythmic force
c)   movement type C = interacting circular strata
d)   movement type D = great contrasts of timbre and pacing.

The four movement types create four progressively deeper qualities of time.
The dynamics that Stravinsky specified for each contrasting layer help to dif-
ferentiate their timbres and to clarify the degree of rhythmic and melodic
compatibility between them. Reviewing a recording of *The Rite of Spring* by
the Orchestre National de la R. T. F., conducted by Pierre Boulez, Stravinsky
remarked that 'though the mediumising of sound levels does only negligible
damage to some music, it deprives *The Rite* of one of its dimensions ...'[31]

The Rite is largely a dialogue between movement types B and C and the
time qualities they create: movement type B varies the pace and power of forward momentum in the present whereas movement type C gradually builds
the deeper 'sacred' time of ritual. This dialogue is preceded in each part of
the work by movements type A and D respectively, to establish the context
in which this dialogue develops. The growing disparity between present time
and ritual time reflects the purpose of the rite, which is to secure a productive interaction between the earth and the celestial regions: the regeneration
of the earth is petitioned in the sacred time qualities of movement type C,
but is made effective in the present by the force and vitality of movement
type B.

In The Augurs of Spring, three passages of movement type C alternate with
movement type B. The musical space enlarges with each passage of movement

---

31   Stravinsky, Igor & Craft, Robert. 1982, 90.

type C: the first four-bar volume (fig. 14) is small and, although it combines several tonalities, the three layers of circular figures are juxtaposed in a simple binary rhythmic relationship. The second passage (figs. 16–18) extends to 12 bars; its three rhythmically-compatible layers are now much fuller texturally and juxtapose duple and triple divisions of the pulse. The third passage (figs. 22–37) grows massively, extending the elaboration of the original 025 ostinato at figure 14 to 101 bars; the depth of time quality fluctuates slightly as the juxtaposition of circular motifs varies in number and they are juxtaposed with Khorovod melodies of different pacing and degrees of irregularity.[32]

Spring Rounds grows from an organically-evolving circular line and trill to a dialogue between two differently-paced circular movements, in which the depth of time quality is increased by the syncopation of one of the layers (fig. 49). The time quality is progressively deepened by the addition of irregular circular Khorovod movements (figs. 50–54) and by the counterpointing of the orchestral patterns with those of the three groups of dancers, until the density is released into the great forward momentum of movement type B at figure 54.

Ritual of the Rival Tribes and Procession of the Sage contain the most dramatic construction of temporal depth in Part One as the dialogue intensifies between the force of movement type B and the depth of movement type C. Great conflict is created by the juxtaposition of differently-paced layers. The forward thrust that begins Ritual of the Rival Tribes (fig. 57) gives way to a brief seven-bar Interlude of circular games (fig. 61) in which an irregular Khorovod melody is juxtaposed with regular circular accompaniment figures. But an elaborate construction of unrelated, irregular circular movements (fig. 64) introduces a mood of brooding tension for the coming of the Sage. At first, the joyful Khorovod melody is set against a heavy, five-note pattern for four tubas (Ex. 13). Both the melodic and repeating patterns vary slightly in bars 3 and 4 as it proceeds.

As the Khorovod dies away, two horns juxtapose a pattern that occurs randomly and unfolds even more slowly, a pattern that has been forming since figure 65 + 2 (Ex.14). The length of its final note settles to five beats from figure 69, but the accent constantly changes to a different beat of the bar.

The vast, time-less musical space that immediately precedes Kiss of the Earth is now expanded to breaking point. These two patterns (fig. 67), 'simmering' with added textures, continue until the sudden addition of a third surface (Ex.15), a regular pattern composed of a triumphant rising figure that is divided

---

32   A Khorovod, Russia's oldest dance, derives from old Russian words meaning 'moving around the sun'. It is danced in a circle, the dancers forming chains and interweaving patterns, and sometimes singing.

EX. 13   Khorovod theme against a varying pattern for four tubas

EX. 14   Juxtaposition of irregular patterns for two horns and four tubas (at pitch)

between the piercing timbres of the piccolo clarinet, trumpets (including piccolo trumpet) and trombones (fig. 70):

EX. 15   Regular patterning for wind and brass against irregular patterns for horns and
               tubas (rhythmic patterns only)

The three patterns proceed inexorably and independently of each other, even as the metre increases from 4/4 to 6/4, finally destroying all sense of time.

The dialogue between movement types B and C continues in Part Two with light circular movements of varying depth in Mystic Circles of the Young Girls. A second massive growth occurs in Ritual Action of the Ancestors.[33] Two circular surfaces form as the six chief elders dressed in bearskins move in circles on the stage (fig. 131). The juxtaposition of a muted four-note melody deepens the time quality (fig. 132). This small volume suddenly opens out into a vast musical space that lasts only two bars as the bears begin to circle and paw at the Chosen One (fig. 134). Here, the Khorovod is heard triumphantly in the horns (some muted) against many circular ostinati. The rest of the movement hurtles forward with surface movement type B before returning to the opening line and trill.

There are just two passages of movement type C in Sacrificial Dance, the second passage of a much deeper time quality than the first. They maintain the sense of 'sacred' ritual time as the Chosen One is offered to the sun god Yarilo (figs. 174–180, 181–186), and are only briefly separated by a passage of movement type B. These passages impinge upon the forward momentum of surface movement type B and its quality of 'gestural time' to affirm the Chosen One's deepening trance-like state in 'sacred time'. The two types of movement almost blend; as Mircea Eliade has written of ritual self-sacrifice: 'Through repetition ... concrete time is projected into mythical time ... Any ritual ... unfolds not only in a consecrated space ... but also in a "sacred time" ... when the ritual was performed for the first time by a god, an ancestor, or a hero'.[34]

The structuring of *The Rite of Spring* by these four types of movement is reinforced by changes of pitch collection. Allen Forte, Claudio Spies, Pieter van den Toorn and many other scholars have shown how Stravinsky moves between diatonic and octatonic pitch collections.[35] Migration between pitch collections and pitch sets with common pitch formations facilitates the changes of pace and time quality between the work's four types of movement; smooth pitch transitions between its starkly abutted sections are essential to its character as a living organism.

---

33 Boris Asaf'yev notes the use of 'chorale' material here. The accompanist and male dancers rehearsing for Millicent Hodson and Kenneth Archer's 1987 reconstruction of *Le Sacre* recognised this melody as a quote from the Mass of the Dead. Järvinen, Hanna. 2013.

34 Eliade, Mircea. 1959, 20–21.

35 Forte, Allen. 1978. van den Toorn, Pieter. C. 1986, 130.

The choreography was conceived to reflect and enhance the musical dialogue between these secular and sacred temporalities. Described, initially at least, by Stravinsky as of the 'utmost importance', the choreography was entrusted to the newly-discovered 'star' dancer Vaslav Nijinsky. If the audience expected to see outstanding displays of ballet technique and graceful movement and to delight in the visual splendour of its scenery and costumes, their expectations were to be confounded. Nijinsky took a great interest in Cubist ideas, stating that 'My new formula of movement emphasises the mechanism of gesture and line. I apply to choreography the theory of Cubist painters'.[36] Consequently, Nijinsky's choreography was realised with great objectivity, in terms of mathematical formations: lines, circles, mandalas, spirals, and the counterpointing of groups. His vision was of a decentralised ballet in which each of the dancers is a soloist with an individual part, though only the Chosen One has a virtuoso part.[37] Working hard at rehearsals in February 1913, Nijinsky described the work as 'really the soul of Nature expressed by movement to music ... It will be danced only by the corps de ballet, for it is a thing of concrete masses, not of individual effects'.[38]

As Stravinsky and Nijinsky worked together on the ballet, Nijinsky specified every detail of the dancers' stylised movements and eliminated every glimmer of individuality and self-expression from them, insisting that the gestures of his choregraphic design, like the Cubist painters' faceted forms, were sufficient. Above all, he emphasised the elemental, grounded nature of pre-historic tribal behaviour, infuriating the dancers by requiring them to abandon their training and dance flat-footed with knees turned in and elbows glued to their ribs, to stomp noisily and to fall about.

Nijinsky's Cubist-style choreography drew attention to the work's changes of time and movement. He took the revolutionary step of contrasting dynamic movement with stillness and immobility, of arranging the floor plans asymmetrically, and of introducing prolonged repetitive movements. Although the Parisians were perplexed by the choreography, the Russian critic Prince Volkonsky, who was more familiar with the current renaissance of ancient Russian culture and with Russian Orthodox ideals of community, was full of appreciation for its mass rhythmic effects:

---

36   Nijinsky: quoted in *Peterburgskaia Gazeta* 15. 28.4.1912. In Jarvinen, Hanna. 2013, 81 (in translation).
37   Hodson, Millicent. 2008.
38   Stravinsky, Vera & Craft, Robert. 1979, 95.

It must be said that the execution of this was wonderful – steady, monotonous, the people did not move, only the lines moved, as if no-one lived
alone, on their own – a human necklace tied by the invisible string of
rhythm.[39]

The actual score that Stravinsky worked on with Nijinsky reveals just how
much the choreography was involved with the musical design: the dancers'
physical gestures sometimes synchronise, sometimes counterpoint the rhythmic emphases and musical phrasing, in order to add another layer of patterning and change the time quality. In Spring Rounds, for example, three groups
of dancers enter one after the other (from fig. 49), each identified with a different rhythm in the orchestra: in bar 4 and bars 7–8 all movement freezes, an
effect that articulates the asymmetric periods of movement.[40] In Ritual of the
Rival Tribes (fig. 60), Stravinsky specified that the women should dance in 4/4
to the new motif in the oboes and clarinets while the men dance in 2/4 to
the counter-rhythm in the English horns. In Mystic Circles of the Young Girls,
the three groups of dancers should each articulate a different metre (figs. 93–
95) to bring out the relationships between the three motifs.[41] In The Augurs
of Spring, Nijinsky gave the male dancers one rhythm with their arms and
another with their feet, and in Spring Rounds there are five counterpointed
movements (fig. 53). Stravinsky conceived this pagan ritual in terms of both
aural and visual rhythmic movements, even specifying that the women dancers should 'walk in a bell-swinging rhythm' in Part Two,[42] and pointing to the
effect of the juxtaposed rhythms in Spring Rounds:

Pendant ce temps, les Adolescentes viennent de la rivière ... Ils se melan-
gent; mais dans leurs rythmes on sent le cataclysme des groupes qui se
forment ... C'est la forme qui se réalise, synthèse de rythmes; et la chose
formée *produit un rythme nouveau*.[43]

---

39   Apollon, June 1913 quoted in Järvinen, Hanna. 2013, 93.
40   Craft, Robert. 1992, 243.
41   Pasler, Jann. 1986, 72, 79.
42   Craft, Robert. 1992, 234.
43   Stravinsky, Igor. In Lesure, F. 1980, 14 (my italics). The article appeared in the journal
      Montjoie, in homage to Wagner (!) in the centenary year of his birth. Stravinsky wrote
      above one of his sketches for *Le Sacre:* 'Music exists when there is rhythm, as life exists
      when there is a pulse'. Craft, Robert. 1992, 245.

[During this time, the young girls come from the river ... They mix; but in their rhythms one feels the sense of disaster in the groups which are forming ... It is form which is emerging, a synthesis of rhythms; and the thing formed *produces a new rhythm.*]

The counterpoint between visual and musical movement in the dialogue between dynamic linearity in the here-and-now and depth of 'sacred' time was an essential part of *The Rite*. Years later, however, Stravinsky described Nijinsky as 'hopelessly incompetent in musical technique' because Nijinsky believed that the choreography should re-emphasise the musical beat and pattern and be constantly co-ordinated with it.[44] Rather than restricting the choreography to mere imitation, Stravinsky thought that choreography should realise its own form, one that was independent of the musical form but measured to the musical unit.[45]

Stravinsky described *The Rite of Spring* as 'architectonic', 'a series of rhythmic mass movements of the greatest simplicity which would have an instantaneous effect on the audience ...'[46] The work may also be seen as embodying a self-organising series of emergent levels of temporality: it imitates the growth of space in the form of sound, as it increases in complexity from a point to a multi-dimensional entity. Just as a geometrical structure in physical space is formed by the juxtaposition of points, lines, surfaces and volumes, so *The Rite's* qualities of musical time grow from an immediate 'now' to great temporal depth in a similar process of juxtapositions. *The Rite* simulates the process by which we experience the growth of many other forms, for example, in nature, mathematics and folk tales.[47]

The stages of this growth movement have a striking effect on the sense of time that is created. Movement types A and B create the measurable time qualities of the physical world. In the Introduction to Part One, in movement type A, the left hemisphere processes each line of movement and – remarkably – also registers and groups the overtones of each individual timbre. The forceful rhythmic energy of movement type B activates areas of the left hemisphere, its homogeneity of timbre, dynamics and texture diminishing the role of the right hemisphere that prefers to compare and relate information. Increased density

---

44   Stravinsky, Igor & Craft, Robert. 1981, *Memories and Commentaries*, 37.
45   Ibid.
46   Stravinsky, Igor. 1975, 48. Stravinsky likened the sensation produced by music to that evoked by the contemplation of the interplay of architectural forms. Op. cit., 54.
47   Regarding the structure of myths, Claude Lévi-Strauss observed: 'Nature has only a limited number of procedures at her disposal, and the kinds of procedure which Nature uses at one level of reality are bound to reappear at different levels'. Lévi-Strauss, 1978, 10.

comes with the conflict between metre and accents as they are processed by neurally separate areas of the left temporal lobe that are in strong competition with one another. A strong rhythmic pulse stimulates areas of the brain concerned with the timing of physical movement, not only the substantia negra and basal ganglia, but also the cerebellum, the oldest part of the brain: connections are also made to the frontal lobes, the amygdala, and other emotion-processing areas.

With movement types C and D attention shifts to timbre and melodic contour, and to the relationships between discrete layers of movement. Movement types C and D make greater appeal to the right temporal lobe in juxtaposing a variety of time-creating movements and also to neighbouring areas of the parietal lobe concerned with movement in space. As contrasts of timbre and rhythm increase and relations become more complex, the sense of present time is diminished in favour of temporal depth and an enlargement of musical space. Movement type D creates the remotest quality of time and the largest musical space by stimulating the right hemisphere to relate lines that are greatly contrasted in pace and timbre.

The choreographic succession of *The Rite* connects into a continuous temporal form as we 'live through' it with the dancers; the centres of attention in the brain change as its qualities of time unfold and fluctuate in depth, and as its dominant musical elements alter. The function of a group ritual is to enable access to new realms of experience, both individual and collective, that are not ordinarily accessible. Although variations in time quality can, of course, be found in music of all periods, the construction of four distinct types of time and movement in *The Rite of Spring* suddenly propelled the relationship between music and time into sharp focus; no previous piece of music had represented the process of 'being becoming' in quite such a direct and forceful manner.

Stravinsky's innovative juxtapositions of rhythmic patterns had touched elemental forces. In March 1912, Stravinsky wrote to Roerich: 'It seems to me that I have penetrated the secret of the rhythm of Spring ...'[48] The *Montjoie* article had explained that 'le cycle annuel des forces qui renaissent et qui tombent dans le giron de la nature est accompli dans ses rythmes essentiels' [*the annual cycle of forces that are reborn and fall into the bosom of nature is achieved in its essential rhythms*].[49] 'Play *Le Sacre*', wrote Stravinsky to Andrei Rimsky-Korsakov, '... I am certain that in time you will begin to feel it ...'[50]

---

48   Stravinsky, Vera & Craft, Robert. 1979, 85.

49   Stravinsky, Igor. 1913. In Lesure, F. 1980, 13–14.

50   Stravinsky, Vera & Craft, Robert. 1979, 25.

Those who first heard *The Rite of Spring* remarked upon the dramatic effect the music had had upon them. In the spring of 1913, after playing the work with Stravinsky in a four-handed arrangement at the house of Louis Laloy, the editor of *La Grande Revue*, Debussy wrote to Stravinsky saying that he was haunted by it 'like a beautiful nightmare' and was trying in vain 'to reinvoke the terrific impression'.[51] Laloy recorded that after this performance they were 'dumbfounded, overwhelmed by this hurricane which had come from the depth of the ages and which had taken life by the roots'.[52] The painter Jean Jeanès, who was present at one of the first performances, wrote to Stravinsky: 'it seems to me that you have expressed one of the elementary forces of Man'.[53]

The philosopher Gisèle Brelet later wrote of the temporal aspects of *The Rite of Spring*:

> L'éternel présent de Strawinsky est bien différent de celui des primitifs: il n'est plus ignorance de la durée psychologique, mais délivrance a son égard; et reconquis sur le temps, il n'est plus forme statique et figée, mais forme toujours actuelle et infiniment féconde; il n'est plus 'magique', mais 'discursif': en lui s'exprime, non plus l'inconscient refus de temps, mais un conscient consentement au temps, enfin compris en sa nature profonde ...[54]

> [Stravinsky's eternal present is quite different to that of ancient peoples: it is no longer ignorance of psychological time, but an escape in that respect; and having won back time, it is no longer a static, stiff form, but a form that is always real and infinitely fertile; it is no longer 'magic', but 'discursive': what is expressed is not the unconscious refusal of time, but a conscious assent to time, its profound nature ultimately understood ...]

Stravinsky thanked Nijinsky for being 'the ideal flexible collaborator' and also Roerich for creating the 'atmospheric pictures' for 'this work of faith'.[55] The *Rite of Spring* marks an important milestone in music's function as a temporal art, recovering that of Renaissance polyphony: Stravinsky later described himself

---

51   Stravinsky, Igor & Craft, Robert. 1979, 50. Stravinsky disputes this date in fn 1.
52   Stravinsky, Vera & Craft, Robert. 1979, 87.
53   Op. cit., 102.
54   Brelet, Gisèle. 1949, 688.
55   Stravinsky, Igor. 1913. In Lesure, F. 1980.

as a 'turning-around' point in the history of music, rather than a revolutionary. Even more fundamentally, *The Rite of Spring's* dynamic representation of growth and changes of temporality draws attention not only to the temporal aspects of human existence, but also to our own relationship with a creative power beyond ourselves.

CHAPTER 5

A Japanese Spring

During the years 724–736 CE, the Japanese court poet Yamabe no Akahito travelled extensively throughout some of the remoter regions of Japan with the Emperor Shomu and his entourage. As he travelled, he recorded his impressions of the wonderful sights and sounds of the natural world in brief, concisely structured poems. In 1912, nearly 1200 years later, Stravinsky was inspired by the temporal aspects of this delicate poetic form, and a poem by Akahito became the first of his *Three Japanese Lyrics.*

By 1909, *Le Japonisme,* the fashion for Japanese art, culture and aesthetics, had been influencing Western Europe for a generation. Since Japanese ports had opened to imports from the West in 1853, and particularly since the Meiji Restoration in 1868, Japanese ceramics, woodblock prints, textiles, bronzes and enamels had been eagerly collected by Western dealers and had rapidly become a source of inspiration for artists. Katsushika Hokusai's woodblock prints were first printed in black and white in the 1860s, while his *Manga,* line-drawn cartoons, famously found their way to Paris wrapped around a consignment of porcelain. At the International Exposition held in Paris in 1867, Japan had its own national pavilion showing Japanese works of art, and Japanese art also featured strongly at the subsequent International Expositions held in Paris in 1878, 1889 and 1900. The Director of the 1900 International Exposition, Tadamasa Hayashi, was one of many art dealers in Europe who, from the 1870s, imported thousands of Japanese prints that subsequently influenced such artists as Manet, Monet, Van Gogh, Gauguin and Toulouse-Lautrec. It was now many years since Whistler's *Purple and Rose* of 1864 and the beginning of a fashion for Japanese costumes that, in 1878, had inspired Monet to paint his wife in a kimono. Van Gogh had painted *La Courtisane* in 1887 after an ukiyo-e print by Eisen had appeared on the cover of *Paris Illustré* in the previous year. Many art critics had travelled to Japan in order to write informed articles: for example, thirty-six issues of a magazine, *Le Japon Artistique,* that commented on Japanese art and culture, were published in Paris between May 1888 and April 1891. Composers also found new inspiration in Japanese subjects: Gilbert and Sullivan had great success with the opera *The Mikado* (1885), and Pierre Loti's novel *Madame Chrysanthème* (1887), about a naval officer who marries a geisha in Nagasaki, became the subject of Puccini's opera *Madam Butterfly* (1904). Debussy was among the many collectors of Japanese woodblock prints, and Hokusai's *In the Well of the Great Wave at Kanagawa* featured on the front cover of the first orchestral score of *La Mer*.[1]

The characteristic techniques of line-drawing in Japanese woodblock prints influenced not only the Impressionists but also the Art Nouveau and Cubist movements. The scenes portrayed in Japanese prints often lack perspective and their rhythmic lines project outside the frame. Coupled with this is a love of asymmetry and irregularity, manifested in a freedom of line and positioning that likes to place the subject 'off-centre'. Japanese prints lack shadow and delight in flat areas of strong colour that make a contrast to the sinuous curves of their lines and patterned surfaces. In Paris, Stravinsky became well acquainted with Japanese art: away from the politics of the Ballets Russes he had found real friendship and encouragement for his latest works in a group of artists, musicians and poets who called themselves 'The Apaches' (The Ruffians).[2] This avant-garde group had been meeting after concerts since 1902 to play their compositions to each other and to read and discuss all things new, including the current fashion for Japonaiserie. The group included Maurice Delage, Florent Schmitt and Maurice Ravel, the three dedicatees of the *Three Japanese Lyrics*. Maurice Delage, the dedicatee of the first of these songs, was a particularly close friend of Stravinsky. Like many other businessmen he had often visited Japan – most recently in the spring of 1912 – and had written a number of compositions as a result of his fascination with that country.[3]

In the summer of 1912, Stravinsky had read a little anthology of Japanese lyrics that had been selected from the old poets. The impression they made was exactly like that made on him by Japanese paintings and engravings. He recalled that the graphic solution of problems of perspective and space shown by their art incited him to find something analogous in music.[4] Much later, during a visit to Japan in 1959, he told an interviewer that he was attracted at the time (1912) by Japanese woodblock prints, a two-dimensional art without any sense of solidity, and that he had also discovered this two-dimensional nature in some Russian translations of Japanese poetry and had attempted to express it in his music.[5]

Although the Japanese poems and prints in his possession were 'two-dimensional' in nature and lacked solidity, nevertheless, like *The Rite*, they

---

1   See Funayama, Takashi. In Pasler, J., ed. 1988, 273–83.
2   See Pasler, ed. 1982, 403–7.
3   The Apaches met at the home of Maurice Delage: Walsh, Stephen. 2002, 186.
4   Stravinsky, Igor. 1975, 45.
5   Stravinsky, Igor 1959. In Craft, Robert. 2007.

TABLE 1   *Waka* poetry during the Nara and Heian periods

NARA PERIOD (710–794 CE)			
Man'yoshu	700 after 759		Yamabe no Akahito (700–736)
HEIAN PERIOD (794–1185 CE)			
	after 850		Minamoto no Masazumi Ki no Tsurayuki – a compiler of Kokin Wakashu
Poetry competitions	885		
Kokin Wakashu	920		
	988		Noin b. Compiled first surviving Utamakura

evoked certain qualities of time, albeit of a very delicate and elusive kind. Recreating the techniques of ancient Japanese poems and 19th century wood-block prints in music became a project very close to Stravinsky's heart.

Stravinsky chose three ancient Japanese poems from his collection.[6] The author of the first poem, Yamabe no Akahito, was writing from 724 CE, during the Nara period (Table 1). He was one of the four great poets to contribute to the *Man'yoshu,* the earliest surviving collection of some twenty volumes of Japanese poems which was compiled sometime after 759 CE.[7] The author of the second poem, Minamoto no Masazumi, contributed to the *Kokin Wakashu* though little is known about him. The author of the third poem, Ki no Tsurayuki, was one of the compilers of the *Kokin Wakashu,* a collection of poems which, like the *Man'yoshu,* ran to twenty volumes.

---

6   Stravinsky's collection of old Japanese poems had been translated into Russian by A.S. Brandt.

7   Akahito contributed thirteen long poems (*nagauta*), and thirteen short poems (*tanka*) as *envois* (*hanka*) to these long poems, to the *Man'yoshu.* The *Man'yoshu* was the single greatest literary achievement of the Nara and early Heian periods, and was important for being written in the Japanese language as opposed to Chinese. With the introduction of poetry competitions (*Uta-awase*) in 885 CE and the commissioning of the *Kokin Wakashu* by the Emperor Daigo in 905 CE, the making of short poems, formerly called tanka but now known as waka, became an important and much prized part of Japanese life.

Waka poetry, as it came to be called, established a genre that became a Japanese court tradition lasting until the 14th century. Over the centuries it created a vast meta-narrative from poetic 'traces' of time that expressed great nostalgia for the Japanese traditions and culture of the past. The art of *waka* (literally, 'Japanese song/poem'), little known in the West, was the art of constructing poems that had rich associations with earlier poems but added some new and interesting aspect to them. These associations were promoted and enriched in three ways: through *utamakura* (reference words), through explicit allusion, and through intertextuality. *Utamakura*, literally 'poem-pillows' on which poets could 'rest' their associated ideas, were usually place names that had acquired a poetic status or objects that had come to have symbolic value. They were collected into a handbook by Noin at the beginning of the 11th century. Explicit allusions to earlier poems could also be made by varying phrases that had come to be sufficiently well-known. Disparate poems could also be simultaneously connected by intertextuality in elaborate networks of finely-wrought associations recalling theme, style or mood.[8]

The spontaneous composition of *waka* poetry became a vital social skill. It could establish one's status at court entertainments and in society generally, and was a necessary embellishment of travel diaries. It developed into a means of shorthand communication between friends and lovers that was greatly prized. At best, *waka* poems are characterised by elegance and beauty and a poignant awareness of the pathos of life (*mono no aware*). Paradoxically, art, elegance and beauty came to be very highly valued in a culture which aspired at the same time to the Buddhist ideal of regarding these things as ultimately of fleeting worth.

Like the 'artisan craftsman' – *homo faber* – philosophy which Stravinsky was later to embrace, the art of composing *waka* poetry is the conscious art of 'poem-making'.[9] Words are carefully selected and arranged with skilful regard to their total effect. Words can have more than one meaning, adding depth to their associations, and the recurrence of similar sounds in homonyms, homophones, alliteration and assonance can set up counter-rhythms within its very concise structure which, sadly, are lost in translation. The genre is chiefly concerned with the passing of time, and tends to blend emotions of remembered moments with those of the present moment and express them within a strict syllabic structure. The themes of *waka* poetry are varied, but their content is usually strictly limited and structured within 31 syllables, with an

---

8   See Kamens, Edward. 1997, 23–62.
9   See Chapter 7:7: Time and Form: Jacques Maritain

upper phrase of 5 plus 7 plus 5 syllables and a lower phrase of 7 plus 7 syllables. Rhyme is considered to be a fault and there is no strict concept of the
'line'.

The two-dimensional effect of this poetic form that had attracted Stravinsky's
interest arises largely through the juxtaposition of two ideas or sentiments,
more often than not with a shift of temporality between the two phrases. For
example, in the first phrase the poet may refer to a geographical place with a
poetic tradition, and in the second phrase, endow it with a new emotion when
he has visited that place. Or the movement between the phrases may be to a
new symbolism to mark the meaningful reappearance of a significant object,
such as a tree that has been buried in the river. The most admired poems have
an implicit ambiguity either in subject or in outcome: the movement of the
poem leaves the reader somewhere between its two temporalities with a feeling of insubstantiality and open-endedness.

The three poems that Stravinsky selected present different perspectives on
Spring, a favourite subject of *waka* poetry. Each poem takes two images and
creates a delicate and elusive temporality by juxtaposing their qualities of
movement: the first tells of snow coming to cover the white spring flowers; the
second describes the arrival of spring and the white foam that rushes amidst
the thawing ice floes like spring flowers; the third describes the confusion
between distant white clouds and cherry blossom. There is also a temporal
progression between the three songs that moves from uncertainty about the
coming of spring to vivid here-and-now sensations of its arrival, and then to
the traditional symbolism of fully blossoming cherry trees.

Stravinsky spoke of 'succeeding by a metrical and rhythmic process'.[10] The
vocal line represents the first flowers of spring in all three songs. It is consistent
in style, with each syllable of its Russian translation set to a single quaver, and
it mostly patterns the interval of a 3rd in 'circular' movements. To ensure that
the temporal quality of each song is created first and foremost by the music,
Stravinsky reduced the power of the literal meaning of the words by putting
the tonic accents of the Russian translation in opposition to those of the musical phrase. He wrote to his publisher, Derzhanovsky, that as there is no such
thing as accentuation in either the Japanese language or in Japanese poetry,
he had eliminated the accents of the Russian translation so as to achieve the
linear perspective of Japanese declamation.[11]

---

10   Stravinsky, Igor. 1975, 45.

11   After composing the textual and musical accents to coincide in the ordinary way,
      Stravinsky moved them an eighth or a quarter note to the right, transforming the words
      into vocal 'sounds' and reducing the power of their literal meaning to create their own

The linear perspective of the vocal line, however, is fragmented and spare, and echoes something of the syllabic discipline of *waka* poetry in that the number of syllables in its successive phrases are in similar ratios such as 5: 3, 6: 4, or 8: 6. Stravinsky also captures the haunting effect of the poems' carefully-placed syllables by setting the text to 'circular' motifs that expand and contract around a few pitches like znamenny chant. He matches resonant vowels to pitches that recur at significant melodic points of the phrase, invoking both the 'natural' mood of Russian peasant singing and the simple purity of nature. By contrast, the instrumental layer that unfolds against this articulated vocal line is continuous, held discrete, and often chromatic in character. In *Three Japanese Lyrics* Stravinsky finds an analogy for the fragile two-dimensional quality of the *waka* poems by juxtaposing two musical lines and distinguishing their movements by greatly contrasting timbres. The bright timbre of the soprano voice occupies the foreground, but is heard only intermittently against a continuous layer of soft, often muted solo instruments.[12] Each layer of sound unfolds at its own pace with its own quality of movement and in its own umwelt, even though the two layers may begin from a similar motif, as in *Akahito*. The action of the poem is embodied in the unfolding of these independent layers.

Stravinsky also became interested in the connection between the two-dimensional effect of *waka* poetry and the two-dimensional, spatial-temporal quality of Japanese prints. During his visit to Japan in 1959, Stravinsky told music critic Hans Pringsheim that he had long been fond of Japanese art and that about 50 years previously he had owned some prints by Hokusai and Hiroshige.

The spatial-temporal quality of the powerful rhythms in Hokusai's engraving *In the Well of the Great Wave at Kanagawa*, for example, has justly made it famous (Illustration 1). The overarching lines of the powerful surf-laden waves on the left hand side form a three-part sequence, threatening three fragile boats

---

time quality: Stravinsky, Vera & Craft, Robert. 1979, 107–8. Stravinsky replied to his publisher's enquiries: 'The most natural course was to shift all the "long" syllables onto musical "short" [beats]'. Richard Taruskin writes that Stravinsky is using the terms 'long' and 'short' in a conventional way to describe Russian tonic scansion which is qualitative not quantitative; he also illustrates Stravinsky's accentual changes. Taruskin, Richard. 1987, 170–171.

12   The small chamber group comprises solo piccolo, flute, two clarinets, string quartet and piano. *Three Japanese Lyrics* had its première on 14 January, 1914 at the Salle Erard in Paris. The programme included *Three Mallarmé Poems* by Ravel, written for the same instrumentation, and *Four Hindu Songs* by Maurice Delage, a pupil of Ravel.

ILLUSTRATION 1   *In the Well of the Great Wave at Kanagawa* – Hokusai
THE METROPOLITAN MUSEUM OF ART, NEW YORK

that are being tossed about in the valleys between them. The boats create a second rhythmic line which leads from the perilous activity in the foreground to the scene's serene background. The almost audible rhythmic pounding of the waves is juxtaposed to the strong silent form of Mount Fuji, the symbol of eternity. The interaction of these rhythmic lines in a two-dimensional medium sets up a fragile and unstable time quality.

A photograph of Stravinsky in his living room at home in Ustilug in 1912 shows four Japanese prints hung vertically on the left hand side of the wall behind him.[13] The bottom print is *Japonaiserie: the Courtesan* by Van Gogh, after Keisai Eisen. The top print appears to be a version of *Festival of Lanterns on Temma Bridge in Settsu Province* by Katsushika Hokusai.[14]

Japanese woodblock artists became masters at creating visual movement and mass with single lines: light, colour and tone were subordinate to the juxtaposition of forms and linear rhythms. Hokusai's *Festival of Lanterns*

---

13   Stravinsky, Theodor, 1975.
14   Hokusai often produced several versions of the same scene.

ILLUSTRATION 2   *Festival of Lanterns on Temma Bridge in Settsu Province* – Hokusai
BROOKLYN MUSEUM, NEW YORK

(Illustration 2) juxtaposes rhythmic lines within a two-dimensional frame, and although at first sight it is harmonious, closer scrutiny proves it to be unreal in its perspectives. The line of the bridge cuts across the middle of the scene, decreasing in size from right to left as does the crowd, though the lanterns do not. The bridge is asymmetrical, having six four-part supports to the middle from the right and only four to the opposite shore. A line of boats decorated with lanterns and carrying carousing locals counterpoints the line made by the bridge; it floats from left to right, increasing rhythmically from a single boat to groups of three and five. There is a third rhythmic line made by the dwellings on the distant shores; they show that the river bends round to the left in the centre of the scene. The picture's rhythmic lines carry the eye outside the two-dimensional framework, so that our sense of space is expanded by the interaction of its rhythms and enriched by a quality of open-endedness and instability. There is a strong temporal effect too, because the print captures a single point in time in the long and rich history of the location.

Stravinsky achieves a similar spatial-temporal effect in *Three Japanese Lyrics* by juxtaposing two streams of rhythmic movement that do not meet or relate to each other. In each song, each line of movement remains constant and distinctive within its own temporal world, proceeding independently against the other in imitation of the movement described in the poem. By this means, Stravinsky creates a musical analogy of the fragile and ambiguous temporalities created in both waka poems and Japanese woodblock prints.

The poem of the first song is by Yamabe no Akahito:

> Waga seko ni
> Misemu to omohisi
> Ume no hana
> Sore to mo miezu
> Yuki no furereba

> To the one I love
> I'd like to show
> The plum blossoms
> Which are indiscernible
> Because the snow fell[15]

In this poem we move from the thought of movement to the actual movement of snow falling to cover blossom. The ambiguity of white on white, snow on blossom, is a favourite device of *waka* poetry.

In this first song, two streams of rhythmic movement move at a moderate speed and at the same quaver pace, but as in the poem, one layer expands in register to engulf the other. The fleeting juxtaposition of these two layers of movement captures the action and time quality of the poem in 46 seconds or so. In the opening bars, the soprano line is heard between the timbres of the flute and clarinet, her bright, fragmented circular motifs at first surrounded by the continuous soft background (Ex. 16).

At first there is little separation between the layers as they pattern a similarly narrow chromatic cluster: simply a haunting alternation of C♭– C♮ against a downward C♭– B♭ in the wind ostinato.

The voice sets the major 3rd E♭ – G irregularly on the 3rd, 2nd and 1st beats of the bar against the regular instrumental ostinato (bars 1–5). As the blossoms begin to be lost to sight, the instrumental group becomes more active,

---

15   Poems translated by Keiko Miyakita. These translations evoke the elusive temporality of
        the text and its two-dimensional quality.

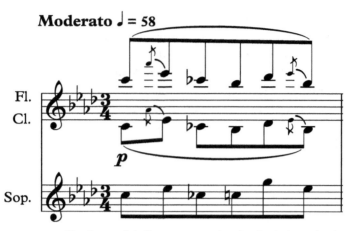

EX. 16   Two layers of similar movement that develop independently

expanding chromatically and with pizzicato notes and harmonics to surround the vocal part. The vocal motifs also rise, continuing to pattern the intervals of a major and minor 3rd. High-pitched staccato quavers for piccolo and pizzicato notes for cello in the low register evoke the falling of snow; the fragile, open-ended time world of the poem vanishes with a single quaver and grace note.

The poem of the second song is by Minamoto no Masazumi:

> Tanikaze ni
> Tokuru koori no
> Himagoto ni
> uchi-izuru nami ya
> Haru no hatsuhana

> With the wind from the valley
> The ice broke
> Through every crack
> Waves spill out
> These are the first blossoms of Spring[16]

16   Its full meaning is: 'The valley wind of early spring starts to break the ice on the river, and between every crack the water spills out making white waves, which must be the first spring flowers'. This poem was printed in the 20th issue of *Le Japon Artistique*.

In this song the vocal and instrumental layers move with a great contrast of pace between them, from *vivo* to *largamente* and back. The furious whirling and whistling of the wind through the valley is evoked by a repeating demi-semiquaver motif, rapid rhythmic figures in irregular groupings, and a great variety of timbres and textures. Anchoring these textures is a harsh D♯ that is sustained intermittently by the second violin *sul ponticello*.

The stately vocal line of *Akahito* reappears at the climactic midpoint of the song to announce the arrival of Spring with similar quaver patterns of minor 3rds. The vocal patterning is briefly elongated (bars 20–21). The actual arrival of Spring is suggested in the final five bars in which the vocal line (as at the end of *Akahito*) rises to pattern alternating major and minor 3rds, the last pattern accelerating towards a soft chord of instrumental harmonics. The contrast between the lively linear activity of the instrumental stream and the slow vocal line announcing the first fragile flowers creates the impression of an extended event in the present, though its performance time is less than a minute.

The poem of the third song is by Ki no Tsurayuki:

> Sakurabana
> Sakini kerashina
> Ashibiki no
> Yamano kai yori
> Miyuru shirakumo

> Cherry blossom
> May be blooming now
> Ashibiki no ('pillow word' – epithet for mountain top)
> between the mountains
> white clouds can be seen[17]

The cherry tree is the national tree of Japan, and from the *Man'yoshu* onwards the tree and its blossom held an almost mystical position in the *waka* tradition. Various comparisons of cherry blossom to white clouds appear in at least five of Tsurayuki's poems. From its origin as a symbol of unity and solidarity among

---

17   This poem particularly captures the Japanese love of Nature and its symbolism. Keiko Myakita writes: 'The poet looked up and saw the white clouds between the mountains and with his longing heart he thought of the cherry blossom buds that must have just opened'.

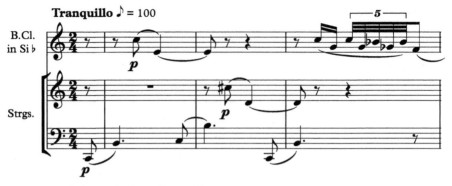

EX. 17   Instrumental layer: Tsurayuki

the people it became an image of shade and peace, its full-blown blossoming a symbol of Man's destiny or immortality.[18]

In the third song, Stravinsky imitates the poem's confusion between blossom and clouds by juxtaposing two similarly paced layers in quavers, as in *Akahito*. But here they create distinctively different time qualities by their contrasting pitch behaviour and pacing at ♪ = 100. The spare, wispy phrases for strings and clarinet spread expansively over three bars and three octaves, tranquillo, with large intervals that bend and sway towards each other like branches (Ex.17).

The vocal layer continues the close patterning of the intervals of a 3rd and a 4th of the first two songs. Their contrast of pace is blended by decorative woodwind flourishes that suggest clusters of blossom on a branch as in a Japanese print.

The temporality changes suddenly to a vivid present as the full blossoming of the cherry trees becomes indistinguishable from the clouds. The vocal patterning again rises in pitch, but is joined by the instrumental line for four bars (bars 14–17). The climax comes with the vocal patterning of the major and minor 3rd as before, the final major 3rd being unaccompanied.

The time world of the song – and the set of songs – is sealed with the soft distant timbres of the woodwind and violin, with the prominent interval of a 4th in bars 9–10 now recalled in stretto entries and with rhythmic diminution. This is the longest of the songs, with a performance time of barely 1 minute and 25 seconds. Despite its brief realisation in clock-time, the coming together

18   In the Preface to the *Kokinshu*, Ki no Tsurayuki writes: '... it is poetry, which with only a part of its power, moves heaven and earth, pacifies unseen gods and demons, reconciles men and women and calms the hearts of savage warriors'.

of two slowly evolving contrasting movements creates a monumental quality that mirrors the long time span of the poem.

In the *Three Japanese Lyrics* of 1912 Stravinsky built on the layering technique that had produced a similarly delicate and elusive effect in the first of his *Two Poems* of 1911, *The Flower*. In this setting of a poem by Balmont, the short articulated phrases of the vocal part also play around a few pitches in a 'circular' movement while the accompaniment imitates the movement described in the poem. The growth of the flower, for example, is embodied in the increase of texture from a trill on a bare 5th to an added ostinato and a skeletal third line. It continues in a relatively long passage, più mosso, in which four layers of patterning are heard simultaneously as the flower blossoms (letter B). Even as early as 1911, Stravinsky juxtaposes four layers of movement with differing degrees of regularity to represent the mature but delicate being of the flower. The vocal part patterns quavers within an octave in asymmetric phrases; of the three accompanying ostinati, one is strictly regular with a heavily dotted demisemiquaver rhythm, one has semiquavers that change their harmonic perspective in every bar, and the third, in the bass, has a slow, irregular pattern that repeats. Stravinsky's empathy with the being of the flower is felt in his setting of the final line, 'Do you hear its thin little voice?' which is left unaccompanied.[19]

In *Three Japanese Lyrics* Stravinsky sought 'something analogous' to problems of perspectives and space in graphic art with which to create the fragile and elusive temporalities of the Japanese poems he had selected. His solution was to mirror their temporal ambiguity by juxtaposing layers that are equal in weight but contrasted in their energy and actions. In July 1954 Stravinsky arranged *Two Poems* for the same combination of instruments as *Three Japanese Lyrics*.

It seems that the question of unfamiliar temporal-spatial qualities and their effect on human consciousness had occupied Stravinsky's thoughts for some time. In 1908, he had bought a picture by M. K. Cuirlionis, a Lithuanian painter whose work interested him greatly. It depicts a row of pyramids in flight towards the horizon, not in the diminuendo of orthodox perspective but in crescendo, i.e. getting bigger towards the horizon. He recalled that the picture had been 'part of his life', but was lost with his other possessions in Ustilug.[20] Stravinsky's techniques for creating fragile temporalities in these songs composed between

---

19   'Thin' meaning high, but not weak. In the second of the Balmont songs, the dove's cooing and fluttering is suggested by a demisemiquaver movement similar to that of the cherry blossom in the third of the *Three Japanese Lyrics*.

20   Stravinsky, Igor & Craft, Robert, 1981, *Expositions and Developments* 27, n.1.

1911 and 1913 may be related to two particular techniques that he may have encountered in his early years when he had wanted to be a painter. Both techniques concern the different ways in which artistic materials are juxtaposed and their effect on the cognitive faculties.

Firstly, the problem of representing three-dimensional movement in a two-dimensional figure had been specifically addressed by Hokusai in his *Manga,* a series of line-drawn cartoons, first published in 1814, which began to circulate in the West after 1854. Hokusai sketched thousands of subjects; in many of his cartoons people, animals and objects appear to be moving because he portrayed them in a position of instability. He drew them as seen in one fleeting moment in the process of change from a static state into a dynamic action. The tension between the perception of a static two-dimensional figure and the three-dimensional movement implied by its unstable position creates an ambiguous visual space.

One hundred or so years after *Three Japanese Lyrics,* neuroscience experiments have corroborated this phenomenon.[21] When observed in fMRI tests, the dynamic bodily actions portrayed in the static lines of the Hokusai *Manga,* with their particular visual cue of instability, activated an impression of movement in the brain.[22] Remarkably, further tests found that even listening to words that merely suggest movement, for example, 'walking', activated the same areas of the brain, even while both eyes were closed.[23] Given the degree of cooperation and overlap between the aural, visual and spatial processing systems, these findings suggest that just as the visual system interprets two simultaneous but contradictory visual perceptions in a new and ambiguous space, the auditory system may interpret two simultaneous but contrasting movements as creating a new and ambiguous quality of time.

Secondly, artists have long known how to create ambiguous spatial effects to access deeper levels of the mind. Following the publication of his Charles Eliot Norton lectures as *Poetics of Music*, Stravinsky thought that a good subject for future lectures, if given by the composer Ernst Krenek, would be *The Psychological Principles of Auditory Form*, since 'something like Anton

---

21   Activity was stimulated in areas including V5, the middle temporal gyrus, left extrastriate body area, left superior temporal sulcus and other related motion-associated areas: Martin, A. et al. PLoS One, 2009. 4(5): e5389.

22   Ibid. Significant activation was found in the bilateral inferior temporal gyrus in the extrastriate cortex (BA19), and in the bilateral inferior occipital gyrus (BA18 and BA19).

23   Research found 'a unique activation in the bilateral extrastriate visual cortices when the participant observed an implicit motion cartoon because of instability'. Osaka, Nauoyuki et al. 2009.

Ehrenzweig's *Psychoanalysis of Artistic Vision and Hearing* was needed by a musician'.[24] Stravinsky's reference to Ehrenzweig's work throws an interesting light on his own musical techniques, and also connects them with his lifelong interest in painting. Ehrenzweig contrasts the function of surface perception – directed to the processing of precise, compact, coherent, biologically relevant and aesthetically good shapes – with the function of depth perception to which other matter is relegated and to which distortions are repressed.[25] Ehrenzweig takes examples from modern art, including the paintings of Picasso, in which the lack of dominant eye-catching features and consequent ambiguity of form stimulate depth perception. Furthermore, he makes an important reference to Henri Bergson's method for achieving an intuitive state of depth perception in the visual arts. To aid the artist in practising depth perception, Bergson had recommended 'the simultaneous visualisation of a diversity of superimposed objects, which in spite of their differences of aspects ... require from the mind the same kind of attention'.[26] There is an important analogy with music here. Visual art, especially that of the Cubists, experiments with the superimposition of equally strong forms in order to depress perception to a gestalt-free, time-free level. Ehrenzweig went as far as likening the gestalt-free vision that results from these superimposed perceptions to Bergson's 'metaphysical intuition'.

Ehrenzweig applies Bergson's method to music and comments on the temporal effect of listening to polyphony, 'where several melodies sound together yet none is strong enough to attract and fix conscious attention exclusively to itself'.[27] Stravinsky's works make a similar distinction between the surface perception of music in clock-time and the holistic perception of temporal depth in which clock-time is overlaid or negated. Stravinsky's time qualities lie on a spectrum between those of the focused present and the timeless: he constructs time qualities by juxtaposing patterns of varied degrees of regularity or irregularity and combining layers that are differently paced, making contrasts of timbre that clarify their individual qualities of movement.

In a later chapter Ehrenzweig observes that while time-order is essential to the forming of identity for surface perception, the depth-levels of the mind are not similarly bound and can identify events without regard to their

24   Stravinsky, Igor & Craft, Robert. 1982, 104.
25   In music, these distortions may include, for example, the unconscious hearing of overtones which are repressed in favour of the more biologically important hearing of tone colours. This supports Eugenie Lineff's suggestion that folk singers were hearing overtones; Stravinsky was also keenly aware of overtones.
26   Bergson, Henri. 1913, 14. In Ehrenzweig, Anton. 1953, 35.
27   Op. cit., 41.

temporal order.[28] He gives examples of composers' 'time-free' holistic hearing, and observes that

> the working of the depth mind is indeed far from chaotic and may excel in its purely technical achievement the gestalt-bound functions of the surface mind: it can adapt itself to the technical intricacies of Bach's fugue construction as well as Schoenberg's 12-tone row.[29]

Ehrenzweig quotes the experience of Mozart who, gradually assembling parts of a work in his mind, inventing and making them 'as in a beautiful dream', could at last see the whole of it at a single glance, not as a succession, but 'all at once'.[30] After composing *Symphonies of Wind Instruments* (1920) and making closer acquaintance with the philosophy of Jacques Maritain, Stravinsky sought to promote this kind of time-free holistic listening by strengthening the clarity and unity of his spiritual works.

---

28   Op. cit., 106–111. Neuroscience research has since confirmed that the brain also recognises the many forms of a serial row as 'family members' of the original row. See Chapter 7.

29   Op. cit., 112.

30   Op. cit., 107–8.

CHAPTER 6

Heaven and Earth

Perhaps more than any other of Stravinsky's works, *Les Noces* (The Peasant Wedding), expresses the 'soul' of Russia and the ethos of the Russian Orthodox Church. Russian Orthodox spirituality is based on the concept of community in its widest sense, as the oneness of worship in heaven with that of the Church on earth. The role of the Church had been summed up by Germanos, the 8th-century patriarch of Constantinople: 'The Church is the earthly heaven in which the heavenly God dwells and moves'.[1] By 1914, Russian Orthodoxy had flourished vigorously for a thousand years or so, its beliefs and customs pervading all aspects of Russian life. *Les Noces* portrays three aspects of the Russian 'soul' as it brings together secular customs and superstitions, personal prayers and ritual laments, and petitions to the saints.

Stravinsky conceived the idea of presenting actual wedding material through quotations of popular verse, and eventually found his ideal material in anthologies of poetry by Afanasyev and Kireyevsky, 'these two great treasures of the Russian language and spirit'.[2] His own libretto, structured as a suite of wedding episodes, was put together almost entirely from songs collected by Kireyevsky, using clichés and fragments of talk typical of these occasions. He came to visualise *Les Noces* as a dance-cantata in four scenes and as a series of ritualised tableaux that would present a peasant wedding as had been established in Russia for centuries.[3] Stravinsky's direct quotations of popular verse were already characterised by a sacred-secular spirituality; the challenge would be to unify the time qualities of the sacred and the secular musically, in an autonomous temporal form.[4]

---

1 Ware, Timothy. 1983, 56. The continuity between earth and heaven is reflected in the structuring of space and details of line and decoration in the design of a Byzantine church. Based on the concept of humanity's place in the cosmos, the church is the place where humankind meets the angels and the lower creation, and where the different reality of a heavenly future is explored.

2 Stravinsky, Igor & Craft, Robert. 1981. *Expositions and Developments*, 115.

3 Stravinsky, Igor. 1975, 106.

4 In response to Boris Asaf'yev, Stravinsky denied all orgiastic tendencies in the work. (Craft, Robert. Foreword to Asaf'yev, Boris. 1929: xiii.) Craft describes Asaf'yev's book about Stravinsky as 'the one crucial book so far published about Igor Stravinsky', but describes Asaf'yev as a dialectical materialist and Stravinsky as a Christian who believed in the divine nature of artistic inspiration: op.cit., vii. Stravinsky refused to promote an English edition of

© KONINKLIJKE BRILL NV, LEIDEN, 2022 | DOI:10.1163/9789004518537_008

EX. 18   Typical figure of the 5th echos with similar patterning to Palchikov: Peasant
                Songs, no. 31

Stravinsky thought that *Les Noces* was even primarily a product of the Russian Church: the melodic formulæ of Russian liturgical chant are blended with folksong motifs, moments of spiritual significance are marked by the sounds of bells of all sizes, saints are petitioned frequently for their blessing on things of everyday life, and a feeling of spiritual serenity results from the quality of *apatheia* (the ordering of the emotions). *Les Noces* presents an intimate picture of Russian customs and Orthodox beliefs.

The secular and the sacred in *Les Noces* are linked melodically by their patterning of a small pitch array (Ex.18). The above motif of the 5th echos, for example, is musically compatible with the patterning of a folksong from Palchikov's collection of 1888, only differing in its rhythmic manners.[5]

Similarly, the 5th echos patterns of strotchny chant that Stravinsky evokes for the 'blessing' of the groom (Ex.19) are readily compatible with the folksong patterns with which they alternate.

In Russia, towards the end of the 16th century, collections were made of the polyphonic strotchny chant that revealed a concept of intervals and growth of substance that also characterises Stravinsky's choral writing in this work. Strotchny chant uses parallel intervals, especially 4ths, 5ths, 2nds and even 7ths, with great freedom, and additional voices simply embroider the chant without altering its character. With regard to the similar embroidering of the choruses in *Les Noces*, Stravinsky remarked that he had gone back to old Russian church music, as well as to Bach and Palestrina, and that in Russia any chorus

---

Asaf'yev's book, stating that any interest in Asaf'yev was misplaced, but he did purchase a copy in Berlin in 1930.
5   Swan, Alfred J. 1926, 365.

EX. 19   Patterning of 5th echos melodic formulæ and folksong motifs

could sing this music because for years they had sung it in the churches.[6] In *Les Noces*, as in strotchny chant and folksong, spiritual beliefs are expressed within a small pitch gamut, the number of voices at any one time is fluid, and melodic contours are matched to resonant vowel sounds.

Although typical of an informal village wedding, Stravinsky's treatment of the text and the simultaneous mixing of speech and song in a multi-layered sound world also recall two ancient practices of the Russian Orthodox Church. By the 16th century, church services had become very protracted by long coloraturas (*anenaiki*) sung to meaningless syllables by rival virtuoso singers. The clergy sought to hurry the office, in case it lasted five to six hours, by singing canticles and saying prayers simultaneously. The practice, known as *tuilage,* or layering, resulted in a complex sound world in which words were scarcely comprehensible, and in which the reading of texts, the invocation of saints, prayers and chanting blended with the cries of mendicants and the disputes of pilgrims. Pierre Souvtchinsky wrote of this practice:

> Sans aucune doute un échafaudage de lignes musicales et une simul-
> taneité de différentes musiques qui se succèdent, ou se répètent en se
> chevauchant, ne peut pas ne pas donner naissance à une émotivité intense

6   Interview Jan.10th, 1925. Stravinsky, Igor & Craft, Robert. 1979, 620 n. 241. Strotchny (poly-
     phonic) chant was given official approval by Patriarch Nikon in the mid-17th century, despite
     serious reservations by many Orthodox clergy that it smacked of Rome and threatened the
     unity of the faith.

et aigue. Donc, si le procédé en lui-même était 'vicieux', il n'en avait pas moins un sens émotif et rituel extrêmement sûr et direct ... Cette simultaneité et, dans un certain sens, cette plénitude de sons, de chants et de mots ne pouvait manquer d'agir sur l'état de concentration spirituelle des masses et de provoquer en même temps une émotion de fête collective.[7]

[Without any doubt, a build-up of musical lines and the sound of different musical lines following each other or repeating and overlapping simultaneously, cannot fail to give birth to a sharply intense feeling. Thus, if the method in itself was 'wrong', there was in it no less of a sense of emotion and of extremely sure and direct ritual ... This simultaneity and, in a certain sense, this fullness of sounds, chants and words could not fail to act upon the state of spiritual concentration in the crowd, and at the same time, provoke a feeling of communal festivity.]

The second church practice, that of adding meaningless syllables to the text, known as *homonie,* developed in church music between the 12th and 16th centuries. It was a phonetic phenomenon related to a phase of language development, and reflected a move towards phonetic exaggeration. It showed a mistrust of the logical meaning of the words, lest the quality of time implicit in the text detract from the sacred time quality of the music. The texts of znamenny chant in the Orthodox liturgy became filled out and sustained by interpolated vowels and the addition of certain words; hitherto mute vowels were marked with neumes, and Kh was added to specific vowels. Certain mute sounds – originally articulated like half vowels – were lost in time, resulting in changes of articulation, the displacement of accents and the general regrouping of sound elements. Even key dogmatic words became deformed: *Bog* (God) became *Bogo, Christos* (Christ) became *Christosos,* and *Spass* (Saviour) became *Sopasso.* These additions were retained by the Old Believers, and although eliminated from the revised liturgy their use continued in popular songs.[8]

Similarly in *Les Noces,* Stravinsky reduces the 'word-sense' to 'sound-sense' by many idiomatic means which are inevitably lost in translation.[9] Distinctive shades of meaning are conveyed by diminutives and the use of dialect words in regional accents, underlining the unpretentious nature of this wedding. The number of syllables is varied to expand or contract the musical patterns: for

---

7   Souvtchinsky, Pierre. 1949/6, 100–101.

8   Op. cit., 96ff.

9   Stravinsky referred to V. Dal's *Explanatory Dictionary of the Living Great Russian Language* as one of the 'sources' of *Les Noces.*

example, the work opens (bars 1–8), with the words of the bride-to-be arranged as meaningless syllables as she establishes the ritual aspect of the wedding by playing with the resonance of the 'overtone' motif – *Kosal moia ko ... Kosa moia kosinka rusaia*! – [my plait, my little braid is strawberry-blond]. The affectionate diminutive for mother – *matushka* – (fig. 1 + 5 – 7), also highlights the dressing of her tresses as a familiar religio-sexual folk custom. The use of old-fashioned 19th century words such as *matushka* and *dusha* – 'soul' (fig. 10 – 2) evoke ritual time and distance the text. There are also regional variations in pronunciation as, for example, when the mother of the bride sings of the interweaving of the red ribbon – *lentu upliatu* – (before fig.3), and examples of 'country yokel' speech, as Fétis Pamfiliévitch is addressed as *sudar* – 'sir' (fig. 12). These idiomatic ways of speaking reclaim the ordinary, everyday time of peasant life. Changes of vowels and constantly alliterative sounds such as 'sh' and 'zh' (before fig. 16) build inner rhymes, end rhymes or even approximate rhymes, helping to structure the phrase. Some words have more than one meaning, and some have invariable epithets that, when repeated, are like verbal 'chords' in different places in subsequent lines of the text, creating waves of movement. Stravinsky commented that even the proper names in the text such as *Palagai* or *Saveliushka*, that belong to no-one in particular, were chosen for their sound, their syllables and their Russian typicality.[10]

Charles Ramuz, who translated the text of *Les Noces* to be sung in French, observed:

> At any given moment there are at least four texts, literary and musical, sometimes interrupted and succeeded by others, sometimes mingled, sometimes resolved in a kind of unison. But the climax of disorder always fits into a most rigorous plan, a mathematical system ... it was difficult [to work it out], even though all I had to do was to arrange the syllables ...[11]

The complex sound world of *Les Noces* also owes much to the resonance of bells, an important element of worship in the various Orthodox churches. In Holy Week in Jerusalem, for example, twelve Gospel passages retelling the Passion of Christ are read in Gethsemane on the afternoon of Holy (Maundy) Thursday: one bell is rung after the first reading, two after the second reading, and so on, as the story of the Passion unfolds. Stravinsky observed this Orthodox ritual at home soon after moving to America: Vera Stravinsky's diary,

---

10   Stravinsky, Igor & Craft, Robert. 1981. *Expositions and Developments*, 115.

11   Ramuz, Charles F. 1929, 73–74.

April 25th, 1940 – Maundy Thursday – records: 'In the evening, Igor reads to me the twelve gospels used in the Russian church service'.[12]

Bells are pealed at the Mount of Olives for the procession to Golgotha on the morning of Good Friday, and bells precede the prayers and singing of the Lamentations of Our Lord in the evening. Bells accompany the procession to the shrouded Gospel symbolising the burial of Christ, and also the celebration of His Resurrection when the black covers are removed to reveal the white covers underneath. All is quiet and dark until midnight on Holy Saturday when the Patriarch emerges with the Light of Heaven, bundles of lighted candles, and announces *Khristos anesti*! (Christ is Risen!) to the joyful pealing of bells.

Moments of special spiritual significance in the Russian Orthodox liturgy have long been marked by the ringing of bells; in particular, the many church bells to be found in St Petersburg offered a depth and complexity of sound that could be 'entered into' by the worshipper. While a typical tuned European bell of the thick-walled, flared-profile variety may sound a minor chord, an untuned bell or large East Asian barrel-profile bell offers a large collection of dissonant partials. They help the vibrancy of the bell's attack and perform an important function in arresting the listener's attention. Dissonant partials considerably enhance the effect of bells swung as a peal, where their less precise pitch relationships add further interest to the kaleidoscope of interacting patterns. This dissonance was much prized in Russia (where some of the world's largest bells may be found), because the Russian style of ringing was based on the beauty of interacting rhythms and timbres at high and low pitches. When Stravinsky notated the bells of St Paul's Cathedral, London, in June 1914, he remarked upon the 'astonishingly beautiful counterpoint such as I have never heard before in my life'.[13]

The dissonant intervals found in untuned bells, particularly the 0–11 interval, produce 'beats' which can be felt physically as pulsations. Stravinsky uses this penetrating interval when he particularly wants to engage the listener's attention at a significant spiritual moment (Ex.20).

Stravinsky uses the major 7th, 0–11 interval, for example, in the 'faith' and 'fire' chords of the first movement of *A Sermon, A Narrative and A Prayer* (1961) as the climax to a repeated refrain, a Stravinskian 'signposting' of a significant spiritual text.[14]

---

12   Craft, Robert, ed. 1985, 114.

13   Stravinsky, Igor & Craft, Robert. 1979, 127.

14   Stravinsky also uses the 0–11 interval to draw attention to significant changes. Regarding changes of movement in *Le Sacre*, Pieter Van den Toorn writes '... note the metric accentuation of the 0–11 span, a downbeating that ... typifies its articulation and that ... renders

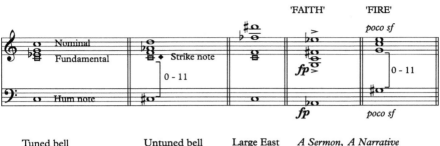

EX. 20   3 types of bell from 'Bell': Percival Price. 1980, Vol. 2, 426.
          Reproduced with permission of the licensor through PLSclear

The frequent use of bells evokes the Russian Orthodox belief in the transformation, not only of the sense of hearing but of all five bodily senses, onto
a transcendent plane. Bell sounds permeate many of Stravinsky's works,
from the bells and funeral gong of *Le Rossignol* to the tolling 'bells' that close
Requiem Canticles.[15] Their complex sound world transforms the secular into
the sacramental, joining earth with heaven. *Les Noces* is not only suffused with
bell sounds but is even framed by 'untuned' bells: the intervals of a minor 9th
and major 7th (0–11) on four pianos establish a resonant sound world as the
bride combs her tresses,[16] while the octave plus the wider major 2nd brings a
peaceful conclusion to the wedding ritual.

Les Noces bridges the secular and the sacred with frequent invocations to
God, the Virgin Mary, the Apostles, Angels and Saints. In particular, petitions
are made to St Cosmas and St Damian, two 3rd-century Eastern saints who
gave free medical help to the people and died as martyrs during the reign of
Diocletian. Recognised as wedding saints in Russia and popularly worshipped
as deities of a fertility cult, these two saints were originally identified with
skomorokhi, or wandering minstrels. Healers by profession, skomorokhi were
respected for their ability to cast spells: they exercised magico-priestly functions at weddings and other rites and sometimes even took precedence in

---

it highly conspicuous in moving from one block or section to the next'. Van den Toorn,
Pieter C. In Pasler, ed. 1986, 133–4.

15   Robert Craft remarked 'the music performed for the composer's funeral in Venice, just
before the ferrying to the grave, reminds me of his experiments with notations for the
different speeds of the city's bells, since their rhythms absorbed him as much as their ring
and the percussive articulation of mallet and clapper'. Craft, Robert. 1992, 259.

16   The 0–11 interval is notated enharmonically as a diminished octave.

processions over the cross-bearing priest of the Church. The relationship of the skomorokhi to the ecclesiastical authorities was highly ambiguous: although they were often persecuted for leading the people astray, drawings of them are to be found decorating the illuminated letters of medieval psalters in religious centres such as Pskov and Novgorod.[17] Unique to Russia, skomorokhi were banished beyond the Ural mountains by Tsar Aleksei in 1648 and finally excommunicated by the Church in 1657.[18] In *Les Noces,* petitions are made to Cosmas and Damian to strengthen the bond between bride and groom, and sacred and secular customs are performed simultaneously as the marriage is blessed with icons, bread and salt. Further petitions are made to these saints in the third tableau as the bridegroom departs.

A deeper influence of the Russian Orthodox Church upon *Les Noces* may be found in the work's serene quality of *apatheia*, a spiritual discipline described in the writings of the Church Fathers. *Apatheia*, or purity of heart is the first of three stages in the spiritual life. It is not an absence of passion, as in the Stoic meaning of insensibility, but a state in which the energy of human (self-centred) passions has been redirected and transfigured into an all-consuming love of God and mankind. St Simeon writes: 'Thus the only possible beginning [of the spiritual life] is the diminishing and taming of passions ... When through the heart's opposition to them, passions are completely subdued, the mind begins to long for God, seeking to get closer to Him, for which purpose it increases its prayer ...'[19]

The second stage of the spiritual journey is to begin to be aware of God in and through Creation, to apprehend the 'being' and inner principle of created things, and to become receptive to the power of meaning in the world. According to St Gregory of Sinai, the ability to perceive being and meaning through achieving passionless-ness was 'true reason, such as man had in the

---

17   Stasov's publication, *Slavianskii i vostochnyi ornament,* shows two skomorokhi decorating two mid 14th-century Novgorod initials (A) from a Psalter and the Liturgicon. In Zguta, Russell. 1978, 71.

18   Op. cit., 63. Itinerant skomorokhi, who enjoyed far lower social status than resident skomorokhi, brought entertainment that was often scandalous, and raided the community before travelling on. Often masked, they read omens such as the sex of an unborn baby and brought with them tame bears that enacted skits on human behaviour. Archpriest Arvakum and Ivan Neronov, two leaders of the Old Believers, played an important part in the excommunication of the skomorokhi. In the 15th century, clergy were instructed that all skomorokhi or those who associate with, or listen to them, should be barred from Holy Communion for a year and declared anathema.

19   Writings from the *Philokalia* on Prayer of the Heart. 1951, 160.

beginning'.[20] The fruit of the first two stages of the spiritual life is the perception of transcendent meaning in Creation.

The third stage is union with God: St Basil teaches that 'A mind not dispersed among external objects and not carried about the world by the senses returns to itself and from itself rises to thoughts of God; illumined by this beauty it forgets nature itself'.[21]

In *Les Noces,* the quality of *apatheia* orders the emotions of the peasant wedding and ensures that the ritual reaches beyond the emotions to assume an objective, ontological quality; the 'staging' of wedding customs and rituals was described as *igrat svad'bu,* 'to play a wedding'.[22] This quality is secured by several means: not only do the quotations and typical wedding sayings of the text have no connecting narrative,[23] but, following Stravinsky's directions, the singers were to be placed in the orchestra pit out of sight. The choreography is expressed in blocks and masses, and individual personalities do not emerge: solo voices impersonate now one type of character, now another. C. A. Cingria wrote of the memorable performance given by one singer, Kibalchich, that 'he was the chorus, not an individual, but a race: the whole of sacerdotal and administrative Russia'.[24] To maintain the quality of *apatheia* and avoid the expression of personal emotions, the bride's changing status is symbolised in the binding of her tresses in red and blue ribbons. The unknown future of the bride and groom is ritualised in a traditional folk game, by voices affectionately impersonating a swan and a goose: these archetypal characters can voyage in both sea and sky, and tell fantastic stories that mirror peasant superstitions.[25]

To ensure the complete objectivity of this folk ritual, members of the wedding party acquire idealised attributes. The guests carry the 'beauty of the bride', symbolised by a head-dress or by a small pine-tree decorated with

---

20   Op. cit., 37.

21   Op. cit., 236.

22   Zguta, Russell. 1978, 12–13. The Grace for the Gorodische wedding feast runs: 'O Lord Christ, bless us, to start the wedding game, to set the tables, to spread the tablecloths, to bring bread and salt and the sweetmeats ... and the mead from the cellar ...' Swan, A.J. 1973, Appendix iii, 213.

23   Proverbs and sayings (as at fig. 122) are often in two-part form, each phrase carefully balanced and paced against the other for effect, with an adjunct word that emphasises the two-fold structure.

24   Craft, Robert, ed. 1985, 111.

25   Stravinsky, Igor & Craft, Robert. 1981. *Expositions and Developments*, 116–7.

ribbons and sweetmeats.[26] The bridegroom is referred to as a prince and his male friends as outriders in the royal train. The best man, or druzhko, is a 'warrior', who keeps all manner of evil away from the bridal couple through magic and the incantation of spells. His role had often been played by a skomorokh, and Stravinsky introduces the 'strumming' of their customary instrument, the gusli, into the score. In many wedding rituals, pagan magic and superstition co-exist with the ethos of the Orthodox Church and evil spirits are driven out or deceived by a multitude of customs, some involving icons.[27] Bread and salt are given to wish the young couple wealth and fertility, whilst two flowers upon a branch, one red, one white, symbolise the bond between the bride and groom.[28] Stravinsky's first draft for the scenario of *Les Noces* even contained an incantation against sorcery.[29]

The quality of *apatheia* also orders the time and place of the laments to preserve the proper relationships between relatives and guests, and emotions are expressed in turn to secure the proper balance between joy and sorrow. Every Russian woman had to learn how to perform a lament and, as with znamenny chant, the traditional formulæ had to be memorised and improvised upon. The job of the professional weepers employed for important ceremonial occasions was to awaken specific emotions and thoughts about the bride and groom and their families with great clarity and detail.[30] Farewells are made not only to relatives but also to material things, as symbols of the stages of life about to be left behind and the unknown personal journeys about to begin. Much of the traditional material for these laments is in the form of dialogue, the favoured form of Russian folk tales.

Stravinsky's assistant, Arthur Lourié, later wrote of the quality of *apatheia* that endows *Les Noces*:

> If *The [Rite of] Spring* proceeded from a breach of balance in form and emotion which characterises it as a heathen act, then *Les Noces* restored

---

26   A wedding was primarily a household proceeding: a daughter-in-law was expected to be not a beauty but a terrific worker, 'to have the strength of an animal and endurance of a horse', as one wedding ritual put it! Sokolov, Y.M. 1966, 203.

27   Stravinsky recalled that after his wedding ceremony Rimsky-Korsakov blessed him with an icon which he then gave him as a wedding present. Stravinsky, Igor & Craft, Robert. 1981, 41.

28   'These symbols reflect the richness of the Russian spirit, not magical elements standing outside ordinary life': they reflect 'something that is contained within it ... that makes up his customs, his mode of life'. Yeleonskaya, E. N. In Sokolov, Y. M. 1966, 466.

29   Stravinsky, Vera & Craft, Robert. 1979, 145.

30   Sokolov, Y. M. 1966, 226–7.

the lost balance. It is a mystery play of Orthodox everyday life built on rhythms and identical in spirit to icon-painting. *Les Noces* is dynamic in the musical sense but in the emotional sphere it is fixed with the tranquility and serenity of an icon ... If it were not for the balance of the inner life ... then *Les Noces* would become a Khlystovian rite.[31]

An icon performs the sacramental function of conveying the divine nature of God in a form that is humanly accessible. Created to act as a kind of spiritual window between the material and the spiritual, the seen and the unseen, it is first and foremost a channel of spiritual insight and communion with the Divine, not an object to be venerated in itself.[32] God's blessing is invoked upon an icon, as upon the Eucharistic elements of bread and wine, to transform the physical materials and human skills employed in its construction into the means of coming closer to God and of carrying prayers to heaven.[33] It depends for its effectiveness upon the skill with which its materials are formally constructed and organised for the senses; in painting an icon, the artist makes a personal act of prayer to whichever Saint or aspect of the Divine he seeks to represent and clears his work of all egotistical attitudes. An icon has no patterns of light and shade and often has a gold background since the fullness of heaven is bathed in the brilliant and unchanging light of God. Sometimes its 'reverse' perspective widens out to carry the beholder into deeper understanding, and the familiar spatial world in which the icon itself has taken form is transcended. Just as the materials of an icon are organised to carry the viewer to a new space, Stravinsky organises the ritual materials of *Les Noces* to create new and unfamiliar qualities of ontological time.

The sacred and the secular aspects of this work are unified by a melodic motif that is able to migrate easily between a diatonic and an octatonic context: the three-note 'Old Believers' motif, the 025 figure found in the harmonic series.[34] With the capacity to pass seamlessly between different harmonic contexts, this

---

31 Lourié, Arthur. 1928. para. 4. The Khlysts were orgiasts as well as demonists; they were persecuted by the church in the 18th century but persisted into the 20th century.

32 Stravinsky composed beneath an icon and had several 18th and 19th-century icons on his bedroom shelf. Over Stravinsky's bed hung a locket which he took with him on his travels; it contained a miniature icon copied from an old master by his son, Theodore. Craft, Robert. 1972, 305. He also had a copy of an icon of St Michael that he had kept since childhood in his Russian Bible. Op. cit., 376.

33 Icons are hung on the iconostasis that separates the sanctuary from the main part of the church, to symbolise the connection between earth and heaven.

34 See Chapter 3: Ex. 11, 12

resonant overtone motif is a principal means of varying the depth of both time and space in *Les Noces*, and of connecting earth and heaven.

Stravinsky was keenly sensitive to resonance, vibrations and the 'echoic value' of words. Some anecdotes about Stravinsky's 'wonderful ear' relate specifically to his hearing of overtones and vibrations.[35] He composed at the piano, which was muted and covered in felt, since he 'needed vibrations not tone', and liked to demonstrate string harmonics at the piano by playing a note so that its fourth partial could be heard.[36] He would sometimes imitate Beethoven's custom of placing one end of a pencil between his teeth and the other on the piano, to demonstrate how Beethoven was able to 'hear' music by feeling differing rates of vibration.[37] Stravinsky could be disturbed by the vibrations that he knew were going on everywhere, from 'the streets, the neighbours, the radios – even when the radios are turned off'. He often noted down the music he heard in the rhythms and intervals of machinery, in street noises, and in hurdy-gurdies and carousels. In this way, both the hard, more resonant sound of the cimbalom and the song of a tipsy passenger in a Vaudois funicular, complete with a 'hocket' made by his friend's hiccups, found their way into *Les Noces*.[38]

Pierre Souvtchinsky said of Stravinsky's 'wonderful ear':

> It would seem that something more than theoretical and speculative thought sustained and guided I.S. It must surely be the phenomenon of his musical ear, incomparably imaginative, evocative, provocative, controlled, demanding and true at the highest level of sound perception, linked in a mysterious way to a fount of intelligence and spirituality.[39]

The resonant overtone motif that generated the movement of *Zvezdoliki* also suffuses *Les Noces* in many forms and contexts. In the ritual laments, its resonance is enhanced either by the dissonant major 7th, 0–11 interval found in untuned bells or by oscillating figures. In the secular choral passages the motif rings out as loud peals of bells, their resonance only slightly clouded by chromatic or 'wandering' bass lines. This overtone motif creates a mosaic in sound, confirming Boris Asaf'yev's early observation that Stravinsky has the ability to

---

35   Stravinsky, Igor & Craft, Robert. 1981. *Expositions and Developments*, 36. Also Stravinsky, Vera & Stravinsky, Igor. 1985, 194.

36   Craft, Robert. 1957.

37   Notes for *The Recorded Legacy*. CBS Records, 1981.

38   Craft, Robert. 1992, 338–9.

39   Souvtchinsky, Pierre. 1982, 23 (translated from the French).

EX. 21   No. 47 from *50 Songs of the Russian People* collected by Liadov in 1901.
                The pitch centre is G, but the melody includes the haunting minor seventh, F♮

EX. 22   Stravinsky's 'Song of the Goose': *Les Noces*.
                This melody swings between two tonic pitches, G & C, with F♮ and B♭ as the minor
                7th degrees of their respective natural scales

create 'a unique complex of intonational "gestures" by which the character and pace of the piece are defined', a passage in the book that Stravinsky marked 'important'.[40]

The 6th overtone, the minor 7th above the tonic, gives resonance to those Russian folksongs that used the natural scale and were sung in just intonation (Ex.21) [41]

The interval of a minor 7th avoids the strong pull of the major triad upon the 5th degree of the scale to resolve onto the tonic and allows the tonic to shift more freely. Russian folksongs may also play around the resonant minor 7th interval upon tonic notes that are changing, which creates a wonderful spatial open-ness, as in Stravinsky's 'Song of the Goose' (Ex.22).

It took Stravinsky several years to find a suitable instrumental accompaniment to the vocal sound world of *Les Noces* because preserving the clarity of its resonant intonations presented something of a challenge. His solution was to support what he called the 'soufflé' elements by an ensemble consisting exclusively of percussion instruments: pianos, timbals (timpani), bells and xylophones, 'none of which instruments give a precise note'. He explained that the sound combination 'was the necessary outcome of the music itself', and that we must look further than the imitation of an orchestrion (which, since Beethoven's time, was often used at peasant weddings) for an explanation of his final choice.[42]

---

40   Asaf'yev, Boris. 1929, foreword by Robert Craft, ix.
41   Alfred Swan describes the major scale with the flattened 7th as a highly popular scale
      formation in Russian folk songs. Swan, Alfred, J. 1943, 505.
42   Stravinsky, Igor. 1975, 105. Also Stravinsky, Vera & Craft, Robert. 1979, 160.

In the 1930s, Stravinsky's sensitivity to the natural structure of sound led him to remark of the works of Schoenberg and his followers that 'the chromatic gamut on which they are based only exists scientifically, so that the dialectic which is derived from this is artificial ...'[43] Stravinsky also remarked upon the expressive 'poverty' of the tuning of the well-tempered scale, and predicted new changes in the appreciation of richness of 'pitch' in the future.[44] Even as an octagenarian, the thought of 'sounds electronically spayed for overtone removal' made him feel, as he quaintly put it, 'bodily ill'.[45]

Les Noces marks another important development in Stravinsky's techniques for embodying time *in* music. The dialogue of temporalities that builds the powerful force of *The Rite of Spring* had largely arisen from rhythmic constructions: clear-cut passages of dynamic forward movement contrasted with the juxtaposition of differing rhythmic layers to deepen the time quality. This dialogue increasingly negates the sense of 'now' as the pagan ritual develops a state of trance, a timelessness that is brutally cut off by the sudden death of the Chosen One. In contrast to the stark rhythmic contrasts of *The Rite,* the more nuanced time qualities of *Les Noces* are enriched with resonances that create depth of spiritual meaning. The bride's symbolic ritual of dressing her hair is given an echoic 'halo' by play upon the harmonic series and an accompaniment of 'bell-strikes' and oscillating octatonic intervals. The petitions to the Saints during the ritual festivities typical of a village wedding create a multi-layered sound world of unpitched speech and heterophonic voices which recalls the atmosphere of the Orthodox liturgy. This sound world is slowly penetrated by 'pealing bells', whose mixed partials are present in the indeterminate pitches of the accompanying instruments. They continue to punctuate the reverberating vocal motif of the concluding scene, extending its time quality into eternity.

1   The 025 Motif and Changing Time Qualities

Much of *Les Noces* is built on ostinati or pedal notes but it is far from static: the patterning of its unifying motif is variously-paced, moving constantly between the pulses of ♪ = 80 and ♩ = 120 to the minute, and between differing depths of secular or ritual time qualities. The resonant pitches of the overtone motif which open the work (Ex.23) immediately establish a deep quality of time ...

---

43   Interview March 12th 1936. Op. cit., 328.
44   Stravinsky, Igor & Craft, Robert. 1981, *Memories and Commentaries*, 121.
45   Stravinsky, Igor & Craft, Robert. 1982, 127.

EX. 23   Opening play on the harmonic series

... whereas contrasting passages of here-and-now dynamic momentum, such as fig.9, harmonise the overtone motif as the 3rd, 5th and 6th degrees of the major scale (Ex.24):

EX. 24   Overtone motif on F♯ harmonised in the key of A major

These different time qualities are bridged by passages of homophonic chanting and fluid polyphonic textures, and by the juxtaposition of several layers of differing rhythmic complexity.

The first ten bars are purely for the ear before the curtain rises; they invite the listener to enter the melodic and rhythmic patterning of ontological time. The bride's 025 motif E – D – B on its fundamental E is enhanced by an acciaccatura on the 8th overtone – F♯. This passage opens a resonant musical space and establishes the remote time of ritual by its antiphonal response to her friends' low-pitched chanting on E. At the choral celebrations (fig. 9) the motif is set in a diatonic context and then at three successive pitch centres, until the motif on the fundamental note F♯ is accompanied by the strumming of the gusli (fig. 14) and juxtaposed with a variant on E in the bass. These layers are reversed and treated antiphonally (from fig. 18). The time quality of sacred ritual returns (fig. 21), but this time through two laments a 5th apart, each with the resonant minor 7th above the tonic. This construction creates depth by its juxtaposition of four planes according to their complexity: a prominent lament on A is set against a less prominent lament on E, a two-note ostinato across the metre and a rapidly oscillating accompaniment. A third voice is added in parallel fourths (fig. 23) in the style of strotchny chant. The first scene concludes with the juxtaposition of two highly contrasted qualities of movement (fig. 25, Ex.25): the bride's lament, an elaboration of the motif on the fundamental D, floats freely

EX. 25   The bride's song against ritual chanting

in elongated movement against the return of rapid chanting, the difference in pace deepening the ritual time quality.

In the second scene, at the groom's house, the overtone motif rings out as joyful bell-strikes on the motif F – G – D (fig. 29 + 2, ending B♭ – A♭ – F, fig. 33 – 2). In contrast, it appears as a haunting figure in the octatonic laments (F♯ – E – D♭ (C♯), fig. 35 + 4), where it is set to a slowly oscillating semitone (Ex.26):

EX. 26   The resonant motif ending the mother's phrases

The motif, also hidden in the folk melody for basses (from fig. 42), is juxtaposed with a cross-metre ostinato in the timpani, and rapidly gathers many other repeating patterns. Two unaccompanied male voices give the blessing (fig. 50) with melodic patterns reminiscent of the 5th echos and the harsher intervals of strotchny chant. The intonations of the 5th echos bring to this simple village wedding associations with the Virgin Mary, described in the Orthodox liturgy as the 'unwedded Bride'.[46] The sacred-secular contrasts continue (from

---

46   5th echos formulæ are used at the Saturday service of Great Vespers. After 10 stichera, the Dogmatikon offers a classical piece of theological teaching drawing parallels between the Annunciation and the story of Moses and the Red Sea. The text reads: 'In times past, the image of the unwedded Bride was inscribed in the Red Sea: there Moses parted the waters; here, Gabriel was the servant of the wonder. Then, Israel rode dry-shod through the deep; while, now, the Virgin hath without seed given birth to Christ. After the passing of Israel, the sea was as ever impassable. After the birth of Emmanuel, the Virgin without reproach, remains uncorrupt'. Translation from the original Greek made at the Orthodox Monastery of the Veil of Our Lady, 89, Bussy-en-Othe, France, p.116. In the early 1950s the Byzantine monastery at Grottaferrata presented Stravinsky with a copy of the *Oktoechos*

EX. 27   Three-layered construction to petition St Cosmas and St Damian

fig. 53) with the resonant minor 7th of the folk melody answered by step-wise chant figures. The textures increase (from fig. 59) over a slow syncopated osti-nato spanning the 0–11 interval, enharmonically notated C♯ – C♮.

At the departure of the bride in the third scene, the overtone motif on F♯ moves to many other pitch centres (E, C♯, G♯, B, B♭, G and F♯) and is juxtaposed with slow ostinati and rapid oscillations. Earth and heaven are joined as this motif moves around the voices, blessing the everyday symbols of bread and salt and petitioning St Cosmas and St Damian. The two forms of the motif are set against the bridegroom's ritual theme first heard at figure 21, in a complex three-layered construction that, like *tuilage*, evokes the multi-layer sound world of the Russian liturgy (Ex. 27).

The motif also permeates the exuberant folk melodies in several forms: the motif on C♯ – B – G♯ alternates with that on F♯ – E – C♯ accompanied by the strumming of the 'gusli' (fig. 75). After a long approach, two lines of lament at the tritone with a fixed oscillating accompaniment return to the resonance of ritual time (fig. 82), each phrase of the laments ending with the overtone motif as before.

At the wedding feast in Part Two the motif is changed into many different forms. For example, a syncopated, extended version on E greets Monsieur Pelagai (fig. 92); the motif on D♭ (for soloists) is juxtaposed against that on E♭ in the piano parts for the traditional symbols of two flowers on a branch (fig. 93); a distorted dominant-tonic form is heard at the arrival of the goose (fig. 94 + 2–3); and the syncopated variant reappears irregularly across the metre against one-bar ostinati as two wedding guests go to warm the marriage bed (fig. 114 + 1).

The reiteration of the central pitch E in the piano parts (fig. 114) generates the first peal of the wedding bells on F♯ – E – C♯ (from fig. 115), before the bells

---

(the eight-note Byzantine system used in the Sunday liturgy) in an Italian translation. Stravinsky, Vera & Craft, Robert. 1979, 619–20.

Final scene of *Les Noces*: overtone motif punctuated by resonant chords

ring out on the motif E – D – B at 'All will go well' (fig. 121 + 4). Variations of
the motif at other pitch centres appear for passages of traditional folk wisdom
(e.g. fig. 122), but as the texture thickens and the pitch world widens to include
spoken voices in the typical church sound world of *tuilage*, the motif is heard
as marcato bell-strikes, with the motif D♯ – C♯ –A♯ heard triumphantly on all
four pianos (fig. 126). As the couple are bedded and the scene begins to 'freeze'
(fig. 130), the variants close to the motif on C♯ – B – G♯ in a syncopated version
sung by a solo bass voice (fig. 133, Ex. 28).

    The motif is punctuated by bell-strikes on B and C♯ for pianos, rattles and
bells that add resonance to the C♯, eventually the B, of each vocal phrase.
As this choreodrama concludes, the overtone motifs are irregularly per-
meated by lengthening silences that stretch time and imply their endless
continuation.

    Les Noces is a complex mosaic in sound of overtone motifs and resonant
syllables that fluctuates in dynamism and density around two related pulses.
It is an icon in sound in which supernatural guidance is sought and freely
mixed with symbolic objects and ritual gesture for the proper ordering of
everyday life and the culture of the community.[47] *Les Noces* also united the
two parts of Stravinsky's nature, the spiritual and the rational, as he ordered
these folk materials into a unified temporal form. Following the impact of
The Firebird, Petrushka and *The Rite of Spring, Les Noces* was a further step in
grafting the musical soul of Russia 'at an angle' on to the traditions of West.

---

47   Many of Stravinsky's large-scale works with a spiritual dimension – *The Rite of Spring,
      Les Noces, Symphony of Psalms, Mass, Canticum Sacrum, Threni* – express the faith of
      the community. After a visit to the convent of San Bernardino in South America, Robert
      Craft observed: 'I have rarely seen I.S. so moved. And it is not only because of the rites, as
      he says, but because the whole community has participated in them ... The whole com-
      munity believes and the whole community belongs ...' Craft, Robert. 1968, 223: diary for
      March 31, 1961. In Guadalupe, which Stravinsky had placed at the top of Craft's itinerary
      as an awesome holy site, Stravinsky knelt to join in prayer with the local community of
      farmworkers. Craft, Robert. 1992, 31.

Eventually performed in Paris in June 1923, *Les Noces* is dedicated to Diaghilev, who loved it more than any other work by Stravinsky. When Stravinsky first played the vocal score to him in 1915, Diaghilev wept and said that of all the creations of the Ballets Russes, the work was the most beautiful and the most purely Russian.

CHAPTER 7

New Patterns for Old

Stravinsky had blended the sacred and secular time qualities of *Les Noces* by patterning a three-note motif in different rhythmic and harmonic contexts. His next work, *Three Pieces for String Quartet* (1914), returned to the effects of juxtaposing regular and irregular layers, particularly those that are differently paced: this was a type of layering which had proved so effective in creating the powerful growth of *The Rite of Spring* and the elusive time qualities of *Three Japanese Lyrics*. *Three Pieces for String Quartet* is innovative in juxtaposing time-creating patterns of movement in three different ways: vertically in layers; as a single linear succession; and horizontally in sections.

The music of Stravinsky is made up of many types of rhythmic and melodic patterns. In music as in everyday life, the brain searches for patterns in both time and space and at every level of perception, in order to make sense of incoming information. Stravinsky was widely read, and some of his references, including those to Nesmelov, Nicholas of Cusa and Anton Ehrenzweig, suggest that he had a lifelong interest in the effects of music upon human consciousness: greater knowledge would further his aim of promoting communion among his listeners, and between the listener and the Divine. Recent research in the field of neuroscience has begun to look more closely at the higher brain functions – how humans think, reason and create – and in particular at the effects of different types of musical patterning upon the brain. The results of research tests in California on Mozart's musical patterning, for example, suggest that the source of Stravinsky's instinctively-constructed rhythmic innovations may lie in the brain's natural patterning processes.[1] It may even be that Stravinsky's innovative juxtapositions of rhythmic layers, involving the simultaneous processing of several different time-creating movements, activate the brain's temporal-spatial reasoning skills at a very high level. This research also begins to throw light on Pierre Souvtchinsky's insightful description of musical creation as an '*innate* complex of intuitions and possibilities'.[2]

---

1 Shaw, Gordon L. 2000, 96–127.
2 Stravinsky, Igor. 1947, 30 (my italics).

1 Cortical Patterning

The above-mentioned research was based on Vernon Mountcastle's organisational principle for cortical function, published in 1978.[3] To simulate activity in the brain, Mountcastle's mini-columns of 'neurons', in interconnected columns of six by six, were run to produce full Monte Carlo pattern evolutions. The columns were programmed to fire at three levels: above average, average, and below average.[4] By enhancing the patterns to a large cycling probability and evolving them from their initial state to the next most probable pattern, hundreds of natural sequences of patterns were generated. These initial states were evolved until repeating spatial-temporal patterns appeared and the patterns returned to their original form.[5] A similar generation of natural sequences of patterning is thought to be inherent in the mammalian cortex.

Two main types of patterning emerged in these pattern evolutions: precise sequential patterning in which patterns were related but prescribed, and more creative patterning in which patterns were related in more freely-evolving and interesting ways.[6] These evolutions were related to a certain 'temperature' parameter, T; as the parameters were varied, a series of transitional states with

---

3 Mountcastle, V. B. 1978. Vernon Mountcastle's organisational principle for cortical function proposed that the cortex is organised into columns, each consisting of between 1,000 and 10,000 tightly interconnected neurons. Each column is made up of mini-columns of 30–100 cells, in six differentiated layers in a cylinder formation of about 0.01cm across, the mini-column being the irreducible processing unit of the cortex. Generally, neurons in the upper layers near the cortical surface have longer-range connections. On a larger scale, the left and right hemispheres of the brain are linked by a large bundle of axons, the corpus callosum, which permits moderating interaction between the two. Thus, there are in the region of ten billion neurons across the cortex, each with roughly 10,000 synapses, acting as a global, cooperative system. The patterning process begins as information arrives from the sensory inputs to the thalamus, a sub-cortical system that is the main gateway to the cortex. The processing of sensory information is influenced by other important subcortical systems, including the amygdala, which has a crucial role in emotions and emotional memories, and the hippocampus, which is essential for forming short-term memories and transforming them into long-term memories. Also important to this sensory processing are the sub-cortical systems involving the release of neuromodulators. Of these, dopamine and serotonin are more influential than the classic neurotransmitters, and act globally on cortical neurons in both space and time. Some input signals from the sensory systems excite neurons and some inhibit them. If the input signals add up to a value greater than the firing threshold of the neurons, they will fire and send out action potentials. Thus, the mini-columns in Mountcastle's model are able to be excited into complex spatial-temporal firing patterns.

4 Op. cit., 93–96 The memory patterns were called 'trions' because of these three levels of stimulation.

5 Op. cit., 96–99.

6 Op. cit., 98.

precise values appeared between these two types of patterning, producing new repertoires of memory patterns.[7] In the human brain, these parameters vary as a result of the action of neuromodulators such as serotonin that bring about similar changes in brain patterning.

The research team proposed that the various symmetry operations performed on an initial pattern might prove to be the key to the higher brain functions of thinking, reasoning and creating. Close study of the memory pattern evolutions found that the higher functions of the brain recognise not only the frequency of recurrence of an initial pattern but also specific types of their related forms in both time and space.[8] Symmetry operators are also inherent in the human brain, which has the innate ability to recognise a pattern, its spatial rotation, mirror reflection and inversion, and its reversal in time. It was quickly noted that, musically speaking, these correspond to the Prime form of a row (P) and its Inversion (I), Retrograde (R) and Retrograde Inversion (RI).[9] These findings suggest the probability – even the inevitability – of Stravinsky's later move to the juxtaposition of serial patterns as a means of further strengthening the relationships of his autonomous temporal structures.

The experiments proved that a high level of cooperativity and structured connectivity exists between groups of neurons. A memory pattern was enhanced by the Hebb learning rule,[10] and with a small break in symmetry, the operations of pattern rotation, mirror reflection, interchanged firing levels and reversal in time resulted in a columnar network's recognition of other members of its 'family' pattern group.[11] The natural activity of the human brain is to generate evolutions of memory patterns that eventually settle down into repeating patterns classifiable into family groups related by symmetries. The recognition of these related forms of patterning is the result of 'broken', or almost perfect, symmetry in which the pattern has been loosened or modified in some way.[12]

---

7   Op. cit., 97.

8   Op. cit., 101–103.

9   Op. cit., 102–107, 232.

10   In 1949 Donald Hebb had proposed that learning and memory takes place through synaptic modification: 'When an axon of cell A is near enough to excite a cell B and repeatedly or persistently takes part in firing it, some growth process or metabolic change takes place in one or both of the cells such that A's efficiency as one of the cells firing B, is increased'. Op. cit., 88.

11   Shaw, Gordon L. 2000, 105. This small breaking of symmetry also allows extremely rapid selectional learning to take place, in contrast to instructional learning which is much slower. Op. cit., 100.

12   Related variations in patterning also form the basis of znamenny chant. Stravinsky commented on this creative use of asymmetry in the mosaics at Torcello: 'Their subject is

The research also found that the symmetry family groups generated by each cortical column formed the fundamental building blocks of an innate cortical 'language' that operates as the columns are coupled into a higher level of cortical architecture.[13] As these firing patterns rotate, they are thought to construct a kind of neural 'grammar', since they fit together with varying degrees of probability and in specific spatial and temporal orders.[14] It is the order in which different memory patterns fit together in a ring configuration that is important to this brain 'language', and interestingly, there are also combinations of memory patterns that do not fit together.[15] When several columns are coupled together, the relationship of the temporal rotations one to another is important, for without temporal phase differences between the same inherent pattern in connected columns, there is essentially no learning.[16] For pattern processing to take place, it is necessary for firing patterns to rotate through all the columns of cells, and for information to be stored in the various memory systems. Rotation also allows for the patterns to be compared, so that familiar objects may be recognised from different viewpoints.[17] This research suggests that the patterning of a close group of pitches including their 'family members' – the organic style that Stravinsky inherited from his native musical forms – is similar in process to natural cortical activity and its ordering of patterns into an intelligible 'language'.

Previous work by researchers on centres of neural coherence recorded by EEG had revealed an intrinsic relationship between patterning and spatial-temporal reasoning:

> ... the trion model proposed that the inherent spatial-temporal firing patterns of highly structured, interconnected groups of neurons, have the built-in ability to recognize, compare and find relationships among patterns ... According to the model, the evolution of these relationships among neural firing patterns into specific temporal sequences for tens of seconds over large portions of cortex allows for the performance of other more complex spatial tasks requiring spatial-temporal reasoning.[18]

---

division ... But in fact, each is the other's complement ... balanced, but not equally balanced. And, the sizes and proportions, movements and rests, darks and lights of the two sides are always varied'. Stravinsky, Igor & Craft, Robert. 1979, 19.

13   Shaw, Gordon L. 2000, 195.
14   Op, cit., 110.
15   Op, cit., 115.
16   Op, cit., 113.
17   Op. cit., 99–101.
18   Sarnthein, Johannes, et al. 1997, 107.

The research team concluded that the brain's ability to discern symmetry relations among patterns and transform them into time sequences was the basis of the higher brain function of spatial-temporal reasoning. This included the complex skills required to process music: tests found that music of a highly patterned and structured type excites and primes the neurons' common repertoire and sequential flow, facilitating and enhancing their symmetry operations.[19] Both kinds of memory pattern evolutions, the sequential and the creative, are involved in spatial-temporal reasoning in proportion to the nature and demands of the task. It was found that listening to musical patterning even enhances the flow of brain patterning, at least in the short term, and facilitates other spatial-temporal tasks.

Patterns of all kinds, particularly rhythmic patterns, engage our attention and invite our involvement in their development. They co-ordinate us with the time world that is created by their frequency of recurrence and the degree to which they are related to other forms in their family group. Music, when presenting both symmetrical and asymmetrical patterns in independent, clearly differentiated layers of movement simultaneously, stimulates complex forms of spatial-temporal reasoning and creates hybrid qualities of time. Stravinsky frequently juxtaposes irregular patterning, that expands or contracts melodically or varies by a few pitches or beats' rest, against the regularity of an ostinato pattern that may also cut across the metre. These combinations of patterning are an important means of regulating the quality of time that is created in music. Because we experience time as a succession of mental qualities that vary constantly between all levels of consciousness, music, as both physical and immaterial, intelligible but untranslatable, is ideally suited to mirroring these changes. As Stravinsky remarked, music is 'the best means we have of digesting time'.[20]

The temporal qualities of *The Rite of Spring* had been created by juxtaposing patterns of differing degrees of regularity and pacing, particularly at Procession of the Sage (from fig. 64). The temporal qualities of *Three Pieces for String Quartet*, first conceived as dances for a biblical story, also arise from Stravinsky's juxtaposition of regular patterns to more creatively irregular patterns, the two types of pattern evolutions studied in the above- reported research. By combining layers and sections of patterning with differing degrees of frequency, regularity and complexity, Stravinsky creates time qualities that

19   Rauscher, Frances H., Shaw, G. L. & Ky, K. N. 1995, 185, 44.
20   Craft, Robert. 1972, 6.

range from those of living gestures to hybrid qualities that are remote or hieratic.

2   Three Pieces for String Quartet (1914)

Jean Cocteau had asked Stravinsky to write music for a ballet on the biblical subject of David and Saul that would be a mix of fairground features and ritualistic elements from the Old Testament. Cocteau visualised this work in terms of 'the acrobatics of a fairground gymnast ... and [with] the three poems, it's all a kind of music hall'.[21] The objective presentation of the ballet as pure movement was important: Cocteau envisaged that 'the dance must not express anything ... the anatomy must comprise a visual curve among the sonorous curves ...'[22] The first dance would show David's victorious battle with Goliath, his triumph by means of a stone in a sling, his difficulty in severing the head, and his dance around it. The second dance would show Saul's jealousy of David for having slain his 'ten thousands'; while dancing, David manages to avoid the spear that Saul hurls at him. The third dance would show David dancing ecstatically around the Ark, the Lord Jehovah having chosen him above all others to be King of Israel. However, Stravinsky did not recreate the mood of the biblical story in which David was reproached for his unseemly dancing by Saul's daughter Michal.[23]

The project for the ballet was never realised: it is possible that Stravinsky redirected his ideas for David into an unexpected commission from the Flonzaley String Quartet. The three movements that he completed construct three contrasting temporalities. The first of the *Three Pieces* juxtaposes differentiated layers of regular and irregular movement vertically, the second patterns linear time with dynamic gestures, and the third movement alternates contrasting sections. They present a kind of architect's model, a miniature summary of Stravinsky's time-creating techniques to date, just as *Requiem Canticles* would do over fifty years later.

The first movement, David's victorious dance at a fast pulse ($\bullet$ = 126), lasts about 47 seconds. Stravinsky constructs the time quality of a bizarre archaic ritual by superimposing four lines of patterning that range from unwavering regularity to large-scale irregularity (Ex.29):

---

21   Walsh, Stephen. 2002, 229.
22   Craft, Robert. ed. 1982, 74.
23   Aschengreen, Erik. 1986. *Jean Cocteau and the Dance*, trans. Patrick McAndrew and Per
      Avsum. Copenhagen. In Watkins, Glen. 1994, 239.

EX. 29   Juxtaposition of regular and irregular patterns, 1st movement, bars 23–26

   The viola's arco and regular pizzicato pattern join the cello's regularly repeating pattern to form a single layer of movement, but its complex relationship
with the two differently patterned cycles of the violins produces a trance-like
quality that would have been apt for David's gruesome dance. The 1st violin has
a diatonic 4-note theme consisting of three phrases of circular patterning that
contract from one phrase of 11 beats to two phrases of 6 beats. Its regularity is
large-scale: it is repeated unchanged four times, and quickly concluded with a
thematic fragment and a coda. The 2nd violin repeats the octatonic tetrachord
descending from F♯ with a large degree of temporal irregularity, the number
of beats' rest between its 'interruptions' varying between 6 and 9. The cello
extends the 2nd violin's octatonic tetrachord downwards to C♮, and its ostinato
of 2 + 3 + 2 beats, together with the regular viola pizzicato, is juxtaposed with
each of the first violin's repeating patterns with changing emphases.
   Rhythmically, the first movement juxtaposes three regular patterns of very
different lengths against one short, irregularly-occurring pattern: the long
10-bar theme for the 1st violin, the short 3-bar ostinato for the cello, and the
viola's short 4-note pizzicato motif are regular, while the 2nd violin – as the
loudest and driest sound – challenges the temporal regularity with a reiterated
motif that is heard once and then twice alternately. Pitch-wise the patterns
are juxtaposed differently: the lower three parts combine to pattern five octatonic pitches against the 1st violin's diatonic tetrachord. The layers are held
discrete by textural, timbral and dynamic contrasts: the lightness of the first
violin's whole bows and the guttural sound of the second violin playing at the
very heel of the bow are set against the drone of the viola, *sul ponticello*, and

the repeating pizzicato rhythms of the viola and cello, so that the distinctive movement of each layer is heard clearly. This mixture of regular and irregular patterning of both pitch and rhythm presents a complex spatial-temporal processing task for the brain,[24] so that the time quality created by this combination of sound patterns is bizarrely unfamiliar.

The second of the *Three Pieces*, proceeding at a fast walking speed ($\downarrow$ = 76), lasts about 1'45", and presents a display of gestural motifs with a vivid here-and-now time quality that was possibly inspired by the movements of the English clown Little Tich. As David dances before King Saul, the style is jerky with moments of suspended elevation (where the clown's long flat shoes become stilts) and sharp chords as he tumbles about. These articulated phrases are 'lived through' by the listener,[25] and would have been an apt portrayal of David as he sought to avoid Saul's attacks. The movement has an ABA structure: Stravinsky patterns four contrasting gestural motifs (bars 1, 5, 14, 16) around two slightly longer episodes (bars 26, 37), connected by a brief lyrical cadenza for the first violin. The structure is 'off-centre', as the title of the later orchestral arrangement *Excentrique* implies, the return of the opening motifs being severely curtailed.[26] Each motif varies slightly: the first motif, rescored at bar 49, sets the viola and cello a 9th higher than previously, leaving the 2nd violin as the bass. Stravinsky also makes a visual joke at bar 34, when the second violin and viola up-end their instruments to play a downward arpeggio pizzicato.

The third of the *Three Pieces* expands ontological time by alternating regular and irregular patterning in sections. With a slow pulse ($\downarrow$ = 40) this movement is the longest of the three with a performance time of 3'47", but its remote time quality belies its notation as just two pages of miniature score. It takes an antiphonal form in which three slightly varied passages of 'chant' are answered three times by a regular refrain (Ex. 30).

The reverent pianissimo quickly establishes a liturgical context, as would be fitting for King David's dance around the Ark in which Moses had placed the stones inscribed with the Ten Commandments. The later orchestral arrangement is entitled *Canticle*.

---

24   See Chapter 10: Music as a Higher Brain Function.

25   Stravinsky empathised in this way during a visit to *Kanjincho*, a kabuki dance-drama in Japan. Robert Craft recorded: 'The vocal noises, the grunts, groans, strangulated falsettos, are a delight to I.S. who tells me excitedly that the unity of sound and gesture is absolute …' Craft, Robert. 1968. Diary for April 8th, 1959, 191.

26   *Quatre Études for Orchestra* (1914–28) arr. from *Three Pieces for String Quartet* and *Étude for pianola* 1917, revised 1952.

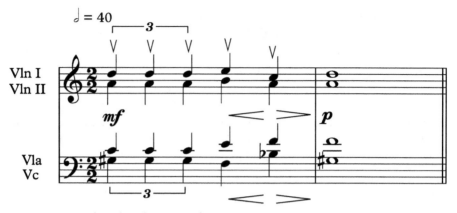

EX. 30   Regular refrain, bars 8–9, 3rd movement

After an introductory 'antiphon', four homophonic phrases expand and contract in the style of znamenny chant as if set to a hidden text. Variations in the scoring, such as a lower pitch for the cello in the second phrase and a rising contour for the first violin in the third, are minimal. Stravinsky specifies the indistinct and distant sound that is produced by whole bows played pianissimo over the fingerboard. Each phrase is answered by a six-note refrain played mezzo-forte and in a normal tone, whose rhythm suggests the liturgical response: *Gospodi pomiluy*: 'Lord, have mercy'.

The second part of the movement turns this dialogue upside down: the dynamic is reduced to pianissimo and the texture lightens substantially as the triplet rhythm of *Gospodi* is transferred to a high register in a new swinging style, with harmonics in the cello line. The original refrain returns in an expanded form at a low register, played very softly over the fingerboard (bar 39). The deepening time quality is dispersed by rests and the transparent resonance of four-part harmonics, and all movement ceases with two barely audible notes for the viola.

3   Chant Dissident (1919)

Stravinsky also juxtaposes regular and irregular patterning to create the remote time quality of *Chant Dissident*. The fourth of *Four Russian Songs* scored for voice and piano, *Chant Dissident* recalls an esoteric part of the Russian religious tradition. A great number of religious verses and chants were preserved

EX. 31   Dméstvenny-style opening of *Chant Dissident*, bars 4–5

by Russian mystical sects such as The Flagellants, Stranniki and God's People.[27] These verses deal with the temptations of the world or the coming of an Anti-Christ and the end of the world; they present allegories of the Sectarian Church, for example, as a garden refuge or as a ship sailing over the sea of life. Many have a satirical character and are aimed at the social order, at the 'innovations' of the Church, or the deficiencies of daily life. An expression common among sectarians was that 'A song is a ladder up to God'.[28]

The style of the opening (bars 1–17, Ex. 31) is that of the highly decorated dméstvenny chant that was preserved by the Old Believers after it gradually disappeared from official church use in the 18th century. Used on festal occasions, the beauty of its many melismas depended upon the improvisatory skills of the singer.

The song draws an analogy between the difficulties of everyday life and the spiritual difficulties of reaching the Kingdom of God: snowstorms and blizzards have closed all the paths to the church.

This spiritual song is constructed entirely from graduated combinations of patterning, drawing the listener away from a sense of the present. As in *Three Pieces for String Quartet*, the juxtaposition of regular and irregular patterning varies in complexity. First of all, the practical obstacles of the journey are lamented in the circular chromatic patterning of a small pitch range against a widely-spaced ostinato that emphasises the interval of a 9th and a tritone (bars 1–11). The song is then shaped by several types of layering that briefly vary the depth of time quality to mark out points of special spiritual significance.

The first type of layering (bars 12–17) honours the Creator who gives life; it juxtaposes two 3- bar vocal phrases of organic patterning against two regular 3-note ostinati at a similarly high pitch. The second type of layering (bars

---

27   In the first sketchbook for *Sektanskaya* (*Dissident's Song*) Stravinsky identifies the text as no. 351, p. 445 from *Songs of Russian Sects*. (Pesno russikh sektantov-mistikha by Rozhdestvensky and Uspensky, St Petersburg, 1912.) Stravinsky substitutes 'Jesus Christ' for 'honor' [*sic*] in the third line from the end. Stravinsky, Igor & Craft, Robert. 1982, 423. At this time, Stravinsky also set two fragments of sectarian music, without text, entitled *Khlyst* (Flagellant). Op. cit., 422.

28   Sokolov, Yuriy. M. 1966, 378.

EX. 32   Overtone motif in *Chant Dissident,* bars 18–20, 26–28

18–20, 26–28) juxtaposes the three-note 'overtone' motif (E♭ – D♭ – B♭) – the 'Old Believers' motif in *Zvezdoliki* and the unifying figure of *Les Noces* – against a pedal point chord of B♭ and C♭ (Ex.32). The resulting second inversion chords give this motif a 'floating' quality.

The first appearance of this construction (bars 18–20) has a melisma on the word *rodimogo,* a word used to express a special emotional link – as, for instance, with our parents who have given us life. It is a particularly intimate and tender way of addressing *rodimyi,* 'my Lord'. Its repeat (bars 26–28) elaborates the word *Bce,* creating a generous resonance to encompass 'all' their loving sisters and brothers.[29]

The third type of layering (bars 21–24, 29–40) opens out to juxtapose two circular melodic patterns, a 3-note step-wise pattern for the voice and a widely-spaced pattern for piano, against a dissonant pedal point that punctuates them with changing emphases. The fourth type of layering (bars 41–45) juxtaposes three circular movements of different width and pacing, the more irregular vocal line juxtaposed against regular consecutive 5ths for the piano.

The doxology (bar 46) is constructed with three layers of circular movement that vary in different ways: freely-evolving stepwise patterning in the vocal line and an irregularly repeating trill-like figure are juxtaposed with a regular quaver ostinato in the bass that varies slightly in its pitch content. The juxtaposition of these three independent movements deepens the time quality as glory is given to God and His Son.

4   Pulcinella (1919–20)

Perhaps Diaghilev imagined, when he gave Stravinsky some pieces by 'Pergolesi', that he would simply orchestrate them as written, but Stravinsky wanted to

---

29   *Rodimogo* and *Bce* are modern transcriptions of the Cyrillic script: some church Slavonic letters were excluded from the Russian alphabet by the Bolsheviks in 1918, in a special decree reforming Russian spelling.

make them his own.[30] He felt compelled, out of love for the music, to heighten their essential dynamism with his own Russian 'accent'. Some years later, in one of the most intimate passages of his *Autobiography,* he spoke, in the context of Pulcinella, of his intuitive awareness of the 'being' of things: 'Love is the single force that penetrates to the very essence of being and is the only potent dynamic force for creation'.[31] He described his love for the disparate movements that became *Pulcinella* as a 'look in the mirror': he felt, perhaps, that in setting these 18th-century pieces he became even more clearly aware of the traits of his own musical personality.[32]

It came as a surprise to Stravinsky that these movements in 18th-century style were based in gesture and dance.[33] He rewrote the pieces, frequently inserting an extra beat or bar to create an asymmetrical phrase, often thickening and spicing their basic diatonic harmonies with dissonance and delayed resolutions, and making colourful use of contrasting instrumental and vocal timbres and extended pedal points. These features removed the original movements from their place in both time and space, bringing a certain objective quality to their stylistic associations and transporting them eastwards.

He countered the scepticism of his publisher, Kling, by asserting that each piece had been recomposed in both timbre and tonality, thereby obtaining 'a block for the whole', and that each had been completely transformed and developed in an original way.[34] Stravinsky had heightened the rhythmic vitality of each movement, recasting the dialogues of instrumental timbres and clarifying the movement of motifs around the orchestra. Instruments had been treated equally, the scoring for bassoons, horns and cellos being as agile or melodic as for other instruments. The trombone and the double bass were even paired in a duet, Stravinsky jokingly pointing to the contrast in size in relation to the volume of sound that each produces. Stravinsky's orchestral string techniques lean towards those of the 19th- rather than 18th-century, and include ricochet bowing in the upper half of the bow, pizzicato harmonics, striking use of the high register of the cello, and flautando bowing to create unusual colours. Double and even triple stopping may be found in the viola parts, and the strumming of the gusli is imitated on several occasions.

---

30   It is thought that these pieces may have been by such composers as Gallo, Wassenauer, Monzo and Parisotti.

31   Stravinsky, Igor. 1975, 81.

32   Stravinsky, Igor & Craft, Robert. 1981. *Expositions and Developments*, 113.

33   Stravinsky, Vera & Craft, Robert. 1979, 185.

34   Stravinsky, Igor & Craft, Robert. 1981. *Expositions and Developments*, 113, also Stravinsky, Vera & Craft, Robert. 1979, 201.

Diaghilev was shocked, but the result of Stravinsky's recomposition was radical and theatrically effective.[35]

Pulcinella is important for marking the beginning of Stravinsky's synthesis of Russian and Western styles of patterning, and for promoting Stravinsky's stylistic move from organic patterning to a greater emphasis on the relationship of the phrase to the structure as a whole. In an article of 1927, *A Warning,* he observed that the one stable element of the Classical period and its basic substance was the quality of 'reciprocal relation' between constituent parts, its purely formal substance as opposed to any individualistic or ultra-musical elements.[36]

Stravinsky did not set out to write a satire, but with hindsight he remarked that it was perhaps inevitable to some extent that it was.[37] Nevertheless, Diaghilev's commission led to a new appreciation of 18th-century classicism on his part, which he felt was an entirely logical step for him.[38] *Pulcinella* offered Stravinsky the opportunity to blend the asymmetric patterning of ontological time characteristic of Russian native forms and the more regular patterning of time found in the Classical music of the West, a juxtaposition that he developed further in *Mavra* (1922). This mixing of musical styles remained a prominent characteristic of his works; as he himself said, *Pulcinella* was not only his discovery of the past, but 'the epiphany' through which the whole of his late work became possible.[39]

5   Symphonies of Wind Instruments (1920) and Cubism

The commission by *La Revue Musicale* of a page of music in homage to Debussy[40] made Stravinsky feel bound to develop 'a new phase of musical thought influenced by the work itself and the solemn circumstances that had led to it'.[41] Stravinsky recalled that his response to the commission was

---

35   Asaf'yev described the instruments as 'treated as characters in the comedy ... the doubles of the figures on the stage'. He also observed that 'The strings in the Toccata are used ... to carry the movement from one register to another'. Craft, Robert. 1992, 265.

36   Stravinsky, Igor. 'A Warning': December 1927. In White, E.W. 1979, Appendix 1, 578.

37   Stravinsky, Igor & Craft, Robert. 1981. *Expositions and Developments,* 112–3.

38   Stravinsky, Igor & Craft, Robert. 1981. *Memories and Commentaries,* 92.

39   Stravinsky, Igor & Craft, Robert. 1981. *Expositions and Developments,* 113.

40   Debussy died on 25th March, 1918. Stravinsky's piece was printed in the December 1920 issue of *La Revue Musicale* as no.7 in a collection of short pieces by different composers in memory of Debussy.

41   Stravinsky, Igor. 1975, 89–90.

to compose a 'choral' piece, a solemn chant in Orthodox style, that expressed his grief at the loss of Debussy's great friendship and the tragedy of Debussy's death while still at the height of his powers.[42] Stravinsky sent this piece to the *Revue Musicale* as a piano arrangement,[43] but it became the final section of *Symphonies of Wind Instruments*, a work which he described as 'an arrangement of tonal masses ... sculptured in marble ... to be regarded objectively by the ear'.[44]

The three tempi of *Symphonies of Wind Instruments* relate in mathematical proportions, suggesting a possible influence on his 'new phase of musical thought'. Stravinsky had become acquainted with Cubist ideas and artists on his arrival in Paris in 1909. He had acquired two paintings by Picasso in 1910, and also worked with Nijinsky's Cubist ideas for *The Rite of Spring* in 1913, but it was not until 1917 that Stravinsky began to develop a close personal friendship with Picasso himself.

Picasso's style, and that of the Cubists, had been much influenced by the mathematical ideas of Henri Poincaré through his disciple Maurice Princet. Stravinsky regarded musical form as in some degree mathematical, and as far closer to mathematics – or 'something like' mathematical thinking and relationships – than to literature: he remarked that mathematics offers the musician 'new tools of construction and design'.[45] Like Ortega y Gasset, Stravinsky considered that 'musical form is mathematical because it is ideal, whether it is, "an image of memory", or a construction of ours'.[46] He endorsed Marston Morse's view of mathematics as 'the result of mysterious powers which no one understands, and in which the unconscious recognition of beauty must play an important part'. It applied to the art of musical composition 'more precisely' than any statement he had seen by a musician.[47] Morse, like Poincaré, regarded the beauty of mathematics as coming from another realm; Stravinsky too, seems to have viewed mathematics as a spiritual art form, remarking that 'out of an infinity of designs a mathematician chooses one pattern for beauty's sake and pulls it down to earth'.[48]

---

42   Arthur Lourié describes this chorale as being in the Orthodox pattern: 'The Music of Stravinsky'. 1926, § 5.

43   The original chorale was a tone lower and had a metronome marking of ♩=100.

44   Stravinsky's programme note for performances in the 1920s. In Taruskin, Richard. 1996, 1486, n. 61.

45   Stravinsky, Igor & Craft, Robert. 1981, *Expositions and Developments*,100.

46   Stravinsky, Igor & Craft, Robert, 1979, 20.

47   Stravinsky, Igor & Craft, Robert. 1981, *Expositions and Developments*, 101.

48   Ibid.

The application of geometrical ideas to the arts was fashionable during the early part of the 20th century, and *de rigueur* among artists at the Ballets Russes. For a staging of *Le Rossignol* in 1917, later withdrawn, Fortunato Depero proposed to put the cast in rigid geometricised suits with geometric protuberances for their whiskers, eyes and mouths, and set them in a garden full of cones, arc segments and discs. Balla's staging of Stravinsky's *Fireworks* featured the play of light on geometrical solids. Coincidentally, at a gala evening in 1917 for the Italian Red Cross at the Teatro Costanzi in Rome featuring *Fireworks*, *The Firebird* and a suite from *Petrushka*, paintings by Picasso, Braque, Natalya Goncharova and the Futurists were exhibited in the theatre foyer.[49]

A close friendship between Stravinsky and Picasso began when Picasso left Paris for Rome in 1917 for preliminary work on the decor and costumes for *Pulcinella*. Like Stravinsky he worked with striking contrasts, designing costumes that made, according to the painter Jean Hugo, 'a certain, perhaps delectable, disagreement between the style of the costumes and that of the decors'. It was here in Rome that Picasso drew the first of his three portraits of Stravinsky.[50] The two artists spent a fortnight in Naples together exploring the town, and were particularly impressed by the *Commedia dell'Arte*, the aquarium and the old Neapolitan water-colours. Postcards from Picasso and his wife Olga Khokhlova in 1920 asking Stravinsky for the manuscript of *Pulcinella* show the degree of intimate friendship that continued between them. They had close mutual friends in Ernst Ansermet and Eugenia Errazuriz, and as part of the artistic group around Diaghilev they frequently met at private performances and suppers together with Jean Cocteau, Baroness d'Erlanger, Misia Sert and the Comte de Beaumont.[51] An informal photo of 1925 shows Cocteau, Stravinsky, Picasso and Olga in relaxed mode together in Juan-les-Pins;[52] Picasso was one of the few with whom Stravinsky used the intimate French form of address, *tu*.[53]

Picasso had been the leader of an artistic group, 'La Bande à Picasso', at Le Bateau-Lavoir in Montmartre, whose members had included, from 1905, the

---

49   For the 1922–3 season, Picasso's close colleague and co-founder of the Cubist movement, Braque, produced 'unforgettable' scenery and costumes for Georges Auric's ballet *Les Facheux*. Braque also gave 'valuable advice' to Stravinsky's son, Theodore, in his career as an artist.

50   A few days later, when leaving Italy for Switzerland, Stravinsky was obliged to surrender the portrait to Italian border police, who suspected it of being a plan of fortifications.

51   Stravinsky, Vera & Craft, Robert. 1979, 614 n.178.

52   Op. cit., 271.

53   Op. cit., 603 n. 38. Picasso gave Stravinsky a traditional French beret, which Stravinsky still liked to wear in America, forty years later. Horgan, Paul. 1972, 140.

mathematician and actuary Maurice Princet. He gave informal lectures to the group. As a keen student of the work of the polymath and mathematician Henri Poincaré, Princet wished to disseminate the ideas expounded in Poincaré's 1902 treatise *La Science et l'Hypothèse* on the new non-Euclidean geometries and the theory of the fourth dimension. Princet became known as the 'mathematician of Cubism'. The Cubist artist Jean Metzinger recalled that Princet 'conceived of maths like an artist and evoked continua of n dimensions as an aesthetician. He liked to interest painters in the the new views of space ...'[54]

Princet introduced Picasso to Esprit Jouffret's *Traité élémentaire de géométrie à quatre dimensions* (1903), with its very clear geometrical illustrations of hypercubes and complex polyhedra, drawn with a high degree of faceting. They were generated by an analytical method for 'rotating' geometrical shapes to obtain different perspectives of their four-dimensional structure as projections onto a two-dimensional plane.[55]

Meditating on these highly faceted illustrations, Picasso realised that new depth of meaning was obtained by depicting their different perspectives, not successively as Poincaré suggested, but simultaneously. Given that perspective distorts our perception of an object, the problem was to give equal validity to each of the differing viewpoints. As Picasso began to juxtapose different perspectives of his subject, his work became increasingly geometricised.[56]

Between 1906 and 1908, Picasso filled sixteen sketchbooks with experimental drawings and paintings that developed into the geometricised primitivism of the female figures in *Les Desmoiselles d'Avignon* (1907) and ultimately into Cubism. The paintings of Picasso and Braque are constructed with juxtaposed planes, overlapping sharply-defined volumes, contrasts of straight lines with curves, cones, cylinders, and inverted perspectives.[57] On Tuesday July 18th 1917, surely one of those serendipitous moments in history when the paths of

---

54   Miller, Arthur. 101, n. 106.

55   For Poincaré the fourth dimension was a spatial dimension: '... in the same way that we draw the perspective of a three-dimensional figure on a canvas of three (or two) dimensions, so we can draw that of a four-dimensional figure from several points of view ... Imagine that the different perspectives of one and the same object succeed one another'. Op. cit., 105, n. 133. In 1910 Manuel Manolo recalled that 'Picasso used to talk a lot the about the fourth dimension and he carried around the mathematics books of Henri Poincaré'. Op. cit., 103–4.

56   The squatting female figure (lower right) in *Les Desmoiselles d'Avignon,* for example, is seen both from the back and in profile simultaneously and is constructed from triangles, squares and circles. The techniques of this painting were so groundbreaking and so shocking that the canvas was hidden away and was not exhibited until 1916, the year that Picasso and Stravinsky met.

57   Gleizes' Cubist portrait of Stravinsky was completed in 1915.

new and radical ideas unknowingly cross, Stravinsky's *Three Pieces for String Quartet* were performed at the Salle d'Antin in Paris. Stravinsky's juxtaposition of contrasting layers and sections to create unfamiliar time qualities were played just as the gallery was exhibiting Picasso's *Les Desmoiselles d'Avignon*, a painting that juxtaposed contrasting geometrical shapes to create new and unfamiliar spaces.

Picasso's painting, *Three Musicians* (1921), shows how he dismantled and rearranged his subject matter, juxtaposing flat planes of unshaded colour and angular shapes in new ways to suggest spatial ambiguities (Illustration 3).

The painting depicts Picasso himself and two poet friends: Pierrot on the left, playing a clarinet, is thought to commemorate Guillaume Apollinaire who had died in November 1918; the singing monk on the right is Max Jacob, who was about to go into a monastery. Picasso is the central guitar-playing figure, Harlequin. The costume of this self-portrait – a favourite depiction – recalls

ILLUSTRATION 3   Pablo Picasso, *Three Musicians*
MUSEUM OF MODERN ART, NEW YORK. © PHOTO SCALA, FLORENCE

Picasso's designs for the Ballets Russes' 1920 production of *Pulcinella*, on which he had worked with Stravinsky. Dark colours frame the lighter, more complex overlapping of light colours in the centre foreground, highlighting the central figure. Like Stravinsky's *Symphonies of Wind Instruments*, the painting has an unreal yet monumental quality. Cubism had a lasting influence on Stravinsky's style: in *Symphonies* he adopted similar 'cut and paste' Cubist techniques, finding a musical analogy in juxtaposing qualities of time and movement as facets of the temporal form.[58] Years later, in 1956, after a morning spent working on *Agon*, Stravinsky still thought and composed in this way, remarking 'A series is a facet, and serial composition a faceting, or crystallising way of presenting several sides of the same idea'.[59]

Stravinsky had wanted to be a painter, and it is quite possible that his juxtaposition of sections in *Symphonies of Wind Instruments* was influenced by discussions with Picasso on dismantling a form and re-assembling its parts: for Stravinsky, the construction of form was of paramount interest.[60] Just as mathematicians bring an ideal form 'down to earth', and artists depict perspectives of a subject simultaneously, *Symphonies of Wind Instruments* takes an Orthodox-style chant, extracts and develops its intrinsic movements, and recombines them to create a 'new' time, in a musical analogy of the Cubist process.

The unity of a work is usually revealed by analysis of its melodic, harmonic and rhythmic materials, and the development of its relationships.[61] In constructing music as a temporal art Stravinsky had added a new consideration: the unity and meaning of *Le Rossignol, Petrushka, The Rite of Spring* and *Les Noces* also depended upon the construction and ordering of their time qualities. The question of how to relate the diverse movement qualities of *Symphonies of Wind Instruments* as a memorial to Debussy – that commemorated Debussy's role in freeing music to be a temporal art – presented Stravinsky with a completely new challenge.

---

58   In August 1917 Bakst wrote to Stravinsky that he had purposely saved some enthusiastic
      letters from the Cubists, 'of whom you are so fond', following his (Bakst's) recent produc-
      tion of *Phèdre* with Ida Rubinstein at the Paris Opéra. Craft, Robert, ed. 1984, 92.
59   Craft, Robert. 1972, 58.
60   Stravinsky, Igor & Craft, Robert. 1981, *Expositions and Developments*, 102–3.
61   For example, see Cone, Edward T. 1962, 18–26. Cone's analysis of Stravinsky's works are
      based on stratification, interlock and synthesis. 'Stratification' describes the tension
      between separated, incomplete ideas or areas and the expectation of their development;
      'Interlock' is the presence of a musical feature that runs through each type of recurring
      idea so that successive segments are counterpointed in time; 'Synthesis' is the reduction
      or transformation of one or more components of the work to reach a cogent goal.

6   Symphonies of Wind Instruments (1920): Temporal Form

Stravinsky's homage was to be in his own language.[62] He had a distinct feeling that Debussy would have been rather disconcerted by his musical idiom, as he had previously been by *Zvezdoliki*.[63] Stravinsky's association of these two works, together with his interest in Cubist techniques, tends to confirm that his new phase of musical thought had more to do with Time and with contrasting the facets of a temporal form, rather than any advance 'in the direction pointed to by the tendencies of the Debussyist period'.[64]

Symphonies of Wind Instruments pays homage to Debussy by the interaction of its different sections: the opening cries cease, and the litanies for mercy, forgiveness and rest are gradually superseded by a joyful hymn of praise. The final solemn chant brings peace and the Christian hope in the *Theotokos* (the 'God-bearer') and the resurrected Christ that is voiced in the dismissal of the Russian Orthodox *Panikhida* (a liturgy for those who have fallen asleep).[65] Stravinsky described *Symphonies* as 'an austere ritual which is unfolded in terms of short litanies between different groups of homogeneous instruments'.[66] The distinctive feature of a litany is a recurring refrain which lends the text a spiral form, as in the *Panikhida* service itself that weaves together biblical readings, the Great Litany, Alleluiahs, Troparia (short hymns), a Kontakion (a hymn on a biblical subject), the Trisagion (a hymn to the thrice-holy God) and several litanies for the departed.[67] *Symphonies* imitates this ritual by weaving together brief, recurring sections. Two litanies (figs. 6, 15) and their return in reverse order are prefaced and briefly interwoven with qualities of movement derived from the original chant; they act as changing perspectives on the chant and are

62   Stravinsky, Igor. 1975, 91.
63   Op cit., 90. *Roi des Étoiles* [*Zvezdoliki*] was also dedicated to Debussy.
64   Op. cit., 89–90.
65   The final chorale is based on a chant in the *Obikhod*, the Slavonic *Liber Usualis*. Craft, Robert. 2006, 248 quoting Taruskin.
66   Stravinsky, Igor. 1975, 95. 'Stravinsky speaks of "the cantilène of the clarinets and flutes taking up their liturgical dialogue and softly chanting it"'. Taruskin: 1996, 1485. The full *Panikhida* service is composed of a Psalm, the Great Litany, Alleluia, Troparion (short hymn) in Tone 8, Troparia in Tone 5, Litany for the Departed, petition for Rest in Tone 5, Psalm 50 (51), Canons in Tones 1, 3, Litany for the Departed, Ikos in Ode 6, Kontakion (hymn with a biblical theme), Ikos in Tone 8, Ode in Tone 9, Trisagion (prayer, an ancient cry from Isaiah), Troparia in Tone 4, Litany and Dismissal.
67   The Hymn of the Departed for example is strophic, with the refrain 'Blessed art thou, O Lord. Teach me to justify thy ways' after each of five three-line verses. Taruskin: 1485 ff. The Requiem Hymns for salvation, forgiveness, restoration, rest and paradise use melodic motifs of the 5th echos, and have the refrain 'Teach me Thy statutes'.

finally subsumed into its original, plain form. Stravinsky said that *Symphonies of Wind Instruments* 'was designed as a 'grand chant', an objective cry of wind instruments in place of the warm human tone of the violins'.[68]

Symphonies of Wind Instruments, like *Three Pieces for String Quartet*, explores contrasts of symmetry and asymmetry in the juxtaposition of regular and irregular patterning: each section is patterned freely with the organic, asymmetric rhythms of Russian native forms, but their pulses are strictly proportioned in the ratio of 3:2. This tension creates a complex spatial-temporal reasoning task that draws the listener away from the here-and-now to time qualities of greater depth.

Stravinsky derived three distinctive qualities of movement from the chant (Ex.33):

a)   the repetition of heavy chords (fig. 65 + 1 – 2)
b)   a swaying movement generated by a legato slur (fig. 65 + 2 – 3)
c)   a 'striding' figure that includes (b) and the distinctive interval of a 4th (fig. 66 + 1 – 2)

EX. 33   Three movements derived from the chant, fig. 65

Stravinsky expands the first three heavy crotchet chords of the chant and aspirates them into a passage of 'sighs' (fig. 1); the swaying slur (fig. 65 + 2 – 3) becomes a brief preview of a hymn of praise (fig. 3), that finally emerges in full at the new Tempo 3 (figs. 44, 46). The 'striding' figure characterised by the interval of a 4th generates the swinging movement which divides the pulse differently (fig. 11) and is juxtaposed to the second litany in metrically-displaced variants (fig. 21). Several brief transition passages that repeat the slurred intervals of a 4th act as links (after fig. 41) and help to unify the work.

The contrast of chordal patterning with melodic patterning is clear-cut (Table 2). Short aspirated chordal movements at Tempo 1 contrast with melodic patterning and counterpoint at Tempo 2 and with joyful homogenous

---

68   Stravinsky, Vera & Craft, Robert. 1979, 225. The 'Great Chant' acquired its name from its wider pitch range, including intervals of a 6th and 7th. 'While traditional znamenny chant contained isolated echoes of the folk song, the folk song cantilena (*raspevnost, pesennost*) has now become the very foundation of the Greater Chant'. Brajnikov, M. 'Russian church singing in XII–XVIII centuries'. In Alfred J. Swan, 1973, 43.

movement in constantly changing metres at Tempo 3. The full statement of the chant returns at Tempo 1.

The proportioned crotchet pulses increase by half as much again from 72 to 108, and then to 144 to the minute. Chordal materials at Tempo 1 evoke articulated cries, sighs and a small fragment (fig.3) that will become a full hymn of praise at Tempo 3. In contrast, the melodic materials at Tempo 2 are made up of close legato patterning in the style of Russian folk song and liturgical chant: the cantilena of the first litany (fig. 6) is supported by legato chords, but the second litany – more melodically wide-ranging in the style of the Great Chant (fig. 15) – is treated contrapuntally. Contrapuntal and chordal patterns are briefly juxtaposed at Tempo 2 at seemingly random moments (figs. 21, 23 + 2, 33, 34 + 2). In contrast, the hymn of praise at Tempo 3 (fig. 46) moves homophonically with asymmetrical rhythms in circular motion.

The chant and the three movement qualities derived from it are thus arranged to create an 'austere ritual'. In a dynamic analogy of Cubism's juxtaposition of geometric shapes, they unfold four spiral movements that differ

TABLE 2   Melodic and chordal patterning at proportioned tempi: *Symphonies of Wind Instruments*

Tempo 1 ♩= 72	*CHORDAL PATTERNING*
	a) The 'Cry': opening, figs. 2, 9, 26 + 2, 37 + 2, 39
	b) Tutti 'sighs': figs.1, 4
	c) 'Hymn of praise' preview: fig. 3
	d) Emerging chant bars 7–9: figs. 28, 42, 56
	e) Chant: fig. 65
Tempo 2 ♩= 108	*CHORDAL PATTERNING*
	a) Chant fig. 66 - 66 + 2 in 6/8 time: fig.11
	b) Links using interval of 4th: figs. 43, 45, 57, 64
	MELODIC PATTERNING
	a) Litany 1: 3 flutes, fig. 6. + bassoon: fig. 8
	b) Litany 2: flute/clarinets: figs. 15, 29
	c) Reverse of litany 1: figs. 38, 40
Tempo 3 ♩= 144	*CHORDAL PATTERNING*
	'Hymn of praise' in changing metres: figs. 44, 46

EX. 34   Second litany, *Symphonies of Wind Instruments*

greatly in their degrees of momentum, temporal depth and musical space.[69] The first spiral (to fig. 6) is brief and tight-knit: it quickly presents the three movement qualities derived from the chant. Its aspirated 'cries' and 'sighs' are answered by a legato movement based on the chant's distinctive interval of a 4th. A brief preview of Tempo 3 is embedded in this spiral at Tempo 1 (fig. 3).

In contrast, the second spiral movement (from fig. 6) describes a single wide revolution that unfolds largely circular melodic patterning much more slowly. Two litanies petitioning peace and rest are briefly interwoven with movements derived from the chant and then reversed in shortened forms. The first litany (fig. 6) simply patterns five stepwise pitches for three flutes and a solo bassoon against a slow sustained accompaniment.[70] The second litany (fig. 15) has a greater pitch range, canonic entries, and a deeper time quality created by two, sometimes three contrapuntal layers for flute and two clarinets (Ex.34).

This litany is preceded and then counterpointed by a joyful variant based on the 'striding' motif of a fourth and swaying movement (figs. 11–24, Ex.35).

This rhythmically and timbrally-contrasted layer of movement seems to continue independently elsewhere, reappearing briefly in 6/8 time against melodic patterning in 3/8 and 3/4 time at Tempo 2 (figs. 21, 23 + 2, 33, 34 + 2).[71]

---

69   See Chapter 9: Mental Imaging, and Chapter 10: Music as a Higher Brain Function.

70   In the original 1920 scoring, two circular patterns, the litany and its accompanying chords, revolve simply in rhythmic cycles of contrasting length (fig. 6), the accompaniment consisting almost entirely of consecutive major 7ths, the resonant bell-like interval, o–11. The 1947 revision slows and smooths the accompanying chords with suspensions, calming the character of the prayer and increasing the contrast with the other time qualities.

71   Tempo 2, half as fast again as Tempo 1, juxtaposes a chordal, compound division of the pulse against the duplets of the litanies.

EX. 35   Joyful variant juxtaposed 'randomly' against the second litany, fig. 21

On their return in reverse, the first litany is interrupted by a final 'cry' (fig. 39). The momentum of this second spiral movement gradually diminishes, with a preview of the new Tempo 3 (fig. 44) contained within a contracted version of the chorale at Tempo 1 (fig. 42), and two transition passages of fluctuating 4ths at Tempo 2 (figs. 43, 45).

The third spiral movement is in the form of a joyful Hymn of Praise that celebrates the present moment with circular figures (fig. 46). Its energy eventually begins to diminish with the appearance of a second fragment of the chant and progressively longer passages of swaying 4ths. The meaning of the work is revealed in this spiral movement as sighs and cries are subsumed and transcended in spiritual joy.

The fourth spiral movement, the original chant, stretches time towards eternity. All contrasts of patterning, pacing and time quality are abandoned as its melodic contours flatten out and its phrases lengthen. *Symphonies* begins in 'clock-time' with mourning but is superseded first by the time qualities of petitionary prayer and then by spiritual joy; its qualities of time and movement finally unify 'out-of-time' as facets of an autonomous but meaningful temporal form. The construction of the work pays homage to Debussy, not only as a friend and colleague, but also to his vital role in freeing music to be a temporal art. It achieves this by embodying time as both *chronos* and *kairos*: *chronos* in the linear, gestural time qualities of sorrow and joy and *kairos* in its shaping of ontological time qualities into an autonomous memorial.

The four contrasting spiral movements create a monumental four-part Litany for the Departed. As in *Les Noces*, emotions in this memorial have not been banished, but are ordered with the quality of *apatheia*. Stravinsky did not aim to compose a work that would please its audience, but hoped that it would appeal, nevertheless, to those in whom 'a purely musical receptivity outweighed emotional cravings'.[72] These spiral forms were the first of several spiral forms in Stravinsky's works, notably the middle movement of *Octet* (1923)

---

72   Stravinsky, Igor. 1975, 95.

and movements in the late serial works from 1952: *Cantata, Threni, A Sermon,* and *Requiem Canticles.*

Symphonies of Wind Instruments looks forward to *Symphony of Psalms,* another autonomous temporal form that embodies a spiritual journey. In 1945, Stravinsky re-orchestrated the concluding chorale of *Symphonies* for a CBS programme that included the *Symphony of Psalms.* Its suitability as a companion piece surely comes not only from its length of performance time and similar instrumentation, but also from its hauntingly beautiful appeal to the human spirit.[73]

Stravinsky's exploration of patterned movement from *Les Noces* to *Symphonies of Wind Instruments* was almost exactly contemporary with the work of the philosopher Jacques Maritain. *La Philosophie Bergsonienne* had been published in 1914; his second book, *Art et Scolastique* (1920) proposed that the transcendent beauty of an art work arises from the 'shining' of form on *proportioned materials. Symphonies* is already a visionary musical realisation of Maritain's philosophical ideas; this work, together with the closer influence of Maritain through Arthur Lourié, largely determined Stravinsky's new musical direction in the 1920s.

7   Time and Form: Jacques Maritain

Stravinsky was in Paris in the first part of 1914 for the first performance of *Le Rossignol* and a concert performance of *The Rite of Spring.* Being an avid reader with a keen interest in new ideas it is quite possible that he knew of Maritain's first book, *La Philosophie Bergsonienne,* soon after it was published. Maritain's philosophy, like that of Nesmelov, was concerned with human consciousness, thought, and the perception of a transcendent reality, subjects of supreme interest to Stravinsky.

Jacques Maritain, a pupil of Henri Bergson, was working on a critique of his teacher's philosophy of 'continuous becoming' as perceived by the intuition. Basing his critique on the precepts of Scholasticism, itself based on ideas from St Thomas Aquinas and ultimately, Aristotle, Maritain was seeking to give greater weight to the intellect and to the stricter ordering of rational schemes. Where Bergson had seen faith as an internal experience, Maritain defined faith

---

73   Stravinsky's re-orchestration was influenced by the forces needed for *Symphony of Psalms.* Stravinsky, Vera & Craft, Robert. 1979, 228–9.

as the result of intelligence, influenced by the human will and imbued with divine grace.

Neo-Thomism had been adopted as the official philosophy of the Roman Catholic Church in 1879, and after the First World War it had quickly gathered force and begun to establish itself as an important strand of modern thought.[74] Neo-Thomism, like Nesmelov's *The Science of Man,* sought to be more scientific in spirit by taking rational thought as its starting point: spiritual revelation had to be supported by reason. From an analysis of natural knowledge, neo-Thomist philosophy moves to synthesise ideas about supernatural knowledge while remaining true to Christian beliefs. St Thomas Aquinas had sought a more reasoned connection between created things and higher truths; he rejected the 'divine illumination' proposed by his teacher, Albertus Magnus, and was the first to assert that all human knowledge reaches the intellect through the senses. His five proofs of the existence of God recognise the limits of natural knowledge and are based only on those manifestations of God's actions in the world that are accessible to human experience.[75]

Aquinas, following Aristotle, believed that the source of all human knowledge lies in the brain's abstraction of universal elements from their material context which it then restores to pure forms. Aquinas also rejected the duality between the soul and the body in which the soul is seen as a largely independent spiritual substance, and asserted that the soul is the form of the body, giving actuality and 'being' to it. Following Aquinas, neo-Thomism emphasises the natural role of the intellect in abstracting the intelligible forms and principles inherent in sensory information, and of giving being to matter through form.

Born in the same year as Stravinsky, Jacques Maritain converted to Roman Catholicism in 1906 and quickly became the foremost French representative of neo-Thomism. Maritain believed that three major degrees of knowledge, scientific knowledge, metaphysical knowledge, and supra-rational knowledge in the form of mystical experience, could co-exist, each having its own place within a grand synthesis. For Maritain, the sensory world embraces notions such as number, space, time and life, that can be known from both scientific

---

74 Pope Leo XIII's encyclical *Aeterni Patris,* 1879, made neo-Thomism the official philosophy of the Roman Catholic Church. Its basic place in Roman Catholic thinking was reaffirmed in Pope Pius XII's encyclical *Humani Generis* in 1950.

75 Aquinas offered five proofs of the existence of God: that there is either an infinite chain of cause and effect or a first uncaused cause; that efficient causes, dependent upon each other, also need a first cause, God; that there is a distinction between necessary and contingent being; that the varying degrees of analogous qualities in things presuppose an absolute source; that all things seek an end in their author, God, to whom they strive to return.

and philosophical perspectives; metaphysics presents a higher synthesis in the idea of Being, where the activity of the brain passes from sensory input to the non-material realms of the mind. By bringing together attitudes of adoration and intellectual admiration the mind gains higher knowledge by reason and by the processes of abstraction and analogy. Higher still are the supra-rational forms of knowledge, in which reason is illuminated by divine revelation without the intermediary of discursive thought, and the soul is brought into loving and intimate union with God.

Maritain's first book, *La Philosophie Bergsonienne,* was based, like the philosophy of Kierkegaard, not upon a priori concepts but upon lived experience. Bergson had rejected both idealistic and mechanistic pictures of the world as having departed from reality, and his philosophy of vitalism saw reality as dynamic, and nature as always becoming. Religion, in his view, must justify itself by taking part in this activity and by being practical rather than theoretical.[76]

Maritain was critical of Bergson on many points, but his own work is nevertheless based on some of Bergson's chief insights, particularly on the role of the 'practical intellect' and the role of intuition. *La Philosophie Bergsonienne* begins by examining Bergson's definitions of these terms. The function of the 'practical intellect' is to 'make' things and 'arrange' matter: 'L'intelligence est une faculté ordonnée à la pratique, et façonnée par la pratique'.[77] [*Intelligence is a faculty directed to the practical, and shaped by the practical.*] The practical intellect breaks up experience into its component parts which it isolates, measures and conceptualises, but it gives only a static picture and remains on the outside of life. The practical intellect breaks up time into separated instants, and its temporal domain is that of measurable clock-time.

Stravinsky was temperamentally suited to Maritain's concept of the practical intellect, since he declared that he had the same attitude as 'the most illustrious masters' in crafting music 'as an artisan', as a shoemaker makes shoes, 'day in, day out, and for the most part, to order'.[78]

Both Stravinsky and Maritain understood the interaction between the human intellect and the physical world as having a mathematical basis. *La Philosophie Bergsonienne* stresses the mathematical aspect of the 'practical intellect':

76　Bergson, Henri. 1911, 186. In Macquarrie, John. 1981, 171. Bergson defines God as 'unceasing life, action, freedom: Creation so conceived is not a mystery; we experience it in ourselves when we act freely'. Bergson, Henri. 1911, 262. In Macquarrie, John. 1981, 172.

77　Maritain, Jacques. 1914, 18.

78　Stravinsky, Igor. 1975, 170 –1. Stravinsky is quoting a letter from Tchaikovsky.

> Or la pratique de l'homme consistant essentiellement à agir sur la mat-
> ière brute et à manipuler les solides, l'intelligence humaine sera essentiel-
> lement géométrique ...[79]

> [Now, as Man's practical faculty consists essentially of acting upon raw
> material and of manipulating solids, human intelligence will be essen-
> tially geometric ...]

In contrast to the practical intellect, Maritain defines the role of intuition as
taking us into the inwardness of life, and perceiving activity, becoming and
flux as duration. It is the means of penetrating the flow of living reality and its
vital impetus (*élan vital*):[80]

> Quel est l'objet de l'intuition bergsonienne? ... c'est précisément *la durée*.
> Cette durée ... inexprimable en termes conceptuels, n'a rien du com-
> mun avec le temps mathématique, ... avec le temps mésurable, ... c'est le
> changement pur ... le changement sans rien qui change ... un écoulement
> qui s'enrichit sans cesse ...[81]

> [What is the object of Bergson's intuition? ... it is precisely *duration*. This
> duration ... inexpressible in conceptual terms, has nothing in common with
> mathematical time, ... with measurable time ... it is pure change ... change
> without anything that changes ... a flow that ceaselessly enriches itself ...]

Bergson believed that 'by the sympathetic communication which it establishes
between us and the rest of the living, by the expansion of our consciousness
which it brings about, [intuition] introduces us into life's own domain, which
is reciprocal interpenetration, endlessly continued creation'.[82] Maritain suggests that this continuous, indivisible becoming has an element of novelty and
creativity that makes spontaneity and free will possible.[83]

Maritain modifies Bergson's emphasis on the role of the intuition by introducing a greater contribution of the intellect. In particular, he points out that

---

79   Maritain, Jacques. 1914, 18.
80   Vera Sudeikina wrote to Stravinsky on March 18th, 1935: 'The only good sign is that if they
      all come to me for consolation, it must mean that my *élan vital* is intact'. Stravinsky, Vera
      & Stravinsky, Igor. 1985, 72.
81   Maritain, Jacques. 1914, 27.
82   Bergson, Henri. 1911, 323. In Macquarrie, John. 1981, 171.
83   These qualities also characterise the improvisatory nature of Russian Orthodox
      church chant.

'becoming' involves both the measuring of interactions and relationships, and memory, both of which are functions of the intellect [*sic*]. By replacing intelligence by intuition and the 'being' of things by duration or pure change, the principle of identity is destroyed. Maritain concludes: 'en bref, il s'agit de *penser* avec les *sens*' [*in short, it's a matter of* thinking *with the* senses].[84]

In *La Philosophie Bergsonienne* Maritain puts forward an insight into time and human existence that is particularly relevant to music as a temporal art.[85] He presents a new way in which the body and soul are linked and interact: the body and the soul are not two different entities existing in space, but are the means by which humankind exists in two different modes of time:

> Toute la relation de l'âme et du corps, de l'esprit et de la matière est donc ... celle d'une durée indivisible qui se conserve intégralement, à une durée qui n'est plus ou presque plus qu'un présent instantané qui recommence sans cesse; des transitions en multitude infinie permettant de passer continûment de l'une à l'autre, et la première agissant et s'actualisant par la seconde. Voilà la grande découverte de la philosophy nouvelle: *distinguer et unir l'âme et le corps, non plus en fonction de l'espace,* comme les Cartésians l'ont fait d'après M. Bergson*, mais en fonction du temps* ...[86]
>
> L'âme n'est plus qu'une certaine manière de durer, le corps une autre manière de durer.[87]

[The relationship of soul and body, of spirit and matter, is therefore that of an indivisible time which preserves its wholeness, to a time which is no more, or nearly no more than a instantaneous present that ceaselessly begins again; an infinite multitude of transitions allowing a continual passage from one to the other, and the first acting and actualising itself through the second. This is the great discovery of the new philosophy: *to distinguish and unite the soul and the body, no longer in terms of space,* as the Cartésians have done following M. Bergson, *but in terms of time* ...

---

84 Maritain, Jacques. 1914, chapter 3.
85 The rise of Christianity brought the problem of Time to the fore. While the Platonic tradition asserted that 'time is the moving image of eternity' and that, having little to do with movement, time is less real than eternity, the Hebrews thought of time as *kairos* 'meaningful time', the time in which God has immersed himself by means of the Incarnation. The Scholastic view of time is that God knows and experiences all points of time simultaneously, thus avoiding the difficulties in attributing to God the foreknowledge of events. Hanson, A.T. 1969.
86 Maritain, Jacques. 1914, 206–7.
87 Op. cit., 208.

The soul is no more than a certain way of being in time, the body another way of being in time.]

La Philosophie Bergsonienne speaks to that blend of rational mysticism which was central to Stravinsky's nature: the geometrical nature of the 'practical intellect' appealed to his rational mind, while the role of intuition in perceiving being and being becoming was in harmony with his spiritual nature. Crucially, it supported his belief that creating music with a transcendent quality was possible through rational musical schemes.[88]

Maritain's second book, *Art et Scolastique,* published in Paris in May, 1920, began to explore the implications of Bergson's philosophy for artistic creativity. He proposed that truth may be expressed in two ways: through the abstract speculative order of metaphysics that isolates mystery in order to know it, and through the practical order of poetry and artistic creation that is always active and uses its findings.

In Thomist philosophy a work of art has to fulfil three conditions in order to please the intellect, through the senses, by its beauty: it should have integrity so that the intellect loves the being of it; proportion so that the intellect loves its order and unity; and *'éclat or clarté'* so that the intellect loves the light and intelligibility of its reason.[89] The Thomist aim is that the artist should 'faire briller l'éclat d'une forme, la lumière de l' être' [*make a form shine with the light of its being*]. Beauty in art arises from 'le resplendissement de la forme sur les parties proportionnées de la matière' [*the shining of form on proportioned materials*].[90] Thus the beauty of an art work is a spiritual quality, as distinct from

---

88   The philosopher Karl Heim (1874–1959) offers a way of understanding how Maritain's two modes of being, the soul and the body, may interact. Heim begins from Heidegger's proposition that time is the basic form of existence. Part of us, which Heim calls the ego, stands both in time (in the 3-dimensional world he calls the 'objectivisable world') and outside the time-series (in a world he calls the 'non-objectivisable' world). We experience the latter, the eternal 'now', in our encounters and relationships with other people, for example, and recognise that it exists simultaneously with the 3-dimensional world that 'passes' from past to future, to which it is linked. The 3-dimensional world of everyday life is the medium onto which our experiences in the 'non-objectivisable' world are projected and communicated. So we live in two inseparable types of time and space simultaneously. Quality of forward movement is important for the part of the ego in time, and quality of relationships for the part of the ego outside time. Thus, to co-ordinate our sense of 'becoming' in the 3-dimensional world with that of 'being' outside time, for example through music, is to unite the two parts of our ego at its most profound point and to facilitate access from one part of the ego to the other. Heim, Karl. 1953.

89   Bergson, Henri. 1920, 37.

90   Op. cit., 38.

aesthetic beauty in which the senses predominate. Maritain's *Art et Scolastique* makes an important departure from Thomist philosophy in proposing that artistic forms may take on a transcendent quality:

> L'éclat de la forme doit s'entendre d'une splendeur ontologique qui se trouve d'une manière ou d'une autre *revelée à notre esprit*, non d'une clarté conceptuelle ... *pour nous,* mais bien quelque chose de clair et lumineux *en soi,* d'intelligible *en soi* ...[91] une participation de la divine clarté ...[92] s'il en est ainsi, c'est que le beau appartient a l'ordre des transcendanteaux.[93]

> [By 'the shining of form' is understood an ontological splendour that is revealed by one means or another *to our spirit*, not a conceptual clarity ... *for us*, but rather something clear and shining *in itself*, intelligible *in itself* ... a participation in divine clarity ... if it is thus, beauty belongs to the transcendental order.]

In *Art et Scolastique* Maritain defines the two levels of an art work: the artist is to arrange raw materials, *matière prochaine,* into an objective form so that it reveals *matière éloignée,* a meta-level of spiritual beauty. Speaking of the *temporal* relation between the two levels of art, Maritain described the length of a poem as relative to its own inner measure,[94] while Stravinsky needed to know how long a piece must take, before it excited him. [95] This arrangement of raw materials requires total objectivity on the part of the artist:

> L'Art ne s'occupe pas du bien propre de la volonté, et des fins qu'elle poursuit dans sa ligne d'appétit humain ... Comme la Science c'est à un objet qu'il est rivé (objet à faire il est vrai, non à contempler).[96]

> [Art is not concerned with the good of one's own free will, and the ends that it pursues in the way of human appetite ... Like Science it is bound to an object (an object to make, it is true, not to contemplate).]

---

91 Op. cit., fn. 42–3 (my italics).

92 Op. cit., 47.

93 Op. cit., 45. '... dans leurs classifications les anciens ne donnaient pas une place à part à ce que nous appelons les beaux-arts' [*the ancients did not make a separate place in their classifications for what we call the fine arts*]. Op. cit., 37.

94 Maritain, Jacques, 1954, 390

95 White, E.W. 1966, 564 . A comparison of their artistic views is given in Chapter 11.

96 Op. cit., 31.

Like the Scholastic philosophers, Maritain sees the artist's arrangement of materials as bearing a particular relationship to the growth patterns of the physical world: he was fond of quoting St Thomas' maxim: 'Art imitates nature in its way of operating'.[97] He believed that it is the way of working that continues God's creativity, and to think of the essential goal of art as the representation of the real, is to destroy it:[98]

> La création artistique ne copie pas celle de Dieu, elle la continue ... la nature est ainsi le premier excitateur et le premier régulateur de l'artiste, et non pas un example à decalquer servilement.[99]

> [Artistic creation does not copy that of God, it continues it ... nature is thus the first instigator and regulator of the artist, and not an example to copy slavishly.]

The second level of an artistic work, *matière éloignée*, has a new quality of brilliance that comes from its materials '... que l'artiste dispose et sur laquelle it doit faire briller l'éclat d'une forme, la lumière de l'être' [... *that the artist arranges and with which he must make a form shine with the light of its being*].[100] All the materials must support the 'light' of the form.[101] But the arrangement of the materials may involve some transformation of their properties by the artist (such as the special treatment of words to diminish their intrinsic temporal implications): 'Mais pour faire resplendir ces rayonnements dans son oeuvre ... même il doit déformer en quelque mésure, reconstruire, transfigurer les

---

97   St Thomas Aquinas: Summa Theologica I, 1.117.a.1.
98   Bergson, Henri. 1920, 78–9.
99   Bergson, Henri. 1920, 89–90 The idea is also found in Dante: 'that your art follows nature, as far as it can, much in the way a student follows his master; so that your art is the grand-child of God'. *The Divine Comedy: Inferno*. Canto XI, lines 103–6.
100   Op. cit., 83.
101   In the first edition of *Art et Scolastique*, Maritain contrasted the 'light' of Gregorian chant and the music of Bach with the darkness of the music of Wagner and Stravinsky. After his first meeting with Stravinsky in 1926, subsequent editions carried a footnote: 'Je m'accuse d'avoir ainsi parlé de Stravinsky. Je ne connaissais encore que *Le Sacre du Printemps*, j'aurais dü voir déjà que Stravinsky tournait le dos à tout ce qui nous choque dans Wagner ... Sa pûreté, son authenticité, sa glorieuse vigueur spirituelle sont au gigantisme de *Parsifal* et de *la Tétralogie* comme un miracle de Moîse aux prestiges des Egyptiens'. 1927 [*I blame myself for having spoken thus of Stravinsky. I knew only* Le Sacre du Printemps, *I should have already seen that Stravinsky was turning his back on everything that shocks us in Wagner ... His purity, authenticity, and glorious spiritual vigour are to the gigantism of Parsifal and the Tetrology, as a miracle of Moses is to the marvels of the Egyptians.*].

apparences matérielles de la nature'.[102] [*But to make the brilliance of his work shine out ... he must even deform* [*the materials*] *in some measure, reconstruct, transfigure the material appearances of nature.*]

Maritain's first two books were deeply attractive to Stravinsky's Old Believers temperament and he subsequently pursued the ideal of attaining a transcendent level in art by continuing to strive for 'light' and 'resonance', and by strengthening the relationships of his temporal forms. Stravinsky and Maritain met for the first time on June 10th 1926 and became personal friends from 1929 onwards. Never one to reveal very much about who or what had influenced him, Stravinsky simply recalled that until 1926 he knew of Maritain 'only through his books'.[103]

---

102   Bergson, Henri. 1920, 88.
103   Stravinsky, Igor & Craft, Robert. 1981. *Expositions and Developments*, 75–6. By 1926 Maritain had also written *St Thomas d'Aquin Apôtre de Temps Modernes* (1923), *Réflexions sur l'Intelligence* (1924), and *Trois Reformateurs* (1925).

CHAPTER 8

Time for Pushkin

Stravinsky felt an intimate bond with Pushkin, describing his genius and all its versatility and universality as 'organically Russian'. He thought that this quality, that had given spontaneous voice to the 'soul' of Russia and to a whole school of thought, had characterised 'the most specific' of Russia's civilisation; it had been Peter the Great's ambition to blend it with the intellectual wealth of the West. Stravinsky revealed that he had consciously cultivated this same mentality, wishing to preserve Russia's national characteristics as found in the art of the people rather than in any 'ethnographic aestheticism'. In composing *Mavra* to Pushkin's poem *The Little House at Colomna,* Stravinsky felt that he was asserting his alliance with the authentic origins of Russian nationalism rather than imposing any academic 'doctrinaire catechisms'. Although he enjoyed the satirical skits of the Moscow Theatre troupe, La Chauve-Souris, in Paris, in a more serious vein he saw Diaghilev and himself as part of the tradition initiated by Peter the Great. This tradition had been continued by Glinka (in *Ruslan and Ludmilla*) and Tchaikovsky (in *Eugene Onegin* and *The Queen of Spades*) and had inspired Pushkin's naturalness and true portrayal of his Russian 'being'.[1] *Mavra* is dedicated to the memory of Glinka and Tchaikovsky.

The 'spiritual nucleus' of *Mavra,* the spirit of Russia, was to be conveyed in the lively genre of opéra-bouffe. By the 1830s Russia was already beginning to recover its native culture from foreign influences and was fermenting with life and vitality; vaudeville and burlesque that made frequent attacks on the corruption and inefficiency of bureaucracy under Tsar Nicholas I were at the height of their popularity.[2]

Pushkin wrote *The Little House at Colomna* in 1830 as he was completing *Eugene Onegin* and at the height of his creative powers. Written in Byronic octaves that rhyme, AB AB AB CC, the poem records an incident in the life of lower-middle class (pomeschik) people in a suburb of St Petersburg. Their speech is a mix of the Slavic language and the vernacular. Boris Asaf'yev describes this type of high-spirited, eclectic Russian speech as differing in style 'according to epoch, rank, society, and the personality of the individual': he

---

1   Stravinsky, Igor. 1975, 97–8.

2   Boris Asaf'yev describes the subject of *Mavra* as an old Russian vaudeville dealing with an incident in the Thirty Years War. Asaf'yev, Boris. 1929, Chap. 10. Pushkin was exiled several times for his literary attacks on the corrupt nature of society.

observes that 'Speech ... may be filled with interjections, exclamations, interrogations, declarations. The problem is to catch its whole excitement ...' With regard to the speech of *Mavra* (and also of *Eugene Onegin*) he remarks that 'Words pour out in unbroken melodic lines, commas are ignored ... and emotional tone and its nuances take precedence over sense ...' Asaf'yev recalls that, in setting this type of speech, Tchaikovsky had also been attacked for his 'misplaced accents, ungrammatical word-couplings, pauses in the wrong places, and metrical confusion'.[3]

Pushkin, like Stravinsky and Maritain, regarded the artist as *homo faber*, and declared that the aim of poetry was poetry.[4] Abandoning the declamatory style of the 18th century, Pushkin had created a new realism that was conveyed in an easy-flowing texture and inflection, with a new economy of style that clarified its pacing. In developing and perfecting the flexibility of the regular tonic metre, his cantos developed a rhythmic unity that may be appreciated both visually and aurally: the rhythmic flow of the narrative is paramount. At the beginning of his *Art Poétique* Pushkin speaks of the innovative poetic techniques in *The Little House at Colomna* that capture this easy-flowing movement, stating that he is bored by the four foot iambic line advocated by Lomonosov, that he will use a five foot iambic line for this poem instead,[5] and that he prefers the caesura to come after the second stress rather than the third, for better orderliness.[6] Although the opera is set to Pushkin's poem in a transcribed version by Boris Kochno, it was Pushkin's structuring of the original text, which Stravinsky described in terms of its 'highly lyrical depth' and its 'poetic structure of rhymes', that encouraged him to seek a musical analogy for its fluidly-changing time qualities.[7] It is hard, however, for Pushkin's 'Russianness', his rhyme schemes, distinctive variations of rhythm, and linguistic idiosyncrasies, to be translated into another language and for his literary genius to be completely understood by non-Russians.

Firstly, Stravinsky emulates Pushkin's nuanced pacing of the narrative by frequently counterpointing the musical stresses and metres with those of the text to obscure the sense of the present and set the action at a distance. *Mavra*

---

3 Asaf'yev, Boris. 1929. In Craft, Robert. 1992, 266.
4 Stravinsky praised Pushkin's 'scrupulous commonsense and matchless lucidity', and his art as 'amply deep and amply mystical in itself': White, Eric W. 1966. Appendix, A, 588–589.
5 Aristotle gives the iambic metre as the metre best suited to satire, lampooning and invective: Aristotle. 1932, 15–17.
6 Boris Kochno transcribed Pushkin's largely narrative tale into dramatic dialogue and action, and his placing of caesura and the lengths of his lines are consequently more flexible than in the original.
7 Stravinsky, Igor 'Pushkin: Poetry and Music'. In White, Eric W. 1979, Appendix 1, 589.

is shaped throughout by incompatible juxtapositions, even to the extent of mismatching the music and the staging, as Arthur Lourié later observed:

> Dans *Mavra* les rapports entre le rythme musical et le texte étaient contraires: certains épisodes de *Mavra* nous présentaient même des formes métriques qui contredisent ouvertement la logique élémentaire du texte. Le mouvement de la musique dans *Mavra* s'opposait sciemment au mouvement scénique.[8]

> [In Mavra the relationships between the musical rhythm and the text were in conflict: certain episodes of Mavra even presented us with metrical forms that openly contradicted the simple logic of the text. The musical movement of Mavra was knowingly contrary to the movement on stage.]

Stravinsky's means of distancing Parasha's opening aria from clock-time to a 'new' objective time are especially innovative.[9] Textual stresses are set in opposition to the musical stresses, the five foot lines of text are shorter than the musical phrases, changes of subject in the text do not correspond to the musical sections, and the articulations of the musical phrases are counterpointed against slightly irregular cycles in the ostinato accompaniment. Stravinsky constructs another kind of 'out-of-time' experience for the love scene between Parasha and the Hussar in Scene 5. The text is syllabified into separate sounds, the pace of movement is expanded and slowed across a repeating rhythm, and their duet, 'two loving hearts' (figs. 125–134), is set with a tension of 2 against 3 that creates the unreal 'time' of a dream.

Secondly, Stravinsky captures the sparkling quality of Pushkin's easy lyricism that comes from his well-observed portrayal of 'being', the natural ways in which people talk and behave. Pushkin's 'zephyr-like quality' of light, satirical humour comes from his brushing together of many different literary styles. He employs a complex mix of styles and a great variety of digressions, literary allusions, and poetic techniques. He does not disguise these creative processes, and in his constant references to literary fashions, literary models, and above all, his own observations, he even makes this *mélange* plain as he narrates the incident with his own particular brand of affectionate satire. These variations in style accelerate and slow the narrative; he also structures the text by retreating from the tale to vouch for some different reality, or

---

8 Lourié, Arthur. 1929, 246.
9 Parasha's prototype was Onegin's Larina: Asaf'yev, Boris. 1929, 221.

by intruding upon it in order to puncture its character and add another level of meaning.

Stravinsky finds a musical analogy for this structuring of pace in Pushkin's sparkling lines, with their mix of literary styles and lampooning of the subject, by juxtaposing typical features of Russian and Western Grand Opera and exaggerating the contrast between them, just as he had added 'Russian' features to the dance movements of *Pulcinella*. Stravinsky sets asymmetrical Russian patterning against the symmetrical patterning of the West in ways that are quite inappropriate: by these means he not only captures the cosmopolitan spirit of the 1830s but also Pushkin's objective quality of satire.

Following the Russian-style patterning of Parasha's aria in Scene 1, the typical bravura style of a 19th century Western European operatic hero (fig. 6) is accompanied by sforzando chords at the heel of the bow that imitate the strumming of the gusli and bring associations with the religio-magical role of the skomorokh. An amusing mismatch of moods occurs in Scene 2 when Parasha's Mother and her neighbour sing earnestly of the weather and God's providence (fig. 44): their vocal lines begin in unison but quickly become heterophonic against the orchestra's light and cheerful responses (fig. 48). As Mother and her neighbour begin to sing at length of the coming winter gloom (fig. 49), and as their vocal patterning becomes more organic, the Tchaikovskian accompaniment becomes ever more sparkling; as they discuss the serious topic of Providence and the gladness and distress it brings, the accompaniment becomes even lighter in weight (fig. 51). In Scene 4, the trio of Parasha, her Mother and a neighbour begins with slow vocal unisons in the style of Western Grand Opera as they mourn their previous cook, observing righteously that 'She always did her duty' (fig. 80), but their duet soon becomes heterophonic against the continuing opéra-bouffe style of the orchestra. After all the Russian-style vocal patterning, the trio ends with an anachronistic perfect cadence at the exclamation: 'She's a lovely girl' (fig. 92 + 3 − 4).

While Russian-style heterophonic folk singing, laments and a polka are set to opéra-bouffe accompaniments, the typical Russian movement of pitch centres by a tone and a semitone is contrasted with diatonic harmony, and metrical accents are displaced against the easy-flowing pulse of their musical accompaniments. Some of the traditions of Grand Opera are gently lampooned by being introduced into many situations of ordinary life: the cadenza in 3rds for Parasha and the Hussar (fig. 21), Mother's lyrical duet with the flute whilst singing of cleaning and laundering (fig. 36), the cook's extended announcement of her name with a great flourish (fig. 75), and Parasha's sudden launch into popular melody at 'And how can I forget those nights?' (fig. 111), are among the many delightfully anachronistic examples.[10] Stravinsky paces the text by melismas, by syllabification, and by grand operatic gestures quite inappropriate to the everyday circumstances of the tale.

The role of narrator in the poem naturally falls to the orchestra who accompany sympathetically or undermine the stage action with a contrasting mood. The momentum of the narrative is sometimes slowed and the time quality deepened by the orchestral shadowing of the vocal parts, sometimes in canon. This device is used to exaggerate the importance of a gloomy situation to comical effect, as in Scene 2 (fig. 28 + 2) where a soaring Romantic melody accompanies Mother's melodramatic lament on her maid's death. It is also used to show empathy (figs. 14–17) or to underline the increasing confusion between the characters as the *dénouement* rapidly approaches (figs. 134–140).

The mix of Eastern and Western European styles is particularly evident in the contrasts of pitch collection and their typical melodic intonations. Asaf'yev notes Stravinsky's use of the intonations of folksong, gypsy music, and romantic songs of Russia's urban culture in the 1820s [*sic*], particularly those of *Vecher*, a popular song of the time that evokes rural life.[11] Parasha meets her mother's concern about wearing a coat, for example, with a typically resonant folksong intonation created by the minor seventh (A) of the natural scale on B (fig. 33 – 1, Ex.36).

EX. 36   Typical folksong motif

This intonation also characterises the neighbour's melody (figs. 48 – 1, 56, 57 – 2), and returns in a number of variants (i.e. fig. 135). Another brief motif sung first by Mother (fig. 28 + 1), later by Parasha (fig. 134) and then by the Hussar (fig. 136 + 2 – 3) when he is trying to please, is typical of the resonant intonations that recur in Russian folksongs.

In contrast, the swashbuckling Hussar is characterised by variants of a diatonic phrase in which a high note is approached very quickly and then held (Ex.37: the melodic cliché is more suited to a heroic tenor in a Romantic Grand Opera (figs. 11 + 3, 17 + 3 – 5):

---

10   *Mavra* is, perhaps, the amusing satire on Romantic opera that Stravinsky had wanted to compose ever since reading *Koz'ma Prutkov* in his student days.

11   Asaf'yev, Boris. 1929, 221.

EX. 37   Motif in the style of Western Grand Opera

These variants recur at inappropriate times (figs. 75 + 3, 89 − 1) and most poign-antly (and amusingly) in the Hussar's later melodramatic aria (fig. 143).

Stravinsky makes musical references, chiefly to typical motifs of Mozart and Verdi, that add an extra layer of associations. The words 'day and night' (fig. 72 + 2 − 3) are tossed around, briefly recalling the astonished exclamations of 'sua madre' in *The Marriage of Figaro*, and as the Hussar prepares to shave we hear the 'ticking' accompaniment typical of Mozart's operatic finales when there is an impending crisis (from fig. 157). In the Pastorale (fig. 93) the change to voices in Verdian parallel 3rds and 6ths makes an amusing contrast to the Russian folksong style of the preceding two scenes. The contrast between East and West in the patterning of pitch brings a sense of spatial-temporal disorien-tation, and increases the objectivity with which we view the characters as local and historical 'types'.

But *Mavra* maintains its essentially Russian musical character by the fre-quent patterning of a small pitch range, the minor hexachord, at different pitch centres: the hexachordal patterning of the three sections of Parasha's opening aria, for example, pass through four pitch centres, B♭ − G − A − B♭. When Parasha's aria returns (fig. 105), it shifts to pattern the hexachord on G♯, a semitone higher. *Mavra* is unified by the recurrence of this hexachordal into-nation just as *Les Noces* was unified by the three-note 'overtone' motif.

The mood of *Mavra* is above all anecdotal, and its light inconsequential nar-rative concludes with humorous 'moral' advice in vaudeville style. The 'weight' of *Mavra*, as a musical analogy of Pushkin's poetic techniques, more than com-pensates for its meagre length in clock-time. Stravinsky later said of the work that he simply wanted to try his hand at the living form of the opéra-bouffe which was so well suited to the Pushkin tale, and to renew the style of these dialogues–in–music.[12]

Stravinsky wrote to Ernst Ansermet in September 1921 that his opera was coming on very well, adding that it was very different from what he was doing. He was proud of the synthesis he had achieved between the spirit of Russia and the Western style, since he wrote again in December to say that his opera

---

12   Stravinsky, Igor. 1947, 58.

had all the signs of being a masterpiece.[13] He was glad to see that he had completely succeeded in realising his musical ideas, and was therefore encouraged to develop them further.[14] Some years later he recalled that only a few musicians of the younger generation appreciated *Mavra*, and realised that it marked a turning point in the evolution of his musical thought.

The work that followed, *Octet*, continued the mix of Russian and Western styles begun in *Pulcinella* and pursued again in *Mavra*, and also developed the objective quality that had 'distanced' both *Mavra* and *Symphonies of Wind Instruments*. Stravinsky's *Octet* would not only have a 'spiritual nucleus' built of many stylistic contrasts, but also its movements would unify into an autonomous musical *object*.

---

13   Stravinsky, Vera & Craft, Robert. 1979, 636, n. 3/4.
14   Stravinsky, Igor. 1975, 103.

CHAPTER 9

The Object Is Time

In *Art et Scolastique* (1920), Maritain had proposed a view of beauty in which the senses and intellect work together. It was a form of beauty that depends upon the degree of order, proportion and perfection of relationships with which the artist fashions *matière prochaine* (raw materials) into *matière éloignée* (the things made present to the spirit). The aim of the artist is to create an object with a form that shines with 'ontological splendour'.[1] At the same time as Maritain was writing *Art et Scolastique*, Stravinsky was realising this concept of the spiritual art-work in *Symphonies of Wind Instruments* by ordering and proportioning its living movement qualities into an autonomous temporal form.

In 1921, Stravinsky was introduced to Arthur Lourié, a Roman Catholic and an ardent disciple of Jacques Maritain. As Stravinsky's musical assistant from 1924–31 Lourié enthusiastically promoted Maritain's work: Robert Craft recalled that 'Stravinsky respected Lourié's musical opinions, was interested in his philosophical ideas and enjoyed his company'.[2] Lourié's letters to Stravinsky were full of religious matters such as prayers that he had copied out for the composer, requests for Stravinsky to pray for him, and glosses on the Evangelists.[3] A letter from Lourié to Stravinsky in 1924 confided that he had just read the spiritual exercises of Loyola and had been thinking 'that if Stravinsky were a theologian he would write in the same way, with the same dry passion'.[4] The letter reveals something of the depth of their discussions at that time, and of Lourié's early understanding of Stravinsky's spiritual nature.

Stravinsky was receptive to Maritain's *homo faber* philosophy and its view of the artist as a craftsman creating an 'object' to appeal to the spirit; these ideas were very much in tune with Stravinsky's aim of developing a 'gift' from God into a temporal form with a transcendent quality.

---

1   Maritain, Jacques. 1947, 38. See also Maritain, Jacques. 1943, 34: '... the primary reason of art, which is to construct, and create through the spirit, objects each one of which is a condensed universe existing for itself'.

2   Stravinsky, Vera & Craft, Robert. 1979, 220. In 1956 Pierre Souvtchinsky recalled that Arthur Lourié was closer to Igor Stravinsky in the 20s and 30s than anyone else, and that Lourié's ascendancy between 1920 and 1926 [*sic*] was nearly total. Craft, Robert. 1972, 62.

3   Stravinsky, Vera & Craft, Robert. 1979, 290.

4   Op. cit., 220.

© KONINKLIJKE BRILL NV, LEIDEN, 2022 | DOI:10.1163/9789004518537_011

The idea of a musical 'object' increased that objective ordering of ontological time qualities which Stravinsky had sought since Act 1 of *Le Rossignol*. As in appreciating the structure of a painting, a musical object shaped by time qualities is to be 'lived through' with in-depth attention. The visual system processes the individual features of a material object in physical space – its lines, volumes, colours, textures, etc. – and integrates them to recreate an image of the object; several objects may be organised in physical space to create meaning.[5] Similarly, the auditory system processes the individual features of a non-material musical object in time – its contours, timbres and qualities of time and movement – and integrates them to build a mental image of its temporal form: several musical objects may be organised in mental space to create meaning. Musical events, if clearly constructed, may be juxtaposed to build an object that may be clearly mentally imaged.

A musical object, in the course of patterning ontological time with varying depths and densities describes a certain shape. Entering into 'the shape of time, and the time of shape', to quote Thomas Clifton's memorable phrase,[6] requires the musical object to be listened to with in-depth attention, and the shape that it gradually describes to be actively mentally imaged. Clifton wrote '... to a considerable extent, therefore, the perception of time strata involves the perception of not only different horizontal spaces but of spaces at varying degrees of depth'.[7] Elsewhere he wrote '... we should properly speak of time, space and play as residing within the musical object'.[8] Clifton also describes the mental image of a work's 'own universe' as having its own boundaries, and, being separate from the world of everyday practical concerns, as only superficially interrupted by them.[9]

As we have seen in Chapter Four, it is the right hemisphere that constructs the sense of depth in both time and space.[10] If the musical object is both shaped by momentum and temporal depths and constructed with Maritain's 'perfect' relationships, its materials will unify into a clear temporal form with its own unique time world. Remarkably, the imaging of any sufficiently strong temporal design such as this is also repeatable to within a very small margin of error, in performance time.[11]

---

5   Merleau-Ponty has defined space as 'the means whereby the positing of things becomes possible'. Merleau-Ponty, Maurice. 1966, 243.

6   Op.cit., 135.

7   Op.cit., 127.

8   Clifton, Thomas. 1983, 79.

9   Clifton, Thomas. 1983, 79.

10   See also McGilchrist, Iain. 2009, 77.

11   See Chapter 10: Music as a Higher Brain Function.

1   **Mental Imaging**

The brain processes information in two distinctly different ways. When told
that there are two objects, one beside the other, and one is smaller than the
other, the brain may process this information using language, in terms of 'large
object – smaller object', or graphically, by mentally imaging the objects themselves.[12] An image, whether an actual drawing or a mental picture, provides
a particularly clear and fast way of obtaining an overview of a great deal of
information and organising it to render it more intelligible.

Stravinsky's clear visualisation of the ways in which he wanted his works
staged reflected his skill, as a graphic artist, in imagining objects and events:
he even described a musical interval as an object, as something outside of
himself, the contrary of an impression.[13] Robert Craft recalled that 'Stravinsky
saw with his eyes as he heard with his ears, and viewed any painting, or scene
in nature, as a composition. Sitting at a table, he would habitually rearrange
the objects on it, placing them in relationships that enhanced their individual
forms and resulted in new designs. His own drawings of people, of Diaghilev,
Picasso and Ramuz, for example, reveal his perception and gift for capturing
essential features. He could have been a brilliant cartoonist. The young Igor
Stravinsky had been a painter and had wanted to study art'.[14]

Stravinsky sometimes entertained friends with his great powers as a 'magus',
conjuring invisible shapes and their qualities of energy and rhythmic behav-
iours. On one occasion in 1958 he reached out to every side of a table top, and
with great care 'scooped and patted' unseen particles of matter towards the
centre ... until his friends were persuaded to see a pyramid take shape in their
imagination. On another occasion in 1963 he described the arrival of an aer-
oplane, joining his hands to make the plane and hunching his shoulders to
suggest its forward energy. His friends saw its long descent to earth, its increase
in size and every loss of speed and height and increase in gravity as it touched

---

12   Hampson, P. J. et al. 1990, 13.

13   Stravinsky, Igor & Craft, Robert. 1979, 17. Stravinsky dreamt of a musical interval as an
        object while composing *Threni* (1957–8). By this dream Stravinsky knew that the interval
        was right. Stravinsky, Igor & Craft, Robert. 1979, 17–18. The artists Jawlensky and Malevich,
        Stravinsky's neighbours in Switzerland during WW1, greatly admired his talent as a
        painter. Craft, Robert. 1972, 382.

14   Craft, Robert. 1992, 30 Describing his economy in the use of trumpets and horns in
        Variations (1964) Stravinsky wrote 'I needed only a spot of red, however, and a spot of
        blue'. White, Eric W. 1979, 537.

down and came to a halt. It was as if 'no experience, however common, was lost upon him, and no report of it was unworthy of a full creation ...'[15]

In *Art et Scolastique* Jacques Maritain had proposed that it was the task of the artist to create an object that embodied a *'new* analogy of beauty'.[16] Stravinsky likened the task of composing to the refitting of old ships, out of which something new could emerge, but added that the artist could say again, in his way, 'only what has already been said'.[17] Stravinsky designs new temporal journeys within the old traditions: he interweaves time qualities in spiral movement (*Symphonies of Wind Instruments, Octet, Cantata, Threni Part 2, A Sermon, Requiem Canticles*) or moves greater weight and density to a central movement framed by dynamic linear motion (*Octet, Cantata, Canticum Sacrum*). Perhaps his most remarkable 'new analogy' is found in his imitation of the natural growth process to mirror a spiritual journey from the here-and-now to timelessness (*The Rite of Spring, Symphonies of Wind Instruments, Symphony of Psalms, Threni, A Sermon, A Narrative and A Prayer, Requiem Canticles*).

Like Goethe and others, Stravinsky compared the structure of music to architecture. In relation to his father's visualisation of music as architectural, Theodore Stravinsky wrote: 'The formal masses and reciprocal proportions, the straight and curved lines and the joints from which architecture derives, speak directly to the imagination and by-pass commentaries'.[18] The mental imaging of Stravinsky's architectural forms is facilitated by their representation of the physical world as rhythmic manners, their structuring of rhythms in organic patterns of growth, and their objective presentation of being becoming: they relate to real life through their imitation of the movement of human time-consciousness. *Symphonies of Wind Instruments* is, perhaps, the first of Stravinsky's larger-scale 'spiritual' works to construct a crystal-clear mentally-imageable object: its clarity of structure co-ordinates the listener with ontological time.[19] Theodore Stravinsky said of his father's music that it is, above all, a means of communion: his music depends upon this communion 'and such communion is possible only at the ontological level'.[20]

---

15   Horgan, Paul. 1972, 122–3, 228–9.
16   Maritain, Jacques. 1947, 67 (my italics).
17   Stravinsky, Igor & Craft, Robert. 1982, 129.
18   Stravinsky, Theodore. 1953, 9.
19   Stravinsky, Igor. 1947, 142.
20   Stravinsky, Theodore. 1953, 1.

2   Octet (1923)

Maritain's list of artistic materials in *Art et Scolastique* includes 'les rhythmes, les sons, les lignes, les couleurs, les formes, *les volumes*, les mots, les mètres, les rimes, les images, matière prochaine de l'art ...' [*the rhythms, sounds, lines, colours, forms,* volumes, *words, metres, rhymes, images, the raw materials of art* ...].[21] In *Octet*, a new contrast of instrumental volumes contributes to the momentum and weight of the work, and helps to clarify its architecture as a unified musical 'object'.

Stravinsky begins his article, *Some Ideas about my Octuor,* with the stark statement that the *Octuor* (*Octet*) is 'a musical object' whose differences of form are influenced by its differences of musical matter.[22] The work is scored for 'objective elements which are sufficient in themselves', and the play of movements and volumes at either forte or piano creates its impelling force, though Stravinsky advises that part of its weight and space will necessarily be lost 'in time and through time'. However, the musical object cannot lose in quality so long as its emotive basis has objective properties and 'keeps its specific weight'. Stravinsky considers the means of constructing an autonomous musical object to be 'the most important question' in all his recent compositions. The means of construction would remain a lifelong concern, his interest always 'passing entirely to the object, the thing made'.[23]

Stravinsky's language of weight in time and space is also found in Arthur Lourié's article of 1925 on Stravinsky's *Piano Sonata*, in which Lourié defines musical time, *temps constructif* (constructed time), as 'cette dimension de la musique ou se déforment les éléments (qui n'a rien de commun avec le temps horaire)' [*that dimension of music in which the elements are distorted (which has nothing in common with clock-time)*], and musical space, *espace constructif* (constructed space), as 'cette dimension de la musique ou se déplacent les éléments' [*that dimension of music in which the elements move*].[24]

As in *Mavra,* the 'weight' of lines and surfaces in *Octet* is varied by asymmetry and a mix of Eastern and Western styles. *Octet* reinterprets three classical Western forms: the sonata, theme and variations, and the rondo. Its qualities of time and movement form an imageable musical object with a new temporal shape, in which a central tightly-constructed spiral movement is framed by vivacious counterpoint of much lighter depth. The outer movements exploit

---

21   Maritain, Jacques. 1947, 82–83.
22   White, Eric W. 1979, 574–6.
23   Stravinsky, Igor 1972, 110.
24   Lourié, Arthur 1925, 100–101.

EX. 38   Circular movements: Introduction to *Octet*

the linear energy of the Baroque and Classical styles, but the middle movement moves through greater contrasts of time quality by juxtaposing musical
styles: the light volumes of a 19th-century March, Waltz and Can-Can alternate
with the first part of the first variation that has great octatonic resonance and
great weight.

The initial Lento introduces two qualities of movement that will appear in
many forms during the work (Ex.38): a swaying, alternating interval of a tone
(fig. 1) and a circular motif (fig. 3 – 3) whose lower notes move by a semitone.

The sonata form Allegro features pairs of instruments, its transparent contrapuntal texture created by dialogues between highly contrasting timbres and
volumes. Both the first subject (fig. 7), and the second subject (fig.12 – 1) based
on the swaying figure from the Lento, are heard in canon with metrically-
displaced accents. In the first movement, thematic fragments are developed
on and between the pulse so that the regularity of the movement is alternately
established and confounded.

The first movement does not follow the classical scheme of modulation, nor
does it enjoy its customary role as the most substantial movement of the work.
Ethan Haimo has pointed out that the pitch centres of the first movement mark
out a semitone pattern around E in the manner of Russian folksong, and there
is 'a correspondence between stability and tonic-assigned diatonic collections
on the one hand, and instability and tonic-less chromaticism on the other ...'[25]

The range of temporal depth in the central Tema and Variations increases
considerably. Its rondo-variation form was described by Stravinsky as a set of
Variations Monométriques. The Tema replaces the Western-style chromaticism
of the first movement with the close pitch groups and resonant symmetry of
the octatonic scale, but also explores wider movement of the central pitch,
opening a larger musical space: the main theme between A – C♯, for example,
has an answering phrase between E – C♮ (fig. 25, Ex.39).

The phrasing is clear-cut but has greater asymmetry than the phrasing of
the 1st movement: the eight-bar Tema for flute and clarinet expands the third

---

25   Haimo, Ethan. 1987, 46.

EX. 39   Tema and answering phrase: 2nd movement, *Octet*

bar by a beat, but it is answered by the trumpet and trombone in a six-bar phrase without the expanded bar.

Variation A, centred a semitone higher on B♭, juxtaposes a faster, denser version of the first four bars (only) of the Tema to fast scales, now changed from the 1st movement into dense 'ribbons'. It lacks the expanded third bar of the original and also the answering phrase. This concentrated variation recurs as the weighty axis of the movement's spiral form after the lighter Variations B and D, but not after Variation C, so that the movement itself has an asymmetric form.

Variation B is a light march with major 3rds and scales in dotted rhythms, with occasional metric asymmetry. Two surface movements in the styles of East and West are juxtaposed: octatonic patterning and organic development is contrasted with the regularity of a diatonic, arpeggiated accompaniment. The sudden concerto grosso-style cadence, with its duet of 'four-square' arpeggios (fig. 31 – 3) recalls the witty vaudeville spirit of *Mavra*.

Variation C, a Waltz in the style of Petrushka's Ballerina, develops the swaying movement and revolving arpeggios of the opening Lento. It too, juxtaposes two layers of patterning: the flute's high, agile movement is set against two slow, intermittent and elaborated versions of the Tema for trumpet in the low register.

Variation D, a Can-Can, follows without a break with a similar pulse but with greater weight and a tauter construction. Again, two qualities of movement are juxtaposed: two octatonic phrases of the Tema for trumpet, the first sustained and elongated, the second with different metric emphasis, are accompanied by circular quaver patterns that descend the chromatic scale. The middle section lightens as it moves to a new pitch centre on F and to the contrasting timbres of flute and clarinet and a new triplet patterning, after which the initial movement qualities briefly return.

Variation E, a brief fugato with the greatest depth and density, was Stravinsky's favourite variation. It swings between the intervals of the Tema, now low-pitched and widely-spaced, in irregular circular 5/8 figures that talk and breathe like znamenny chant, with changing emphases of pitch. Opposing surfaces are now brought together in homogenous movement and the depth of

EX. 40   Syncopated jazz and Russian Khorovod rhythms: 1st and 3rd movements, *Octet*

time quality is increased by accumulating textures. Its weight is gently released by a succession of organically-evolving circular figures.

The rondo Finale returns to dynamic linear movement and the lively counterpointing of diatonic scales and arpeggios, circular figures, and semitone changes of pitch centre. The theme of the Finale, like that of the first movement, is built on intervals of a 3rd and a 7th, and its second subject (fig. 61 + 2) recalls the swaying movement of the opening Sinfonia. The Western jazz rhythm heard in the first movement (figs. 12, 18) is balanced by a Russian Khorovod rhythm of 3 + 3 + 2 (fig. 66) in the third movement (Ex. 40); in developing an aspirated, homogenous quality, it disperses the weight and energy of this musical 'object' and seals its form.

Arthur Lourié defended Stravinsky's reinterpretation of Classical and Baroque forms:

> Mais ce retour n'est pas un abandon de l'expérience acquise. Les formes classiques originelles catalysent en lui des idées neuves, totalement comprises dans les formes neuves ... et l'oeuvre ainsi accomplie constitue un organisme en soi.[26]

> [But this return doesn't abandon acquired experience. The original classical forms catalyse new ideas in him, totally understood in new forms ... and the work thus accomplished constitutes an organism in itself.]

In his article about Stravinsky for the journal *Versty*, Lourié includes *Octet* as an example of the change in Stravinsky's style to the animating of lines and surfaces, and compares it to Picasso's recent change from Cubism:

> La Sonate, l'Octuor et le Concerto abandonnent la construction dans le volume et le timbre pour entrer dans l'espace linéaire, incolore. L'animation de la ligne est préponderante en cette periode. Analogie dans le domaine

---

26   Lourié, Arthur. 1925, 103.

de la peinture: abandon du cubisme pour les compositions en surface (Picasso).[27]

[The Sonata, the Octet and the Concerto abandon the construction of volume and timbre to enter a linear, colourless space. The animation of the line is of greater importance in this period. Analogy in the area of painting: the abandonment of cubism for compositions using surfaces (Picasso).]

Lourié also remarked on Stravinsky's new animation of linear constructions with regard to the *Piano Sonata*:

> Conquête sur l'espace, elle affirme dans cette dimension une construction linéaire ... Auparavant les deux problèmes du mouvement et de construction du volume sonore étaient resolus par Stravinsky simultanément ... La méthode dialectique instrumentale est rendue à la musique avec une sève nouvelle, où la force et la logique font penser a Bach.[28]

[Conquering space, in this dimension it affirms linear construction ... Previously, the two problems of movement and the construction of sonorous volume were resolved by Stravinsky simultaneously ... The dialectical instrumental method is restored to music with a new vigour, whose force and logic remind one of Bach.]

Lourié concluded his article with some words of Pascal:

> Qu'on ne dise pas que je n'ai rien dit de nouveau: la disposition des matières est nouvelle ... Et comme si les mêmes pensées ne formaient pas un autre corps de discours par une disposition différente, aussi bien que les mêmes mots forment d'autres pensées par leur différentes disposition.[29]

[Let it not be said that I have said nothing new: the arrangement of materials is new ... And just as the same thoughts would form another body of

---

27   Picasso and Stravinsky first met through Eugenia Errazuriz, in Rome in 1917, where the Ballets Russes were performing *Fireworks*, *The Firebird* and *Petrushka*. Both Stravinsky and Picasso had great respect for the past, wishing to revive its vitality with fresh vision, and both artists were exploring the dimensional aspects of art. Picasso was also a gifted sculptor and many of his paintings reveal his thinking in three dimensions.
28   Lourié, Arthur. 1925, 104.
29   Ibid.

discourse by a different arrangement, the same words as well, would form other thoughts by their different arrangement.]

In 1924 Picasso wished to construct a *représentation plastique* to accompany Stravinsky's *Octet* for a 'kind of Music Hall spectacle', but Stravinsky withheld permission from the use of his music, reasoning that 'already as a symphonic piece the work is presented to the auditor in a plastic form'.[30]

3   Oedipus Rex (1926)

Composed as a 20th-anniversary present for the Ballets Russes, *Oedipus Rex* continued Stravinsky's focus on the animation of musical lines and surfaces and the process of 'making' a musical object. The work's temporal form was inspired by the objective lines of movement in Sophocles' play: in a musical analogy, the 'fatal development' and 'geometry of tragedy' resulting from the 'inevitable intersecting of lines', could be represented by musical lines of contrasting energy and temporal depth. Clearly differentiated qualities of time and movement could build an objective portrait of the individual 'as a victim of circumstances' and show Oedipus' growing self-discovery in the face of inexorable forces pursuing Truth.[31]

Stravinsky was drawn to Aristotle's ideas on the nature of tragedy, which were based on the importance of objective action and plot rather than any psychological element:

> ... the end aimed at is the representation not of qualities of character but of some action: and while character makes most men what they are, it is their actions and experiences that make them happy or the opposite ... The plot then is the first principle and as it were the soul of tragedy: character comes second.[32]

The action, Aristotle stated, was to be represented by a pattern, coherently arranged by the artist:

---

30   Stravinsky, Vera & Craft, Robert. 1979, 182–3.

31   Stravinsky, Igor & Craft, Robert. 1981, 24.

32   Aristotle. 1932, 25–27. Robert Craft wrote of Stravinsky: 'He used logic formally and relied on it to explain things that have long since gone over to psychology. The latter simply did not exist for him; no other contemporary creator has been so entirely uninfected by "psychological modes" '. Craft, Robert. 1957, 8.

Life presents to the artist the phenomena of sense which the artist 'represents' in his own medium giving coherence, designing a pattern. Selection and design are necessary for any work of 'representation'.[33] ... Moreover, in everything that is beautiful, whether it be a living creature or any organism composed of parts, these parts must not only be orderly arranged but must also have a certain magnitude of their own.[34] ... the poet must be a 'maker' ... since he is a poet in virtue of his 'representation' and what he represents is action.[35]

The action of *Oedipus Rex* was embodied purely in the movement of its musical lines and surfaces. No one 'acts', and the narrator is the only performer to move, showing his detachment from the other stage figures who address themselves directly to the audience. Stravinsky's ideas for lighting and masks, even puppets, ensured a static representation that focused as much as possible on the 'fatal development' of the play: he wanted to portray, not the fate of the person, but the 'person of the fate and the delineation of it which can be achieved uniquely in music ... Cross-roads are not personal but geometrical'.[36] In line with this aesthetic, Theodore Stravinsky's stage design for the work had 'the advantage of having no depth ... everything takes place on one level'.[37]

The intersecting lines of Stravinsky's musical object were again realised with a mix of Eastern and Western styles: Oedipus' subjects, through whom the gods are working, have broad surface movements in Western style with straightforward diatonic content that simply varies in textural complexity, while Oedipus himself has extensive patterning in Russian liturgical style and greater depths of time quality (Ex.41):

EX. 41   Oedipus' first entry in dméstvenny style

33   Aristotle. 1932, 27.
34   Op. cit., 31.
35   Op. cit., 37.
36   Stravinsky, Igor. 1982, 24.
37   Foreword: Boosey & Hawkes 1949 Edition, iv.

These two streams of movement are distinguished not only by rhythmic manners, style and pacing, but also by changing forms of the minor 3rd that first appears as an ostinato (fig. 2) and increases in complexity in Act 2. It generates a variety of both melodic and harmonic forms that regulate forward movement and depth of time quality. An ostinato figure on a seminal minor 3rd, B♭ – D♭ appears early in Act I (fig. 2): subsequently, intervals of a 3rd are combined in increasingly convoluted melodic figures derived from their vertical grouping as chords of the 7th and 9th, patterning time with greater density and unifying the work.[38]

Stravinsky pointed to the effect of the harmonic dominant that is so often in the minor, negating the pull of the dominant chord in the major to resolve on the tonic: this chord leaves the harmonic movement open-ended and inconclusive.[39]

In shaping the form of *Oedipus Rex*, Stravinsky's animation of lines and surfaces underwent a new form of discipline. Arthur Lourié observed that, in contrast to *Mavra*, the rhythmic manners of *Oedipus Rex* are completely subordinate to those of the text, and that each movement has proportioned metres:

> Le mètre impose une certaine forme au mouvement; il le transpose d'une forme dans une autre, plus rapide ou plus lente, dans un rapport mathématique determiné. L'unité monometrique du mouvement persiste toujours à travers tous les changements.[40]

> [The metre imposes a certain form on the movement: it transforms it from one form to another, faster or slower, in a determined mathematical relationship. The monometrical unity of the movement continues through all the changes.]

Lourié also remarked upon Stravinsky's new harmonic approach to variable density:

> Jusqu'au *Oedipus Rex* ... le compositeur s'attache au développement des lignes musicales, à leur solidité et à leur densité, leurs rapports constructifs. Dans *L'Oedipus Rex* ... le centre de gravité se déplace et c'est l'harmonie qui domine ... La signification dialectique des harmonies d'*Oedipe* dépend de la force et de la vitalité de l'énergie polyphonique qu'elle recèle, car la polyphonie n'est ici que la projection de cette harmonie ... la

---

38   Chords of the 7th contain three intervals of a 3rd.
39   Stravinsky, Igor & Craft, Robert. 1982, 28–9.
40   Lourié, Arthur. 1929. Vol. 10, 246.

puissance dialectique de cette technique consiste dans la façon dont elle se réalise en même temps en plans et en volumes, en lignes et en couleurs (couleurs harmoniques et non de timbres).[41]

[Until Oedipus Rex ... the composer pays particular attention to the development of musical lines, to their solidity and their density, to their constructive relations. In Oedipus Rex ... the centre of gravity shifts and it is the harmony that dominates ... The dialectical significance of Oedipus' harmonies depends on the force and vitality of the polyphonic energy that it contains, for here its polyphony is simply the projection of this harmony ... the dialectical power of this technique is found in the way in which it is realised simultaneously in surfaces, volumes, lines and colours (harmonic colours, not timbral colours).]

With regard to the text, Stravinsky was inspired by St Francis' hieratic use of the Provençal language and finally determined on setting the text to Ciceronian Latin. He wished to leave the play, as a play, behind, and to distil the dramatic essence in a purely musical dramatisation: in composing an autonomous musical object he did not want an action drama, but a 'still life'. He warned his librettist, Jean Cocteau, that he needed a conventional libretto with arias and recitatives. After many revisions, what was left of Cocteau's libretto was 'less the shape of it than the gesticulation of the phrasing'.[42]

Stravinsky rejoiced in the objectivity of Latin as a language of 'convention' for he no longer felt dominated by the phrase or the literal meaning of the words: the text had become purely phonetic material. He recalled that this had for centuries been the Church's attitude towards music and 'had prevented it from falling into sentimentalism, and consequently into individualism'.[43] Pierre Souvtchinsky described the objective setting of a text as originating in the old Russian chant. Formerly, the text had no longer spoken to the imagination but had become an intonation contributing to the musical flow: the technique had been

> ... une sorte de glossalalie où l'élément sonore et musical prévalait sur le sens logique des mots et les reduisait en series de syllabes qu'on rajoutait ou répétait selon les circonstances en obéissant aux exigences musicales.[44]

---

41   Op. cit., 244–245.
42   Stravinsky, Igor & Craft, Robert. 1982, 21–23.
43   Stravinsky, Igor. 1975, 128.
44   Souvtchinsky, Pierre. 1949. In Brelet, Gisèle. 1949, 542.

[... a sort of glossolalia in which the element of musical sonority prevailed over the logical sense of the words and reduced them to a series
of syllables that were added to or repeated according to circumstances in
obeying the musical requirements.]

It was in the context of *Oedipus Rex* that Stravinsky affirmed that he had been
concerned with questions of musical manners all his life, and that he had
worked and thought in exactly the same way in Russia: for him, 'the musical
manners and the thing said are the same thing'. He observed that the principal
source of dramatic tension comes from the rhythms used in each main line of
action, reflecting Sophocles' particular use of metre, and that they are 'more
static and regular than in any other composition of his to date'.[45] Stravinsky
imitates Sophocles' varying metres to distinguish the protagonists: Créon
sings in dactyls in 4/4 time, like the chorus, for example, because 'he too is
on the side of the gods'.[46] Both the rhythmic manners, the inexorable interaction of its lines, and Sophocles' dramatic use of static rhythms are 'frozen' into
Stravinsky's setting of this myth.

The temporal form of *Oedipus Rex* follows the pacing of Sophocles' play: the
action moves at a steady pace in Act 1, but fluctuates widely in depth and pace
in Act 2 between Oedipus' stormy encounter with Jocasta, the revelations of
the Messenger and Shepherd, and the three monumental announcements of
Jocasta's death that puncture the choral commentary. The autonomous time
world of *Oedipus Rex* is sealed by an ostinato figure on the minor 3rd with
which the work began.

Stravinsky became aware of the 'manner' question as he composed Oedipus'
first aria, and feared that he may have established it too exaggeratedly and
too conventionally: Oedipus' line is set apart by its stiff, highly ornate dméstvenny patterning, a stylistic reference that establishes the King's authority as
a 'sacred' figure but also hints at the 'tail-feathers of his pride'.[47] His tenor line
makes a striking contrast with the simple homogenous style of the opening
chorus, having important changes of dynamics, and melismata that must be
given strict and full rhythmic value.[48] The contrast of his Baroque-style dotted

---

45   He sets the simple choriambics, the anapaests (two short syllables) and dactyls (one long,
       two short syllables) rather than the glyconics and dochmii. Ibid.
46   Stravinsky, Igor & Craft, Robert. 1982, 29. Créon sings in 4/4 time but the metre of the
       chorus varies.
47   Boris Asaf'yev observes that the melody of Oedipus' monologue resembles the ornamen-
       tal 'jubilation' of ancient ritual. Asaf'yev, B. 1929, Postscript. Stravinsky had previously
       evoked dméstvenny chant in *Chant Dissident* (1919).
48   Stravinsky, Igor & Craft, Robert. 1982, 29.

arpeggio accompaniment brings a disorientation of time and place and deepens the time quality. Stravinsky finds a compassionate analogy for Sophocles' renowned quality of dramatic irony: he associates Oedipus with another victim of Fate, Desdemona at prayer, through the Verdian device of four unaccompanied cellos (fig. 22 – 1).[49]

The momentum of Oedipus' line begins to be held back in his second aria (fig. 45): convoluted melodic figures around the intervals of a 3rd and a 7th portray his disturbed state of mind. Differently accented 'off-beat games' in the trombones disturb the time quality (fig. 50) and although the defiant scales that follow bring moments of forward momentum, the dméstvenny style returns, and the aria lengthens over an E♭ pedal point and comes to a standstill.

Oedipus' third aria (fig. 83) disperses the energy generated by Tirésias' recent revelations. The close patterning of a related tempo reduces the momentum further, as do more widely-spaced 3rds and 7ths and declamatory scales. Forward musical movement is reduced to a passage of pitchless *clamando*, and Oedipus' piteously reiterated minor 3rds finally bring his line of movement to a halt.

Between Oedipus' three arias the Spirit of Truth strides out with increasing confidence. Créon's line is in C major, in 4/4 time with dactyls and simple binary rhythmic divisions, and with diatonic arpeggios and scales reinforced by strong and regular orchestral rhythms. The momentum of the orchestral accompaniment is at first restrained (fig. 34), but the 'wildly divergent' and inappropriate *Folies Bergères* tune (fig. 40) and the strong rhythms and repeated figures from the chord of the 7th that accompany Créon's final semibreves begin to reflect the increasing urgency and confusion.

Tirésias continues this line of movement, but his vocal line in 2/2 time is not so wide-ranging in pitch and has more *gravitas* than that of Créon as the situation begins to become increasingly serious. It includes wide-ranging chains of melodic 3rds and figures from the chord of the 7th, their widely-spaced twists and turns portraying his dilemma as Oedipus' envoy to the Oracle. The orchestral accompaniment develops from a jerky figure (fig. 75) into the emphatic marking of the crotchet pulse with aspirated triplet quavers.

In Act 2, the pacing of these two opposing lines of movement diversifies exponentially as the dénouement approaches: not only do the rock-like rhythms of Oedipus' 'line' increase after Jocasta's opening aria, but the patterning of the interval of a 3rd also intensifies. In Act 1, major and minor 3rds had

---

49   Philip Gossett has remarked how Jocasta's Cabaletta mirrors the Cabaletta of Verdi's
        Otello (trio in Act III): Otello and Oedipus are both caught in a web. In Pasler, Jann. 1986,
        Introduction xii, n.4.

Joc

[98] Nonn' e‑ru‑be‑ski‑te al‑ter ca‑ti‑on‑i‑bus, re‑ges?____ Co‑ram o‑mni‑bus cla

ma‑re, co‑ram o‑mni‑bus do‑mes‑ti‑kos cla mo‑res, cla‑mar' in ae‑gra ur‑be, re‑ges,

[99]

EX. 42   Convoluted figures composed of intervals of a 3rd

eased the rhythmic flow away from the attractions and resolutions of classical tonality, as had the dominant minor. In Act 2, intervals of a 3rd now frequently accumulate into figures derived from chords of the 7th and 9th to impede the rhythmic flow and intensify the deep time quality (Ex. 42).

At the start of Act 2 momentum is severely restrained: Jocasta's 3rds spread across the interval of a 9th and even a 10th, and the slow duple pulse of her Da Capo aria (fig. 96 + 1) is patterned with emphatic semitone steps. Sweeping triplets oppose the granite-like movement of her arpeggios (fig. 100), while a threatening four-note rhythmic motif echoes her first marked enunciation of 'oracula' (fig. 103) and her revelation that Laius was killed 'in trivio' (fig. 109 + 1). All momentum is 'paused' as the chorus reflect on this information and Oedipus' horrified suspicions are answered by an increasingly menacing figure for timpani (fig. 119).

The intensely rhythmic duet for Jocasta and Oedipus in the here-and-now (from fig. 121) resumes this tightly chromatic movement and triple division of the pulse, but widens out to a tenser dialogue in 4/4 (fig. 127) and then stretches present time with the introduction of a triplet crotchet figure (fig. 129 + 1). In contrast, the Spirit of Truth proceeds calmly and inexorably. The crucial revelations are distanced by a mix of styles: the Messenger announcing Polybus' death is supported by the male chorus that is unaccompanied for the first time, and his solemn sequential scales are accompanied by a light classical Alberti-bass for solo horn, part of Stravinsky's *Merzbild* of 'whatever came to hand' (fig. 135 − 1). Any further sense of momentum or distraction from the Messenger's single-minded purpose is dispelled by the inexorable opposition of metre and accents between the voice and the orchestra that negate clock-time (fig. 139, Ex. 43):

EX. 43   Opposition of metre and accents

This opposition is continued by the chorus and the orchestra (fig. 144).[50]

The Messenger's lapidary rhythms contrast with the Shepherd's lyrical testimony (fig. 147) in which the pitch is lowered and the tense time quality is
deceptively relaxed to a pastoral swing in 6/8 time, enhanced by the rustic timbres of two solo bassoons.

Oedipus' previously florid style is now somewhat simpler, diatonic and
accompanied by Handelian arpeggio figures (fig. 155), while the bass line
restrains momentum with the alternation of a minor 3rd or arpeggios. A long
section based on D, including a D minor triad (fig. 159) and a pedal point
(fig. 162), restrains all forward momentum as the details of the story confirm
the prophecy. At the moment of Oedipus' complete enlightenment, the pedal
point D becomes the third of the chord of B minor; the bi-tonal ambiguity of
a D minor chord in the strings against a suspended second inversion chord of
B minor for woodwind and timpani (fig. 167) not only greatly diminishes the
sense of clock-time but also creates a floating musical space.

It is a prominent theme in Greek tragedy that the gods are inscrutable and
that it is impossible for fragile and fallible humans to anticipate the future
with accuracy. The one-octave scales that began the work now return and
sweep majestically across five octaves, emphasising the inevitability of the
crushing victory of the forces 'who watch us from the other side of death'.[51]
The Messenger's three 'circular' 8-bar announcements of Jocasta's death are
juxtaposed to the circular motion of rapid 1-bar octave scales on G. Its hieratic
quality punctures the mood of the triple-based swing of the following 'mortu-
ary tarentella', Mulier in vestibulo (fig. 173), and the change to 2/4 metre and
the return to Baroque-style accompaniment. With the return of the stately 6/8

---

50   Stravinsky, Igor & Craft, Robert. 1982, 27.
51   Prologue to *Oedipus Rex*.

movement with which the work opened, the 'geometry of tragedy' is complete and the temporal form sealed; its rhythmic energy is gradually dispersed into a bare G – B♭ ostinato, the interval of a minor 3rd from which the work's harmonic vitality has sprung.

4   Apollo (1928)

In contrast to the Delphic Oracle's horrific prophecies, the myth of Apollo and the Muses on Mount Parnassus above offered refinement and beauty. The subject suggested a more abstract web of relationships: not a plot, with the large-scale linear interactions of *Oedipus Rex*, but a more closely patterned musical 'object' whose relationships would be generated by a single intervallic motif and rhythmic idea.[52] This highly-nuanced work is constructed with the simplest of materials: an arpeggio in its first inversion, a diatonic vocabulary, and a single poetic foot – the iamb – in many rhythmic forms. The ballet is a presentation of Apollonian order, as realised in the patterning of ontological time by the living gestures of mime and dance.

The god Apollo has a particular link with the lute, and his patronage of music was characterised by a harmony and order that united all his divine powers, including his important role in healing, purification and prophecy.[53] Apollo was chiefly a benevolent presence for good, but on occasion he could defend his own interests aggressively, so that the Greeks also described him as 'he who shoots from afar', his essential nature being understood as objective and distant. Apollo is already a master beyond instruction so that the three Muses that Stravinsky selected, Calliope, Polyhymnie and Terpsichore, simply show him their arts for his approval.[54]

Stravinsky had hoped that, in keeping with his first ideas, Apollo would be danced in short white ballet skirts in a severely theatrical landscape devoid of all fantastic embellishment.[55] In the end, he thought the scenery for the ballet looked somewhat *Rousseau-esque*, but Georges Balanchine did arrange the dances in accordance with the Classical school, which was exactly what Stravinsky had wished. At the time, it was the first attempt to revive academic

52   Stravinsky, Igor & Craft, Robert. 1982, 32–33.
53   The lute is the instrument traditionally carried by Apollo in the ballet.
54   Ibid, 34.
55   Stravinsky, Igor. 1975, 144. The original decors of the ballet also paid tribute to the French 17th century by incorporating the emblem of le Roi Soleil: a chariot, three horses and a sun disc.

dancing in a work actually composed for the purpose.[56] In this work, there is no mixing of Russian and Western styles. Wishing to clear away 'many-coloured effects and all superfluities', and to recover a 'melodic principle' based on 'sustained psalmody' that was free of folklore, Stravinsky made his 'largest single step towards a long-line polyphonic style'.

In *Mavra,* Stravinsky had found a musical analogy for Pushkin's poetic techniques and their creation of 'zephyr-like' movement. To pace the delicately nuanced ontological time qualities of *Apollo,* Stravinsky based the work on the iambic foot (short-long) and its reverse form, according to the principles of Greek versification. The principle metre of Greek drama was the iambic trimeter, or Alexandrine, consisting of six iambs: additionally, the first, third or fifth iamb in the line could be replaced by the tribach (three short syllables), the spondee (two long syllables), or the dactyl (one long and two short syllables). The immense variety of rhythmic movements in *Apollo* is created from this single source: the iambic foot and its reverse form in various rhythmic durations, together with the alternative tribach, spondee and dactyl rhythms.[57] The background structure of the Alexandrine line does become prominent in places (as in Calliope's Variation) but Stravinsky did not know whether the idea was pre-compositional or not. In its use of Alexandrines, the work is also a tribute to the French 17th century in general and in particular to a couplet by the poet Boileau that Stravinsky placed at the head of Calliope's Variation.[58]

Like the *Octet,* the musical architecture of *Apollo* is clarified by contrasts of instrumental volumes, which Stravinsky thought were all too rarely recognised as a primary musical element.[59] But *Apollo's* volumes are created with the more homogeneous timbres of the string orchestra, and finely-nuanced as they range from solo instruments to thickly scored double-stopping for all parts. The work is scored for six string parts instead of the more usual five, comprising first and second violins and violas, with cellos divided into two parts, and double basses. The division of the cellos changes the usual balance of a string ensemble, allowing greater variety in the weight of the bass line and

---

56   Op. cit., 143.
57   Stravinsky, Igor and Craft, Robert. 1982, 33.
58   Que toujours dans vos vers, le sens coupant les mots, Suspende l'hemistiche, en marque le repos. (*L'art Poétique.* I, 105f.)

      [That always in your verses, the meaning, cutting across the words, stops at the half line, and marks a resting point.].

59   Stravinsky, Igor & Craft, Robert. 1982, 34. Stravinsky remarked that the real joke in the *Pulcinella* duet is that the trombone has a very loud voice and the string bass has almost no voice at all.

in the range of possible textures.[60] Stravinsky emphasised the importance of strict rhythmic articulation in this music and cited many specific bars where the rhythms should be double-dotted and where strict attention should be paid to the dynamics.[61] He would also have liked to have marked every note as to whether it should be played on or off the string, and to have fixed certain bowings.

This musical object is shaped in the outer movements by strong rhythmic variants that show the power and mastery of Apollo, while the three central dances of the Muses and the Pas de Deux have fewer variants and are more delicately scored, each having its own particular character and time world.

Stravinsky specified that the introduction to the birth of Apollo should be double-dotted, evoking the formality of the 17th century overture that set the scene for a stately court entertainment in honour of a divine figure. Apollo's character is established by the juxtaposition of two strong forms of the iamb (fig. 4), a distant melody, piano, answered by a repeating demisemiquaver iamb, pianissimo, for thickly scored violas and cellos (Ex. 44).

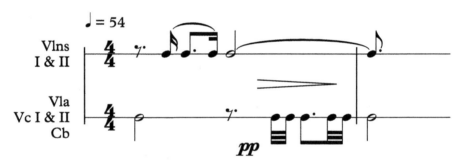

EX. 44   Strong forms of the iambic foot preceding the birth of Apollo

Apollo is born quickly with the juxtaposition of two rhythmically contrasted circular surfaces (fig. 6), and quickly reaches maturity with strong, expansive forms of the reverse iamb in wide-ranging arpeggios and a more slowly paced cantabile melody against the reversed iamb and light crotchet arpeggios (fig. 9). Momentum wanes and the time quality deepens as three differently-paced layers of movement are combined (fig. 13 – 1) and elongated, cross-accented

---

60   At a rehearsal in Berlin conducted by Otto Klemperer, it became clear that the number of instruments to each part needed to be in a certain proportion to ensure the clarity and plasticity of the musical line. Eventually it was decided that the ratio of eight first and eight second violins, six violas, four first and four second cellos, and four double basses produced the desired sharp and precise effect.

61   Stravinsky, Igor & Craft, Robert. 1982, 35.

EX. 45   Forms of the reverse iamb: Pas d'Action

iambs are set against two forms of arpeggio. After the return of the opening section Apollo's regal nature is re-established by rich double-stopping, thickly scored cello parts, and the iambic rhythm in grandly homogeneous movement.

Apollo's 'first essay in verse', as he learns to play the lute, patterns 'gestural' time: double-dotted reversed iambs, phrased ambiguously, also suggest the iambic foot. His lightly-scored Variation is slowed in the final bars by descending iambs in the bass lines that are tied across the bar-line.

In Pas d'Action, in which Apollo meets the three Muses, the reverse iamb appears in changing forms, one of which is a metrical change (Ex. 45).

Introduced by spondees, the opening melody elongates the reversed iambic foot in a slow waltz, accompanied by both the spondee and tribach. Momentum increases with the change to duple time (fig. 28) and a different accentuation of the foot. The tribach forms two graceful passages (figs. 30 – 4 and 31 + 3), the second of which accompanies the (tutti) cellos with the opening theme in 2/4 time *au dehors* (fig. 31 + 3). At a final change to 4/4 metre (Ex. 46), the iambic figure undergoes augmentation and diminution in a canon for three real parts over arpeggiated quavers (fig. 35, one of Stravinsky's favourite passages):

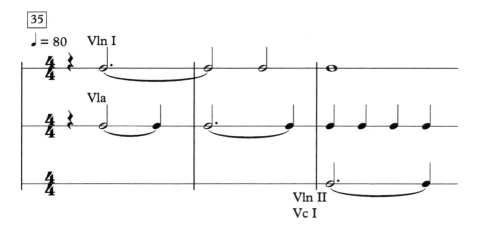

EX. 46   3-part canon: Pas d'Action

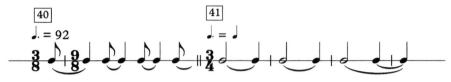

EX. 47   Metrically different forms of iambic foot: Calliope's Variation

The time quality deepens towards extended time qualities as Apollo's melody returns.

Calliope, called 'she of the beautiful voice' by the Greeks, was assigned to the art of heroic song, which was heard only at night as she processed to her father on Mount Olympus. In *Apollo*, she personifies poetry and its rhythmic techniques, inspired by a couplet from Boileau's *L'Art Poétique* in which he advocated the division of the meaning of the words at the midpoint of the line.[62] This variation presents several poetic techniques: the twelve 'syllables' of the Alexandrine are heard in groups of both 6 and 12, both the iambic foot and its reverse form are patterned, sometimes the 'mid-line' break is observed, and the syllables are frequently set with a change of metre. The first part introduces the new triple division of the pulse at a slightly faster speed, but the middle section (fig. 41) transforms the rhythm into 3/4 metre and extends the reverse form into a graceful melody for a solo cello accompanied by tribachs, revealing Calliope's beautiful voice in a 'little homage to Saint-Saëns' (Ex. 47).

This passage was one of Stravinsky's first musical ideas for the work, inspired by a Russian Alexandrine, a couplet from Pushkin. The coda (fig. 43) reverts to the triple division of the pulse.

Polyhymnie, 'she of many hymns', was the Muse assigned to the art of storytelling: here, she holds a finger to her lips and represents mime. The strong reverse iamb which opens the movement is answered by chattering semiquaver movement and accompanied by reverse iambs. Her Variation combines both iambic forms in eloquent narrative gestures (fig. 48) and ends humorously with a single f-p iambic foot. The movement has a single time quality and Polyhymnie's dynamic outward-going personality is framed by a light arpeggiated accompaniment throughout. Stravinsky drew a Russian cross at the end of his sketches for this movement.

---

62   Boileau's *L'Art Poétique* (1674) is composed of four poems. The first deals with inspiration, reason and the cultivation of form. Lines 103–12 of the first poem advocate respect for the reader's ear, having care to the rhythm, the break at the half line and the avoidance of hiatus and cacophony.

Terpsichore combines the rhythms of poetry and the eloquence of gesture and reveals dancing to the world. 'She who enjoys dancing' was also the Muse assigned to the art of the lyre. Returning to the pulse of Calliope's Variation, there is a single temporal quality to this presentation too: its graceful long-line duet for violins is composed of iambs in its reversed form ambiguously phrased in iambic rhythms, and is lightly accompanied (fig. 53). Presently, the iamb and the reverse iamb are tied 'back to back' and emphasised by consecutive down bows in the first violins against an expressive iamb for second violins (fig. 54). The repetitive swaying movements leading to the four brief pauses allow a series of expressive gestures.

Apollo's second Variation, Stravinsky's favourite, presents a strong contrast to those of the Muses. The tempo of Apollo's birth ($\quarternote$ = 54) and the formal style of the 17th century are recalled by two introductory spondees and a powerful form of the reversed iamb in a double-dotted quaver and (demi)semiquaver motif elaborated with trills (fig. 58, Ex. 48).

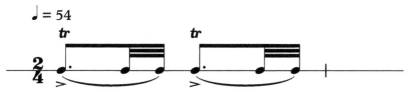

EX. 48   Apollo's powerful character: Apollo's 2nd Variation

There is greater variation in this movement, both in the pacing of the foot as more freely elongated forms (figs. 59 + 6, 61 + 4) and in its greater range of textures, from the thickly scored commanding opening to the delicate and transparent use of harmonics and pizzicato (fig. 60).

With the Pas de Deux for Apollo and Terpsichore, the work returns to the art of dancing: this lushly scored movement creates a deeper, more intimate time quality than the other Variations. The descending reversed iambs of Apollo's 2nd Variation (fig. 58 + 2), now softened and muted (fig. 64 + 2), are answered by a graceful legato melody based on the reversed iambic foot (fig. 65 + 2). A highly lyrical form of the iamb is accompanied by arpeggios, pizzicato (fig. 67), and tribach rhythms, lightly decorated with acciaccaturas (fig. 68). The division of the cellos allows for a very light and delicate bass line.

The Coda for Apollo and the three Muses has the reversed iamb at its fastest tempo ($\dottedquarternote$ = 112) and plays with binary and triple division of the pulse. After the grand opening in 2/4 metre, the reversed form is heard in a new playful 6/8 metre (fig. 73). The iamb appears in several new forms: a tied triplet version in 2/4 (from fig. 78 – 2), an elongation of the reversed form in 6/8 (fig. 79 + 1), and a jazzy passage in which tied iambs are heard alternately in 3/4 and 6/8 against an accented beat in 3/4 time (figs. 83–86). A contrastingly lyrical passage is created from an extended legato reverse form (fig. 89) before momentum slows (fig. 94) to approach the final iambic cadence.

In the Apotheosis at the original tempo ($\bullet$ = 54), Apollo leads the Muses towards Mount Parnassus with Terpsichore at their head. The iamb, *forte* in the upper strings, is answered very softly by three-part chords in the cellos and basses, creating great distance and a remote time quality.[63] The theme that established Apollo's character (see ex. 48) returns over a pedal note, D, with unmeasured tremolos as Apollo and the Muses process into the distance (fig. 99 – 1). Momentum wanes and a greater depth of time is created by the juxtaposition of three circular motifs of differing lengths (fig. 101 – 1): the 1st violins and 1st cellos elongate the long syllable progressively from 5 beats to 8, the 2nd violins and violas slow their 4-crotchet beat cycles to minims and semibreves, and the 2nd cellos and basses lengthen their cycles from crotchets to semibreves.

Stravinsky spoke of *Apollo* as the start of something new in his work with respect to form.[64] *Apollo* achieves the closer relationships necessary to create 'ontological splendour': the spiritual quality and unity of *Apollo* derives from its perfect balance between similarity and variety, that 'harmony of varieties' of which Stravinsky was to speak in his lectures on the poetics of music some ten years or so later. Constructed without his former contrasts of pitch collection and eclectic mix of styles, the temporal form of *Apollo* has a new flexibility, shaped by some two dozen different notations of the iamb and its reverse form, both on and between the pulse.

The patterning of ontological time by a wide range of iambic patterns and their 'family members' – from brief (hemidemi)semiquavers to the extended five-beat effect at figure 13 in the opening movement – perfectly illustrates the balance between variety and similarity necessary to achieve unity. Thoughts on this issue followed Stravinsky's discourse on different types of time in music in his *Poetics of Music*. He observed that music based on ontological time is generally dominated by the principle of similarity, while psychological time is based on contrast. Stravinsky noted that contrast is everywhere and has an immediate effect: it is the element of variety that 'divides attention'.

---

63   Stravinsky returned to this means of creating remote time and distance (as in Charles
      Ives' *The Unanswered Question* (1908)), for the Dies Irae of *Requiem Canticles* (1965–6).
64   'An interview with Igor Stravinsky', 1957, NBC.

Similarity is hidden and has to be sought out, but strives for unity. He set all the problems of art, knowledge and Being, in the context of the One and the Many, recalling the philosophical debate between Parmenides and Heraclitus on the nature of the cosmos. Like Stravinsky, both of these pre-Socratic philosophers sought to understand the relationship of what they felt to be an underlying unity to the familiar experience of change and movement in time.[65] Parmenides believed the underlying reality to be single, timeless and unchanging and that all appearances, all changing forms and motion, are illusory appearances of this single, eternal reality. His belief that true being and knowledge is discovered by the intellect based on the senses, and that it is important for proof to be reasoned, influenced both Plato's theory of forms, and the philosophy of Aristotle. Heraclitus viewed reality as flux and in a constant dynamic process of becoming: he believed the world to be a coherent system subject to perpetual change and that objects change their nature with the flow of time. Moreover, he believed that all things come into being by the conflict of opposites and that it is the tension of opposites that constitutes the unity and harmony of the One. Stravinsky thought that although common sense and supreme wisdom affirm both positions, the One preceded the Many.[66] He remarked: 'How much more natural and more salutary it is to strive towards a single, limited reality than towards endless division!'[67] For Stravinsky, variety, though perfectly legitimate, was only valid as a means of seeking similarity.[68]

Lack of variety may of course be monotonous, but conversely, the quality of similarity may gain in richness, strength and solidity as the 'seductions' of variety are avoided. Stravinsky related his search for this richness to the words of the Areopagite, who maintained that the greater the dignity of the angels in the celestial hierarchy, the fewer words they use: the most elevated of all pronounces only a single syllable.[69]

In his article, 'A propos de L'Apollon de Stravinsky' (1927), Arthur Lourié commented on Stravinsky's newly-refined methods of constructing a unified and spiritual form:

---

65   It is thought that Parmenides (born in 515 BCE), the founder of the Eleatic School of philosophy, and Heraclitus, born in Italy (535 BCE), responded to one another.
66   Stravinsky, Igor. 1947, 32.
67   Op. cit., 141.
68   Op. cit., 32. Chapter 11 compares Stravinsky's lecture notes with the text published as *Poetics of Music*.
69   Stravinsky, Igor. 1947, 141. The Desert Father, Dionysus the Pseudo-Areopagite, was writing c.500 A.D. probably in Syria.

Surmounting the individual element – the animal principle – Stravinsky's music tends, more and more, toward the spiritual. By this same token, it aims at the unity of the moral and aesthetic principle, a unity long since lost.[70]

Apollo shines with the beauty of Maritain's *matière éloignée*; Diaghilev wrote to Serge Lifar that 'somehow the music [is] not of this world, but from somewhere above'.[71]

5   Lourié's Understanding of Stravinsky

Arthur Lourié had immeasurable influence on Stravinsky during the 1920s, in promoting the philosophical ideas of Jacques Maritain. His article 'The Music of Stravinsky', published in Paris in 1926 in the Russian journal *Versty*, is of interest historically since it reveals his early understanding of Stravinsky's peculiarly Russian spirituality, his patterning of ontological time, and his role in the restoration of music as a temporal art.[72]

In the first section of his article, Lourié discerns that the 'enthusiasm for emotional experience is changing into an enthusiasm for human consciousness', and that a new style is emerging.[73] He sees the striving towards self-expression as always egocentric, as fatally bound to time in the 'calendar' sense, and as always leading to self-assertion. In contrast to this, there is geometrical thinking (which is purely musical), the true expression of which reveals itself as plastic realism and recognises the classical or the religious. This way is theocentric and leads to the affirmation of stability and unity. It lies in the escape from 'calendar' time into the concept of 'musical time'. Lourié perceives that

---

70   Lourié, Arthur. 1927, 118 Lourié promoted the idea of Schoenberg and Stravinsky as thesis and antithesis in his article 'Neo-Gothic and Neo-Classic', *Modern Music*, Mar/Apr 1928. Other philosophical writings by Lourié on music include: 'An Enquiry into Melody', *Modern Music*, 1929, vol.3; 'A Crisis in Form', *Modern Music*, 1931, vol.3; 'The Russian School', *The Musical Quarterly*, XVIII, 1932, 519; 'The Dehumanisation of Music', *Ramparts*, NY Jan 1965, 39; 'Profanation et Sanctification du Temps, Essays et Memoirs', Paris, 1966.

71   White, Eric W. 1979, 342.

72   Lourié, Arthur. 1926. Translated from the Russian by Natalia Dissanayake.

73   Raissa Maritain later reminisced: 'The artistic conscience was truly purifying itself, tending towards that "discovery of the spiritual in the sensible", which not only defines poetry but defines the soul of every art, painting as well as music and the theatre.' Maritain, Raissa. Oct. 1943, 33.

'Stravinsky ... recreates the lost balance – formal and spiritual – and leads one directly into the musical essence of the world'.

Lourié describes the dialectics of Stravinsky's recent work as 'so strong ... after removing all superficialities ... he returns us to the long-lost joys of an art founded on the skill of craftmanship'. Maritain's concept of the artist as *homo faber* colours Lourié's language as he contrasts the 'proportional distribution of energy' in each of Stravinsky's works with that of the Romantics, and describes his music as 'realistic and utilitarian'.

In the second section, Lourié points to the extremely refined methods of timbral design in the second and third acts of *Le Rossignol* (completed 1914), and to the *dimensional principles* of *Le Sacre du Printemps*.[74]

In the third section, Lourié sees *Petrushka* as marrying elements of the folk way of life with those of the urban petit bourgeoisie to create a musical portrait of the 1830s. Like Asaf'yev, he points to Stravinsky's 'penchant for refining a baser form of music' in *Petrushka,* and also to Stravinsky's dramatic effect in pitting folk epic elements against the emotional experience of the individualist, Petrushka. In *Les Noces* this separation is overcome: the chorus is the hero, while the heroes are part of the chorus. *Petrushka* is a dramatic work, *Les Noces* is a religious mystery play.

In this third section, Lourié sees the basic element of *Petrushka* as timbre, which is not used to flavour and colour, but is an element of construction:

> The famous counterpoint of the Ballerina and Moor's waltz, constructed by combining patterns of different timbre in simultaneous movement, is very characteristic in this sense ... not a matter of taste but of construction ... The subsequent development of Stravinsky's mastery is going in the direction of the greatest possible objectivity ... This notorious objectivity was not invented by Stravinsky. Since Glinka's time it has always been the formal foundation of Russian musical culture ... He has restored objectivity in Russian music and given it new strength.

As for *The Spring* [*The Rite of Spring*], discussed in the fourth section:

> The very essence of the sound language is free from any submission to formal Western principles that had previously existed in Russian music ... Here, the Scythian aspect of Russia was embodied in music for the first time ... [and was] a rupture from everything that was hostile to this

---

74   My italics. The *dimensional principles* of *The Rite of Spring* are discussed in Chapter 4.

spirit not only in the West but in Russia as well ... Stravinsky straightens the hereditary line coming from Mussorgsky and destroys the pseudo-Russian traditions established by Balakirev and Rimsky-Korsakov.

Lourié considers that

> with regard to musical movement, *The Spring* is static: the enormous dynamism it contains is of a biological nature. It is the organic growth of resonating matter ... its rhythm is more noumenal than musical. 'Breathing' is intrinsic to the forms of movement in *The Spring*. If *The Spring* proceeded from the destruction of balance of form and emotion which characterises it as a heathen act, then *Les Noces* restored the lost balance: it is a mystery play of Orthodox everyday life, built on rhythms identical in spirit to icon-painting. *Les Noces* is dynamic in the musical sense but in the emotional sphere it is saturated with the tranquillity and 'quietness' of an icon ... If it were not for the balance of that inner life, with which Stravinsky endows this work with such perfection and which is not broken for an instant – then *Les Noces* would become a Khlystovian rite.[75]

In the final section, Lourié comments on the traces of 'biological' growth still to be found in *Symphonies of Wind Instruments*, and on its chant which is close to the Orthodox style. He then traces Stravinsky's development from the involuntarily-created forms of the period of *The Rite of Spring* and *Les Noces* to Stravinsky's conscious return to the Classical basis of Western Europe. Stravinsky's use of wind instruments since *Symphonies of Wind Instruments* has become a principle of construction. As for *Mavra*, Lourié considers that its 'enormous significance is beyond doubt', and that it may be 'the most remarkable of anything created by Stravinsky in recent years'. For the West, *Mavra* restores to life the pure form of opera which has been forgotten and lost: for Russia, it revives the line of development from Glinka and Tchaikovsky.

Lourié points to Stravinsky's return to pure 'instrumentalism' and to his connection with the dialectics of Bach, beginning with the finale of *Octet*. For Lourié, musical dialectics are the pure development of musical thought, i.e. something self-sufficient and in its own way unassailable, like the proof of a theorem.

---

75   The Khlysts were one of the mystic religious sects in pre-revolutionary Russia whose most notorious representative was Grigory Rasputin. They believed that Christ was born within them in their erotic ecstasies.

Lourié marks out Stravinsky's route, from the 'organic method' and Scythian spirit of *Le Sacre du Printemps*, through an interest in abstract mechanical relationships, to the closed texture and classical canon of the recent works. He sees that, after breaking the link with the Western tradition which then existed in Russia, Stravinsky returns to it and restores it on very different principles.

But by 1930, as Stravinsky composed *Symphony of Psalms*, Lourié was already distancing himself from Stravinsky's creative direction, feeling that to strive for the complete objectivity and autonomy of a work was to deprive it of its humanity. Almost foreshadowing Stravinsky's search for greater lyricism in the early 1930s, he particularly deplored the move away from melody, which he saw as music's most spiritual element. Melody, he wrote, was 'apt to reveal some intimate truth, the genuine psychological and spiritual substance of its maker. It is melody that discloses the nature of the subject, not the object'.[76]

---

76   Lourié, Arthur. 1929–30, 7/1, 3–4.

CHAPTER 10

A Journey to Hyperspace

Like Diaghilev's commission of *Pulcinella*, Stravinsky's invitation from the Boston Symphony Orchestra to compose a work for their 50th anniversary was timely: he had long wanted to compose a symphonic piece of some length. Retaining the periodic order of a symphony but not conforming to the various customary models, *Symphony of Psalms* (1930) would be a work of 'great contrapuntal development' and create an organic whole.[1] Stravinsky envisaged the work for forces on an equal footing: a SATB chorus (that should include children's voices) and an orchestral ensemble without upper strings.

Symphony of Psalms is the first of Stravinsky's large-scale spiritual works to be based on biblical texts. Arthur Lourié's recent settings of religious subjects – *Sonata Liturgica* (1928) with its Byzantine plainsong-type melodies, and *Concerto Spirituale* (1929) with its remarkable use of low registers – may have prompted him to choose a similarly explicit spiritual subject.[2] Stravinsky turned to the words of the Psalms since they had been written for singing, and because they are the most universal expression of the Church, the foundation of the church's prayers, orisons and chants. The Psalms express many strong and universal spiritual experiences from exaltation to anger, judgement and even curses; Stravinsky deeply regretted that people had lost the capacity to treat the Holy Scriptures 'other than from the point of view of ethnography, history or picturesqueness'. He felt that these 'side-issues' were a serious obstacle to understanding their 'essence and substance'. It was in the context of setting the essence of the Psalms that Stravinsky re-emphasised that music has an entity of its own. He made a strong plea for people to love music for itself and to 'listen with other ears'; only then could its intrinsic value be realised on a higher plane.[3]

Stravinsky selected the texts of *Symphony of Psalms* from Psalms 38, 39 and 150 in the Vulgate version.[4] The texts record the Psalmist's spiritual journey

---

1 Stravinsky, Igor. 1975, 161.
2 Lourié set *Sonata Liturgica* for alto voices and chamber orchestra, and *Concerto Spirituale* for piano solo, voices and orchestra, without woodwind or upper strings. Stravinsky's first sound image for *Symphony of Psalms* was of an all-male chorus and orchestre d'harmonie: woodwind, brass, percussion and double bass. Stravinsky, Igor & Craft, Robert. 1982, 46.
3 Stravinsky, Igor. 1975, 162–3.
4 *Book of Common Prayer*: Psalm 39. 13–15, Psalm 40. 1–3, and Psalm 150.

© KONINKLIJKE BRILL NV, LEIDEN, 2022 | DOI:10.1163/9789004518537_012

from repentance to salvation and from despair to praise and adoration, and they progress through the traditional attitudes of prayer: confession, supplication, thanksgiving, praise and blessing.

The sense of clock-time begins to diminish in the first movement as accumulating textures accompany prayers of confession and supplication; the time quality deepens significantly in the second movement as fugal structures symbolise God's response and the Psalmist's salvation; great depth of time and space is created in the third movement as different aspects of praise and adoration are presented. As in a symphony, each movement has its own character, but progressive growth across the work as a whole both unifies the work as a musical object and embodies a musical experience of spiritual transformation that is personal to the Psalmist but also universal.

The texts which Stravinsky eventually set in Latin suggested a variety of speeds but no shape, so that the primary question of musical order lay in the relation between tempo and meaning. A brisk pulse of ♩ = 92 in the first movement, slows to a calm tempo of ♪ = 60 in the second movement. The tempi of the third movement alternate between slow praise at ♩ = 48 and rapid movement at ♩ = 160, before coming to rest at ♩ = 72 and recalling the meditative opening. Stravinsky thought that, as a matter of 'rhythmic manners', God was not to be praised in fast, forte music, even if the text seemed to specify it: he always preferred to talk about the action of a musical sentence rather than its style.[5]

Symphony of Psalms makes a strong spiritual impact by extending the natural growth process of *The Rite of Spring* to a new level of complexity. The first movement grows from an initial 'point' to a full surface. At the opening of the second movement lines of high-relief interact in a fugal construction to create a dense musical volume. This volume surrounds the more slowly developing fugal structure representing the Psalmist and works within it to bring the movement to a point of equilibrium (fig. 17). In the third movement, sections of highly contrasted qualities of time and movement are interwoven as facets of a hyperspace to take the listener on a journey around the heavens. In its growth from a single chord to a multi-dimensional musical unity, which Stravinsky described as an 'edifice' built with 'sound material', the work embodies a spiritual progression from the here-and-now of confession and repentance to the timeless meditation of adoration and praise. Its successive qualities of ontological time unify to create an autonomous temporal form with a spiritual meaning, illustrating Maritain's proposition that the primary

---

5   Stravinsky, Igor & Craft, Robert. 1982, 44–45.

purpose of art is 'to construct and create through the spirit, objects each one of which is a condensed universe existing for itself'.[6]

1   1st Movement

Stravinsky recalled that the music of the first movement was composed in a state of religious and musical ebullience.[7] In the first part of this text: 'Hear my prayer, O Lord ... hold not thy peace at my tears', the Psalmist comes before God to reflect on his sin and confess that he has continually fallen short of his good intentions.[8] The Psalmist's plea, from Psalm 38.13–14, begins with a sharply accented 'point', the chord of E minor, and continues in a three-stage expansion of lines of low textural relief to form a wide surface movement. The initial chord punctuates the musical growth six times, emphasising the urgency of the Psalmist's petition; in later works Stravinsky uses a similarly piercing chord to signpost 'listen' at significant spiritual points, with the meaning 'He that hath ears to hear, let him hear'.[9]

Symphony of Psalms grows from the root idea of two minor 3rds joined by a major 3rd that is derived from the trumpet and harp motif in the third movement (figs. 3 + 5 − 7). The first movement begins at a thoughtful pace with twisting forms of the interval of a 3rd that betray (as with Oedipus) the Psalmist's wretched state of mind. As the surface movement increases in texture, the lack of contrast in the musical elements ensures that the surface character is maintained and that its momentum does not acquire any great depth. After the first climax (fig. 10 − 1), the musical surface suddenly lightens but quickly increases again, with the Psalmist's pleas marked by longer note values and three layers of motivic textures. The Psalmist can only entrust himself to God's kindness and mercy: 'For I dwell only as a guest with thee, and am a sojourner like all my fathers'. In the third part of the text (fig. 12 + 3), the orchestral texture has a new fullness based on both minor and major 3rds, and the chorus recall the pleading semitone from the opening petition. The textures of the surface movement are fully inflated at the text 'Look away from me ... before I depart and be no more',[10] but the movement continues inexorably, maintaining its tension towards the

---

6   Maritain, Jacques. 1945, 34.

7   Stravinsky, Igor & Craft, Robert. 1982, 45.

8   I am indebted to Artur Weiser for his theological commentary on these Psalm texts.

9   Jesus used this phrase to draw attention to the importance of his teaching, e.g. Matthew 11.15.

10   Jacques Handschin wrote to tell Stravinsky that he had missed out 'peccata mea' after 'remitte mihi' between figs. 12 and 13. Craft, Robert. 1985, 135.

final chord of G major, the dominant of the key of the next movement. The first movement is left open: its growth represents the Psalmist's increasingly terrifying impression of how God views his sin, and the hope that God will no longer look upon him in anger before he dies.

2   **2nd Movement**

In response to the Psalmist's cry for help, God is symbolically present in a high-pitched fugue for solo flutes and oboe in which the unifying motif of 3rds is presented in a widened form (Ex. 49).

EX. 49   Intervals of a third widened as a fugal theme: 2nd movement, *Symphony of Psalms*

The theme is characterised by wide-spread minor 3rds at a calmer pace, and the fugue in four, eventually five close parts, creates an increasingly dense musical volume. The text of this movement from Psalm 39. 2–4, expresses the tension between having the assurance of faith but also striving for it: 'I waited ... he inclined to me and heard my cry. He drew me up from the gruesome pit out of the miry bog and set my feet upon a rock ...' This tension is reflected in the length of time in which the Psalmist contemplates the deep quality of God's presence as God surrounds and saves him.

Stravinsky described the interaction of the equal instrumental and choral forces in this Psalm as making the most overt use of musical symbolism in any of his music before *The Flood* (1961–2). God's response to the Psalmist becomes clear as the fugal theme is heard lightly staccato in the bass register strongly underpinning the new countersubject for sopranos and horns (fig. 5, Ex. 50).

The following choral fugue increases in confidence as motifs from God's fugue in this 'upside-down pyramid' penetrate it.[11] As God brings the Psalmist up out of the mire, the motif of 3rds rises through the distinctive timbres of brass and horns, directing expectation to the coming act of salvation (fig. 8 + 1). The choir is heard a cappella as the Psalmist's feet are set upon a rock and

---

11   Stravinsky, Igor & Craft, Robert. 1982, 45.

EX. 50   God's fugal theme surrounds the Psalmist

given a firm footing (fig. 10). The fugal theme rises through the brass and horns for a second time, the trombone announcing a new joyful dotted semiquaver version of the theme (fig. 13). Two silent beats allow the new situation to register and resonate. The Psalmist accepts that everything he is and has is a gift from God: 'He put a new song in my mouth ... Many see it ... and put their trust in the Lord'. The new song endows the Psalmist with new strength: the dotted 3rds motif is heard fortissimo and the vocal lines are now set to wider intervals (fig. 14). This densely orchestrated passage is frequently pierced by the motif of 3rds, in both its dotted and original form, as a symbol of the new inclusive Covenant between God and His people. God has granted the Psalmist's prayer, bringing him up from the 'pit of tumult' and the 'miry bog' (images probably used originally of the underworld). In this Psalm it is not the details of the Psalmist's personal experience that are emphasised but the divine aspect of God's help.[12]

The chorus, united in their hope and trust in the Lord, converge on the central pitch, E♭, a semitone below the central pitch of the first movement (fig. 17). The quality of time has increased in depth throughout the first two movements: the sense of expectation now deepens as the work's stately momentum is stilled in a transparent construction that rocks between E♭ and E♮ as it searches for equilibrium. Five lines of movement of contrasting pitch range and rhythm are juxtaposed: two differently-paced swaying movements for flutes and oboes are set against a slow syncopated E♭ for the chorus, a wide-ranging bass ostinato pivots between E♭ and E♮ in quavers, and the distinctive timbre of a piccolo trumpet marks out the fugal theme at half speed,

---

12   Weiser, Artur. 1979, 335.

pianissimo. The trumpet's slow enunciation of the fugue motif symbolises the Psalmist's new 'at-one-ment' with God. The final pentatonic chord leaves this movement open, emphasising the continuing journey.

3   3rd Movement

The recognition, in Psalm 39 v. 3, that the Psalmist has a new song, is affirmed by the slow 'Allelujah' that opens the third movement. Eager to counter the many composers 'who had abused these magisterial verses as pegs for their own lyrico-sentimental feelings', Stravinsky gave up the idea of Psalm 150 'as a song to be danced, as David danced before the Ark' in order to treat the final movement 'in an imperative way': its essential importance is given due authority by the introduction of Elijah.[13] The contrasting time qualities of the heavenly spaces are treated as facets of a musical hyperspace and alternated in a monumental spiral form as in *Symphonies of Wind Instruments*. The adoration of the slow opening Allelujah is twice contrasted with the fast-moving journey of Elijah's chariot as it speeds across the Heavens before a transitional bridge passage of praise returns to the time quality of the opening bars.

As the Psalmist enters a new quality of time and space, slow, widely-spaced orchestral chords with prominent movement through G – A – B♭ are answered by a slow choral Allelujah that moves through C – D – E♭. At this new slow tempo, two circular movements, for choir and instrumental ostinati, create a slight increase of momentum at 'Laudate Dominum' (fig. 1) by revolving against each other with minimal rhythmic contrast. The false relations between E♭ and E♮ that hovered expectantly at the end of the second movement (fig. 17) set up rich overtones as the chorus sings of the holy places (fig. 1 + 6), and the musical space enlarges as the number of musical layers increases for the 'firmaments of his power' (fig. 2). This section's stately tempo and mood of authority expresses the Christian belief that 'In praising God the meaning of the world is fulfilled ... [the] community join ... to bear witness to God's mighty deeds, which entail the realisation of the salvation ... of the whole world.'[14]

The meditative adoration at 'Laudate Dominum' (fig. 1), originally composed to the words 'Gospodi Pomiluy', is a prayer before the Russian image of the infant Christ with orb and sceptre, and Stravinsky recalls this text and

---

13   Stravinsky, Igor & Craft, Robert. 1982, 44.

14   Weiser, Artur. 1979, 841: 'Everything that breathes is called upon to join in the praise of God'. Stravinsky decided not to use an organ, and declared that the breathing of wind instruments was one of their primary attractions for him.

the initial Allelujah in an apotheosis.[15] The opening section concludes with a widely-spaced chord on C that retains the flattened 7th of the natural scale, a single B♭ in the cello part that lends the chord the spatial resonance of the harmonic series (fig. 3 – 3). This continues for another six bars, leaving the first section open as though it continues to sound praise as we move away.

The appearance of Elijah (fig. 3) is associated with the coming of the Kingdom of God in two ways. Firstly, the sight of Elijah's translation into heaven was a test of Elisha's spiritual fitness to succeed him:

> Aware that his end was near, Elijah paid farewell visits to the prophetic communities at Gilgal, Bethel and Jericho. The two prophets [Elijah and Elisha] then crossed the Jordan, its waters being driven back miraculously so that a passage was provided; and from his departing leader Elisha asked a double portion of the first-born so that he might be his successor in office. The fact that his request would be granted only if he had a vision of Elijah's translation implies that spiritual gifts can be transmitted only to those who are fit to receive them; he had the vision, received the gift and picked up Elijah's cloak that had fallen from him.[16]

Stravinsky's introduction of Elijah's chariot climbing into the heavens affirms that the whole community of worshippers have indeed been endowed with the spiritual gifts to bear witness to God's mighty deeds.

Secondly, the expectation arose in biblical times that Elijah would return and restore all things before the advent of the Messiah.[17] Jesus himself believed that this had happened, and taught that Elijah had reappeared in the form of John the Baptist.[18] Stravinsky also introduced Elijah and his chariot into this hymn of praise out of his ardent desire for the imminent coming of the Kingdom of God: he dedicated *Symphony of Psalms* 'a la Gloire de DIEU', and pasted a drawing of the Crucifixion, inscribed 'Adveniat Regnum Tuum' in the flyleaf of his sketchbook. He hoped that the audience, listening to it 'with other ears' would understand why he had composed the work.[19]

---

15   Stravinsky, Igor & Craft, Robert. 1982, 46. The Orthodox Church understands Christ as Sovereign of the world.

16   Mauchline, John: Commentary on 2 Kings 2.1–18. In Black, Matthew and Rowley, H.H., eds. 1967, 348.

17   'Behold, I will send you Elijah the prophet before the coming of the great and dreadful day of the Lord': Malachi 4.5.

18   'For all the prophets and the law prophesied until John. And if ye will receive it, this is Elias, which was for to come. He that hath ears to hear, let him hear': Matthew 11.13.

19   Stravinsky, Igor. 1975, 163–4.

At a new, faster speed the motif of minor and major 3rds and ensuing triplets (fig. 5 – 2) are projected in brassy timbres in high-relief.[20] While the exhilarating pace of Elijah's journey across the skies is maintained, the pulse changes to two in a bar for the re-entry of the chorus (fig. 6) as they continue their praise with the resonant Bb – C intonation left behind at figure 3. Their songs of praise alternate in style between slow circular motifs juxtaposed to orchestral ostinati and highly rhythmic aspirated chanting, whose staccato quaver style is reminiscent of Jocasta's 'Oracula, oracula' in *Oedipus Rex*. The two textures join as voices and instruments build a vast paean of praise (from fig. 9).

The opening Allelujah is recalled at the original tempo but with a new tonality, presenting a new facet of the musical hyperspace (fig. 12): the original movement through C – D – Eb is answered by Gb – Ab – Bb. The vision of Elijah returns, but in a modified version. The momentum is slowed (fig. 20 – 3) not only by a new tempo ($\downarrow$ = 60), but by the juxtaposition of the keys of F and F# majors, as a rhythmically reiterated chord is set against a slow succession of 3rds.

A smoothly dotted passage of arpeggios at a stately minim pulse increases in density to introduce what Stravinsky was 'embarrassed' to describe as a final hymn of praise to issue from the skies (fig. 20). As octatonic scales rise in the sopranos (fig. 21) against a rising arpeggio figure on Bb, the increasing momentum slips easily into the final facet of the heavens, a large musical space whose layers revolve freely. Two streams of lightly non-compatible patterning create the deepest time quality of the work (fig. 22): the choir's circular figure, patterning a short pitch range in a triple pulse, moves serenely against a more percussive four-minim ostinato for pianos, harp and timpani (Ex. 51).

EX. 51   Juxtaposition of two metrically different circular patterns: 3rd Movement

---

20   The brassy timbres evoke a 'literal' picture: God revealed Himself in fire on Mount Carmel and translated Elijah in a chariot of the same element.

Tenors and basses briefly lengthen the expression of their praise to synchronise with the four-note ostinato (fig. 24) before the original passage of two
revolving layers returns. The movement is sealed (fig. 29) with a brief recall of
the first two perspectives on the heavenly realms: passages of 'Allelujah' and
'Laudate' resolve onto a chord of C major that consists simply of the major
3rd. In tracing the spiritual journey of the Psalmist from penitence to participation in the everlasting praise of the community of believers, the growth
of musical time and space has been constantly paced by motifs of major and
minor 3rds.

It has often been remarked that a performance of *Symphony of Psalms* creates an atmosphere of great prayerfulness and peace and has a deep effect
upon the spirit. Ingmar Bergman, for instance, wrote to Stravinsky to tell him
that the work had been a source of spiritual power in his life for many years.[21]
The ability of a musical setting to create a spiritual experience in the listener is
a well-established phenomenon but it raises questions about the relationship
of the spiritual in music to religious faith and beliefs.

Although Stravinsky composed *Symphony of Psalms* to be listened to 'on
a higher plane', both he and Pierre Souvtchinsky were concerned to make
an important distinction between the spiritual experience that may be had
through music, and the spiritual growth that comes from personal faith; music
cannot provide any kind of substitute for religious belief. The spiritual experience of prayerfulness and peace that results from the close unity of a musical
structure is not proof of the Divine, but, as in many other great works of art this
structural unity may be an important vehicle to a new perceptive space. This
perceptive space may indeed reveal what Stravinsky termed a 'system beyond
Nature', and may begin to present the listener with the possibility of accepting
religious beliefs.

Speaking of his reaction to seeing *Parsifal,* where he had experienced the
performance as 'an unconscious aping of a religious rite', Stravinsky explained
that what he found 'revolting' was the principle of putting a work of art on
the same level as the sacred and symbolic ritual which constitutes a religious
service. It was in complete contrast to the spirit of the medieval mystery plays
that had 'religion as their basis and faith as their source'. Contained within
the bosom of the Church, 'such aesthetic qualities as they might contain were
merely accessory and unintentional, and in no way affected the substance', for

---

21   Stravinsky, Vera & Craft, Robert. 1979, 461.

the faithful could see the objects of their faith presented in palpable form, like the statues and icons that were put in the churches.[22]

Diaghilev had wanted to stage the Mass, but Stravinsky had refused, finding the concept of art as religious and the theatre as a temple, unseemly and sacrilegious.[23] He felt that the two domains were incompatible and not to be confused: the attitude of a theatre audience is critical and the material there to be evaluated, accepted or rejected, but the attitude of the believer in a religious ceremony is one of acceptance, or at least, of receptivity to the possibility of further enlightenment.

This important distinction between spiritual experience in music and religious beliefs raises the further question of how music can be a bridge to a higher reality. Pierre Souvtchinsky wrote:

> [D]ans l'expérience de la vie spirituelle il est des choses qui ne sauraient non plus ni ne devraient être traduites ou 'exprimées' par la musique. La musique a des thèmes qui lui sont propres, une vocation et une expérience à elle, tant créatrice qu''auditive'. Cette dernière ne peut se définir que partiellement, en tant que 're-sensation' de la musique; dans sa substance, elle doit se baser sur l'entendement de la réalité ontologique du processus musical – c'est à dire sur le temps musical ... Seule cette musique peut être un pont qui nous relie à l'être dans lequel nous vivons, mais qui, en même temps, n'est pas nous.[24]

> [In the experience of the spiritual life there are things which could neither be known nor should be translated or expressed by music. Music has themes of its own, its own vocation and experience, that is as much creative as 'auditory'. The latter can only be partly defined, as the 're-experiencing' of the music; in its substance, it must base itself in the understanding of the ontological reality of the musical process – that is to say in musical time ... Only this music can be a bridge that connects us to the being in which we live, but who, at the same time, is not us.]

The *Symphony of Psalms* functions as a bridge – or an icon in sound – in widening the listener's perceptions to allow new experiences of time and space. It does

---

22   Stravinsky, Igor. 1975, 39.
23   Stravinsky, Igor. 1975, 39ff. Stravinsky, Igor & Craft, Robert. 1981, *Memories and Commentaries*, 48, n.1.
24   Souvtchinsky, Pierre. 1939, 80 (320).

so particularly effectively because the process by which it deepens the sense of time is that by which the sense of space is ordinarily deepened in the physical world: the work progresses directly through deepening time qualities created by successive juxtapositions of movement that allow new time qualities to emerge. Its straightforward temporal construction engages the brain in a logical spatial-temporal reasoning task whose process may be clearly mentally imaged.

The progressive temporal structure of the *Symphony of Psalms* lends itself to some preliminary investigation into the musical processes that create spiritual experience. Chapter Seven reported briefly on research into the ability of the brain to process patterns and their 'family members' and record their frequency of recurrence in time and space; this processing contributes to the formation of our sense of time, not only in daily life but also in the temporalities of artistic constructs such as *Symphony of Psalms*. But recent research into other aspects of musical cognitive abilities has drawn attention to the fact that this process-ing of patterns activates the brain at many frequency levels simultaneously. One possible explanation for the spiritual effect of *Symphony of Psalms* may lie not only in the balance of response between the hemispheres, but that centres of coherence are created between neural networks across a very wide range of higher brain frequencies. This hypothesis is put forward in the light of an increasing body of scientific research into the effects of performing high-level spatial-temporal reasoning tasks, such as listening to music of different styles, mentally imaging music with or without a physical stimulus, score-reading, and musical composition.

4   Music as a Higher Brain Function

By the 1990s data was accumulating from research using EEG spectral anal-ysis which detailed the location, power, and coherence of this cortical activ-ity. In Vienna in 1993, for example, research was carried out on subjects as they listened to music of different styles for periods of five minutes each and performed various musical tasks.[25] The 39 subjects studied (19 male and 20 female) were between 13 and 68 years old and differed in the amount of musi-cal training they had undergone and in their attitudes towards music. The tests aimed to establish the degree of engagement of each hemisphere in the pro-cessing of different styles of music by recording the centres of activity in the

---

25   Although the EEG (electroencephalogram) gives a more diffuse picture of brain activity, information is instantaneous, as opposed to the fMRI (functional magnetic resonance imaging) method that records a more precise location but within a time-spread of several seconds.

brain and the frequencies at which they stimulated this activity.[26] The interrelatedness of brain areas when performing various musical tasks was measured by the increase or decrease in the number of centres of coherence both within each hemisphere and between the hemispheres. Even taking into account that response to music is highly individual and depends upon such crucial factors as interest, emotional or intellectual engagement, musical training, gender, right or left-handedness etc., some interesting general characteristics could nevertheless be identified.

For this research, Hertz (Hz) frequencies were divided into five bands: Theta: 4–7.5 Hz; Alpha: 8–12.5 Hz; Beta 1: 13–18 Hz; Beta 2: 18.5–24 Hz; Beta 3: 24.5–31.5 Hz.[27] Generally speaking, as subjects listened, with eyes closed, to a jazz piece and to works by Bach, Mozart, Beethoven and Schoenberg, all of which had widely differing dominant musical elements and characteristic patterning, both hemispheres were activated, chiefly in the pre-frontal, parietal and temporal areas, but not symmetrically. Greater engagement in the music significantly increased the number of centres of coherence. The results showed that the beta bands – and particularly their uppermost ranges – seem to play a major role in the processing of music; the hemispheric engagement, however, was not necessarily the same for each frequency band, and no hemisphere was seemingly preferred. The fewest significant coherence increases were found in the beta 1 band and the most in beta bands 2 and 3. Laterality changed with the musical style, but when the same tasks were repeated at several weeks' intervals, a fairly large degree of consistency was found.[28]

The theta band was thought to have little to do with music, and the number of significant coherence increases in the alpha band within and between the hemispheres was more equal, and often larger than that in the beta bands: the beta bands were thought to be the frequencies that reflected mental processes. The upper and lower parts of the alpha frequencies were thought to have different purposes however, frequencies up to 10 Hz having more to do with

---

26   Petsche, Helmut, Richter, Peter, Von Stein, Astrid, Etlinger, Susan. C., Filz, Oliver. 1993, vol. 11, no. 2, 117–151. This method records part of the spontaneous electrical activity of the brain, a spatio-temporal electric continuum generated mainly by the nerve cells or grey matter in the cortex: 19 electrodes were placed on the scalp giving 171 possible readings. Coherence is the measure of the degree of similarity between two EEG signals, or of the electric kinship of two brain regions with respect to frequency. When there is no correlation, coherence is '0', when the signals are synchronous, coherence is '1'. Coherence can be every possible value between the two limits.

27   Op. cit., 122. Researchers arbitrarily partitioned the beta frequency range into three bands of equal width to give more detailed information.

28   Op. cit., 117.

general attention, the upper range to 12. 5 Hz being more concerned with specific data processing, and possibly emotional states. Generally speaking, distinctive differences between the hemispheres were more apparent in one or
more beta bands with the most differences in beta bands 2 and 3, depending
on the musical style. Sometimes fairly sharp boundaries were seen between
the frequency bands, and it is worth noting that the research team thought
that 'there was even reasonable suspicion that further essential information
might be expected in data from beyond 32 Hertz', the limit of the method.[29]
This may well prove to be an important factor in recording the effects of juxtaposed patterns that are more complex than those of the composers studied
in the tests.[30]

Several individual cases were of interest in the light of the extension and
diversity of the mental processing that was recorded when subjects listened to
music. A 52-year-old man who listened to the music of Mozart three times, for 1
minute each time with eyes closed, alternated his listening with a mental arithmetic task, also for 1 minute each time. The arithmetic task involved adding up
consecutive numbers beginning with 1. Not only did the tasks activate different centres of coherence in different frequency bands but the arithmetic task
required fewer and less extended cerebral networks than listening to music.
The music of Mozart was found to activate more neural pathways and require
a larger degree of freedom in its processing than the mental arithmetic task.

One set of test results proved intriguing with respect to the processing
of time qualities and musical structure. A 30-year-old male, amateur musician listened to the first movement of Mozart's *Piano Sonata in B♭ major* and
Schoenberg's *Six Little Pieces op. 19* (1911), both works that he knew well.[31] While
listening to both pieces, there were generally more intrahemispheric increases
of coherence in the right hemisphere in all beta bands, with the maximum
increase in beta 3. When listening to Schoenberg's atonal pieces, the number
of increases within the right hemisphere and the number crossing between
the hemispheres was larger than when listening to Mozart in all bands except
theta.[32] But conversely, listening to the first movement of Mozart's sonata

---

29   Op. cit., 123–7.

30   See Sills, Helen. 2001. 'Some temporal implications of the patterning of Mozart and
      Stravinsky in the light of recent neurological research into spatial-temporal reasoning'.
      Marlene P. Soulsby and J.T. Fraser, eds. 2001, 111–126.

31   Probably Mozart's Sonata in B♭ major K.498a (1st movement). Mozart composed three
      sonatas in B♭ major: the sonata used in the research is not specified in the paper, and is
      also described as being in B♭ minor, a key very rarely used at this time.

32   The last movement was written at a time of deep grief at the death of his friend and men-
      tor, Gustav Mahler, on May 18, 1911.

involved the left hemisphere more often in more frequency bands than listening to the pieces by Schoenberg.

The subject explained that he simply enjoyed the isolated sound patterns in Schoenberg without paying much regard to their structure in time, but when listening to Mozart's highly-patterned sonata he enjoyed both its vertical and horizontal aspects in remembering and anticipating its architecture. Schoenberg's *Six Little Pieces op. 19* play with colour and form and are free from formal or temporal constrictions: they are aphoristic, disjointed and atonal, and sometimes feature independent dynamics between the hands.[33] Conversely, Mozart's sonata patterns the scale, triad and arpeggio in many ingenious ways according to a proportioned formal design: variations in the quality of time, however, are more to do with mood, to be brought out in performance by the skill of the pianist.

Other tests on a 54-year-old male professional musicologist and composer involved listening to piano pieces of similar tempi and loudness for periods of five minutes, with eyes closed. The pieces selected were Bach's *Prelude & Fugue in A minor* from Book 1 of *The Well-Tempered Clavier,* the 1st movement of Beethoven's *Sonata in A♭ major,* Schoenberg's *Two Piano Pieces Op. 33,* and a jazz piece, *Amalgame.*[34] Strong centres of coherence were recorded in both the theta and alpha bands, but in the beta bands coherence increases were focused more on specific areas of the hemispheres. The research team found not only clear and very diverse patterns of cortical activation with regard to each hemisphere, but also different concentrations of activity at each frequency band.

It is interesting to note how these centres of coherence differed between composers and between the different frequency levels. The *Prelude and Fugue* by Bach produced strong centres of coherence in all three beta bands with many connections from frontal to posterior areas in the right hemisphere, and a concentration of posterior areas in the beta 2 band. The sonata movement by Beethoven produced far fewer concentrations of coherence that were also less strong, but with a greater number of coherence centres in frontal areas in the beta 3 than in the beta 2 band. During the jazz piece, the centres of coherence were strongest in the beta 2 frequencies, but also with a strong concentration of coherence in the left hemisphere in the beta 3 band. Schoenberg's *Two Piano Pieces,* with a moderate number of coherence centres at the beta 1 and 2 levels, produced the greatest number of its strongest connections across the

---

33   See Chapter 13 for Schoenberg's conception of musical time.
34   Petsche, Helmut. et al. 1993, 135–140.

hemispheres in the beta 3 band.[35] Speaking very generally, the results appeared to reflect the musical elements that were dominant in a work, the strength with which the frequency bands were activated, and whether the musical style was more specialised for one hemisphere than the other.

The Vienna research was wide-ranging and also studied the effects upon the brain of performing other complex tasks such as the mental imaging of music. Mental imagery of all kinds has been described as 'clearly the product of more abstract higher-level structures which provide the top-down computations to generate particular images'.[36] Greater understanding of the neural basis of mental imagery began to emerge in the 1980s, and was seen to be the efferent activation of visual areas in the prestriate occipital, parietal and temporal areas of the cortex. The same kinds of specialised visual information were found to be involved in imagery as in perception. In addition, different components of imagery processing appeared to be differentially lateralised. The generation of mental images from memory depended primarily upon structures in the posterior left hemisphere, and the rotation of mental images depended primarily upon structures in the posterior right hemisphere.[37]

Previous research in Vienna in 1988 with subjects who had some musical training, showed that not only was there an exchange of information between the two posterior parts of the temporal lobe (that are important, among other things, for musical memory), but also that there were interhemispheric increases in coherence between the parietal regions in the beta 2 range and partly also in the occipital regions involving areas of the visual system.[38] With regard to the four-dimensional structure of music, the research team remarked that

> These changes that are also seen during silent reading ... and during mental cube rotation ... are probably related to the fact that music, as an acoustic temporal structure, requires some spatial abilities in the listener to be fully appreciated.[39]

Like composing, imagining music seems to cause a greater number of coherence increases in general and a greater number of interhemispheric increases

---

35   Op. cit., 136.

36   Hampson, P.J., Marks, D.F. & Richardson, J.T.E., eds. 1990, 11.

37   Martha J. Farah. 1984.

38   The dorsal pathway, processing visual movement, contains the middle temporal region, also known as V5.

39   Petsche, H., Lindner, K., Rappelsberger, P. 1988, vol. 6, no 2. 157.

in particular than in music perception. As part of the 1993 research programme, a 30-year-old female cellist listened to the first movement of Brahms' *Cello Sonata in E minor Op. 38* and mentally replayed it after 20 minutes. Both temporal regions were involved but in different ways; imagining the movement caused more increases in the upper beta bands and more intrahemispheric increases of coherence than when simply listening to it.

The mental imaging and composition of music clearly differed from simply listening to music by activating many more coherence increases in the beta bands and by an increasing percentage of hemispheric interactions.[40] The process of composing music produced the greatest number of interhemispheric increases, with an interesting difference between composing tonal and atonal music: composing tonal music increased the number of coherence centres in beta bands 2 and 3 in the left hemisphere, while composing atonal music increased the number of centres in the right hemisphere and also activated many centres of coherence across the whole cortex.

In view of these findings, and taking into account the differing forms of patterning in the test pieces that ranged from Bach to early Schoenberg and jazz, the mental imaging of Stravinsky's temporal forms and their complex flux of juxtaposed layers seems likely to activate coherence centres at the high beta frequencies and promote the closest cooperation between the hemispheres. These speculations apply particularly to his late 'spiritual' works with their patterning of 12-note row forms that are closely related by rotation.

Stravinsky's juxtapositions of patterning may well make a strong appeal to the analytical skills of the left hemisphere as a higher spatial-temporal reasoning task, but it was his expressed aim to co-ordinate the listener with time, involving not only the close cooperation of the hemispheres but also the right hemisphere's spatial skills. The close synthesis that Stravinsky achieves between objectivity of musical form and 'living' changes of time quality suggests that the spiritual dimension of his works arises from a fine balance between the hemispheres at the high beta frequencies and involves both sides of the brain in equal measure. This fine balance may account, at least partially, for the feelings of serenity and peace that arise from listening to *Symphony of Psalms* and many others of his works.

The co-ordination of the listener with qualities of time necessitates the forming of a clear structure, but the ability to mentally image a temporal form from memory also involves an important cognitive skill concerned with time and timing. The brain has the ability to 'replay' an auditory image in mental space

---

40   Petsche, H. et al. 1993, 117–118.

with great temporal accuracy, and possesses the remarkable skill of remembering and reproducing different qualities of time.[41] The above-mentioned research in Vienna, for example, found that a 68-year-old, male amateur musician who had learnt the first movement of Mozart's *String Quartet KV 458* (The Hunt) from memory, was able to listen to and then mentally image the movement in a time that differed from the recording by only five seconds.[42]

It is a recognised phenomenon among trained musicians that in the course of mental rehearsals, the mental imaging of a musical form will become increasingly accurate and settle to a constant performance time. Musicians even find that, in the absence of an instrument or orchestra, enactive imagery of a work can have a greater beneficial effect on the actual performance than that achieved by physical rehearsal.[43] Music is, of course, not the only high level cognitive skill to engage in mental imaging: it is also routinely practised by athletes, pilots, dancers, surgeons and others, where it is important to maintain a highly accurate performance.

Musical skills draw upon a wide range of cortical areas, largely engaging the temporal lobes and temporal-occipital, temporo-frontal and motor areas. Music of very different styles may draw upon more distant brain areas. The more attention is engaged in music as a fully four-dimensional experience, the greater the number of coherence centres both within and between the hemispheres. Music that is highly patterned, such as *Symphony of Psalms,* not only stimulates the neural networks to carry out complex spatial-temporal reasoning tasks at the higher brain frequencies, but also facilitates its mental imaging, both during its performance and without sensory input, in its replay from memory.

---

41   See Shaw, Gordon, L. 2000, 147–154.

42   Petsche, H., Richter, P., von Stein, A., Etlinger, S., Filz, O. 1993, 140.

43   The pianist Phyllis Sellick told an interviewer: '... a tremendous amount of score-reading should take place before sitting down to play the music ... Gina Bachauer studied Brahms' *Piano Concerto No.2* for about a month before she played it. By that time she could play it from memory'. Sellick, Phyllis. February 1999.

CHAPTER 11

Faith Matters

Stravinsky had not been a communicant member of the Russian Orthodox Church since leaving St Petersburg in 1910, but in 1926, soon after he had settled in Nice, he reconnected with his spiritual roots. The reasons for his return were probably many and complex. He had frequent contact with members of the Orthodox émigré community at the Alexander Nevsky church in Paris, where he received news of recent events in Russia; this kept alive his fears concerning his homeland, members of his family and also his possessions, which had been swept away in the social turmoil there. This church, the centre of the Soviet church-in-exile, played a very important place in his life during the 1930s.[1] Around the time of his return to the Orthodox Church as a communicant member his knowledge of Catholic spirituality was deepened through his friendships with Arthur Lourié, and Jean Cocteau, who had recently converted to the Catholic faith.

The church's 'bad music and worse singing' prompted Stravinsky to compose a *Pater Noster* and a *Credo* for use in the Russian liturgy there. [2] In 1934 there followed an *Ave Maria,* which though it is found in several liturgies, was composed as a concert piece.[3] All three are to texts in Old Slavonic, which for Stravinsky had always been the language of prayer.[4] Although he later disclaimed any knowledge of Russian Church music, the sounds of the liturgy and music of the Russian church in Kiev and Poltava stayed with him from childhood, and he did acknowledge that perhaps some early memories of

---

1   Stravinsky, Igor & Craft, Robert. 1972, 41.

2   Op. cit., 40. Stravinsky gives the date of his re-entry into Communion as 1925, the year before composing the *Pater Noster*. The Orthodox Eucharistic liturgy, like that of the Roman Catholic Church, has three parts: the Liturgy of the Preparation, the Liturgy of the Word, and the Liturgy of the Eucharist itself. The Niceno-Constantinopolitan Creed and the *Pater Noster* (Lord's Prayer) come in the Liturgy of the Eucharist, the *Pater Noster* just before Communion. The most commonly used liturgy in the Russian Orthodox Church is the Divine Liturgy of St John Chrysostom, the Divine Liturgy of St Basil the Great being used on festive holy days, during Lent, and from Holy Thursday to Easter Day.

3   In Paris in the mid-1930s, Stravinsky began a fourth a cappella chorus, *Of the Cherubim,* also in Old Slavonic, but only completed a few bars. Stravinsky, Vera & Craft, Robert. 1979, 628, n.18.

4   Stravinsky, Igor & Craft, Robert. 1981. *Expositions and Developments*, 76. Stravinsky inserted a handwritten paper containing a prayer in church Slavonic at the back of his Russian Orthodox Prayer Book, which he had signed 'Igor Stravinsky. 1926, Nice'. Craft, Robert, ed. 1985, 349.

© KONINKLIJKE BRILL NV, LEIDEN, 2022 | DOI:10.1163/9789004518537_013

church singing survived in the simple harmonic style that he aimed at in these liturgical pieces. In his *Pater Noster, Credo* and *Ave Maria,* he had hoped to find deeper roots than those of the Russian Church composers who had merely tried to continue the Venetian (Galuppi) style from Bortniansky.[5]

Stravinsky's new religious fervour as a member of a worshipping community is glimpsed in a letter to Diaghilev on Tuesday 26th April 1926, in Russian Holy Week. Although he had not fasted in Lent for twenty years, he now felt an extreme mental and spiritual need to do so and to ask forgiveness of everyone he could before going to confession. In particular, he asked Diaghilev, with whom he had worked these past years 'without repentance before God', to forgive him his transgressions.[6] Stravinsky took a great interest in Diaghilev's trip to Mount Athos two years later, asking him to bring him several icons (en oléographies)[7] and a wooden Cross, and to have them blessed at the same place.[8]

Stravinsky wrote the brief *Pater Noster* in Old Slavonic while he was working on *Oedipus Rex* in Latin.[9] He began to date his manuscripts on Saints' days, and later remarked that this was during his 'most earnest period of Christian Orthodoxy'. He claimed that, after praying in a little church on his way to play his *Piano Sonata* in Venice, he had been completely healed of a suppurating abscess in his right forefinger. He believed it to be a miracle, brought about by what he called 'a system beyond Nature'.[10]

For a period of five years from 1924, Archpriest Nicolai Podosonov (Father Nicholas) of the Orthodox Church in Nice was a member of Stravinsky's household, living in a separate apartment in their spacious Villa des Roses. Stravinsky purchased an extraordinary number of religious objects and lent a large number of them to be used in the Russian church in Nice for as long as Father Nicholas remained its Father Superior. These included the Cross behind the altar, a framed photograph of the Turin Shroud, images of the Virgin Mary, Saints, Martyrs and the beheading of John the Baptist, robes for priests and canons, cloths and coverings for the altar and lectern, banners, candlesticks and a bronze chandelier. Stravinsky's son Theodore and daughter Milène painted images of the Annunciation and the Four Evangelists, and also of Christ's Birth, Presentation in the Temple, Baptism and Ascension on thick wooden plates to

---

5   Stravinsky, Igor & Craft, Robert. 1972, 40.
6   Craft, Robert, ed. 1984, 40.
7   A type of print that has been textured to resemble an oil painting.
8   Craft, Robert, ed. 1984, 44–45.
9   Stravinsky, Igor & Craft, Robert. 1982, 26.
10   Ibid.

be put on the altar. Following Father Nicholas' suspension, Stravinsky wrote to the Metropolitan Vladimir in Paris in 1931 in an attempt to recover his possessions from the church, explaining that he intended eventually to build a chapel at his home, after which he would want these objects restored for his own use there. He added that this was well-known among the parishioners.[11]

Visitors to Stravinsky's homes in Nice and Paris noticed that he kept a flame burning in front of an icon of the Blessed Virgin, *La Vierge de Perpétuel Secours* (Our Lady of Perpetual Help).[12] He surrounded himself with religious objects in his working studio, and many of his manuscripts carry inscriptions and dedications of a religious nature. Entries in his sketchbooks (after Polymnie's Variation in *Apollo,* for example) and on his printed music are sometimes followed by drawings of the Russian Cross, and occasionally the Saint's day is recorded, as on a first sketch for the theme of the *Piano Concerto.* The cover of Stravinsky's performing copy of *Serenade en la* is inscribed 'Nice, April 9th 1926, after Confession and Communion', and on the first draft for part of *Oedipus Rex* (figs. 198–200) Stravinsky wrote 'March 13th, after my Confession and Communion, Father Nicholas at home'.[13]

After Stravinsky's re-entry into Communion, the teaching of the Christian Church became explicit in both his writings and his works. But his rejoining of the Orthodox community was hardly a 'conversion': Stravinsky did not believe in extrapolating absolutes from experience, but certainly from his own childhood awareness of God he recognised the validity of Max Scheler's phenomenological argument 'that allows for a personal God as well as for an *ens a se*'.[14] Nor did he believe in 'bridges of reason' and recalled that he was neither reasoned into discovering 'the necessity of religious belief' nor swayed by any priestly influence; it was rather that for some years before 'a mood of acceptance' had been cultivated in him 'by a reading of the Gospels and by other religious literature'.[15] Stravinsky was not inclined to elaborate upon the many

---

11   Craft, Robert, ed. 1982, Appendix 1, 386–8. Photographs of Stravinsky at home at the end of his life, show a locket over his bed containing a miniature icon copied by his son Theodore that Stravinsky carried on all his travels, and which was admired by Diaghilev. The shelf beyond the bed displays a collection of 18th and early-19th century icons, a picture of the 'Zurbarán' Lamb in the San Diego Museum and a Christ image from a Roman catacomb. Craft, Robert. 1967.

12   Stravinsky, Vera & Craft, Robert. 1979, 211. This celebrated 15th century Byzantine icon originated in the Keras Kardiotissas Monastery near Kera in Crete but has been in Rome since 1499.

13   Ibid, 211–2.

14   Stravinsky, I. & Craft, Robert. 1981, *Memories and Commentaries*, 75.

15   Ibid.

influences, creative and spiritual, that brought about changes to his life and work, but although he claimed that Maritain had no 'direct' influence on him and certainly had no role in his 'conversion', he did acknowledge that he knew of Maritain's work through his books.[16] This may well be an understatement of the true position: the parallel direction of their development, in moving from a Bergsonian approach to one of greater order and proportion, is striking.

1   Pater Noster (1926)

The Orthodox liturgical tradition prohibited the use of instruments, so this *Pater Noster* is a simple vocal setting in homophonic style. Like the ancient znamenny chanters, Stravinsky patterns ontological time with asymmetric phrases, and matches melodic contours to haunting vowel sounds to penetrate the acoustic.

The piece is based on two melodic formulae that are patterned as in znamenny chant. The first, C – D – E♭ addresses the heavenly places. Both of the first two phrases (bars 1–8, 9–15) proceed to the dominant chord of C minor via two memorable intonations: the denser chord of II7 (bar 4), and the introduction of an A♮ (bars 6, 10, 13) to prepare the impact of three significant words: *Imia* (name), *Tsarstviie* (kingdom) and *Volia* (will). Their resonant vowel sounds are set to the dominant minor chord of the key of the dominant chord (bars 7, 11, 14) a harmonic effect that Stravinsky drew attention to in *Oedipus Rex*.

The second motif consists of just two notes, C and B♭, the drop to a tone below recalling the natural scale (bar 16 – end). The motif expands in patterning as the first two petitions for material and spiritual food, and forgiveness are made, each phrase ending with longer note values. The melodic pattern at the third petition 'as we forgive our debtors' has the largest expansion, rising to include the E♭ and the resonant A♮ of the first motif.

The homophonic setting and organic flexibility of Stravinsky's *Pater Noster* reflects an attitude of gentle trust in God as Abba, a loving Father.

2   Russian Credo (1932)

The Creed expresses the Christian faith in God and Jesus Christ. This *Credo* tilts between A major and five successive modulations, three to F♯ and two to C♯

---

16   Op. cit., 76.

minor, and has a simple homophonic setting like the Credo of his *Mass* (1944–48). Belief in God the Creator ('by Him all things were made') is linked with a vision of His future reign ('His kingdom will have no end') by its similar setting. Each statement of faith creates a different pattern from the same small pitch range, and the phrases are nuanced with resonant vowel sounds and momentary dissonances from internal voice-leading. After the fourth cadence (fig. 35 + 1), the parts move from Christ's crucifixion to a climax at 'whose Kingdom shall have no end' with a steady rise in pitch and increased activity. The way in which the Orthodox Church and the Catholic Church regard Christ's crucifixion differs slightly: the Orthodox Church places greater emphasis on the glory of his resurrection from the dead. While Western worshippers meditating upon the Cross feel deep sympathy with the Man of Sorrows, the Orthodox Church, whilst remembering his human suffering and desolation, is more concerned to celebrate his great victory over death: Christ is the Victor, the King, reigning in triumph.[17]

3   Ave Maria (1934)

The Archangel's greeting to Mary, *Ave Maria*, follows the Old Testament reading at the end of the Orthodox service of Vespers, signifying the coming of Christ and the fulfilment of God's promise to his people. Stravinsky's setting of this greeting to the *Theotokos*, 'the God-bearer', expresses this spiritual idea in variants of a single musical idea.[18] The melodic motif in the upper voice is contained within a 4th, F – B♭, and the homophonic setting in close harmony flows between the chords of B♭ major, D minor and G minor, highlighting recurring vowel sounds. The tonal ambiguity of this piece, the opposition of E♭ (B♭ major) to E♮ (D minor), introduces a heightened temporal-spatial effect and gives the structure a haunting, floating quality. In contrast, *Blagosloven* (holy) is set melismatically, providing a rare moment of contrast to the syllabic setting.

In 1949, Stravinsky prepared Latin versions of *Pater Noster*, *Credo* and *Ave Maria*, revising *Ave Maria* in the process. When Stravinsky sent the Latin versions of *Pater Noster* and *Ave Maria* to Nadia Boulanger, he told her that

---

17   Ware, Timothy. 1983, 232–3.
18   'Hail, Birthgiver of God, Virgin Mary, full of grace, the Lord be with Thee; blessed art Thou among women and blessed is the fruit of Thy womb, for Thou hast borne the Saviour of our souls'.

although he had arranged this version for use by a Catholic group, he hoped it would be used by the Protestant churches as well.[19]

4   Tests of Faith

Stravinsky's life gradually became more difficult in the 1930s. Diaghilev had died in August 1929, leaving Stravinsky, despite their quarrels over the years, bereft of a close friend, kinsman and devoted promoter of his work. More generally, since the economic crash of 1929, the financial situation in Europe was becoming increasingly bleak and Germany would be close to bankruptcy within a year or two. For Stravinsky and many other musicians this meant an increasing shortage of engagements and recording opportunities, especially in Germany. Anti-semitic feeling was on the increase as was the persecution of artists with Jewish connections, especially after Hitler was appointed Chancellor of the Reich in 1933. The Nazis introduced a policy of promoting only German art so that theatre and concert promoters, uncertain of the situation, began to avoid booking foreign artists and their works. Even Stravinsky, who trod cautiously with a strong sense of artistic self-preservation and financial pragmatism, found himself accused of 'degenerate Bolshevik art'. Learning that he was on a list of those with Jewish connections, he provided his publisher, Willi Strecker, with a strong statement about his ancestry. Only in Paris, for the moment at least, was artistic life relatively normal.

Stravinsky was also beset with deep personal worries concerning the ill-health both of his family and himself, and financial matters regarding his many dependents, his publishers and copyrights and his Russian property (now confiscated), as well as the promotion of his two sons in their respective careers. More than ever, his life involved time-consuming travel, whether performing as a duo with the violinist Samuel Dushkin, as a pianist with his son Soulima, or conducting performances of works which had already brought him fame. He became quite discouraged at always conducting the same few works, and at seeing others conduct or 'interpret' them. In a few short months during 1938–9 he lost his mother and then both his wife Catherine and daughter Ludmilla to tuberculosis. In 1940 he emigrated yet further westward to America, marrying Vera Sudeikina and seeking a new way forward in both his personal and his creative life.

---

19   Craft, Robert, ed. 1982, 245–6.

Throughout all these upheavals, Stravinsky continued to wait upon Divine 'gifts'. Despite setbacks, he could still assert that first ideas are very important since 'they come from God. And if after working and working, I return to these ideas, then I know they're good.'[20] But Stravinsky's music was also becoming increasingly misunderstood, and he himself was coming under attack for what was seen as regressive 'Neo-Classicism'. In Stravinsky's tribute to the 'magnificent work of his great contemporary, Picasso', written in 1932, he aimed fire, perhaps, at his own critics by quoting Picasso's response to his critics, taken from La Fontaine's fable, *Le Villageois et le Serpent*:

> Croyez-vous que vos dents impriment leurs outrages
> Sur tant de beaux ouvrages?
> Ils sont pour vous d'airain, d'acier, de diament.[21]

> [Do you think that your teeth will imprint their insults
> on so many beautiful works?
> For you they are made of bronze, steel and diamond.]

5   Perséphone (1933)

After hearing Stravinsky and Dushkin play the *Duo Concertant*, C. A. Cingria wrote to Stravinsky: 'The music is wise … in a way achieved by no one before … It is Petrarch. You have captured the equivalence. Set Petrarch in the same voice as that of the *Duo Concertant*. Perhaps that title would even make people understand …'[22] Stravinsky was enchanted by Cingria's subsequent gift of his recently published *Pétrarque,* not only because Petrarch's mastery of poetic form and metre affirmed his own increasingly structural approach but also because it was characterised by a particular quality of lyricism: Petrarch had developed the sonnet into a highly regulated and disciplined form that was nevertheless able to express passionate but 'sacred' emotions. Stravinsky underlined two passages in Cingria's book: 'Le lyrisme n'existe pas sans règles … autrement ce n'est qu'une faculté de lyrisme et elle exist partout'. [*Lyricism does not exist without rules … otherwise it is only a capacity for lyricism and that exists everywhere.*] And 'Oui l'art … bien que divin parce-que soumis aux

---

20   Dushkin, Samuel. 1949. In Corle, Edwin. 1969, 185.
21   Tribute to Picasso: *Cahiers d'Art*, 7e année, 1932. Appendix 1.
22   C. A. Cingria became one of Stravinsky's closest friends; they first met in Paris in May 1914.

cordes, doit être astucieux et difficile'. [*Yes, art ... although divine because held in check by cords, must be artful and difficult.*]

Stravinsky was particularly taken with the mordant humour of Petrarch's *Dialogue Between Joy and Reason* with its satirical perspective on music and emotion, and began to set it for two voices and a keyboard instrument. The *Dialogue* begins with Joy's professed delight in song and stringed instruments to which Reason replies 'Mieux te serait rejouir en larmes et en soupirs, car il vaut mieux par pleurs venir en joye que par joye venir en pleurs et en gémissements'. [*It would be better for you to rejoice in tears and sighs, for it is better to come to joy by weeping than to come to tears and groans from joy.*] To Joy's description of music as soothing and comforting, Reason replies: 'L'araignée ... adoulcit devant qu'elle morde, et le barbier avant qu'il frappe ...'[23] [*The spider soothes before she bites, and the barber before he strikes ...*]

Stravinsky felt that *Apollo* had been generally dismissed as light and empty. Even many years later he defended the depth of feeling expressed within its musical Alexandrines, and pointed to its truly tragic moments such as Apollo's birth, and his ascent to Parnassus in the apotheosis. He remarked wryly that, of course, Racine and he himself were both absolutely heartless people, and 'cold, cold'.[24] The challenge of his next large-scale spiritual work, *Perséphone*, would be to shape its time qualities with greater lyricism. The highly disciplined lyric quality which Cingria had brought to Stravinsky's notice in *Pétrarque* could offer a way forward.[25]

The opportunity arose for a more lyrical multi-temporal composition in collaboration with the French writer André Gide. Gide enjoyed talking with Stravinsky about Pushkin and all things Russian, and his favourite conversational topic was religion, although Stravinsky was not a good target for his proselytising Protestantism. Stravinsky wrote to Gide to say that he was too seduced by the beauty of the magnificent text not to aspire with all his power to erect a very substantial monument in sound to go with it.[26] The last of the Homeric hymns, *Hymn to Demeter,* which Gide had previously elaborated into an extended poem in French, provided the perfect subject for an autonomous musical object in ontological time: a celebration of the mystery of Time itself,

---

23   Craft Robert, ed. 1982, 370.

24   Stravinsky, Igor & Craft, Robert, ed. 1982, 34.

25   Stravinsky had probably discussed the matter of lyricism with Jacques Handschin also, for Handschin wrote to Stravinsky telling him of a centre for Gregorian singing in Seine Inférieure, and later sent him examples of medieval melodies. Letters of April 1st and October 1st, 1933: Craft, Robert, ed. 1985, 137–8.

26   Craft, Robert, ed. 1985, 189.

recounted in syllabic language. Its subject lent itself to interpretation on several levels: it was both a myth about time as the rhythm of the seasons and the 'death' of time before regeneration, and also an allegory of spiritual rebirth into a 'new' time. It was a subject that could encompass both ancient Egyptian cults and Christian revelation but which also lent itself to the lyrical portrayal of compassion and self-sacrifice, qualities not explicit in the original Greek myth.

In contrast to *Symphony of Psalms* and its growth process into the heavenly realms, *Perséphone* offered Stravinsky the opportunity to explore the construction, not only of different qualities of time, but also the *absence* of time. In the ancient myth, Perséphone descends voluntarily into Hades each Winter to be the spouse of Pluto out of compassion for the sorrowful, faithful spirits whom she has seen there, wandering without hope. She returns to Earth each year to bring the return of spring. As a Christian allegory, the story symbolises the completion of Jesus' mission before his resurrection. The early Jewish tradition held that all those who had died, whether righteous or unrighteous, went to Sheol. The early Christians took over the later Jewish tradition, making a distinction between Sheol as the place of the righteous, and Gehenna as the place of the damned who would not be saved. But the early Christians believed that after his crucifixion Christ, as both human and divine, went down into Sheol out of compassion for the righteous.[27] Here he released the souls who were imprisoned and awaiting him there in the bosom of Abraham, thus opening the gates of heaven for the just souls who had gone before Him. It is the custom of the Catholic Church to read an ancient homily on the subject of the Lord's descent into Hell during the Office of Readings on Holy Saturday (Easter Eve), while the Eastern Orthodox Church typically commemorates the Harrowing of Hades on that day by reading the Paschal Homily of St John Chrysostom.

Stravinsky persuaded Gide to omit all the episodic scenes of his poem, and in so doing, reduced the story to a single narrative and strengthened the work's temporal form. He also felt that it was important to mark the seasonal cycle: in this way, he defined the multi-temporal structure of the work more clearly. As was Stravinsky's custom, he reduced the text to syllables so that the dominant experience would be the time quality-creating movements of the music. *Perséphone* was Stravinsky's first large-scale syllabic setting of the French language and he warned Gide in advance that he would stretch and stress and otherwise 'treat' French as he had Russian. Gide understood Stravinsky's ideal text to be syllable poems; even so, he could hardly have been prepared for the

---

27   I Peter 3.19 and in the Apostles' Creed.

extent to which Stravinsky disregarded the verbal accentuations of his text in order to negate their implicit time qualities.

Stravinsky timed this masque-dance-pantomime precisely to a fixed plan of stage action to determine the unusual pacing of this work in which action and movement are minimal. Eumolpus' narration is supported by bass lines that change slowly by only a tone or semitone, and the asymmetrical phrases and changing metres of the lyrical melodies for the chorus are accompanied by short regular ostinati that hold back development.

The choreography for male and female dancers portrays the action of the tale while it is narrated by Eumolpus, the son of Poseidon and priest of the Eleusinian mysteries, and mimed by Perséphone, daughter of Demeter. The effect is monumental: the orchestra is out of sight, Eumolpus and the chorus are as immobile as the characters in *Oedipus Rex,* and Perséphone's longest soliloquies are musically motionless. Pluto, the King of the Underworld, alias the Devil, only dances: as a mute presence he is even more awesome and terrifying, and his very arrival is greeted with a long pause. Later, Stravinsky thought that the role of Perséphone should be shared by two performers, so that the separation of speech and mime would allow greater freedom for mimetic movement. An illusion of motion could then be established between Perséphone, standing at a fixed point on the stage, in relation to Eumolpus, and the staging worked out entirely in choreographic terms.[28]

The Greeks recognised only three seasons, summer, winter and spring. In *Perséphone* the seasons do not correspond to its three scenes, since Perséphone returns to earth in the middle of Scene III. Eumolpus' opening salutation as priest-narrator (Ex. 52) contains the work's two seminal motifs: the 'lower mordent' figure, E – D♯ – E, and the 'Old Believers' motif, E – D – B, which is heard against its fundamental note, E, giving the opening of the work great spatial resonance:

EX. 52   Unifying motifs derived from Eumolpus' initial announcement

Scene I in summer is set in the remote time of dreams. There is a small temple on the stage consecrated to Perséphone, where 'the tree of dreams extends

---

28   Stravinsky, Igor & Craft, Robert, ed. 1982, 37.

its metallic foliage'. Her maidens, their song moving within a small pitch compass over an ostinato, B – D, beg Perséphone to stay and play in this timeless
place. In contrast to the syllabic treatment of the text, the phrase 'the first
morning of the world' stands out with its longer note values (fig. 14 + 1). The
chorus 'Ivresse matinale' (fig. 23), in which Perséphone is advised 'to let the
future wash over her', suspends time with lapidary rhythms that are aspirated
and cross-accented, recalling the Messenger's rigid rhythmic line in *Oedipus
Rex*.[29] Eumolpus warns that anyone who leans over the narcissus' calyx or
breathes its perfume will see the 'unknown' underworld. *Le calice*, or calyx,
also means chalice ('cup of bitterness') and introduces a significant Christian
connection with The Last Supper. Eumolpus' proclamation of Perséphone's
destiny is accompanied by Verdi-style scales as for the downfall of Oedipus.

After the dream-like movement of Scene I, Scene II is set in the underworld
and begins with the severe dotted arpeggios of *Apollo* and a slow march for
Pluto. This scene evokes a sense of the 'death of time'. Male voices sing 'Ici rien
ne s'achève' [*Here nothing is completed*] and 'chacun poursuit sans trêve ce qui
s'écoule et fuit' [*everyone pursues without respite that which slips away and vanishes*]. Eumolpus announces 'Ici la mort du temps fait la vie eternelle' [*Here the
death of time makes life eternal*].

The maidens' lullaby 'Sur ce lit elle repose' alternates the metres of 2/4
and 3/4, and negates time in similar cross-accented ways to Parasha's opening aria in *Mavra*.[30] The maidens' five-bar melody, consisting of three cross-
accented four-beat phrases, is repeated nine times in all, but with different
patterns of elided syllables that highlight the central pitch B, and a contraction
of Eumolpus' opening motif: E – D♯ – E – D♮ – B. Stravinsky sets this melody
against two widely-spaced ostinati, the upper ostinato regular in its three or
four pitches, the lower one slightly varying. The hypnotic combination of these
three different layers of movement negates the sense of clock-time and linear
progress, particularly as it gains in texture with a second part. Between the
fifth and sixth repetitions, and to continuing widely-spaced ostinati, Eumolpus
announces that here life eternal equates to the death of time.

The juxtaposition of asymmetric and cross-accented melodic patterns at
'Les ombres ne sont malheureuses', is repeated five times with slight changes

---

29   Fig. 139: *Reppereram in monte puerum Oedipoda.*

30   Stravinsky had originally composed this *Berceuse* for Vera Sudeikina to his own words
      in Russian: Stravinsky, Igor & Craft, Robert. ed.1982, 38. The lyricism of 'Les baisers des
      ruisseaux' and 'Nous apportons nos offrandes' in Scene III is reminiscent of the Maidens'
      chorus in Act I, Scene 3 of Tchaikovsky's *Eugene Onegin*. Stravinsky had adapted the
      music of Tchaikovsky for *Le Baiser de la Fée* six years earlier.

EX. 53   Asymmetric and cross-accented patterns on a pedal note negating time

to an irregular ostinato (fig. 93 + 1, Ex. 53)). It continues to restrain movement, evoking the absence of time: the souls in the underworld have no other destiny than to begin again endlessly.

Eumolpus' solemn announcement of Perséphone's destiny and his offer of 'the cup of forgetfulness' (fig. 121) is briefly reminiscent of Oedipus' florid dméstvenny style although here it is diatonic. Strictly rhythmic, dense movement at the display of underworld treasures (fig. 124) stultifies around repeated pedal note figures. Even Eumolpus' uncharacteristically animated narration of the offering of a pomegranate to Perséphone changes to a new *dolce* vocal style but it is set to a three-note ostinato for 12 bars (fig. 145 − 1). The still centre of the work is created as Perséphone is urged to look again into the calyx of the narcissus in the hope of reversing her plight. Movement is minimal around a central pitch C as she gazes upon the desolate, frozen Earth, and the following passage accompanied by string quartet is among the most poignant passages of music that Stravinsky ever wrote (from fig. 152 − 1). Movingly, the triad-based figures of *Apollo* return intermittently as she watches her mother, Demeter, searching for her. As the solution to Perséphone's plight unfolds, the bass line develops from an initially taut two-note ostinato into 'random wandering' and then into pedal notes (fig.171 − 1).

To begin Scene III, Eumolpus returns with the style of the opening and its central pitch, E. In contrast to the absence of time, a lyrical Easter hymn, 'nous apportons nos offrandes' (fig. 207), has a strong Russian character with many melodic intervals of a 4th and a 5th and asymmetric phrase lengths (Ex. 54).[31]

---

31   Stravinsky acknowledged the Russian character of this chorus and jokingly referred to the work as *Persefona Ivanovna*. Craft, Robert, ed. 1984, 475, Appendix 2, n.3.

EX. 54   Asymmetric Russian Easter hymn against a 3-beat ostinato

This joyful choral invitation to Perséphone to return heralds the coming of Spring and new life. Marked *piano*, with constantly changing metres and changes of emphasis, it is cross-accented against a three-beat ostinato that continues to hold back forward momentum: Perséphone has yet to be freed. Perséphone's return to earth is proclaimed dramatically with a repeated lapidary rhythm over a pedal note: 'Il est temps' finally becomes 'Printemps' (fig. 220) with a crack worthy of the sudden breaking of ice on the River Neva.

But the conclusion to Scene III remains 'other-worldly' as Perséphone accepts her destiny. Stravinsky loved the music of the final chorus when it was played and sung in tempo and quietly, without a general crescendo.[32] Eumolpus' narration rises above the chorus who have the same text, but who shadow the beginnings and endings of his phrases, creating the cloudy 'echo' effect with which the work fades away.

Perséphone is unified by Eumolpus' opening motifs. The lower mordent figure E – D♯ – E is transformed into the sturdy chant at 'Ivresse matinale' (fig. 23), and into a powerful prelude to the display of Pluto's treasures (fig. 124 + 1). It is inverted for the Introduction to Scene II and the frozen rivers of winter (fig. 160), double-dotted at the beginning of Scene III (where it develops into Perséphone's 'motif'), recalled in the maidens' welcome of Perséphone (fig. 232), and restored for Eumolpus' final narrations. Stravinsky's favourite interval of a minor 3rd, heard initially as B – D, grows as the underlying ostinato figure of Scene I, and highlights the proclamation 'Ici la mort du temps fait la vie eternelle' [*Here the death of time creates eternal life*] in Scene II (fig. 83 + 3). The use of this minor third motif connects the death of time to 'Cependant sur la colline qui domine le présent and l'avenir ...' [*However, on the hill that dominates the present and the future ...*] in Scene III (fig. 200 + 1). It evokes Perséphone's desolation (fig.152 – 1) as she prepares to contemplate winter on

---

32   Stravinsky, Igor & Craft, Robert. 1982, 38.

Earth, and it reappears as ostinati on B♭ – G (fig. 224) and G♭ – E♭ (fig. 250 – 1) to slow forward movement. Also prominent from Scene II onwards are the dotted triad-based figures recalling *Apollo*, and in Scene III, a recurring motif for Perséphone's return, A – G♯ – A – G♯ – G♮ – D – C♯, which has developed from Eumolpus' opening figure.

In the 1960s, well after his adoption and development of serialism, Stravinsky felt that although *Perséphone* begins tentatively, the B♭ music in 3/8 metre near the end is long, and the melodramas beget large stretches of ostinato, he still loved the music.[33] He defended the score of *Perséphone*, stating that it was an indissoluble whole in which many previous compositional tendencies were renewed, and that it was the present link in a continuum of works from *Oedipus Rex*, whose autonomy had in no way been diminished by his abstention from the spectacular.[34]

Stravinsky's article on *Perséphone* protests that music is not thought, waxing and waning according to the 'temperatures' of the action, but is given only to put things in order, to pass from an individualist, anarchic state to an ordered one, perfectly conscious and 'pourvu de garanties de vitalité at de durée' [*furnished with guarantees of vitality and life*].[35] He commanded the editors of *Excelsior,* who had omitted the last paragraph of his article on *Perséphone*, to reinstate and reprint it, asserting that he was on a perfectly sure road and that the projections of things that were felt and true were not 'mere caprices of his nature'. Drawing an analogy between his art and a nose that is not manufactured but just is, he declared that something that is functioning is not open for discussion or criticism.[36]

Paul Valéry, 'a deep source of intellectual and moral support' to Stravinsky on two important occasions in his life, wrote to Stravinsky after attending a performance of *Perséphone* to say that he was only a profane listener, 'but the divine detachment of your work touched me ... The point is to attain purity through the will ... LONG LIVE YOUR NOSE'.[37]

---

33   Ibid.

34   Interview 29 April and 1 May, 1934. In White, Eric W. 1985. Appendix 1, 581.

35   Op. cit., 580.

36   Op. cit., 581.

37   Stravinsky, Igor & Craft, Robert. 1981: *Memories and Commentaries,* 76. Later, Stravinsky asked Valéry to read and criticise the literary style of his lectures on the poetics of music, to be given in French at Harvard University. Referring to a conversation between St John Perse and Einstein about chance, Stravinsky said he simply did not understand chance in art: 'One has a nose. The nose scents and it chooses. The artist is like a pig snouting truffles'. Craft, Robert. 1972, 148.

6   Darker Times

Robert Craft was of the opinion that in the years around 1944 Stravinsky was undergoing a period of intense spiritual searching.[38] Hitherto, Stravinsky had often adapted techniques for organising rhythm and movement from extra-musical sources, particularly poetry and the visual arts, but his spiritual reading at this time suggests that he was seeking new directions. Whilst preparing his lectures on the poetics of music to be given at Harvard 1939–40, Stravinsky had turned again to Nesmelov's *The Science of Man*, and also the writings of Bishop Nicolas of Cusa (1401–64); both writers were deeply involved in explicating the relationship of human consciousness to the transcendent.[39]

Rooted in the thought of Dionysius the Areopagite and the neo-classical, humanist and scholastic traditions, Nicolas was an influential writer and church reformer who was concerned to unite the various factions of the Roman Church. His writings, which are of a metaphorical nature, concern the cognitive functions of the human mind and the 'knowability' of God. Nicolas believed the human mind to be an image of God's mind: just as God's mind, 'Divine Simplicity', *en*folds the true natures of all the things *un*folded from it, so the human mind enfolds concepts while unfolding them in a conceptual universe. Created things have oneness and unity in the mind of God, but are unfolded in the plurality and variety of Creation; similarly, human beings unfold a variety of concepts that unite in the realm of knowledge.

Bishop Nicolas meditated on the concept of God as 'the coincidence of opposites'. In a celebrated example he cites the interaction of a circle and tangent to show how humankind can think beyond the limitations of material things to the Divine.[40] He imagined a tangent approaching a circle so that the circumference of the circle appears to be increasing; if this movement is extrapolated to infinity, the circumference of the circle will appear less and less curved and the two will eventually be able to join together. Nicolas used this (mathematically impossible) image as an analogy of how created beings may move towards the Creator and how all things may eventually coincide in God as nothing but God.

Stravinsky's interest in Bishop Nicolas' writings lay, perhaps, in two particular areas of his thinking. Firstly, Nicolas saw the human mind not only as an image of God's mind but that there was a constant connection between them. He perceived the human mind as a measure that sets the limit of all things and

---

38   Stravinsky, Vera & Craft, Robert. 1979, 356.
39   Craft, Robert. 1992, 82.
40   God is Absolute Unity and Oneness: there is no opposite to the ineffable Infinite.

believed that the 'knowability of God' may be explored through mathematical ideas. He considered the arithmetic, geometry, numbers, planes and solid figures constructed by the human mind – often moving or constructing other mentally-imageable figures – to be the most certain form of knowledge of God.[41] He presents mathematical ideas as a paradigm of how the oneness of the human mind is gradually unfolded to create a conceptual universe: the number series unfolds units in the human mind just as God unfolds his Creation. Bishop Nicolas' thought 'joins the concept of an enfolding God and an unfolding universe to the certainty of mathematics and to the Christian tradition that everything is created in the divine word or *Logos*'.[42] Perhaps Stravinsky thought of Nicolas' mathematical metaphors as a possible source of new designs for temporal forms to connect the human mind with the Divine. In the course of this creative activity, human beings would also become participants in God's creativity, a concept central to the writings of Jacques Maritain.[43]

Secondly, Nicolas endeavours to make the transcendent, infinite God, whom he calls the 'maximum', more accessible to his Creation, whom he calls the contracted 'minimum', who are limited images of God. He perceives that we are assimilated or likened in some way to the objects of our knowledge, and in this way we are able to liken ourselves to our Creator. In response to a request from the Benedictine monks of Tegernsee he set them the spiritual exercise of looking at an image of the suffering Christ in which his eyes are looking straight forward out of the picture. Nicolas teaches them to apprehend the divine through this icon and expounds upon the workings of the human mind. Jesus' gaze invites them to enter the world of the picture and to look beyond him as the transparent image of God, to God. Although this quickly becomes the dominant experience, Nicolas tells the monks that they will simultaneously understand that Jesus' eye contact is not really taking place: the mind moves backwards and forwards across a great distance of time and space between the depth of the image and the realisation of the illusion. This juxtaposition of two opposing perceptions creates an ambiguity that allows the human mind to escape the familiar limitations of time and space and to experience a transcendent reality.[44] It was a technique that Stravinsky had instinctively

---

41   The Book of Wisdom 11.20: 'but you have set all things in order by measure and number and weight'.

42   Cusanus, Nicolaus [Nicolas of Cusa]: Stanford Encyclopedia of Philosophy.

43   At the end of his life Stravinsky wryly remarked that his 'human measure' was absolutely physical and immediate. He was made 'bodily ill … by sound electronically speyed for overtone removal'. Stravinsky, Igor & Craft, Robert. 1982, 127.

44   The method recalls the technique of Hokusai's cartoons.

employed, for example, in juxtaposing two independent lines of movement to capture the elusive time quality of *Three Japanese Lyrics,* and two differently-paced circular surfaces to evoke the heavenly realms in the third movement of *Symphony of Psalms.*

Like Isaiah, Nicolas sees Creation as in a dynamic, dialectical relationship with God, in which things proceed from, and return to God simultaneously, a concept also found in the final words of Stravinsky's *Poetics of Music.*[45] Nicolas' philosophical ideas seem to have offered Stravinsky some timely comfort in his search for new musical structures with a mathematical or proportional basis with which to create new perceptive spaces.

Stravinsky's reading at this time also included the militant Catholic writers Léon Bloy (a friend of Jacques and Raissa Maritain) and Georges Bernanos, as well as parts of the *Summa Theologica* of St Thomas Aquinas. After a sudden conversion to the Catholic faith, Léon Bloy had been inspired by the report of a vision of Our Lady of La Salette, whom he believed to have delivered an apocalyptic message about the 'end times'. Like Stravinsky, he was a man of strong views: his writings attacked rationalism, and in particular the contemporary business community, as being too worldly. Although making many enemies through his explosive temper, Bloy exerted considerable influence on succeeding writers.[46] As with Stravinsky's brief period of sympathy for Mussolini, Bernanos renounced his enthusiasm for fascism after seeing the effects of the War in Minorca, and emigrated to Brazil, from where he mocked the Vichy regime. A former soldier, wounded in the First World War, he was a strong supporter of the Free French Forces under Charles de Gaulle.[47]

Much given to writing in the margins of books, Stravinsky criticised C. F. Ramuz's *Questions* for its 'Protestantism', and approved C. A. Cingria's Roman Catholic views. But it was his almost daily reading of Jacques-Bénigne Bossuet's *Méditations sur L'Evangile,* that continued to shape his spiritual formation.[48]

---

45   Isaiah 55. 10–11, and Stravinsky, Igor. 1947, 141–2.

46   Léon Bloy (1846–1917) has had a strong influence on writers including Graham Greene, Jorge Luis Borges and John Irving, and in 2013 was quoted by Pope Francis in his first homily as Pope. According to the historian John Connelly, Bloy's radical interpretation of chapters 9–11 of St Paul's Letter to the Romans influenced theologians at the Second Vatican Council (1962–5) to change the Catholic attitude to Judaism.

47   In 1947 Bernanos was approached to write the screenplay for a film based on a novella by Gertrud von Le Fort, about the execution of the Carmelite nuns of Compiègne in 1797. Although not adopted at the time, Bernanos' literary executor secured its publication in 1949 after his death, entitling it *Dialogues des Carmelites*. Poulenc adapted this screenplay for his opera of the same name in 1957. Georges Bernanos (1888–1948) won the Grand Prix de Rome for *Diary of a Country Priest* (1936).

48   Stravinsky, Vera & Craft, Robert. 1979, 356.

Bishop Jacques-Bénigne Bossuet (1627–1704), a theologian and court preacher to Louis XIV of France, was appointed tutor to the Dauphin in 1671 before becoming Bishop of Meaux in 1681. His *Méditations* (1694–95) comprise four volumes of short sections to be read daily in which he expounds texts from the Gospels. In 1913, the *Catholic Encyclopedia* ranked Bossuet even higher than St Augustine and St John Chrysostom as the greatest orator and preacher of all time. Bossuet's writing has a simple down-to-earth eloquence that focuses on ethical rather than doctrinal matters. Beginning with the Sermon on the Mount, and 'the eternal joy proposed under different names in the eight beatitudes', his short chapters include meditations on the Lord's Prayer and the Last Supper and a variety of other spiritual matters. Day 21, for example, meditates on 'Prayer, and the presence of God in secret', a matter, perhaps, close to Stravinsky's heart. Bossuet taught that Jesus' disciples must not only follow His words and examples, but pray for the continual influence of divine Grace. The fourth volume begins with a commentary on the farewell discourses of Jesus at the Last Supper as recorded in the Gospel according to St John, chapters 15–17. In this text, Jesus uses the analogy of a vine and its branches to describe his relationship to his followers. He teaches them that the Father is like a gardener, who prunes barren branches and cleans fruiting branches to make them more fruitful still. Jesus assures them that those who remain in him, like the branches of a vine, will bear much fruit, but those who do not remain in him are like branches that are thrown away and wither. Those who remain in Jesus and in his words may ask whatever they wish and it will be done, to the Father's glory.[49] This text, together with Bossuet's commentary, would have spoken to Stravinsky's deep faith and encouraged him as he persevered, despite fierce criticism, in his musical mission. The text continues with Jesus' commandment to his disciples to love one another as God has loved Him and as He loves them,[50] a new Christian understanding of God that is proclaimed in the text from the *First Letter of John.* Stravinsky later set this text at the heart of *Canticum Sacrum* (1955).[51]

At this time Stravinsky was also given a copy of Bossuet's *Elévations sur les Mystères* (written in the same years as *Méditations sur L'Evangile*) by Abbé Fortrier, who had been particularly impressed on hearing Stravinsky's 1944 *Sonata* for two pianos performed by Nadia Boulanger and one of her pupils.[52]

---

49   John 15.1–8 (New English Bible).
50   John 15.12.
51   First Letter of John 4.7 (Vulgate version).
52   Stravinsky, Vera & Craft, Robert. 1979, 648.

In 1944, Stravinsky also visited Santa Clara, the convent of the Dominican sisters in Sinsinawa, Wisconsin, and was often in the company of Jacques Maritain.

After Stravinsky's *Poetics of Music*, the spiritual substance of his works became increasingly explicit. Unusually, his work had even begun to be influenced by external events: the first movement of his *Symphony in Three Movements,* begun in 1942 as a 'concerto for orchestra', was affected by a documentary about scorched earth tactics in China, as was its third movement by newsreels and documentaries showing goose-stepping soldiers.[53] Stravinsky had also been approached to write the music for Franz Werfel's film, *Song of Bernadette* (1943), in which Bernadette Soubirous, a schoolgirl in Lourdes, had reported eighteen visions of the Virgin Mary near the Massabielle caves. Following Our Lady's instructions, Bernadette had opened up the waters of a spring that had brought miraculous cures. After intense scrutiny of the Virgin's appearances by sceptical church authorities, Bernadette had eventually been canonised. Stravinsky, as both a believer in miracles and the beneficiary of one, began to compose serenely beautiful music for the Virgin's first appearance that eventually became the second movement of *Symphony in Three Movements* (1943–5).

7   Babel (1944)

In March 1944 Nathaniel Shilkret, a staff composer at MGM, commissioned Stravinsky to contribute to a composite work: six Creation stories recounted by the Yahwist plus an Introduction, to be set by seven different composers.[54] This work, *Genesis Suite*, was to be recorded on six 78-rpm discs. Schoenberg (originally Hindemith) was asked to write the first movement, a wordless choral-orchestral Prelude; Shilkret himself would write the story of Creation, Tansman, the story of Adam and Eve, Milhaud, that of Cain and Abel, Castelnuovo-Tedesco, The Flood, Ernst Toch, the Covenant of the Rainbow, and Stravinsky, the final movement, the story of the Tower of Babel.

Set for male chorus, orchestra and male narrator to words from the first Book of Moses (Genesis 2. 1–9), *Babel* lasts about seven minutes. The story illustrates Man's hubris, his rebellion against God and God's response, a subject close to Stravinsky's heart. Welding many traditions into one primeval history,

---

53   Stravinsky, Igor & Craft, Robert. 1982, 50–52.
54   The opening books of the Old Testament combine different sources. The Yahwist is the name given to one, or a school, of these authors who used the name Yahweh to refer to God.

the Yahwist records that originally humanity was united and had one language and one vocabulary. A great migration of people came to settle upon a plain in Shinar in Babylon; they built a city called Babel, which means 'Gate of God'. They wished to establish a nation, to build a city to show their strong self-reliance, and to erect a great tower with its top in the heavens in order to make a name for themselves. Here, the Yahwist's choice of words brings out the irony that the people, rejoicing in their inventiveness, built the tower with bricks, not stone, and used bitumen for mortar, thus building something which, from the very first, was essentially unsatisfactory and perishable.[55]

The first section of *Babel* at the slow tempo of $\downarrow$ = 42 evokes the long chronological time of the migration: Stravinsky constructs it with a sinuous figure of five quavers which cuts across the metre and moves, rapidly but erratically, from cellos and basses in a very low register to the violins four octaves higher. Above it, the contrasting timbre of the solo oboe's bare tonic-dominant figures (fig. 1) opens a large musical space, diminishing the sense of the present moment and distancing this first section into a remote historic era.

The narrator suddenly announces 'And the Lord came down!' This ancient way of speaking evokes God's great distance, and by contrast, the work of humankind as tiny. Stravinsky, always against any 'literal' representation of God, Jesus Christ or the Virgin Mary, sets God's words for a two-part male chorus in the style of strotchny chant: solidly homorhythmic, it has a large number of open and dissonant intervals of a 4th, 5th, and 7th, even a sustained augmented 4th.[56] The quality of movement in this second section contrasts with that of the first section, the dense texture of this passage having little melodic, rhythmic and timbral variety. Although a substantial presence, God remains 'outside' time in an other-worldly haze of tremolos and triplets. The tremolos cease as God takes action (fig. 13).

The tower is not completed; it stands as a symbol of the people's inability to build a stable and intrinsically valuable society. God confuses the language of the people and scatters the people abroad 'upon the face of the earth' into

---

55   von Rad, Gerhard. 1981, 150–1. In the second millenium BCE, Babylon was the heart of the ancient world and its central power. The Babylonians built cult buildings of gigantic proportions. The ziggurat Etemenanki, for example, stood, 'a marvel of coloured, glazed tiles, over 297 feet high ... founded on the breast of the underworld ... its pinnacle reaching to heaven'. Ibid.

56   In 1935, Stravinsky considered collaborating with Charles Chaplin, to film a Passion play in a nightclub, but had felt that Chaplin's suggestion that Christ be represented on stage would be sacrilegious. In 1944 Stravinsky was invited by Mercedes de Acosta to compose the music for the stage production of her play *The Mother of Christ*, but Stravinsky insisted that the Virgin Mary be represented on stage, not by a human actress, but by a light.

many nations. The contrasting momentum of this third section marked *con moto* ($\bullet$ = 120) is reminiscent of Elijah's flight in *Symphony of Psalms*. Although musically descriptive of scattering, its two layers of movement, based on the intervals of the first section, are juxtaposed with one layer twice the speed of the other (fig. 19). This not only detracts from the pointillistic effect but creates great depth, drawing attention to the grave outcome of this story. In the final section, Stravinsky slows the forward movement with one last reference to 'Elijah's' motif, and sustained chords.

8   Mass (1944–48)

Some writers on Stravinsky have expressed surprise that, as a communicant of the Russian Orthodox Church, he wrote a Catholic Mass. The Catholic Church is in full or partial intercommunion with other churches, but Pope Paul VI defined the relationship of the Catholic and Russian Orthodox Church as so profound 'that it lacks little to attain the fullness that would permit a common celebration of the Lord's Eucharist'.[57]

There is only one point of doctrinal difference between the Orthodox and Catholic churches: the *filioque* clause. The Eastern Church uses the original form of the Nicene Creed which reads 'I believe … in the Holy Spirit … who proceeds from the Father'. The Western Church inserted an extra phrase: 'who proceeds from the Father *and the Son*' (*filioque*), which the Orthodox Church regards as heresy. Despite Stravinsky's uncompromisingly dogmatic beliefs this doctrinal difference does not seem to have been a difficulty for him: the *Russian Credo* of 1932 (revised 1964) sets the Eastern form, while the Catholic *Credo* of 1948 includes the *filioque* clause.

Although there are differences of emphasis and understanding between the Orthodox and Catholic churches owing to the original differences of temperament between Latins and Greeks, it is quite possible to feel at home in both traditions. The differences in emphasis have been described by Bishop Timothy Ware:

> In the early Church … Latin thought was influenced by juridical ideas, by the concepts of Roman Law, while the Greeks understood theology in the context of worship and in the light of the Holy Liturgy. When thinking

---

57   Pope Paul VI, 14.12.1975: 13–18. Full communion is defined as 'those bonds of communion – faith, sacraments and pastoral governance – that permit the Faithful to receive the life of grace within the Church'.

about the Trinity, Latins started with the unity of the Godhead, Greeks
with the three-ness of the persons; when reflecting on the Crucifixion,
Latins thought primarily of Christ the Victim, Greeks of Christ the Victor;
Latins talked more of redemption, Greeks of deification; and so on ...
each had its place in the fullness of Catholic tradition.[58]

There was also a difference of understanding with regard to the organisation of
the Church: the Eastern Church did not assign universal supremacy and infal-
libility to a Pope, but held that, in matters of faith, the final decision rested
with a Council representing all the bishops of the Church. Stravinsky clearly
toyed with the idea of formally embracing Roman Catholicism, but his cultural
roots and his childhood love of Old Slavonic as the language of prayer largely
determined his continuing allegiance to Russian Orthodoxy. He had thought
'many times' about why he had never become a Roman Catholic; he had 'a
great feeling' for Rome, and had often thought about the Latin language and
the apostolic history of the papacy.[59]

Stravinsky believed in the authority of the Pope and rejoiced in his friendship with Cardinal Roncalli, the Cardinal Patriarch of Venice, later Pope John
XXIII.[60] In 1956, Roncalli invited Stravinsky to present the world première of
Canticum Sacrum in the Cathedral of San Marco in Venice.[61] Six years later as
Pope John XXIII he signed the patent creating Stravinsky a knight commander
with the star of the Papal Order of St Sylvester. At the ceremony following a performance of his *Mass*, Stravinsky, 'never more serious in his bearing', received
the blessing of Rome, an accolade almost invariably reserved for Roman
Catholics. Stravinsky valued this honour very deeply, to the point of dressing in
the full insignia of his Papal knighthood on his last birthday, June 18th 1970.[62]
Moreover, Stravinsky had chosen the church of ss Giovanni e Paolo in Venice
and the island cemetery of San Michele as the place of his funeral and burial

---

58   Ware, Timothy. 1983, 56. Ware uses Catholic in the sense of universal.
59   Horgan, Paul. 1972, 203.
60   Talking of the Church with the Evelyn Waughs, 'S. shines, showing himself to be at least as
      ultramontanist as Mr W ... and as prone to believe in the miraculous emulsification of St
      Januarius' blood'. Craft, Robert. 1972, 8.
61   During one of Stravinsky's visits to the Vatican, Pope John XXIII, who enjoyed quizzing
      Stravinsky about the latest books, artists and composers, entreated Stravinsky, rather
      reproachfully, to 'call him up' next time he was in Rome. He also asked Stravinsky for
      his autograph, at which Stravinsky was somewhat nonplussed. Horgan, Paul. 1972, 137–
      139. Horgan also records Stravinsky's visits to the Catholic Archbishop Edwin Byrne,
      Archbishop of Santa Fe, and their affectionate friendship: Op. cit., 146, 218.
62   Op. cit., 276.

long before his death, because it had been Roncalli's parish.[63] Stravinsky would receive another Papal decoration in 1965, this time from Pope Paul VI before a performance of *Symphony of Psalms* in the Vatican.

Stravinsky hoped that his setting of the Mass would be an effective challenge to the decline of the Church and a protest against the Platonic tradition of music as anti-moral, for 'music praises God ... it is the Church's greatest ornament'.[64] He thought that this falling away from God in the character of Church music was reflected in 'religious' religious music and 'secular' religious music which is 'inspired by humanity in general, by art, by *Ubermensch*, by goodness, and by goodness knows what'.[65] Theodore Stravinsky, after describing his father as 'One for whom a Truth exists, a truth outside of self – necessary, transcendent, independent of "self" ', also observed that his father considered the 'modern' world to have committed apostasy.[66] Church music of the past had expressed penitence, humility, joy and adoration, and without the richness of all of its forms, Stravinsky feared that parts of the musical spirit were in disuse and would disappear with the form.[67] For him, qualities of the spirit, such as the joy of the Doxology (*Symphonies of Wind Instruments*) and the serene glory of the Laudate (*Symphony of Psalms*) were all but extinct, and did not exist in secular music. He held that one had to be a believer to compose the musical forms of the Church: the attitudes of prayer and penitence, and the sense of impending judgement that would characterise Stravinsky's late works, *Canticum Sacrum, Threni* and *Requiem Canticles*, could not be secularised. In his *Mass*, Stravinsky restores these spiritual qualities by creating a meaningful passage through time qualities appropriate to each of its movements, from the focused 'now' of the Credo to the timelessness of the Sanctus and Agnus Dei.

At this time, Stravinsky was being introduced to the medieval and renaissance music of the West. Nadia Boulanger, a champion of Stravinsky's music from the days of *The Firebird,* had introduced him to the music of Guillaume

---

63   Op. cit., 275.

64   Stravinsky, Igor & Craft, Robert. 1979, 124.

65   Ibid.

66   Stravinsky, Theodor. 1953, 18. Robert Craft wrote: 'Having lived close to Stravinsky for nearly a quarter of a century ... I knew him to be ... "profoundly religious". He believed in the Devil Incarnate and in a literal, Dantesque Hell, Purgatory, Paradise. And he was deeply superstitious, forever crossing himself and those around him, wearing sacred medals, and performing compulsive acts without which the auguries for the day were certain to be unfavourable. Furthermore, he believed in miracles, both large and of the Houdini sort, and never questioned the provenance of any sacred relic. Dogmatism was another part of his religion, as it was of Stravinsky himself ...' Craft, Robert. 1992, 288.

67   Ibid.

de Machaut and the isorhythmic motet, and also to the music of Josquin des Prez, Lassus, Byrd and Monteverdi. Robert Craft, too, had introduced Stravinsky to a large repertory of 'old' music, from Machaut and Josquin des Prez, to Lassus and Schütz.[68] Stravinsky came to see the history of the Western Church as a series of attacks against polyphony, the polyphonic marvels of Josquin, Ockeghem, Compère and Brumel being the true musical expression of Western Christendom. Even so, his own Mass setting expresses each spiritual quality with a mix of styles: homophonic movement, chordal chanting, dméstvenny-style melodic lines, two-part strotchny chant and antiphonal canonic constructions. Only short sections are treated contrapuntally: Christe eleison, the 'Amen' of the Credo, Pleni sunt coeli et terra, the final Benedictus qui venit (fig. 51), and the first two choral statements of the Agnus Dei.

The purpose of the Mass is to make effective in the present the power of Christ's self-sacrifice on the Cross, so that, in this work above all others, Stravinsky sets the text with total clarity. 'Partly provoked' after playing through some 'rococo-operatic sweets-of-sin' Masses by Mozart, Stravinsky scored his setting for mixed chorus and the 'cooler' timbres of a double wind quintet.

8.1   Kyrie

The retention of a Greek invocation at the beginning of a Latin Mass (divorced from the litany of which it was once the refrain) represents an early attempt to unite the Eastern and Western parts of the Church in worship. Thus, it is particularly appropriate that Stravinsky sets the Kyrie with both the 19th century homophonic style of Russian Orthodox worship and Roman Catholic polyphony. Prayers are made to the Trinity: three petitions each to God the Father, God the Son, and God the Holy Spirit. They express the desire for forgiveness, so that the community can proceed as one body to praise and glorify God.

The first and third petitions of the first Kyrie and the first Christe petition are preceded by 'bell-strikes' on E♭. As at the moment of consecration in the Mass, bells command attention, create resonant sound waves, and mark the moment as sacred. Each of the three initial Kyrie petitions resolves differently, the third Kyrie elongated on a second inversion chord before leading into the three petitions to Christ. The counterpoint of the second Christe Eleison is accompanied by repeated staccato figures that are taken up by the voices in the third Christe Eleison. The texture recalls the 1st movement of *Symphony of Psalms* and the staccato accompaniment to the Psalmist's plea for forgiveness. An instrumental Interlude allows time for meditation on these prayers before

---

68   Craft, Robert. 2006, 250, 189.

EX. 55   Opening of the Gloria (at pitch)

the three final Kyries continue the repeating staccato figures more urgently. The many second inversion chords give the movement a floating quality.

8.2   *Gloria*

In this movement the Christian community seeks a transcendent space in which to praise God's glory. This space stands in contrast to the constrictions of the physical world and celebrates the unique blend of divinity and humanity to be found in the person of Jesus Christ. Stravinsky's stark contrasts reflect both the difference between the earthly and heavenly spaces, and the dual nature of Christ. The opening bars for oboe and trumpet suggest a medieval pneuma or a festive dméstvenny chant, and continue above the solo alto (Ex. 55).

The solo soprano (bar 12) is accompanied by a bassoon in its high register, the cor anglais forming the bass line. These constructions open a floating musical space and negate the sense of clock-time. In an abrupt change of pitch and density, this opening is contrasted with the chanted praise of those on earth (fig. 13): the chanting introduces asymmetric metres within a strictly regular pulse and the natural accents of speech are alternately emphasised and counterpointed by a repeated chord in the brass. The alternation of the light musical space and the dense, chanted surface becomes much more rapid as heaven and earth are brought closer (fig. 19). Each of the three final attributions of Jesus as Holy, the Lord, and the Most High is followed by a repeated chord for reed instruments, whose open spacing has the penetrative power of a striking bell.

8.3   *Credo*

The Credo returns to the here-and-now for the expression of doctrinal beliefs. Stravinsky made it clear that the word 'religious' did not correspond in his mind to states of feeling or sentiment, but to dogmatic beliefs.[69] He felt that 'religious music without religion was almost always vulgar', and, when asked if one had to be a believer to compose music for the Church, he replied, 'Certainly, and not merely a believer in symbolic figures, but in the Person of the Lord, the Person of the Devil, and the Miracles of the Church.'[70]

The Creed expresses belief in the Trinity and in the resurrection of Jesus Christ as an assurance of the continuing alliance between earth and heaven. Stravinsky sets this movement in an inexorably homophonic style. Both the *Russian Credo* in Old Slavonic (1932) and this Credo in Latin, have a consistently austere syllabic style, but where the former was diatonic, this movement is shaped by contrasts of harmonic clarity and non-diatonic density.

Stravinsky accentuates certain important beliefs in both settings. The 1932 *Credo* has a semitone clash at 'Boga istinna' [*true God*] (bar 20), while the 1948 Credo has a semitone clash at 'Deum verum de Deo vero' [*true God from true God*] (fig. 27). The note values are slightly lengthened in the 1932 setting at bars 29–30 and also in the Mass setting at figure 27 + 4 to mark the significance of God's Incarnation. In both settings, as in znamenny chant, Stravinsky connects spiritual ideas with variants of a single motif: the 1932 *Credo* simply connects belief in the three persons of the Trinity (bars 1–3, 9–11, 57–59), while the 1948 Mass setting repeats the opening phrase and connects it to 'Patrem omnipotentem', 'Et in unum Jesum Christum' (fig. 26 + 1), 'Et ex patre natum' (fig. 27 – 6), and 'Et resurrexit tertia die ... et ascendit in coelum, sedet ad dexteram patris' (fig. 33). The Latin text includes the controversial *filioque* clause, and the opening motif is not recalled until the Holy Spirit is worshipped and glorified with the Father and the Son (fig. 37), thus completing the Trinity.

While the 1932 *Credo* has a steady momentum, the pacing of the 1948 Credo is more varied. After the witness of the Prophets, three doctrinal beliefs are chanted emphatically on a single chord: belief in the Catholic and Apostolic Church, belief in one baptism for the forgiveness of sins, and belief in the resurrection of the dead and the life to come. These beliefs are highlighted in the musical flow as particularly important articles of faith.

Stravinsky sets the Creed to facilitate the declaration of beliefs, and the effect of its inexorable rhythmic homogeneity bears out his quip that 'there is much to believe'. The slightest departure from this austere style stands out clearly: note values are extended for Christ's incarnation, that is also marked by a brief Interlude for reflection in the wind parts (fig. 31); the elongation of

69   Stravinsky, Igor & Craft, Robert. 1982, 26.
70   Stravinsky, Igor & Craft, Robert. 1979, 124–5.

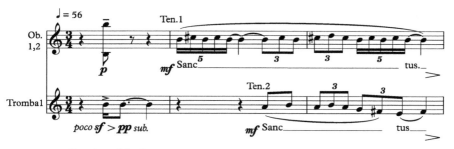

EX. 56   Opening of the Sanctus

syllabic motion on 'Et vitam venturi saeculi' [*And the life of the world to come*] (fig. 41) prepares for the reflective amen.

8.4   *Sanctus*

The Sanctus expresses the Christian view of the world as an expanding reflection of the Divine, and contemplates Being and Love as both present in the world and transcendent to it. In contemplating the holiness of the Lord of Hosts, the community of believers also contemplates the holiness of Creation itself, 'not as elevation and distance in space but as an elevation of quality which does not exclude the most intimate presence'.[71]

This expanding reflection opens with a 'bell-strike' on B, and three sharply accented alternations of 'Sanctus' on B and C♯ for two tenors in dméstvenny style that evoke the spreading of sound waves throughout the world (Ex. 56).

Each phrase, including that of the following solo quartet, ends with a different harmonisation of the central pitch B at a slow crotchet pulse (♩= 56). Stravinsky's setting of 'Pleni sunt coeli et terra' [*Heaven and earth are full (of your glory)*] as stately dotted rhythms for solo duet increasing to a solo quartet is a perfect illustration of his insight that 'abundance is a quality not a quantity'.[72] The increasing fullness of heaven and earth is accompanied by two sustained and widely-spaced lines for brass. The much faster Hosanna (♩= 98) returns to the central pitch B, and the patterning of two 'circular' surfaces: the heterophonic vocal parts within a short pitch range are juxtaposed to lively cross-accented chords in the wind and brass, the increased rhythmic complexity expressing boundless joy in Creation.

---

71   Zundel, Maurice. 1943, 164.
72   Vera Stravinsky's diary, October 27th, 1946: Craft, Robert, ed. 1985, 138.

Stravinsky's solemn Benedictus contemplates the mystery of the Incarnation with a dignified double-dotted bass line in the bassoons. The final phrase, tutti, relaxes and expands into a slow rate of harmonic change towards the return of the Hosanna. This Hosanna, a variation on the first, is even more joyful and ends assertively by juxtaposing slower cross-accented voices to slowly changing chords in the wind and brass.

8.5   *Agnus Dei*

In the Agnus Dei the Christian community meditates on the deep mystery of Christ's sacrificial self-giving. The vocal and instrumental forces, with contrasting timbres but similar density, are heard antiphonally, creating a spiral movement: they are equal and complementary for the first time in this Mass setting. The opening instrumental 'prayer' occurs three times, forming the central axis of the movement and acting as a meditative refrain from which the voices venture further afield with each entry. The opening theme, a step-wise cadential figure that suggests both Agnus Dei and 'amen', is arranged to alternate between the timbre of trumpet and oboe. The first choral response presents a canon at the 9th between female and male voices, while the second reverses the entries. At the third choral response, the final prayer petitioning peace is set homophonically.

The opening theme and its reverse form rise through the brass and wind parts, sealing the structure with a timeless meditation upon the mystery of the 'one perfect and sufficient sacrifice'. The dense canonic writing of this Agnus Dei creates great depth of time quality appropriate to the Lamb of God as the offering of the temporal to the timeless.

Throughout these more difficult years Stravinsky's commitment to time in music diversified, his energies focussing on certain specific areas. He continued to work on the structural relationship of parts of a form to the whole, but his 'spiritual' works also made a variety of important statements. His composition of a *Pater Noster, Russian Credo* and *Ave Maria* recovered the haunting intonations of the old Russian chant and folk song that preceded the 19th century western harmonies of composers such as Bortniansky; his Mass for the Catholic Church recovered the spirit and the forms that were in danger of being lost in more secular times. *Perséphone* rose to the double challenge of composing music that was both lyrical and objectively sacred in character, while simultaneously embodying both the *absence* of time and the process of regeneration from winter to spring. Conversely, in writing the brief work *Babel*, Stravinsky demonstrated his temporal skills in conveying both the long time-span of the migration and scattering of the people, and the intervention of God outside time, in the here-and-now. The important topics of his writing in this period – principally his notes for the lectures that were published as *Poetics of Music* – are concerned with the co-ordination of mankind and Time. In the 1930s and 1940s, throughout these explorations of time in music, Stravinsky enjoyed the friendship and support of Jacques Maritain.

9   The Poetics of Stravinsky and Maritain

In 1938, some years before writing *Babel* and the *Mass*, Stravinsky had been approached to give some lectures on the poetics of music at the University of Harvard. In June of that year, the text of the lectures was nearing completion; they had been written by Roland-Manuel and Pierre Souvtchinsky after meetings with Stravinsky and with the help of his somewhat cryptic notes. Souvtchinsky wrote to Stravinsky, apparently in response to Stravinsky's forlorn confidences concerning his spiritual and creative life, to offer him some comfort and advice: 'Do not even dream that you have reached a "dead end". In the first place, what is happening to you is a transition from one cycle to another.'[73]

Stravinsky's notes for the first of the lectures are full of his frustration at not being understood: reactions to his work, he said, had been violent, misdirected, misaddressed, and demonstrated the 'vice' that resides in the whole musical conscience. With his early works things had changed, not on the aesthetic level but 'in the mode of expression': the popular interpretation of his creative development as 'Revolution at the time of Sacre and assimilation of the revolutionary conquests now' was wrong.[74] The published text makes the point that the ideas that Stravinsky is developing will continue to serve as a basis for musical composition because they have been developed in actual practice. It adds that Stravinsky's creative work 'is the fruit of his conscience and his faith', and recounts Stravinsky's plea that credit be given to the speculative concepts that have engendered his work and that have developed along with it.[75] Many of these 'speculative concepts' are not only expanded upon in

---

73   Craft, Robert. 1992, 90.

74   Stravinsky's lecture notes are given in Craft, Robert. 1992, 93–98.

75   Stravinsky, Igor. 1947, 7. Stravinsky chose a native French speaker, Roland-Manuel, to transcribe his notes into French after reading his review of Stravinsky's *Autobiography*. Roland-Manuel was a professional musician (composer) and author-critic. There is not a single complete sentence by Stravinsky in the final text of *Poetics of Music*: Craft, Robert. 1992, 82.

the text, but clearly echo the views of Maritain as expressed in *La Philosophie Bergsonienne* and *Art et Scolastique*.

Stravinsky's notes for the first lecture include the 'making' of music as speculation in sound and time, and analysis of the elements of time and movement as *Chronos* – Maritain's *matière prochaine*. This 'making' is achieved through a dialectic between contrast and similitude in both music and creation, and realised as polychromy and monochromy. A potentially important note concerning 'meditation in active and passive music (author – listener)' is not taken up in the final text. Both the notes for this first lecture and the published text conclude by stating that he will single out general principles and particular facts in a method of 'synchronisation', for the real hierarchy of phenomena and also the relationships of things take form on a completely different level. This 'synchronisation' is a complex reference both to the ideas of Propp and Lévi-Strauss on myth and ritual, and to the spiritual perception afforded by Maritain's *matière éloignée*.

Stravinsky's notes for the second lecture also reflect Maritain's views on the two levels of art. His materials include movement in time, metre, rhythm, the sonorous scale, and the sonority of sound as pitch, register and timbre, while the phenomenon of music is defined as 'sounds organised by the conscious action of man'. In amplifying Stravinsky's notes, the published text of chapter two echoes Maritain's contemporary work on 'creative intuition' and a transcendent level of art: music is the result of the appetite of the artist who is 'gifted for that task with a very special aptitude' for putting nature's many voices in order.[76] It is reason 'enlightened by instinct (intuition)' that can 'lay hold of the phenomenon of music at its origins',[77] music 'that will make us participate actively in the working of a mind that orders, gives life and creates'.[78] The chapter continues by discussing the 'exclusively musical experiencing of time'. Stravinsky's note (j) refers to scheme, form and system and the co-existence in a mechanical or organic unit of different forms: in the text this becomes a reference to the framework of classic tonality 'in the scholastic sense of the word'.[79]

Stravinsky's notes for the third lecture refer to the making of a 'piece' by an artisan, as opposed to a 'composer', which is seen as a pejorative term. Roland-Manuel's text refers to Maritain by name, and describes the artist's

---

76   Stravinsky, Igor. 1947, 23.
77   Op. cit., 24–5.
78   Ibid, 24.
79   Op. cit., 35.

task as essentially practical activity.[80] Stravinsky's notes (c) to (f) list invention, imagination as self-expression and intellectual imagination, the will and the accidental in the creative process, and the nature of inspiration; he reports that at a certain moment in the process of creating, creation begins to happen automatically. The text discusses the true nature of music as free speculation, the unhampered play of a work's functions, and artistic invention as the full realisation of a lucky find. An echo of Maritain's language of appetite, intuition, being, and 'light of intelligence' can be heard in the text in the references to practical activity, balance, and calculation through which the wind of the Spirit blows; were Stravinsky to be given a work in a perfectly completed form he would be embarrassed and nonplussed by it as by a hoax.[81]

The fourth lecture borrows the title *Musical Typology* from Pierre Souvtchinsky's 1938 article,[82] but deals, not with qualities of time, but with the problem of defining musical style, its continuity and discontinuity, the determinacy and indeterminacy of its evolution as musical history, and its arbitrary classifications. Stravinsky's notes turn to submission and ascendancy, 'the law to which any art must subject itself', while the published text of chapter four refers to the anarchic individualism which isolates the artist from his fellow-artists and from the public, and produces an age which seeks uniformity in matter and in which all universality in the realm of the spirit is shattered. The text states that universality stipulates submission to an established order and, echoing the philosophy of Maritain, that it is only by 'exalting the competent workman in the artist that a civilization communicates something of its order to works of art and speculation'. The good artisan 'dreams of achieving the *beautiful* only through the categories of the *useful* ...'[83]

Stravinsky's note on 'modernism' as an 'ineffectual' word becomes, in the published text, a comparison of art and spirituality; modernism is defined radically as a form of theological liberalism which is a fallacy condemned by the Church of Rome. It was Stravinsky's strong opinion that modernism in the arts would be open to an analogous condemnation.[84] The notes conclude with

---

80   Op. cit., 51–2. Asked if he agreed that writing music was a 'spiritual process', Stravinsky replied that it was a vocation. Stravinsky, Vera & Craft, Robert. 1979, 389.

81   Ibid, 53.

82   In December 1938, Stravinsky had read Pierre Souvtchinsky's essay, 'Reflections on the Typology of Musical Creation: The Notion of Time and Music' and had recommended it to Charles-Albert Cingria for publication in *La Nouvelle Revue Francaise*. Craft, R. 1992, 84.

83   Stravinsky, Igor. 1947, 75–76.

84   Theodore Stravinsky also speaks of the 'inestimable damage' caused by the false idea of modernism that has retarded the understanding of both contemporary art and Stravinsky's music. Stravinsky, Theodore. 1955, 17–18.

the statement that he is neither a revolutionary or a conservative, and (with important implications for Stravinsky's current legacy) that *he is not a modernist*. He states emphatically that he has always been taken for what he is not.

Stravinsky's notes for the fifth lecture simply state, 'Folklore and musical culture. Plainchant, sacred and profane music', but the published text refers to Balakirev, Mussorgsky, Borodin, Rimski-Korsakov and César Cui, who all 'seized upon popular melodies and *liturgical chants*'.[85] The text in chapter five refers to research undertaken into Russian historical and religious life, chiefly by Leontiev, Soloviev, Rosanov, Berdyaev, Fedorov, Nesmelov, and Diaghilev's Mir Iskusstva. The notes for the fifth lecture conclude with the importance of ordering art with the intellect, without which 'music has no value, or even existence, as art'.

Stravinsky's notes on performance for the sixth lecture return to the subject of time, specifically the different temporal levels involved in a work's realisation: 'Being, nothingness, and reality are simultaneous in a musical work'. The published text elaborates on the musical sins that militate against the faithful realisation of a work. The final notes (that also form the final words of *Poetics of Music*) declare the heart of Stravinsky's message: 'The true meaning of music. Like all the creative faculties of man, music is a quest for unity, communion, union with fellow beings and Being [illegible word], Monism, the Creator'.

While Stravinsky was preparing his lectures on the poetics of music, Jacques Maritain was working on his book, *Creative Intuition in Art and Poetry,* in which he defines the higher quality of an artistic object as 'l'expression ou la manifestation, dans une oeuvre convenablement proportionnée de quelque principe secret d'intelligibilité qui resplendit' [*the expression or manifestation, in a suitably proportioned work, of some secret principle of intelligibility that shines forth*].[86] Like Stravinsky, he believed that this intelligibility is created when 'la musique imite avec des sons et des rythmes ... "les moeurs", comme dit Aristote, et les mouvements de l'ame, le monde invisible qui s'agite en nous ...' [*music imitates ... "our ways" with its sounds and rhythms, as Aristotle said, and the movements of the spirit, the invisible world that stirs within us ...*][87]

Maritain had written several pages on 'creative emotion' or 'creative intuition' – 'something entirely different from the expression of feelings' – in *Frontières de la Poésie,* published in 1926.[88] He proposed that by means of

---

85   My italics.
86   Maritain, Jacques. 1947, 84.
87   Op. cit., 81–2.
88   Stravinsky, Vera & Craft, Robert. 1979, 222 where the title is wrongly given as *Funèbres de la Poésie.*

creative intuition, and without being aware of it, the artist speaks to himself in his work as God does in the act of creation. 'Only God can create', Stravinsky once remarked, 'I make music from music.' But Stravinsky, too, had felt that he created an object 'because God makes me create it, just as he has created me ...'[89]

Maritain proposed that [the artist] must 'subdue to his own purpose all these extraneous elements from the external world' in order to 'manifest his own substance in his creation',[90] just as Stravinsky felt that 'The need for restriction, for deliberately submitting to a style, has its source in the very depths of our nature ...'[91] As for expressing himself, Stravinsky liked Oscar Wilde's observation that 'every author always paints his own portrait'. Part of his admiration for Pushkin lay in the fact that 'being a poet to the finest fibres of his soul, Pushkin ridiculed all false, pseudo-philosophical ideologies, and adhered only to his art and true portrayal of his inner self'. Speaking at the end of his life about the precognitive sense he had of his material, Stravinsky added: 'one's forms are a stamp of oneself, of one's physical, bilateral apprehension of experience, and form and function are the same'.[92]

Maritain gave six lectures on creative intuition at the National Gallery of Art in Washington in the spring of 1952. A comparison of Stravinsky's views on the poetics and transcendence of art with those of Maritain taken from *Creative Intuition in Art and Poetry* (1953) (Table 3), illuminates the shared vision that nourished their friendship over many years.

Maritain continued to work on the idea that we exist in two modes, the body in clock-time and the soul outside time in eternity. Writing in *Art and Poetry* (1945) he suggested that '... music should cease only by emerging into a silence of another order ... where the soul for a moment tastes that time no longer is'.[93] The 'emerging into a silence of another order' would be an apt description of the experience that follows the conclusion of many of Stravinsky's works from *Les Noces* to *Requiem Canticles*.

Maritain's *Approches de Dieu* [Approaches to God] was published in 1955. Here he suggests that the thoughts and operations of the speculative intellect are not subject to 'the flux of impermanence' since they emerge 'above' time: Man therefore 'escapes' time by this activity to experience 'a succession

---

89   Stravinsky, Vera & Craft, Robert. 1979, 195.
90   Maritain, Jacques. 1954, 113.
91   Stravinsky, Igor. 1975, 131–2.
92   Stravinsky, Igor & Craft, R. 1982, 28 n.4.
93   Maritain, Jacques. 1954, 57.

TABLE 3   A comparison of Maritain and Stravinsky's views.
           Page numbers for Maritain are from *Creative Intuition in Art and Poetry*;
           Stravinsky's views are taken from *Poetics of Music* (PoM), *Themes and Conclusions*
           (T&C), *Conversations* (Conv), *Stravinsky in Pictures and Documents* (P&D),
           Autobiography (Auto), and *Dialogues* (Dial)

MARITAIN	STRAVINSKY
Poetry is that intercommunication between the inner being of things and the inner being of the human self which is a kind of divination. (3)	The profound meaning of music and its essential aim ... is to promote a communion, a union of man with his fellow man and with the Supreme Being. (*PoM* 18)
An abstract work of art returns to man a quality of the mind which is concealed in it: number and proportion make the senses rejoice in a property of their own. (6)	Something in my nature is satisfied by some aspect of an auditive shape. (*Conv.* 15) Musical form is mathematical because it is ideal. (*Conv.* 20) Is it possible to discover a reflective system between the language structure of the music and the structure of the phenomenal world? ... well, yes, perhaps eventually. (*T&C* 146–7)
Poetic objects exist as vehicles of actual, ideal communication, where two minds meet. (12) The oriental artist does not manifest subjectivity but meditates on life force (11). Oriental art is the opposite of Western individualism and never says 'I'. (19)	My further, personal belief is that the [Beethoven] quartets are a charter of human rights. (*T&C* 147) Individual caprice and intellectual anarchy ... isolate the artist from his fellow artists. (*PoM* 73) All that we are able to do is to surrender ourselves to the course of the experiment that is being conducted in and by us. (*P&D* 196)
Art ... while being aware of the supra-human, divine or magic or Dionysian power inherent in things, strives after the Intelligibility of things and intends to bring out their connivance with Reason. (20)	For here in classical dancing I see ... the eternal conflict in art between the Apollonian and the Dionysian principles. (*Auto.*100) Music unites the contrary attributes of being both intelligible and untranslatable. (Lévi-Strauss, *Introduction to Anton Webern: Perspectives.*)

TABLE 3   A comparison of Maritain and Stravinsky's views (*cont.*)

MARITAIN	STRAVINSKY
Truth, in speculative knowledge, is the conformity of the intellect with Being: truth in practical knowledge is the conformity of the intellect with the [creative] appetite. (47) Art is an inner quality that raises the human subject and his natural powers to a higher degree of vital formation and energy. (48)	All the problems of art … including the problem of Knowledge and Being revolve ineluctably about this question [the co-existence of the One and the Many]. (*PoM* 32) From the formal but intense and prolonged operation of our intelligence is derived a spiritual force, just as electricity comes from a generating plant. (*Tempo* 97, 71)
The poet knows himself only on condition that all things resound in him: a kind of revelation, both of the Self of the poet and of some particular flash of reality in the God-made universe. (114–5)	The more [the artist] eliminates all that is extraneous, all that is not his own, or 'in him', the greater is his risk of conflicting with the expectations of … the public. (*Auto* 175) The composer in me has been partly formed by interactions of choice with the phenomenal world: the entelechy of these choices has made me different from other composers. (*Dial.* 70)
What is looked for by the painter in visible things must possess the same kind of inner depth as his own self: the same secret meanings, correspondences, echoes and communications which the poet catches in the universe of Being. (130)	Familiar things, things that are everywhere attract [the true creator's] attention. He observes it to draw inspiration therefrom. (*PoM* 54–5) I was not attracted by any folklore element in Petrushka, always being tempted, in the life of things, by something very different from that. (*P&D* 66)
Melody has the property … of discovering the original reality, both psychological and spiritual, of the one who creates the melody. Melody (contrary to harmony and rhythm) is essentially irrational. (252–3)	The capacity for melody is a gift. This means that it is not within our power to develop it by study. (*PoM* 39) In the horizontal, one arranges the file as one wants but the vertical assemblages are something else. They must justify themselves before God! (*P&D* 248)

TABLE 3   A comparison of Maritain and Stravinsky's views (cont.)

MARITAIN	STRAVINSKY
The action of a play is the focus or aim of psychic life from which the events, in that situation, result. (356)	I consider this static representation a more vital way to focus the tragedy ... on the 'fatal development' that, for me is the meaning of the play (*Oedipus Rex*). (*Dial* 24)
A work unfolds in poetic space: beauty *does* as beauty *is*. The essence is a greater mystery than the action. (364)	It is through the unhampered play of its functions then, that a work is revealed and justified. (*PoM* 49) The only forms which are worth anything are those which flow from the musical material itself. (*Le Sacre, Dossier de Presse,* 76)

of fragments of eternity'.[94] When reason and intuition are involved with the practical organisation of an intelligible object, both functions of the intellect [*sic*] are united in a common purpose, lifting Man 'above' time to participate in transcendence. Like Stravinsky's vision of promoting communion with the Supreme Being through music, Maritain believed that when we enter into what is most basic and profound in perfected works created by the artist's creative intuition, then we can know the Divine Essence, by virtue of an analogy which achieves its intrinsic properties.

Maritain states that the three criteria for the Beauty that reveals the Divine – integrity, proportion and light – have 'a perfection ... which transcends things and ... makes them fit to give joy to the spirit. It is a reflection in things of the spirit from which they proceed ... God is subsistent Beauty and the being of all things derives from the divine beauty'.[95]

Despite the similarity of their vision and their friendship over many years, personally, Maritain and Stravinsky held each other in somewhat critical

---

94   *Approaches to God,* chapter 3, where Maritain adds to Aristotle's five ways of approaching God. He argues for a sixth way: the pre-existence of the Self in God, which is then born into time. (See also Dante's *The Divine Comedy: Purgatory.* Canto IV, 7–12).

95   Maritain, Jacques. *Approches de Dieu,* 96, in Daley, M.F. 1966, 97–98. Maritain quotes St Thomas Aquinas, *Comm. in Divinibus Nominibus.* C4, lect. 5.

esteem. As a closer friend of Stravinsky from 1929, Maritain later published his opinions of Stravinsky's music:

> [T]he more he becomes himself, the further he removes himself from magic. Compare the *Rites* [*sic*] and the *Wedding*, where so many spirits of earth and of the water still haunt him, to other masterpieces like *Apollo* or that *Capriccio* of which the brilliant poetry depends in its entirety on the made object.[96]
>
> He fears the eternal laws, this ferocious intellect in love with the song of the daughters of men ... With Stravinsky the spirit or poetry of the work is not consubstantial to its soul, but transcends it. But it is the spirit proper to the composer, his dominating intellect, his own will.[97]

Maritain referred to what he saw as the tendency of both Stravinsky and Paul Valéry to describe themselves as mere engineers in the manufacturing of an artefact:

> In reality the spiritual content of creative intuition ... animates their artefact despite their grudge against inspiration ... But because it is scanty in them, or arises only from some secret stir in the working reason of a touchy Muse, they make good this very aridity, and manage to side-track us, by magnifying it ... For all that, Stravinsky is not a narcissist but a genuine creator ...[98]

Stravinsky, in turn, recommended Maritain very highly but described him as:

> one of those people of superior intelligence who are lacking in humanity, and if Maritain himself does not deserve this judgement certainly it applies to a great deal of his work. Maritain is still attached to the nihilism of his youth and this can be sensed in all his books, despite the great value of his work in Christian and Thomist thought.[99]

96   Maritain, Jacques. 1945, 72–3.
97   Op. cit., 49 & 72–3.
98   Maritain, Jacques. 1954, 62.
99   Stravinsky, Vera & Craft, Robert. 1979, 632, n. 52.

CHAPTER 12

A Matter of Time

'Salut au "making"', wrote Wystan Auden to Stravinsky after their first collaborative session on *The Rake's Progress* (1948–51). Stravinsky's dedication to making a musical object was understood and appreciated by his librettist: Auden found Stravinsky to be a professional artist, 'concerned not for his personal glory, but solely for the thing-to-be-made'.[1] Both men of Christian faith, Auden and Stravinsky frequently discussed religious matters but arrived at their faith differently; while Stravinsky's beliefs were dogmatic and his relationship with God personal, Auden's faith was grounded in reason, logic, and theological concepts that often took the form of Scholastic propositions.[2]

Stravinsky and Auden worked on the plot together. Between 1732–33, William Hogarth had illustrated the downfall of a fictional character, Tom Rakewell, a rake in debt-ridden fashionable London society. In Hogarth's first picture Tom inherits a fortune from his father, evidence of whose miserly ways can be seen all around the room, even down to the starving cat. Auden suggested that the fortune arrive instead from an unknown uncle so that, as in a fairy tale, the riches are completely unexpected. The fairy-tale quality is further enhanced by Auden's addition of 'Mother Goose' and the 'Ugly Duchess' and by the agreement with Nick Shadow that he will reckon with Tom after the notional 'year and a day'. Hogarth's second and third pictures show Tom in fashionable London society, first holding a levée in his house, and then attending an orgy.[3] The fourth picture shows Tom's arrest for debt on his way to St James' Palace to attend Queen Caroline's birthday party, but he is saved by his former servant, the faithful Sarah Young, who, out of love for him, gives him her meagre earnings. In the fifth picture, Tom is shown marrying an old woman for her fortune, while Sarah, now deserted, is held back at the church door and prevented from reaching him. In the last three pictures, Tom loses everything in a gaming house, and is sent to the Fleet prison for debtors, where the faithful Sarah visits him with their child. Finally, Tom is sent to the Bethlem Hospital, where it was the custom in the 18th century for fashionable ladies to go for a day's pleasure outing to observe the antics of its poor mad occupants.

---

1   Stravinsky, Igor & Craft, Robert. 1979, 397.
2   Op. cit., 400.
3   Tradesmen come to offer their services to the newly rich Tom Rakewell. Hogarth included a figure seated at a keyboard which is thought to be Handel.

© KONINKLIJKE BRILL NV, LEIDEN, 2022 | DOI:10.1163/9789004518537_014

As Stravinsky and Auden worked on the plot, following Hogarth closely, their own narrative 'began to assume a different significance' and to take on Christian meanings.[4] Hogarth's pictures show Tom's financial downfall in 18th century London with horrific social realism, but Stravinsky and Auden focused instead on the gradual destruction of Tom's soul as he ignores his conscience in pursuit of his own individual will. This is a recurring theme in Stravinsky's writings, both at the level of the individual and that of contemporary society: his Orthodox background and teaching of the Church Fathers on *apatheia* had a deep influence on both his creative work and his spiritual life.

Hogarth's narrative shows the perils of fashionable society and the love of money, particularly with respect to gambling and debt,[5] but Tom Rakewell's far deeper troubles begin when he is hubristic and lazy and would sooner trust to Fortune for money. Rather than be an 'industrious apprentice in a copybook', he takes the extreme view (espoused by Calvin and others) that 'good works are of no avail, for Heaven predestines all'.[6]

At this, Nick Shadow quickly appears to present Tom with three temptations, just as the Devil tempted Jesus Christ three times in the wilderness. Tom's first temptation, following Hogarth, is to pursue his duty to himself, to follow Nature and enjoy a life of pleasure with his new-found affluence. But the second temptation, rather than to marry for a fortune like Hogarth's Rake, is to seek happiness in asserting his free will and choosing his own path in life. Nick Shadow cleverly builds on Tom's subsequent disillusionment with pleasure by suggesting that he can differ from the 'giddy multitude' who are 'driven by the twin tyrants of appetite and conscience'.[7] Tom's progressive turning away from his conscience as he delights in individual choice is encouraged by his ideas of predestination: his third temptation, rather than to gamble for a greater fortune, is to gain power and glory by god-like powers. It is at the moment of this third temptation that Nick Shadow is revealed as the Person of the Devil.

In the first scenario for the opera, the 'Villain' had wheeled in a fantastic apparatus for making gold out of sea water, which can be Tom's if only he will sell his soul in a Faustian bargain. Stravinsky and Auden later changed this into a crude apparatus for making bread out of stones in a direct reference to Christ's temptation to satisfy Man's material, rather than spiritual needs: Christ could gain the world for himself rather than for God, by displaying spectacular

---

4   Stravinsky, Igor & Craft, Robert. 1981: *Memories and Commentaries*, 156.
5   Hogarth's father had written a paper on how to remedy the National Debt, which is shown at the bottom right-hand corner of picture 7: *The Prison.*
6   Act 1, figure 28.
7   Act 2, figure 33 + 1.

powers. Poor deluded Tom is tempted to believe he can banish all want by his own skills and restore earth to its former state as an Eden of goodwill.[8]

Stravinsky immersed himself in four operatic scores by Mozart, particularly *Cosi fan tutte,* having recently heard a performance of this opera in Colorado in July 1948. *The Rake's Progress* is partly Mozartian in style, its heavenly music belying events on stage that are significantly more horrifying than any of those depicted in Hogarth's pictures. Stravinsky, like Mozart, skilfully balances the portrayal of troubled emotions with a mood of deceptively easy wit and gaiety. By the final scene of *Cosi fan tutte,* for example, the four lovers have gained new, if painful, knowledge about themselves and each other. With Mozart, Enlightenment thinking wins the day: the moral, announced playfully in the final chorus, commends those who meet trials and tribulations with Reason.[9] *The Rake's Progress* borrows some of Mozart's rhythmic manners, and also its fine balance between the serious and the witty, but explores deeper spiritual issues from a Christian moral perspective as Tom pursues his mistaken path through life: as unexpected riches trigger the emergence of Tom's shadow side he meets trials with false Reason, and ultimately loses his mind.

Like *Perséphone* (but unlike *Cosi*), *The Rake's Progress* looks at the nature and purpose of time, which is realised both in the opera's imaginative events and its musical techniques. The libretto by Wystan Auden and Chester Kallman in verse form combines a serious moral about using one's time on earth wisely, with the imaginary time of fairy tales in which anything can happen, and also with an unreal present in which everything is a game. Stravinsky recalled that Auden seemed to regard the making of poetry as a game, albeit to be played in 'a magic circle', and that all his conversation about Art was, so to speak, *sub specie ludi*.[10] Stravinsky matches this sense of play, for example, in Tom Rakewell's aria 'Since it is not by merit we rise or we fall', by evoking the changing wheel of Fortune:[11] he sets the words to a merry canon at the octave, a beat apart, which is reversed and differently accented when it returns.

Speaking some twenty years later, Stravinsky named *The Rake's Progress* as an example of one of his remote-in-time subjects.[12] Not only is *The Rake* distanced by its original setting in the 18th century and its objective treatment, but

---

8   Matthew 4. 1–4
9   In *Cosi fan tutte,* Fiordiligi and Dorabella almost 'marry' their new admirers, but their betrayal is distanced both geographically and psychologically, and given an exotic twist by the disguise of their 'new lovers' as Albanians.
10   Stravinsky, Igor & Craft, Robert. 1981: *Memories and Commentaries,* 157.
11   Act 1, figure 31–8.
12   Stravinsky, Igor & Craft, Robert. 1982, 108.

as in *Petrushka,* its temporal levels also resonate deeply across historical time. *The Rake* reaches back more than two thousand years to the myth of Venus and Adonis, and transfigures the original story: in the final scene, the chorus comment that 'not every rake is rescued at the last by Love and Beauty'.[13] As in Hogarth's engravings, Love is redemptive: Venus transcends the erotic love with which she is traditionally associated, and also Adonis' poor treatment of her, by a higher quality of love.[14] Both Hogarth's Sarah and Stravinsky's Anne love the Rake faithfully through thick and thin and support him in a Christian spirit of forgiveness. In their opening pastoral duet Tom and Anne sing of the 'Cyprian Queen', Aphrodite (Venus), who will bring love to restore 'the age of gold'.[15] Like Adonis, Tom will turn from the love that is offered him to pursue his own pleasures, but by the end of the opera, he will realise that he 'hunted shadows disclaiming thy true love'.[16] He is not physically killed like the mythical Adonis but Nick Shadow has one last trick: he all but kills Tom's soul, his very being, which deprives him of his sense of present reality and of all sense of Time.

The spectrum of time qualities in *The Rake* ranges from the elusive time of the lovers' dreams in spring and a new out-of-time quality as the tragic lovers symbolise Venus and Adonis, to the focused here-and-now of vaudeville created by the auctioneer's patter and Baba's chatter. But even in the present, Nick Shadow, like the Charlatan who oppresses Petrushka, has the power to suspend time and to reverse it to prevent Tom's life from realising its full potential. Tom Rakewell's spiritual 'progress' is measured by his awareness of time in all its qualities. The cuckoo clock (with its inscription TEMPUS FUGIT) on the wall of Mother Goose's brothel strikes one as Tom realises that he wishes to go home 'before it is too late', but at a sign from Nick Shadow, the clock turns backwards to strike twelve. To speed up Tom's moral disintegration, Shadow observes that it is his prerogative to deny the temporal dimension of his life: 'Time is yours. The hours obey your pleasure. Fear not. Enjoy. You may repent at leisure'. In the churchyard, Shadow announces that Tom has 'run his race', ironically echoing the sentiments of St Paul [17], but he obligingly halts the clock after the ninth

---

13   Act III, figure 289 + 1.

14   Venus has an erotic character in Ovid's *Metamorphoses* (Book 10), in Shakespeare's first published poem of that name in 1593, and in her depiction by Titian (1553–4). Botticelli's painting *The Birth of Venus* (c.1486) shows her as graceful, modest and delicate.

15   'Time will run back and fetch the age of gold': On the Morning of Christ's Nativity: The Hymn. John Milton, st.14, l.135.

16   Act III, figure 244 + 2.

17   The Second Letter of Paul to Timothy: 4.7.

stroke to give Tom just a little more time to decide how he will kill himself. The clock strikes once after each correct answer, but the extended intervals between the last three strokes both expand and suspend the sense of clock-time. In the first scenario for the opera, Tom simply played the game of chance to regain chronological time, to recover his lost past, innocence and love before finding hope in the future. The first version of his lament concluded with 'Let it strike. Time doesn't frighten me anymore. For love there is no past or future, only the present'.[18] The final version is a good deal stronger in its message, but based on the same distinctively Christian understanding of Love as reaching beyond time and being stronger than death. The word 'Return', understood spiritually as repentance and turning away from evil, runs through the opera, drawing attention to Tom's recurring chances to reform. Although Shadow has taught Tom that there is no Return, Tom risks all on this word and on his sudden realisation that Love is the greatest power: Love can plunder Hell of its prey and always renews life in the eternal process of forgiveness. Emotionally and spiritually, the poignant music for string quartet and symbolic striking of the clock in the churchyard scene, prepares us for the deepest part of the opera, and, significantly, was the point at which Stravinsky began composing.[19]

As in other stage works, *Mavra, Oedipus Rex* and *Perséphone*, the different time worlds of the characters are distinguished by Stravinsky's rhythmic 'borrowings'. Stravinsky added scansion marks (or occasionally, the musical metre) to each section of the libretto to establish its tempi, rates of harmonic and rhythmic change and rhythmic manners, and then memorised the lines whilst pacing up and down and repeating them aloud. Having decided the most suitable tempo for the substance of each section he would time its length most precisely.[20] Where a particular behaviour and time world had found perfect musical expression in the past, Stravinsky 'borrowed' and reinterpreted its essential features, adding its associations to his work. The strictly dotted rhythms, vocal coloratura and wide intervals of the 18th century, for example, already perfectly express a strong and resolute state of mind in grappling with a conflict between love and duty.

---

18   Stravinsky, Igor & Craft, Robert. 1981: *Memories and Commentaries*, 174.
19   Act III, Scene 2. During a recording session of the graveyard scene in *The Rake's Progress*, Stravinsky remarked of the bells: 'I dreamed once in Switzerland that sound'. Stravinsky, Igor & Craft, Robert. 1981, *Expositions and Developments*, 61. He also remembered the effect of the trumpet solo in *Don Pasquale* from his St Petersburg days: Stravinsky, Vera & Craft, Robert. 1979, 417.
20   Stravinsky, Igor & Craft, Robert. 1979, 361.

The customary role of an opera orchestra is to support, belie or comment on the stage action; the strong dotted rhythms that accompany Tom's first protest against work mock his unworthy resolve,[21] while the large intervals and straightforward rhythms of Anne's C major Cabaletta reveal her true heart just as plainly as Fiordiligi's initially firm stand in *Cosi*.[22] The Mozartian introduction to Tom, Anne and her father's first meeting with Nick Shadow mocks their relationship with a gracious formality reminiscent of the wedding procession in *The Marriage of Figaro*.[23] The very brief suggestion of Cherubino's aria 'Non so più' in *The Marriage of Figaro* at the beginning of Tom's aria 'I have waited' immediately communicates his new state of youth and innocence.[24] The frequent passages of pedal point, as in the duet 'In a foolish dream', evoke the cantata style of a former age in which a pedal point arrests a sense of forward movement to offer a moment of rest and reflection on the situation.[25]

Some of the most poignant moments in *The Rake's Progress* achieve the same blend of irony and tender sympathy that Mozart captures. In *Cosi fan tutte*, the unreal time world of deceitful lovers vowing to write and be faithful is perfectly captured by a throbbing staccato bass and soft off-beat semiquavers around a legato falling semitone. Stravinsky uses the same musical configuration to express the whores' insincere sorrow that Tom did not keep his vow to Anne. The wave-like semiquaver figure that accompanies *Cosi's* Fiordiligi, Arabella and Don Alfonso as they gaze at the lovers' departing ship, recurs in various forms in *The Rake's Progress*, notably as Anne comes to search for Tom outside his London home.[26] The dotted quaver-demisemiquavers figure of Tom and Anne's opening aria permeates the work whenever either of them refer to their lost love. In a new form it introduces Anne's beautiful Cavatina about love that is betrayed, whose pulsating bass notes are reminiscent of the opening of Bach's *St Matthew Passion*.[27] These moments of refined pathos are contrasted with the wit of songs in street-ballad style that evoke the world of Hogarth and *The Beggar's Opera*. Stravinsky's borrowings from the past serve the same function as the rich associations and layers of meaning, gathered over many years,

---

21   Act 1, figure 27.
22   Act 1, figure 193. Stravinsky titles the aria Cabaletta, drawing attention to its rock-like rhythmic character.
23   Act 1, figure 51.
24   Act 3, figure 239.
25   Act 3, figure 243.
26   Act 1, figure 81.
27   Act 1, figure183.

that characterise the *waka* poetry that he set in *Three Japanese Lyrics*. These
musical references, revisiting traditional rhythmic expressions of 'being', add
historical depth to the many temporalities of the opera and enrich the work's
spiritual impact.

Ingmar Bergman staged *The Rake's Progress* in Stockholm in the same year
that it was completed.[28] Stravinsky liked the way that, at the beginning of the
last scene in Bergman's production, Shadow sat on the tombstone with a sil-
houette of three Gothic steeples in the background. At first the audience was
only aware of three spires as ominous presences, but as the action developed
the spires gradually became clearer and stronger, so that by the end it was
clear that they represented Golgotha and the three crosses at the crucifixion
of Christ.[29] The production was also acclaimed as having great significance in
the history of Swedish opera, for most of the changes of scenery took place
without bringing down the curtain: the cast froze in their positions until the
new sets had been lowered into place. Bergman said that he dispensed with
the conventional use of the curtain to separate the scenes in order to break
down the intense realism that often develops in portraying the Rake's downward path. When the audience is especially moved, he explained, the mood
must be broken, 'because Stravinsky wants to tell you "something" and that
"something" is the moral of the morality play'.[30]

Like the itinerant *skomorokhi* who ended their theatrical presentations with
the 'moral' of the piece in verse form, the principal characters of *The Rake's
Progress* bounce back at the end of the opera to relieve the intense mood with
a moment of light vaudeville. In a striking parallel with Stravinsky's visionary
ideas on the purpose of music, the practical message of *The Rake's Progress*
concerns the co-ordination of Man with Time: 'For idle hands and hearts and
minds, the devil finds a work to do.'

The Rake's Progress is a prime example of the deep spiritual impact that
a multi-level temporal structure can have on all who participate in it. It
appears that for the orchestral players, on one occasion at least, the spiritual
quality of *The Rake's Progress*, and indeed of Stravinsky himself, quite transcended his somewhat inadequate conducting of it. Recalling a rehearsal
of the work at the Metropolitan Opera House in New York, the cellist Janos
Starker described how, in spite of a lack of a conductor's 'traditional duties',
the musicians started together and breathed together in a 'rare session of

---

28   Stravinsky, Vera & Craft, Robert. 1979, 461.
29   Stravinsky, Igor & Craft, Robert. 1972, 117.
30   Stravinsky, Vera & Craft, Robert. 1979, 462–3.

spiritual communication' with Stravinsky. At the end of the performance of this 'remote-in-time' opera, something like a grin appeared on the maestro's face: 'perhaps he was not even there, perhaps only his spirit, or his image, appeared'.[31]

---

31   Op. cit., 651.

CHAPTER 13

Stravinsky, Schoenberg and God

Although Stravinsky and Schoenberg were both men of deep faith and dedicated to composing works that promoted the perception of a transcendent reality, the nature of their faith was very different. In his early life Schoenberg had been drawn to the temporal aspect of music as a means of expressing psychological feelings. Inspired by the work of such contemporary psychoanalysts as Sigmund Freud and Joseph Breuer he had approached a young doctor, Marie Pappenheim, to write the libretto for his opera *Erwartung* (1909). Although only a half hour in length, the heroine conveys a great range of emotions through the wide spacing of atonal dissonances, constantly changing timbral colours, transparent orchestration, and large fluctuations of movement that condense or expand psychological time. As Schoenberg explained:

> In *Erwartung* the aim is to represent in slow motion everything that occurs during a single second of maximum spiritual excitement, stretching it out to half-an-hour, whereas in *Die glückliche Hand* a major drama is compressed into about twenty minutes, as if photographed with a time-exposure. My third opera, *Von Heute auf Morgen*, is also relatively short; it lasts about an hour, but uses only the customary theatrical methods of condensing and expanding time.[1]

Schoenberg came to eschew all extra-musical Expressionist tendencies, and in 1921 announced a new system for organising the twelve semitones of the octave. During the 1920s, as Stravinsky sought new means of unifying contrasting qualities of time into an autonomous temporal form, Schoenberg saw the future direction of music as lying in the pure, atemporal world of intellectual relations. He maintained that his serial system could replace all the former functions of tonality, reanimate the old classical forms of the sonata, variation and da capo, and ensure the supremacy of German music for the next one hundred years.

Relations between Stravinsky and Schoenberg, at first cordial, deteriorated in the mid-1920s. Stravinsky saw Schoenberg for the last time in 1949 at

---

1 Schoenberg, Arnold. 1975. 'New music: My music', 99.

© KONINKLIJKE BRILL NV, LEIDEN, 2022 | DOI:10.1163/9789004518537_015

a concert at which Schoenberg read a delicately ironic speech acknowledging the honour of being awarded the freedom of the city of Vienna. In spite of having previously described Schoenberg as 'a chemist of music', Stravinsky wryly remarked that this honour had just been conferred on Schoenberg, 'a half century too late'. On hearing of Schoenberg's death, Stravinsky immediately sent a telegram to Schoenberg's widow saying that he was 'deeply shocked by saddening news of terrible blow inflicted to all musical world by loss of Arnold Schoenberg'. Six days later, during a visit to Alma Mahler-Werfel, Stravinsky was visibly moved at being the first to see Schoenberg's death mask.

Although Stravinsky acknowledged the many differences between Schoenberg and himself with respect to the nature of their faith and their aesthetics, he had a deep fellow feeling and respect for Schoenberg. Unlike Schoenberg, Stravinsky believed that the purpose of music was to establish an order in things and, in particular, to co-ordinate humankind and time. He drew interesting contrasts and parallels between Schoenberg and himself, but it is revealing that he is totally silent in these comparisons about their respective attitudes to the temporal aspects of music.[2] This fundamental difference between the two composers may explain in part why, for a long time, Stravinsky showed no interest in Schoenberg's serial system.

Dismissing the description of Schoenberg and himself as thesis and antithesis as a 'parlour game, no more', Stravinsky proposed a number of parallel points that he thought 'more interesting'. Although seemingly alike in faith and musical purpose, consideration of his first and sixth parallel points reveals some fundamental differences.

Stravinsky's very first point of comparison concerned their spirituality: their common belief in Divine Authority, the Hebrew God and biblical mythology, and Catholic culture.[3]

---

2   Stravinsky, Igor & Craft Robert. 1982, 108–9. Theodor Adorno had also criticised the developmental aspect of Schoenberg's music: 'The continuum of subjective time experience is no longer entrusted with the power of collecting musical events, functioning as a unity, and thereby imparting meaning to them ...' Adorno, Theodor, W. 1948, 60 'The question which 12-tone music asks of the composer is not how musical meaning is to be organised but rather, how organisation is to become meaningful.' Op. cit., 67 'The function of the work of art lies precisely in its transcendence beyond mere existence.' Op. cit., 70. 'Now, intervals have become nothing more than building stones, and all experiences which are encompassed in their differentiation are seemingly lost.' Op. cit., 76.

3   Stravinsky, Igor & Craft, Robert. 1982, 108.

1   Belief in Divine Authority

Stravinsky had an uncompromising belief in Divine Authority and a strong sense of accountability to God. He had always regarded his talents as God-given, and even from his earliest years he had prayed to God for the strength to use them. He sensed the musical ideas that came to him from God were 'gifts', and he waited in trust for them even though the waiting was anguish. He felt accountable to God for what he called his 'vertical assemblages', though all he was able to do, he said, was to surrender himself to the experiment that was being conducted in and by him.

Schoenberg's strong belief in Divine Authority is revealed in his many writings about music and spiritual matters. Born a Jew, he briefly converted to Christianity and the Lutheran Church from 1898, but returned to the Jewish faith by 1922 (formally affirming it in 1933), feeling increasingly that in the current political situation in Germany he could not escape his racial and religious heritage. He confided in a letter that he had found great support in his belief in something higher, beyond, and that it had brought him comfort 'in increasing measure' in the years between 1915–22 during which he was composing *Jacobsleiter*.[4] Schoenberg's picture of God was severe; he saw Him as a kind of Supreme Commander who had to be obeyed. Schoenberg described the Ten Commandments as one of the first declarations of human rights, adding that they nevertheless denied humankind freedom of faith, because there is only one God.

Schoenberg's writings contain many references to his relationship with God: for example, he remarked that Italian national music was being written on higher orders, 'whereas I, in my reactionary way, stick to writing mine on orders from The Most High'.[5] He believed that music has only one content which all great men wish to express: the longing of mankind for its future form, for an immortal soul ... the longing of this soul for its God.[6] Like Stravinsky, Schoenberg felt that musical ideas came from God: 'if [a composer] has done his duty with the utmost sincerity and has worked out everything as near to perfection as he is capable of doing', he remarked, 'then the Almighty presents him with a gift, with additional features of beauty such as he never would have produced by his talents alone'.[7] Like Stravinsky, he felt himself to be a channel,

---

4   *Jacobsleiter* was composed 1915–17, 1918–22. Stein, Edwin, ed. 1964, 71.
5   Schoenberg, Arnold. 1975, 175.
6   Op. cit., 464.
7   Op. cit., 86.

'merely the slave of a higher ordinance under whose compulsion he ceaselessly does his work'.[8]

Both Schoenberg and Stravinsky felt that the Authority of God was manifest
in the effect that music can have on the spirit. The closing words of Stravinsky's
Poetics of Music see the unity of a work as having a resonance, caught by
the soul, that flows back towards its source in the Supreme Being. Similarly,
Schoenberg felt that 'the artist is only the mouthpiece of a power which dic-
tates what to do', and that music 'conveys a prophetic message revealing a
higher form of life towards which mankind evolves. And it is because of this
message that music appeals to men of all races and cultures'.[9] Schoenberg felt
that it was his historic duty to write what his destiny ordered him to write.[10]

2   Belief in the Hebrew God

Both Stravinsky and Schoenberg believed in God as He was first known by the
Hebrews, but the very different nature of their faith arose from their opposing
perceptions of the relationship between God and the dimension of Time. The
Hebrew people saw God as the Lord of history who acts within time, using people and events to work out His purpose for His Creation. They perceived that
His nature was being progressively revealed through the prophets, and that it
was purposeful in guiding His people towards greater spiritual understanding.
For the Hebrews, this process of revelation was continuous: God was always
ahead, leading His people on pilgrimages of discovery into what has always
been, so that truths of a fuller reality are revealed to humanity as long as traditions are open to reflection and change.[11]

As we have seen, Stravinsky's lifelong Christian faith was incarnational: he
believed that God was immanent in everything around him and that the most
ordinary thing could be the source of creative inspiration. He believed that God
was loving and accessible and that He was fully revealed after the prophets in
His Son, Jesus of Nazareth. Although transcendent to His Creation, God was
working within it to reconcile everything to Himself. Stravinsky's late works,

---

8   Reich, Willi. 1971, 46.
9   Schoenberg, Arnold. 1975, 136.
10   Stein, Edwin, ed. 1964, 250.
11   Westermann, Claus. 1979, 13. Westermann suggests that we lose much of the richness and
     diversity of Biblical mythology as historical revelation by regarding it as a collection of
     static thought forms (emphasising nouns like 'salvation'), rather than as a record of con-
     tinuous actions (through verbs like 'saving') between God and His people.

Cantata and *Canticum Sacrum,* celebrate God's profound involvement with humanity in the life of His Son, and show Stravinsky's personal commitment to Christ as both human and divine: Stravinsky places the narration of Jesus' mission and teaching at the heart of both works. *A Sermon, A Narrative and A Prayer* and *Abraham and Isaac* both illustrate the transformative power of faith. In his writings Stravinsky displays a belief in the work of the Divine Being in time and through time, and the renewal of revelation through traditions.

Stravinsky owned many Christian objects of devotion; he prayed constantly before icons, and composed beneath an icon in his study. God as Love was the single source of creation and of creative inspiration and enabled the essence of things to be entered into through empathy; for Stravinsky, God was a lifelong source of creative energy and directly accessible through intercessory prayer. By extension, he regarded the canons of the Christian faith as just as necessary for music as for everyday life. The musical means of penetrating what he called 'A system beyond Nature' lay in the important question of Time: in the ordering of the time-creating rhythms of being, and the juxtaposition of time-creating movements to escape time, space and causality.

Between 1908–21, by contrast, Schoenberg was part of the *Blaue Reiter* group of artists who were interested in occult, oriental and theosophical writers. He also had a deep faith in a Hebrew God, but after his reaffirmation of the Jewish faith, Schoenberg's intellectual understanding of God owed much to the philosophy of Schopenhauer. He had first encountered Schopenhauer's ideas as early as 1913 and his spirituality developed from the expression of raw emotions in *Erwartung* and *Die glückliche Hand* to embrace Schopenhauer's understanding of God as 'Will', and the created world as manifestations of the Will in 'Representations'.[12] Schopenhauer understood the underlying reality beyond the physical world as a driving force, an energy lying outside space, time and causality. It strives to realise itself, like Plato's Ideas, as particular representations in the created world, we ourselves being among its many manifestations. But this underlying reality, this endless striving of a unity that lacks all distinctions and tension between opposites, is objective, passionless and totally inaccessible; Schopenhauer believed that the closest experience of it is to be had in the experience of our own bodily striving, both physical and mental.

Schopenhauer, like Schoenberg, believed in a high calling and a visionary purpose for music. Schopenhauer believed that music differed from the other arts: unlike sculpture, painting and literature which needed intermediary physical materials, music could bypass the expression of Ideas, such as Love

---

12   Schopenhauer, Arthur. 1966.

and Truth and be a copy of the underlying reality itself. Music was able to penetrate to the very essence of this reality and have a powerful effect upon the spirit. Contrary to Stravinsky's belief that a composer's personal emotions had no place in patterning ontological time in music, Schopenhauer believed that the underlying reality could be manifested in music as the ebb and flow of human emotions; not as particular emotions but as the fluctuating movement of normal human consciousness. But Schopenhauer linked human striving with the achievement or non-achievement of satisfaction, and thus with suffering. He was essentially an atheist who did not believe in faith and hope and the continuation of life after death. In the final analysis, Schopenhauer's high conception of music, as the contemplation of Ideas lying outside time, the appreciation of pure beauty, merely provided a temporary means of escape from the inevitable fact of death.

The texts that Schoenberg wrote himself, especially for *Jacobsleiter* and *Moses und Aron,* reflect Schopenhauer's essentially pessimistic philosophical language. In *Moses und Aron,* Moses exclaims: 'God of my Fathers, God of Abraham, Isaac and Jacob, who has reawakened their Ideas in me'. Schoenberg had added these last few words to the biblical text in Exodus 3 v. 6.[13] For Schoenberg also, the 'Will' is a noumena which can never be known: Moses cries out: 'Inconceivable God! Inexpressible, ambiguous Idea!'[14] Schoenberg believed that awareness of the divine can only come through direct revelation or through the intuition or instinct. The central conflict of *Moses und Aron* is the tension between God as Will and the world as Representation, a 'distance' difficult to bridge, for no Image must be made of God. In contrast to Stravinsky's personal relationship with a loving, incarnational God, Schoenberg had great difficulty with the direct revelation of the Will: in *Moses und Aron,* Moses' meeting with God at the burning bush has first to be communicated to Aron and the priests, and only then to the people. Moses, a speaking part, has difficulty in articulating his mystical vision, whereas the more extravert Aron, who does not understand visions, demands signs and miracles from God to justify his faith.

Moses und Aron is also autobiographical, expressing Schoenberg's own despair at the impossible task of representing something of the Will through music, which he nevertheless believed the 'Will' – God – required of him. Revelation of the 'Will' came both personally and through tradition but its representation in music was problematic. Stravinsky had experienced God in

---

13   White, Pamela, C. 1983, 74–5.
14   Ibid.

Creation and in the being of created things as time and movement, and represented them rhythmically. Schoenberg does not seem to have experienced time and movement as keenly, or at least in the way that Stravinsky did; he did not even consider ballet and its direct patterning of time by movement as a musical form. Schoenberg experienced the dilemma of the artist who draws his inspiration from pre-existent archetypal images on 'another plane', but feels unable to achieve their full expression. He could only strive continually to come near to expressing his vision in music for it was hindered by 'style', and lost much in the act of expression itself. For Stravinsky, Schoenberg was the 'hedgehog', who turns out his prickles at criticism as he struggles with his impossible task.[15]

Schoenberg struggled constantly to express the inexpressible God in music; on a personal level, too, his prayers to God were the difficult means to mystical union with Him.[16] The text that Schoenberg wrote for the first of his *Modern Psalms* in 1951 (the only one he actually set) questions his significance as an individual in the great objective scheme of humanity yet expresses the necessity of prayer to maintain faith.

But both Stravinsky and Schoenberg were grounded in time in the sense of tradition. Stravinsky believed that revelation of the Hebrew God was not only personal but comes through artistic traditions which, in his view, operate upon the artist as a living, dynamic force that animates and informs the present. The substance of what is being said remains true for all time but its new form of expression is nourished and revitalised by the past forms in which it must continue to be firmly rooted. He believed that tradition, far from implying repetition of what has been, presupposes the reality of what endures,[17] and observed that ' "Modern" music ... does not exist because we say the same things as our ancestors, but because it expresses them differently'.[18] He saw tradition as undergoing a life process, from birth through growth and decline, to rebirth, and as always in contradiction to another concept.[19] Tradition and renewal create a living dialect;[20] tradition, he said, is an heirloom[21] that carries the good

---

15   Stravinsky, Igor & Craft, Robert. 1982, 107.
16   Arthur Lourié's 1928 article 'Neogothic and Neoclassic' makes a harsh and uncompromising comparison between Schoenberg's 'egocentric conception' in which aesthetic expression takes the place of the religious and art becomes 'a kind of substitute for religion', and Stravinsky's 'limitation of the ego and its subordination to superior and eternal values'.
17   Stravinsky, Igor. 1947, 56–7.
18   Stravinsky, Vera & Craft, Robert. 1979, 209.
19   Stravinsky, Igor & Craft, Robert. 1981, *Memories and Commentaries*, 126–27.
20   Stravinsky, Igor. 1947, 117.
21   Op. cit., 57.

artist on its shoulder as St Christopher carried the Lord.[22] Stravinsky described himself as the 'fox', borrowing eclectic musical means to build on spiritual traditions and insights of the past.[23] Even so, Stravinsky did wonder whether he was merely trying to refit old ships, while the other side – Schoenberg – sought new forms of travel.

Schoenberg also saw it as his God-given mission to develop the new out of tradition, and that he had a duty to develop his ideas for the sake of progress in music.[24] He thought that no new technique in the arts is created unless it has had its roots in the past.[25]

Both Stravinsky and Schoenberg sought to organise sounds to touch the spirit, but Schoenberg believed that music has the power to influence occult parts of our soul and/or our sentimental spheres if it is organised to be agreeable to the ear and comprehensible to the intelligence.[26]

3   Belief in Biblical Mythology

Stravinsky and Schoenberg's fundamental differences of faith in the Hebrew God are also revealed in their settings of biblical texts. Stravinsky believed that the ancient Hebrews' understanding of the nature of God developed in the course of the Old Testament, and culminated in a new Covenant with a loving God through the events of the New Testament. This important evolution in the understanding of God is the subject of the biblical texts at the heart of *Canticum Sacrum*.

Schoenberg's works with biblical texts are from the Old Testament and are vehicles for expressing all that dwells inside him: their complex relationships are for the mind, by which he endeavours to know the unknowable directly.[27] Stravinsky described Schoenberg as a 'cabalist', interpreting biblical mythology in a mystical way and within an esoteric tradition.

For Schoenberg, the biblical idea of the Jews as God's Chosen People was connected with Schopenhauer's concept of suffering as the 'unfulfillment' of the human will. At the individual level, the artist is the Chosen One who has

---

22   Craft, Robert. 1994, 72.
23   Stravinsky, Igor & Craft, Robert. 1982, 107.
24   Schoenberg, Arnold. 1975, 53.
25   Op. cit., 76.
26   Letter to Walter Koons (NBC) 1934: Op. cit., 73.
27   Schoenberg extended the game of chess by playing on a board with 100 squares instead of the usual 64, and using extra pieces.

to suffer a lack of fulfilment and accept the destiny which has been imposed on him.[28] There is much in Schoenberg's spirituality that relates to his own negative experience of life: with musical rejection on account of his 'emancipation of tonality', and with racial rejection as a Jew living at this particular time in Vienna with its strong Catholic culture and heightened atmosphere of anti-Semitism. Schoenberg described his personal spirituality as 'without any organisational fetters'.[29] He was more at home with 'inwardness' and 'a chaste, higher form of emotion', than a great display of passion in performing music, and wrote that he was proud to be a mystic.

It is revealing to compare the difference of approach between Schoenberg's mystical interpretation of *Jacobsleiter*, his first Old Testament setting, and Stravinsky's brief setting of *Babel*, which juxtaposes highly contrasting time qualities.[30] The Bible tells how Jacob lay down to sleep at a certain place between Beersheba and Haran (later to become the cultic place called Bethel), and dreamed that there was a 'ladder' set up on the earth.[31] The angels of God ascended and descended the ladder, the top of which reached 'the gate of heaven'. The ancient world view was that all interaction between the earth and the divine world took place at the 'gate of heaven'; God's messengers did not bear prayers to God, but fulfilled divine commands or supervised matters on earth.

Schoenberg's *Jacobsleiter* (begun in January 1915) goes far beyond the biblical story and becomes a mystical and symbolic vision about successive lives progressing towards God. Jacob's ladder becomes a symbol of spiritual progress, on which a chain of human souls stretching in evolutionary terms from the lowest to the highest are striving in successive lives to grow towards union with their Creator.[32] Schoenberg saw his 'new music' as part of this 'evolutionary' process, regarding it as a more highly evolved language that would speak to the greater spiritual consciousness of future generations of listeners.[33]

---

28   When Schoenberg was asked by his army commander if he was really the composer Arnold Schoenberg, he replied, 'Somebody had to be, and nobody else wanted to, so I took it on, myself'.

29   Stein, Edwin, ed. 1964, 71.

30   *Babel* is discussed in Chapter 11.

31   von Rad, Gerhard. 1981, 10–22.

32   This doctrine originated with Plato's *Timaeus* and the Neoplatonism of Plotinus.

33   Schoenberg would have liked to have made the Israel Academy of Music 'a counterblast to this world that is in so many respects giving itself up to amoral, success-ridden materialism', producing students who must be 'truly priests of art ... making our souls function again as they must if mankind is to evolve any higher'. But many of Schoenberg's own works remained unfinished: out of fifteen items in his collection of Psalms, Prayers, and other Conversations with and about God, he set only one complete item to music.

Stravinsky admired *Jacobsleiter,* and despite criticising the work's orchestration and also its incompleteness, called the existing segment 'one of the highest achievements of our music'.[34]

4   Belief in Catholic Culture

The third part of Stravinsky's first point of comparison of himself with Schoenberg strikes a more ambiguous note. Stravinsky's spiritual home is Russian Orthodoxy but he is also a bridge between the Orthodox East and the Catholic West: although he always retained his 'Russian-ness' he had an affinity with Western culture, especially those of the Latin races, and accepted Catholic culture as the milieu in which he could best express his gifts. He felt part of the tradition, coming from Peter the Great, that sought to blend Russian culture with that of the West, and the circumstances of his life brought him within the orbit of neo-Thomism and the Catholic circle of Jacques Maritain and Jean Cocteau and their resistance to what they saw as German decadence.

Schoenberg also worked with the forms of Catholic culture but in 1938 he wrote a fine work for speaker, chorus and orchestra, Op. 39, that includes the ancient *Kol Nidre* theme of the Jewish liturgy. Part One of the liturgical ceremony for the eve of *Yom Kippur,* the Day of Atonement, opens with evening prayer at which the Book of Sohar is opened and the Rabbi, in the name of those above and those on earth, gives permission for the community to pray with those seeking to be freed from promises which might lead them away from God. *Kol Nidre* means literally 'All Vows' and in the second part of the ceremony, after reference to the Kabbala and the announcement 'Let there be Light', the chorus 'repent that these obligations have estranged us' and absolution is given from 'whatever binds us to falsehood'. At this point, the first bars of the *Kol Nidre* theme are heard, a theme that originated as a Catalan song of the 16th century and has since been influenced by both Catholic and Protestant musical cultures. As with Stravinsky's expression of Orthodox spirituality in *Les Noces,* this Jewish liturgy and its evocative folk theme drew a special response from Schoenberg as one of his best works.

Schoenberg saw himself as continuing the musical tradition coming from Beethoven and Brahms. But in composing with serial techniques alone,

---

34   Stravinsky, Igor & Craft, Robert. 1982, 60.

without a text or any other means of shaping the work, he faced the problem of structuring a large-scale form. Past forms of Catholic culture were based on contrasts of melody and tonality and on the return of recognisable large-scale symmetries. The series, on the other hand, was more of a resource to be quarried for melodic invention. Despite the prolific use of contrapuntal devices and the division of the row into reflecting parts or motifs allowing brief moments of tonality, the problem of structuring a large form from a series remained. As Charles Rosen has shown, the dichotomy between serial organisation and the tonal phrasing of 19th century could not be bridged 'because Schoenberg obstinately [saw them] as governed by the same principle: the invention and variation of themes'.[35]

With respect to the temporal aspect of music, Rosen also points to a deeper problem arising from the unexpected periodicity that was imposed on a form by the row:

> The series has a rhythm of its own opposed to the classical forms in that it is periodic, constantly recurring. By this quality it transcends its inner organisation. The periodicity ... is totally independent of pulsation, unrelated to a measurable tempo. Since different forms of the series in one work may overlap, and may be played with the different notes spaced out or grouped all at once in a chord, the period many not be easily measurable as we normally understand that, but ... [it] creates an invariance of its own ... For this reason, once the periodicity of the series is heard, it ... overrides them all ... it makes the strict and regular rhythms of the neoclassical period sound anachronistic, and it can be heard through them as through a grid.[36]

The problem of constructing a large-scale form by means of serial techniques would be resolved by Stravinsky as he developed serialism to embody the 'living' variations of time consciousness; the solution lay in Stravinsky's ordering of row forms, their rotations and segments, to function as his former patterning of layers had done. Stravinsky organises serial rows just as he had organised diatonic and octatonic pitch patterns to construct qualities of time from the here-and-now to timelessness. Serialism prompted the final development of his style.

---

35   Rosen, Charles. 1976, 109.
36   Op. cit., 114–5.

5   Devotion to The Word

Stravinsky's sixth point of comparison between himself and Schoenberg
makes a play on 'The Word' as both divine creative action – 'In the beginning
was the Word ... and the Word was God ... All things were made by him'[37] – and
the word as a means of human communication. In bringing these two powerful images together Stravinsky pointed out that they had each written some
of their own librettos (*Moses und Aron, Die glückliche Hand, Jacobsleiter, Les
Noces, Renard*) to express the Word in words: through these works, the Word as
a powerful communication from God to mankind is transformed into words as
a means of human communication. But although Stravinsky pointed to their
common devotion to The Word, their treatment of the word as speech and text
could not have been more different.

    In this comparison Stravinsky seems to be speaking from a particularly Old
Testament understanding of 'The Word'. In those times The Word was not primarily understood in terms of content, as in modern theology, but as an action
between a speaker and a listener. It was understood both as a communication
from God to humankind, and as an effective creative power in the world. The
Hebrews, with their genius for worship and theological insight connected their
experience of the transcendent properties of words and language as sounds
with their experience of the divine creative spirit, though the effective power
of the divine Word was on an immeasurably fuller and deeper plane. The
action of the Word was often described as a sound which penetrated the heart
and resonated there, bringing light and understanding.[38] It was understood
as an action or event that came as a prophetic and personal revelation to certain men at certain times and places throughout history rather than a direct
verbal message. The child Samuel, for instance, was called four times by The
Word before he realised the divine nature of the call, for Samuel 'did not yet
know the Lord, neither was the Word of the Lord yet revealed unto him'.[39] The
call was described in terms of sound but sound whose intelligibility required
Samuel's recognition and response.[40]

---

37   John 1.1–3.
38   'The entrance of thy Words giveth light; it giveth understanding unto the simple'. Psalms
      119, 130.
39   1 Samuel 3.7.
40   '... the predominant form in which God appears is in terms of sound, in words. This is
      what contrasts biblical mysticism, for example, with other forms of mysticism. Here the
      peak of religious experience is the reception of a word from God rather than of an iden-
      tity between mystic and the divine ...' Ihde, Don. 1970, 232–251.

In Old Testament times, words were seen as having the power to create meaning in another sphere of reality. Both the Hebrews and the Greeks recognised a qualitatively different power of words in which the word and the object it named were not clearly differentiated but fused as if on the same level of being. Greek words, for instance, were almost tangible in their solidity, and their rhythms and melodiousness were so powerful that they could even affect men at a physical level. Stravinsky was keenly aware of this quality of words, feeling, like Hermogenes, that all names possess 'echoic value'.[41] Words as resonant sounds were a prime source of musical inspiration: the texts of *Les Noces* and *Oedipus Rex* had suggested melodies, motifs, rhythms, intervals and chords.[42] In ordering resonant sounds to construct a work to touch the spirit, 'In the beginning was The Word' was, for him, 'a literal localised truth'.[43]

But poetry and prose bring their own qualities of time to a work and when combined with music their semantic power needs to be controlled. The ancient Russian chant had reduced the words to a series of syllables that were filled out or repeated, often with drawn-out vowels, in a kind of 'glossalalie', according to the musical requirements.[44] Referring to the need for beautiful, strong syllables in the text of *Perséphone*, Stravinsky called the syllable a 'constant' in vocal music.

The natural stresses of a language were also important for Stravinsky, either combined with melodic intonations to enhance their resonance, or diminished and even negated in favour of the musical flow. The prosody of works sung in a language other than the one in which Stravinsky had composed it differed too much; he remarked, for example, that when sung in French, *Les Noces* failed to render the character of the rhythmic accentuation which constitutes the basis of the Russian chant of this work.[45] Stravinsky forbade any translation of the Hebrew text in *Abraham and Isaac* because the accentuation and timbre of the syllables are 'a precisely fixed and principal element of the music'.[46] He made a plea that the sound and stress of words should not be changed in performance.[47]

---

41   Stravinsky, Igor & Craft, Robert. 1966, 112.
42   Stravinsky, Vera & Craft, Robert. 1979, 144.
43   Stravinsky, Igor & Craft, Robert. 1982, 22.
44   The ancient Russian chant adopted the melismatic style of the Greek Orthodox church in the 11th century. Souvtchinsky, Pierre. 'Un Siècle de Musique Russe'. In Brelet, Gisèle. 1949, 542.
45   Stravinsky, Vera & Craft, Robert. 1979, 145.
46   Stravinsky, Igor. Programme note for the Festival of Israel in 1964. In White, Eric W. 1979, 529.
47   Stravinsky, Igor & Craft, Robert. 1979, 34.

Renard began with the syllables of the verse,[48] and it was in setting these popular Russian texts, in which the accents are ignored when sung, that Stravinsky made 'one of the most rejoicing discoveries of his life'.[49] He realised that the meaning of the text could be reduced to a succession of syllabic sounds and emphases in a sentence; *Renard* is phoneme music, and phonemes are untranslatable.[50] Stravinsky's ideal texts were syllable poems, such as the *haiku* of Basho and Buson, in which the words do not impose strong tonic accentuation of their own.[51]

Pierre Souvtchinsky described Stravinsky's treatment of the word as 'à la fois la conception classique et populaire' [*the idea found in both classical and folk culture*]. He continued: 'le mot ... se désagrège en articulations sonores qui s'incorporent intégralement au rhythme, à la mélodie et à l'intonation musicale' [*the word is broken up into sonorous parts which fully blend with the rhythm, melody and pitch*].[52] The ancient textual techniques of folk singers and znamenny chanters also influenced Stravinsky's word setting of *The Rake's Progress*: as Robert Craft helped him with the English prosody of the libretto he found that Stravinsky was 'not so excessively concerned with the demands of strong syllables or the tonic accent in English. What did concern him was the possibility of singing the words, placing such a vowel in such a register, the relationship between the word and the timbre of the voice and vice-versa'.[53]

The juxtaposition of 'The Word' and 'the word' in this comparison is an aetiology, a linguistic technique beloved of the ancient Hebrews that brings words together to create a new meaning. Like the literary forms of parable and paradox it depended on etymology and upon a play on words, and was a means of understanding otherwise inaccessible and inexpressible truths. A word loses a certain amount of its semantic impact by being brought into relationship with another word or by being reduced to its original value where it may become a

---

48   This scandalous skit against the Orthodox church had been made popular by itinerant skomorokhi. The fox who is full of tricks dresses all in black as a nun; in Russia nuns were regarded as inviolable.

49   At a performance of the Kabuki theatre's Kanjincho play Stravinsky was told that the verbs are syncopated, held over the barlines, and that the syllables are grouped into rhythmic quantities that tend to obscure sense. Stravinsky, Igor & Craft, Robert. 1971. *Memories and Commentaries*, 274.

50   Stravinsky, Igor & Craft, Robert. 1981: *Expositions and Developments*, 121. It was in this context that he pointed to the changes in meaning which can occur when different words are emphasised, quoting Kierkegaard's example, 'Thou shalt love thy neighbour', that changes its meaning according to whether the stress comes on 'thou', 'shalt' or 'neighbour'.

51   Stravinsky, Igor & Craft, Robert. 1981. *Memories and Commentaries*, 274.

52   Souvtchinsky, Pierre. *Musorgsky*, 88. In Brelet, Gisèle, 1949, 539.

53   Craft, Robert. 1958. In Boucourechliev, André. 1987, 234–5.

series of sounds which then form new meanings and associations. The utterances of the Hebrew prophets, for example, were full of wordplay and were charged with hidden meaning for 'those with ears to hear'. Ambiguity was not avoided and if a phrase contained several possible references then the utterance was thereby enriched.

Aetiology was one of Stravinsky's favourite linguistic techniques. As early as 1914, he had spoken to Romain Rolland of *Pribaoutki* as '*Dicts*, a form of very old Russian popular poetry consisting of a succession of words which have almost no sense, and which are connected by association of images and sounds'.[54] When composing *The Soldier's Tale*, Stravinsky read the Russian text line by line, counting the syllables and giving a word for word translation. Charles Ramuz described the final text as rich 'avec des trouvailles d'images (non-logiques) des rencontres de son d'une fraîcheur d'autant plus grande que tout sens (logique) en était absent' [*in creative mental images (not logical) of sound coming together with a freshness as great as all (logical) sense was absent*].[55] It seems that Stravinsky adapted the principle of etymological wordplay to the juxtaposition of varied time qualities to create a temporal form, for he had told Romain Rolland that he 'liked to make sudden contrasts in music between the portrayal of one subject and another completely different and unexpected subject'.[56]

Stravinsky described the word, although 'a cumbersome intermediary', as standing between the actual music and the style that bathes the work, channelling the otherwise dispersed thought and complementing the discursive sense.[57] By contrast, Schoenberg felt that his style or method was his private affair, and it was his message that he wanted to be understood and accepted: 'A Chinese philosopher speaks Chinese', he said, 'but what does he say?'[58] For Schoenberg the word was a vehicle for logical, intellectual thought with a mystical meaning. It is interesting that he chose briefly to adopt the Lutheran faith with its greater emphasis on the power of the word as a vehicle for The Word, rather than to adopt the Catholic faith with its greater emphasis on liturgy and ritual.

Schoenberg's understanding of the word as Representation of The Word developed rapidly with each of his religious works. Schoenberg thought that the basic unreality of events in *Die glückliche Hand* (1910 –13), inherent in

---

54   Stravinsky, Vera & Craft, Robert. 1979, 131.
55   Ramuz, Charles F. 1929, 37–38.
56   Stravinsky, Vera & Craft, Robert. 1979, 131.
57   Stravinsky, Igor & Craft, Robert, ed. 1985. Appendix 2, 479.
58   Stein, Erwin, ed. 1987, 223.

the words, would lend itself to being brought out by film. He explained in a letter to Emil Hertzka that the work must never suggest symbols or meaning or thoughts, but simply the play of colours and forms: 'Just as music never drags a meaning around with it ... even though meaning is inherent in its nature, so this too should simply be like sounds for the eye ...'[59] As he adhered increasingly to the philosophy of Schopenhauer he wrote to Henri Hinrichsen at Peters music publishing house in 1914 saying that he wanted his next work, *Jacobsleiter,* to be 'the expression in sound of the human soul and its desire for God'.[60] Schoenberg now seemed to identify himself with a Chosen One: in finding subjects and substance for his work, a Chosen One must leave behind some 'word' as a representation of The Word to complete his God-given task.

Schoenberg's most explicit connection between the world as Representation and the Word as the unrepresentable Will occurs in *Moses und Aron.* When the people are saved despite their apostasy, Moses voices Schoenberg's own personal theology: 'Will you allow this Interpretation? ... So I have created an Image, false, as only an Image can be? ... O word, thou word that I lack!'

Schoenberg also struggled with the impossible task of representing the unrepresentable in words when writing the text of the first of the *Four Pieces for mixed Chorus Op.27*, in 1925:

> Thou shalt make unto Thyself no Image! For an image restricts, limits, grasps, that which should remain unlimited and unimaginable. An image demands a name!

For Stravinsky, The Word was above all active in the world: his description of the action of a unified musical structure on the soul is strikingly similar to Deutero-Isaiah's description of the action of God's Word in the world:

> [A]s the rain and snow come down from heaven and do not return until they have watered the earth, making it blossom and bear fruit, and give seed for sowing and bread to eat, so shall the word which comes from my mouth prevail; it shall not return to me fruitless without accomplishing my purpose or succeeding in the task I gave it.[61]

---

59 Op. cit., 44.
60 Edition Peters: Contemporary music catalogue. New York, 1977, 86.
61 Isaiah 55.10–11 (*New English Bible*).

Thus the consummated work spreads abroad to be communicated and finally flows back towards its source. The cycle then is closed. And that is how music comes to reveal itself as a form of communion with our fellow-men – and with the Supreme Being.[62]

In a later footnote about *Jacobsleiter* and *Die glückliche Hand,* Stravinsky thought that nearly all of Schoenberg's texts were appallingly bad, some of them so bad as to discourage performance of the music.[63]

6   Synthesis

It was Robert Craft's view that after 1950, Stravinsky regarded Schoenberg 'not as the embodiment of an antithesis but as a great colleague from whom he could and did learn'.[64] The coming together of Stravinsky's keen awareness of time and all its qualities, and Schoenberg's serial relationships for the intellect, redirected Stravinsky's creative inspiration. Although Stravinsky later confessed that he had lapsed from being a regular communicant of the Orthodox Church in the 1950s – 'more because of laziness than of intellectual scruple' – he remained sincerely devout and single-minded with regard to his spiritual purpose for music.[65] The major works of Stravinsky's last years develop the temporal aspects of serialism and are explicitly religious: they explore the themes of sacred and secular love (*Cantata, Canticum Sacrum*), the journey to faith (*Cantata, Canticum Sacrum, Threni, A Sermon, A Narrative and A Prayer*), and stories of Old Testament figures who were faithful to God's commands (*Threni, The Flood, Abraham and Isaac*). His last major serial work, *Requiem Canticles,* captures each spiritual attitude of the Burial Service in ascetically-concise qualities of time as the radical climax not only to his

---

62   Stravinsky, Igor. 1947, 141–2.
63   Robert Craft observed: 'To Stravinsky, the personality, as expressed in the music and in what he had read about Schoenberg was not sympathetic. The real reason for Stravinsky's avowals of admiration later on was his indignation at the neglect and ill-treatment Schoenberg had suffered'. Craft, Robert. 1992, 41.
64   Craft, Robert. 1992, 7.
65   Stravinsky, Igor & Craft, Robert. 1981: *Expositions and Developments*, 76. In 1959–60, before performances of *Threni* and *Symphony of Psalms*, people noticed how Stravinsky genuflected and crossed himself in the Russian manner (touching the right shoulder instead of the left at the word 'Holy') in passing an altar, a crucifix, or a shrine. Horgan, Paul. 1972, 136. 'His respect and decorum for the outward symbols of faith were unselfconscious, humble and sincere'. Op. cit., 182.

'living' patterning of serial forms but also to the development of his whole life's work. In some indefinable way, Stravinsky's adoption of Schoenberg's serial system to shape the religious works of his last years stands as a monument to the deep faith and dedicated sense of mission that characterised them both.

CHAPTER 14

New Wine

Stravinsky's adoption of serial techniques was sudden. During his tour of Italy, Germany and Switzerland in 1951 he had displayed no visible reaction to recordings of Schoenberg's *Violin Concerto Op. 36* (1936) and the Dance round the Golden Calf from *Moses und Aron* (1923–37), but at the beginning of 1952 he had been deeply impressed by Webern's *Quartet Op. 22* (1930).[1] In February 1952, after the first of Robert Craft's rehearsals of Schoenberg's *Septet-Suite Op. 29* for a concert in the 'Evenings-on-the-Roof' series at the University of South California, Stravinsky asked numerous questions about its construction.[2] Following this, and beginning at the most profoundly spiritual point of his latest composition, *Cantata* – the Ascension of Christ in the penultimate verse of the Sacred History – he set the text to a serial row, arranging its forms with great symbolism.

Stravinsky continued to compose as he had always done. He recalled that thirty years before he had known little about the 12-tone method and would probably have thought it too academic.[3] Hitherto, his rhythmic manners had been rooted in Russian spirituality as expressed in the organic patterning of chant and folksong; during his final period of creativity, these inherited ways of patterning come to the fore in his organisation of serial rows, their hexachords or trichordal segments, albeit arranged with wider melodic contours. He continues to juxtapose layers differentiated by timbre to vary the depth of ontological time, organising their degree of rhythmic regularity or asymmetry, melodic compatibility or dissonance, momentum, complexity and resonance to contribute to the unity of the whole. He continues to make sudden contrasts between dynamic linear movement and layered constructions that hold back development to allow contrasts of temporal depth. These layered constructions are often crafted from serial

---

1   Craft, Robert. 1957.
2   Stravinsky, Vera & Craft, Robert. 1979, 422 After a rehearsal of Schoenberg's *Septet-Suite* in Venice in 1937, Stravinsky had told interviewers that this was an experiment, not music. Craft, Robert. 1992, 46. Shortly after Craft's rehearsal of the *Septet-Suite* in 1952, however, Stravinsky momentarily broke down, referred obliquely to the work's powerful impression, and said that he wanted to learn more. Op. cit., 39.
3   Morton, Lawrence. 'Stravinsky at home'. In Pasler, Jann. 1986, 344.

forms that are differently paced; they vary the temporal form of the work at significant spiritual moments. Serial organisation, the intrinsic patterning of patterns by related forms of themselves, presented Stravinsky with the opportunity to tighten the pitch relationships and increase the concentration of temporal densities; while completing *In Memoriam Dylan Thomas* (1954), he remarked that although he resisted the academic approach of the serial method, he found it interesting to *experience,* so long as the harmony was correct.[4]

Stravinsky's last larger-scale works are made up of contrasting formal shapes: self-contained temporal forms such as a spiral, a linear narrative, and a timeless monolith whose time qualities unfold, as in *Symphony of Psalms*, to represent a spiritual journey. His development of serial techniques in the 1950s continues the search for Maritain's perfection of formal relationships. All former stylistic influences, the patterning of folk song and chant, the mathematical faceting of the Cubists, and Maritain's ordering of proportioned materials, are now integrated with serial techniques to construct clear, mentally-imageable works that resonate with a spiritual quality.

Stravinsky's final creative phase was also characterised by the search for what Maritain had called 'new analogies of beauty'. The inspiration that he found in Webern's *Quartet Op. 22* for violin, clarinet, saxophone and piano (dedicated to the minimalist architect Adolphe Loos) may well have come from the translucent clarity of its time world. Webern's *Quartet* also unfolds an innovative formal shape: its two movements play with the tension between structure and freedom in different ways but are complementary, in that the formal unity of the first movement is perfectly balanced by the almost improvisatory character of the second. The first movement in sonata form (that repeats both its exposition and its development and recapitulation) closes with its opening section in reverse, a sealing of the form that Stravinsky was to favour. Its two movements also experiment with contrasts: both the three motifs of the first movement and the ABA form of the second movement employ stark contrasts of texture, timbre, dynamics and melodic range. The *Quartet* is relatively brief, but the extreme transparency of its timeless, self-contained temporal world becomes increasingly characteristic of Stravinsky's late works, culminating in *Requiem Canticles.*

---

4   Ibid (my italics).

1   Cantata (1952)

Cantata portrays two aspects of Love, sacred love and human love. Though somewhat alien to the modern way of thinking, the weaving together of sacred and secular love is as ancient and widespread as the association of religion and dance in the central movement, 'Tomorrow shall be my dancing day'. Wishing to set the English language in a 'purer, non-dramatic form', Stravinsky selected four popular anonymous lyrics of the 15th and 16th centuries for their great beauty and syllabification and also 'for their construction which suggested musical construction'.[5] Stravinsky described three of the poems as semi-sacred, and the fourth poem as a love lyric, saying that 'the *Cantata* is therefore secular', but in fact all four poems interweave sacred and secular ideas.[6]

Stravinsky selected four poems of contrasting qualities of time and movement with which to shape its temporal form. He was concerned lest the term *Ricercar* mask the true dynamic function of the canons and his programme notes give an analysis of the work's structure.[7]

Cantata unfolds Stravinsky's favourite spiral structure: it is unified by eight verses of a lyke-wake dirge, a lament sung by women in the late Middle Ages to keen the souls of the dead upon their way. It tells of the passage of the soul toward Purgatory, warning of the torments that await those who have not responded to their neighbours with love and charity.[8] Stravinsky learnt from Auden that the Whinny-Muir of verse 2 is the gorse moor where souls are ceaselessly nettled, 'a familiar landscape of the time', and that the Brig o'dred of verse 6 is the narrow bridge to Purgatory from which the wicked topple into Hell.[9] Stravinsky set this poem quite undramatically, however, composing the two-part female chorus in the Phrygian mode to distance the work to a remoter time. As a prayer, the stresses of words and music only lightly conflict and its circular figures largely prevent any sense of progress: rather, similarly set succeeding verses create points of rest and relief from the accumulating intensity of the intervening movements.

---

5   White, Eric W. 1979, 469.
6   Stravinsky, Igor. Programme note for the first performance. In White, Eric W. 1979, 469.
7   White, Eric W. 1979, 469. The theme of a *Ricercar*, a 16th/17th study in imitative counterpoint, was sometimes slow and lacking in rhythmic and melodic vitality.
8   Though the oral tradition of the dirge would be much older, it was first printed by Walter Scott in *Minstrelsy of the Scottish Border*, 1802. A lyke is a corpse; the Anglo-Saxon word 'lic' gives rise to 'lych-gate'.
9   January 21st, 1953. Craft, Robert. 1972, 43.

In Ricercar I, 'The maidens came', the soprano soloist hints enigmatically at the situation of a young girl who was probably rich ('I had all that I wolde') and about to be married ('How should I love and I so young?'). Her young, immature love is contrasted with the self-sacrificing love of Jesus Christ, since the refrain of her song 'the bailey berith the bell away, the lilly, the rose, the rose I lay' (fig. 2) is associated with the text of a 15th-century carol that originally celebrated the mystery of Corpus Christi. The young girl briefly recalls a mystical text which tells of a 'knight' lying on a bed in a hall in an orchard with the Virgin Mary weeping at his side.[10] The description of the sun shining through the glass window ('As the sonne shone thro' glas, so Jesu in her body was') is also a reference to the Virgin Mary: in poems of the 14th and 15th centuries, Mary's sinless conception of Jesus was compared to sunshine which passed through the glass of a window without being changed.[11]

The sacred and the secular are differentiated by quality of movement. The soprano sings of the girl's present situation against a theme for flute and its inversion in canon for cor anglais that pauses on an 0–11 interval (fig. 2): Stravinsky's signposting for 'listen'. The denser contrapuntal character of this first section contrasts with the refrain 'the bailey berith' which has the easy-flowing movement of a carol. In the refrain, the theme's rising hexachord and its imitative entries for flute and oboe are accompanied by circular movements of an 8ve and a 10th for flute and a light, pizzicato bass line. After shortened repeats of these two sections, the first section returns with more complex movement and a deeper time quality: the passing reference to 'games joyous' (fig. 6) is made with voice and flute in a closer canon against an inversion of the theme by the oboe, with a syncopated bass line that helps to brake forward momentum. The section deepens further towards the sacred subject of the next verse: the solo

---

10   I an indebted to Professor Raymond Chapman for this and the following: The refrain 'the bailey berith the bell away' became associated with the text of the Christmas carol 'Down in Yon Forest there stands a hall', collected by Vaughan Williams and included in the Oxford Book of Carols no. 61: OUP, 1956. But the earliest text of this carol, to which this poem probably alludes, is that found in the Richard Hill manuscript of 1500, printed by Dyboski and others. This text runs: 'Lully, Lulley, Lully, Lulley! The falcon hath borne my make away. 1. He bare him up, he bare him down, He bare him into an orchard brown. (Refrain) 2. In that orchard there was an hall, That was hanged with purple and pall. 3. And in that hall there was a bed, It was hanged with gold so red. 4. And in that bed there lieth a Knight, His wounds bleeding day and night. 5. By that bed's side kneeleth a may, And she weepeth both night and day. 6. And by that bed's side there standeth a stone, "Corpus Christi" written thereon'. The mystical meaning of the 15th century original text was probably Eucharistic.

11   Renaissance paintings of the Annunciation often show sunlight passing through a window.

dedication to Queen Elizabeth I is made with strictly rhythmic phrases that develop into the florid style of dméstvenny chant (fig. 7). They introduce the densely contrapuntal prayer to Christ for the souls of the dead ('grant them a place eternally to sing').[12] The depth of time quality that has been established is then lightened by the next two verses of A Lyke-Wake Dirge.

Tomorrow shall be my dancing day, like the middle movement of *Octet*, forms the densest part of the work, alternating nuanced qualities of time and movement in a much tighter spiral form. From the start, Stravinsky's adoption of serialism was cautious and on his own terms: the 'series' for the Sacred History (derived from 'We will therfor [*sic*] now sing no more' in 'The maidens came') is composed of 11 notes including repetitions of the pitch E (Ex. 57).[13] It patterns the short pitch gamut with the same laser-like intensity as a priest's close intoning of dméstvenny chant at the beginning of a festal liturgy, to penetrate the acoustic and establish a resonance.

EX. 57   Close festive patterning of the serial row: Tomorrow shall be my dancing day

'Tomorrow shall be my dancing day' brings the sudden contrast of strictly ordered relationships of rhythm and pitch in dense counterpoint after the lighter time qualities of canonic movement and the modal tonalities of the opening movements. The text of 'Tomorrow shall be my dancing day' comes from an English carol of the Middle Ages found on early printed broadside sheets in which Jesus speaks of his Incarnation on earth as his 'dancing day' and the Church as His love. The reference to 'the legend of my play' probably comes from performances of medieval Mystery plays that lasted about three or four days, each day ending with dancing to the music of minstrels. Just as

---

12   This second stanza had been added by the Chaucer scholar, E. Talbot. Stravinsky read everything he could about Queen Elizabeth 1st and this dedication probably influenced his choice of text. Craft, Robert. 2006, 172.

13   Stravinsky's fifth point of comparison (Stravinsky, Igor & Craft, Robert. 1982, 107–9) reveals that like Schoenberg Stravinsky regarded numbers as 'things'. Stravinsky was interested in Cabbalistic numbers, for example, ringing the prime numbers 17 and 29 in his sketches for the Sacrificial Dance in *The Rite of Spring*. Forte, Allen. 1978, 115, n. 67. The shorter row may symbolise the cutting short of Schoenberg's life, or may symbolise the absence of Judas.

God was not to be praised in loud music, Stravinsky creates a paradoxically still, timeless quality for the history of Christ's Incarnation as 'dancing'. He does this in two ways. Firstly, any sense of progression is negated by the serial and canonic treatment of the verses; only the tonal, non-canonic setting of the ritornello 'to call my true love to the dance' allows a little forward momentum. Secondly, after the first two verses, the more expressive and symbolically-complex even-numbered verses are followed (as in *Octet*) by the recurring 'weight' of the plainer odd-numbered verses; this gravitational pull not only checks any sense of development, but underlines the significance of Christ's Incarnation as continuing for all time.

This movement is distanced from the here-and-now and presents a remote but finely-nuanced timeless quality. Stravinsky spoke of being constantly located in time in a tonal-system work, but of only 'going-through' a polyphonic work, whether it be Josquin's *Duke Hercules Mass* or a serially-composed non-tonal-system work. He confirmed that his choice in serial composition was made just as in any tonal contrapuntal form and that he composed as he always had, composing vertically and hearing harmonically: in the horizontal, he arranged the 'file' as he wanted, but the 'vertical assemblages' had to justify themselves before God.[14] Stravinsky defined 'hearing harmonically' (for example, in Boulez's *Deux Improvisations sur Mallarmé* and *Le Marteau sans maître*), in terms of hearing densities, which, he observed, had become a strict serial matter, an element for variation and permutation like any other.[15] He added that this all went back to Webern.[16]

The Prime row form (P) consists of just six different pitches within the close compass of a diminished 5th. Initially it is connected seamlessly to its Retrograde (R), Inversion (I) and Retrograde Inversion (RI) forms at a slower Tempo I (♪ = 108), marked 'Cantus Cancrizans'. For the first two verses, the row is in the priestly style of dméstvenny chant, as is the refrain 'Sing oh, my love, oh, my love'. Christ's tonal ritornello, 'To call my true love to my dance' moves forward more easily at a faster Tempo 2 (♪ = 66), as if underlining the urgency of His purpose. The story of Christ's life on earth begins in verse 3 at the faster Tempo 2 that is maintained to the end of the movement. In verse 3 the harmonisation of the tonal ritornello changes and it is more densely scored.

From verse 3 the verses are accompanied solely by two oboes and a cello, the two flutes being recalled only for the new ritornello. The odd-numbered verses, though differing rhythmically in the vocal part to accommodate Stravinsky's

---

14   Stravinsky, Vera & Craft, Robert. 1979, 248.
15   Stravinsky, Igor & Craft, Robert. 1979, 24–25, 128.
16   Stravinsky, I. and Craft, R. 1979, 128.

setting of the text, present the row forms in the same order, I – R – P, each time with the same accompaniment of P forms. But in the second line of each of these odd-numbered verses, the R form in the tenor is lowered and the P form in the oboe part is raised, to bring about a closer juxtaposition of discordant tritones and draw greater attention to the text: in verse 3 it marks out Jesus' poverty; in verse 5 His fasting; in verse 7 Judas' covetousness; in verse 9 the glancing spear; and in verse 11 Jesus' position at the right hand of God.

The row in the even-numbered verses is treated much more descriptively and Stravinsky creates a rich array of symbolic devices to illuminate the text. Like his medieval predecessors, he does not resist arranging the canonic forms to create a pun.[17]

In verse 4, as the Holy Ghost alights on Jesus at his Baptism and the voice of God the Father is heard, Stravinsky sets the row forms around a central pitch, B♭, symbolising the oneness of the Three Persons of the Trinity. Apart from verse 3, where the row forms are held distinct until Jesus is laid in a manger and 'wrapped', verse 4 is the only verse in which lines of text and row forms overlap and in which row forms pivot seamlessly around the central pitch. The three vocal forms, R (a major 2nd lower), P and I, connect smoothly, the latter two beginning on the final note of the preceding form. Set against widely-spaced transpositions of the row for instruments, all row forms are held clearly discrete. The open structure and light time quality of verse 4 reflects the transcendent nature of Jesus' Baptism: the musical space enlarges, and its movement changes significantly as each line is extended to four bars (compared to three bars in other even-numbered verses), and the R and RI forms between the oboes are elongated to last for three lines of text.

In verse 6, where the Jews make 'great suit' with Jesus, the conflict is expressed by the tenor's transposed and aspirated I form and its disjointed connection to the following RI form (at the original pitch) against densely presented I forms in the oboes and a continuously jerky cello line. As they make 'great variance', the instrumental rows set against the tenor voice cease. Finally, 'darkness' is symbolised by the juxtaposition of three widely-spaced P forms, with two forms in canon against the third form at a conflicting pitch.

In verse 8, in which Jesus is condemned, the tenor's P form is accompanied, agitato, by widely-spaced and florid P and I forms for oboes and cello. The release of the robber, Barabbas, is marked out by being the only place in

---

17   Musical puns in the riddle canons of the 14th and 15th centuries often involve retrograde motion: i.e. 'Ma fin est mon commencement': Machaut, 'Canit more Hibraeorum' (sung as the Hebrews read i.e. from right to left), 'Vade retro Satanus' (Retreat, Satan). Apel, W., ed. 1970, 728: 'Retrograde'.

which the vocal part does not have the row. The climax at 'For they scourged me and set me at nought' is set to three juxtaposed statements of the P form to represent 'nought', but are distorted at their beginning and end: the tenor line a semitone lower, the first oboe at the octave above at a slower pace, and the second oboe, a sixth below, are accompanied by fierce demisemiquaver figures in the cello.

In verse 10, in which Jesus descends into Hell, the row forms of the first two lines (R and P against RI and R) are set at the original pitch to make the greatest contrast with the third line announcing his Resurrection. At the text 'he rose again on the third day' (Ex. 58), Stravinsky raises the P and I forms a semitone higher against the R form at the interval of a 5th. This raising of pitch brings a new spaciousness and depth: the regularity of the phrase lengths is interrupted by repeated words and elongated note values to evoke his transformation into a new quality of time and space.

EX. 58   The new time quality of Jesus' resurrection

The Sacred History creates a uniquely spiritual time world with recurring patterns of circular movement, juxtapositions of row forms that constantly vary in degrees of ease and compatibility, and a deepening of time quality at spiritual moments of special significance. Withdrawal from its vast time-scale is achieved by returning to the familiar circular movements and modal tonality of The Lyke-Wake Dirge.

Stravinsky's setting of the fourth poem, Westron Wind, contains much imitation but not the formal canons of the other pieces.[18] The poem draws an analogy between human love and sexuality and the love of God in sending wind and rain to sustain his Creation, and has, like the *Song of Songs*, long enjoyed a sacred context. Taverner, Tye and Shepherd used a 16th century English tune for this 'secular' poem as a Cantus Firmus for their settings of the Mass.

The 'wild agitation' of the wind (and the sweeping power of love) in this tonal duet for soprano and tenor arises from the light interaction of the 'ostinato song-style accompaniment' in the cello, with compatible instrumental rhythms and widely-spaced vocal figures at the same rate of change.[19] The

18   White, Eric W. 1966, Appendix 1, 471.
19   Ibid.

movement continues the withdrawal from the deep time quality of the Sacred History, and the work concludes with the two final verses of The Lyke-Wake Dirge, and a return of the first verse to seal the structure of this temporal form.

2   Stravinsky, Webern and God

As Stravinsky embarked upon what he described as his 'long slow climb up the fifties', the time worlds of Webern's crystalline structures increasingly drew his interest; he described Webern as a perpetual Pentecost for all who believe in music. Robert Craft recorded that between 1952 and 1955 Stravinsky listened constantly to the music of Webern and that he was familiar with the sound of Webern's cantatas and instrumental songs at a time when some of these works had not yet been performed in Europe.

Webern also saw his work as a compelling musical mission in the service of a higher reality. Although Stravinsky found the sentiment of Webern's two late *Cantatas* alien, he identified with Webern's religious attitude to composing and thought him supremely important as the discoverer of a new distance between the listener and the musical object, and of a new measure of musical time. Stravinsky described Webern as profoundly religious, not only institutionally but (like himself) religious 'in the simple holiness of his feeling towards each of God's essents (a flower, a mountain, 'silence')'. But he did find it extraordinary that Webern should compare the six movements of his second *Cantata* to a Kyrie, Gloria, Credo, Benedictus, Sanctus, and Agnus Dei.[20]

'Let's speak no more of Art, but of Nature!' Webern's spirituality was expressed as 'the endeavour to discover the laws by which Nature in the specific form of Man is productive', so that 'something else appears: the *essential*'.[21] Like Stravinsky and Schoenberg, Webern sought to create coherent musical schemes that would bring spiritual insight, believing that 'if interrelationship and coherence are everywhere, the comprehensibility is also guaranteed'.[22] Webern considered the Lord's Prayer to be the greatest model for Art, since

20   Stravinsky, Igor & Craft, Robert. 1981: *Memories and Commentaries*, 103–4. Stravinsky compared Webern to a village priest, content in his immediate locality. Stravinsky thought that he himself had been born out of time, in the sense that by temperament and talent he would have been more suited for the life of a small Bach, living in anonymity and composing regularly for an established service and for God. Stravinsky, Igor & Craft, Robert. 1982, 123.
21   Boulez, Pierre: 1978, I: Aesthetic.
22   Op. cit., VI: Language.

it achieves the greatest comprehensibility, clarity and unambiguousness.[23] Stravinsky thought that for Webern, music was a mystery he did not seek to explain, and that no other meaning existed for him but music.[24]

Webern compared his own compositional method to that of the Parthenon frieze: 'always the same thing in a thousand different ways'.[25] His metamorphic forms imitate the 'law of Nature', capturing the 'being' of natural things such as flowers and crystals in terms of their structures. Webern described his way of working in writing to the poet Hildegard Jone: 'Many metamorphoses of the first shape produce the theme; this as a new unit, in turn undergoes as many metamorphoses; these welded into a new unity, make up the form of the whole'.[26]

The row of Webern's *Variations for Orchestra Op. 30* (1940), for example, that Stravinsky particularly admired, is made up of three related tetrachords in which all the intervals are either minor 2nds or minor 3rds. The whole work is generated by a 4-note phrase of two semitones separated by a minor 3rd in which one note is always shorter than the other three. It generates the greatest possible unity of row forms, intervals, motifs and chords. The form is structured and unified by the constant reflection of related cells within the row to create a mosaic in sound, just as Stravinsky had ordered variants of a single three-note motif to unify *Les Noces*, combinations of intervals of a 3rd to unify *Oedipus Rex*, variations on a first inversion arpeggio and a single rhythmic foot to unify *Apollo*, and a 'two-part' motif to unify *Perséphone*.

In *Variations Op. 30*, Webern juxtaposes rhythmic lines of widely disparate pace, and contrasts scattered row fragments with 4-part chords. He promotes a new flexibility in the 12-tone system by varying both density and flux within the tempo. *Variations* is shaped by tempo controls: each metamorphosis of the motif has its own tempo, and tempo is also linked to dynamics. Stravinsky was interested in tempo controls, and he cited the central movement of Boulez' *Le Marteau sans maître* as an important innovation. In this movement the beat is precisely quickened or held back to basic fast or slow metronome speeds, controlling the ritardando and accelerando. Stravinsky admired the fact that the movement was always en route to a new tempo, creating a 'wonderfully supple kind of music'.[27] One of the chief characteristics of Stravinsky's 'long slow climb up the fifties' was the increasing flexibility of his temporal forms.

---

23   Op. cit., VIII: Personality.
24   Stravinsky, Igor & Craft, Robert. 1981: *Memories and Commentaries*, 103.
25   Op. cit., 104.
26   Ewen, David. 1968, 898.
27   Stravinsky, Igor & Craft, Robert. 1979, 110.

At the end of the 1950s, Stravinsky described Webern's later instrumental works and the songs that came after the first twelve opus numbers and before the *Trio* as perhaps the richest music he ever wrote. This may be partly because all the songs from *Op. 15* to *Op. 18* (except the first of *Op. 18*) have a religious text, including meditations on the sufferings of Christ and the Virgin Mary. Stravinsky also remarked upon the 'entirely new principle of order' that appeared in the brief *Songs Op. 18* (1925) which he thought would in time be 'conventionalised'. He does not elaborate on this new principle of order but the songs play with rhythmic juxtapositions. Each of the three *Songs Op. 18* has a different rhythmic character, the beat being divided into 2, 3 or 4, and lines being superimposed to create a state of flux: patterns are continually demolished and then reassembled as different versions of the same patterns. No one pattern returns, yet all are related as 'family members', creating an intensely close-knit texture. In the two *Songs Op. 19* that follow, Webern creates a 'rhythmic dissonance' that matches the angular character of the pitch organisation: here the pulse is divided 2 against 3, 4 against 6, and different rhythmic lines are juxtaposed.[28]

Stravinsky described Webern as 'having opened many doors',[29] and later acknowledged him as the first 20th century composer to distinguish between the passive act of 'hearing' and the active process of 'listening' that enters fully into a work's relationships.[30] Stravinsky acknowledged the debt that composers owed Webern in the vocabulary of rhythm, in the measurement of time, and in the general raising of sensibility to these things.[31] But he also reflected on Webern's time-scale as tiny, his quantity as minute, his variety as limited. However, Stravinsky considered that if scope were concerned with depth, for example, and not merely with width and expanse, Webern's scope can be very great, and is perfectly circumscribed.[32]

Stravinsky, by contrast, needed to feel a 'dynamic passage through music' and 'a physical here and there and not only a now, which is to say a movement from and toward'.[33] Always favouring a dialectical form of musical argument, he later admitted that Webern seems to put a low premium on the listener's

---

28   Stravinsky observed that the *Beklemmt* episode in the Cavatina from Beethoven's *String Quartet* Op. 130, for example, acquired a new dimension a full century later because of the rhythmic rediscoveries of Webern and others. Stravinsky, Igor & Craft, Robert. 1972, 188.

29   Stravinsky, Vera & Craft, Robert. 1979, 430.

30   Stravinsky, Igor & Craft, Robert. 1979, 130.

31   Stravinsky, Igor & Craft, Robert. 1972, 96.

32   Op. cit., 92–3.

33   Stravinsky, Igor & Craft, Robert. 1982, 127.

sense of involvement: 'Not only is the music wholly unrhetorical,' he observed, 'but it does not invite participation in the argument of its own creation as, say, Beethoven's does …' Emphasising the importance of a temporal journey in music, he described each opus of Webern as 'offering itself only as a whole, a unity to be contemplated'. Stravinsky found Webern's music essentially static, and thought that the cost in subjectivity was high.[34]

3   Canticum Sacrum (1955)

In this work Stravinsky's true musical legacy, the synthesis of Eastern and Western styles and the restoration of music as a temporal art, came into focus. His ambition of grafting Russian culture onto that of the West was even symbolised by the work's première in St Mark's Basilica in Venice, a building that combines the glories of the West and Eastern exoticism. Its five compact movements, constructed with a fine sense of symmetry and proportion, take the listener on a journey that reflects a tour of the Basilica. Like Monteverdi's *Vespers,* which Stravinsky admired for its rhythmic invention, *Canticum Sacrum* is composed of a variety of styles, a *mélange* that ranges from Orthodox chant to serialism, and which disorients any recognition of its place in time and space. This autonomous musical object is shaped by time qualities that reflect the spiritual progression of the texts, unified by its serial treatment of pitch, and sealed by the return of the first movement, Euntes in Mundum, in reverse.

The themes of sacred and secular love, interwoven in *Cantata,* are explored again in *Canticum Sacrum* through biblical texts that recount divine invitation and human response. The texts come from both the Old and New Testaments, and the text of Caritas, taken from the First Letter of John, connects the two parts of the Bible in a new and vital way. The texts describe a circular movement: the risen Jesus' command to the disciples to preach the Gospel in all the world moves back in time to an early allegory of God's love, followed by the story of a father's personal transformation through belief, and the disciples' transformation into Apostles who then go forth to heal and witness to the world. The work describes the same movement of regeneration from heaven to earth and back that is made in the final words of Stravinsky's *Poetics of Music.* This movement is embodied in a monumental crystalline structure; there is a fine balance and symmetry between the solo voices and chorus, chordal and contrapuntal movements, and the musical styles of East and West.

---

34   Stravinsky, Igor & Craft, Robert. 1972, 93.

EX. 59   Close circular layers of verset: Euntes in mundum

Canticum Sacrum opens with a musical 'narthex'. It unites East and West before the sacred history begins: two male soloists dedicate the work to the city of Venice and its Patron Saint, St Mark, with the bare, dissonant intervals of strotchny chant, their proclamation accompanied by Gabrielli-style trombones with two-part Renaissance counterpoint in contrary motion. The musical space opened up by this narthex is enlarged by the extreme contrasts of Euntes in mundum, in which loud tutti forces alternate with a soft five-voice verset, nine bars long, for organ and bassoons (Ex.59).

This is Stravinsky's only writing for organ, perhaps included in the ensemble as appropriate for the acoustics of the vast basilica, and also to commemorate its glorious musical past. The contrast between these two qualities of movement creates great depth of musical time and space in which Jesus' command to preach in 'all the world' can resonate.[35] *Canticum Sacrum,* like St Mark's itself, is a meeting place between heaven and earth in which the present is joined with the timeless.[36] Stravinsky's setting reflects this duality: rapidly repeating semiquaver chords beat upon the acoustic in an early 17th century Venetian-style *concitato,* shimmering like the mosaics and *Pala d'Oro* of the building itself. Juxtaposed to an irregular ostinato composed largely of a minor

35   'Go ye into all the world, and preach the gospel to every creature', Mark 16.7 in the Vulgate
      version, comes in Mark 16.15 in modern editions of the Bible. Contemporary scholars now
      generally agree that the original Gospel of Mark ended at chapter 16.8, so this text, the last
      words of Christ to his Apostles, are part of a later addition.

36   It was well-known that the five domes of St Mark's basilica suggested the five-movement
      form of the *Canticum Sacrum,* and that Stravinsky was also influenced by Palladian prin-
      ciples, such as surrounding a central axis with rooms of sequentially different sizes. Craft,
      Robert. 1992, 9.

3rd, these chords restrain movement but vibrate, *forte*, giving depth to the present. This deep 'now' contrasts with the timeless serenity of the soft verset (bar 17), a modal passage that allows time not only for this body of sound to clear but also for the implications of Jesus' command to register. The 'heavenly' effect of this verset – heard unchanged on two separate occasions – lies in the stately crotchet movement of its five independent lines within a small pitch range: the changes of chord are smoothed by suspensions, evoking a quality of ever-changing changelessness.

Jesus' command is followed by a poetic declaration of God's love: the text of Surge, Aquilo comes from the *Song of Songs* and has been widely, if at times controversially, recognised as an allegory of the love of God for His people, the love of Christ for His church, or the love of the divine Logos for the faithful soul. This collection, or cycle, of songs, whose title means 'loveliest song', has occasioned much piety and religious teaching throughout history.[37] The book was part of the Second Canon by the first century CE and was appointed to be read at the Passover, the solemn but joyful celebration of God's salvation of his people. Israel recognised that all aspects of human life have a full and rightful place in God's purpose, so that these poems, an allegorical dialogue between a bridegroom and his bride, explore the simplicity, gentleness and strength of human love and marriage with great insight.[38]

Surge, Aquilo deepens the remote time world that has been established. Introduced by Stravinsky's first use of tetrachords from the row as four-part chords, its row forms are then presented in the close-knit decorative style of dméstvenny chant (Ex.60):

EX. 60   Serial row of Surge, Aquilo in festive style of dméstvenny chant

---

37   The view of this poem as an allegory of God's love for his Creation has a long history going back before Origen (c.184–253 CE); St Bernard of Clairvaux, for instance, wrote eight sermons on the first two chapters alone. By contrast, this poem, which is also known as *The Song of Solomon*, is now viewed by most modern scholars as describing human love, believing this to be its original meaning. See Barton, John 2020, 345.

38   Christians writing about spiritual love in Greek could not use the ordinary word for love because of its erotic associations, but in Hebrew, the same word is used for the love of God and for human love. *Peake's Commentary on the Bible*, 1967, 468–70.

The many repeating dyads for solo tenor and flute (as in bar 2) not only set up resonant pitch centres that highlight the row's intervals of a tone and semitone, and even its Old Believers' motif (E♭– D♭– B♭), but also stretch time with asymmetrical phrase lengths. The delicately-scored accompaniment for harp, wind and double bass, often in harmonics, enhances the exotic text with transparent textures.

The bridegroom's invitation to his beloved to attend the feast is given in descriptive melismas that create a free-flowing, hypnotic quality.[39] Surge, Aquilo makes a historical parallel with the first motet, Nigra sum, of Monteverdi's *Vespers* (1610), also written for performance in Venice, by being a 'new' kind of monody and accompaniment. The final pitch, A, links this allegorical love poem about the love of God for His people to the important new spiritual insight of the next movement by becoming the first note of its related row.

Ad Tres Virtutes Hortationes is the dense heart of the work's temporal form but also embodies a gradual opening of the spirit in its progressively fluid treatment of the row. Stravinsky reverses the biblical order of Faith, Hope and Love so that the theme of Love continues from the second movement, and the third section, Faith, leads to the story about the power of belief. Following Surge, Aquilo and its theme of God's love for his people, the first text of Caritas, from Deuteronomy (6.5), recalls that the Hebrews were commanded to love God with all their heart, soul and might, for He had redeemed them from slavery in Egypt. The second text of Caritas comes from the First Letter of John (4.7) and introduces a new command: 'Beloved, *let us love one another*: for love is of God'.[40] John expresses an important new understanding: pointing to the act of 'loving' as God's chief characteristic, he suggests that we in turn must love each other and treat others as God treats us.[41] In repeating the first part of this text to enlarge the section Stravinsky emphasised the importance of this 'new text'.[42]

---

39 Jacques-Bénigne Bossuet points to the important fellowship that comes from sharing food and drink, and also its symbolism in the Eucharist: *Lettres Sur L'Evangile* LIIième Jour, Vol. II, 137. The reference to the garden conveys that the bride is modest and chaste, and the description of her as 'my sister' and 'my spouse' denotes psychic nearness and tenderness as found in Egyptian love poems. Myrrh was much used for incense and perfume, and the honeycomb and honey describe the sweetness of her words (Proverbs 5.3). 'The beloved' are the friends invited to the wedding feast.

40 This text is now thought to have been written by John the Elder, author of the three Epistles of John, and not by John the Apostle. (My italics.).

41 C. H. Dodd described these words as St John's (sic) 'outstanding contribution' to Christian theology: *The Johannine Epistles,* 1946 quoted by G. Johnston. In *Peake's Commentary on the Bible,* 1038.

42 Stravinsky, Vera & Craft, Robert. 1979, 431.

In the organ ritornello that opens Caritas the intervals of the RI form are arranged so that each hexachord begins compactly but then widens. It leads to a light, widely-spaced and melismatic instrumental meditation on the R form in preparation for the choral entry. The two texts that mark the new understanding of humankind's relationship with God are set identically to widely-spaced row forms in canon for the three upper voices. The light and compact choral counterpoint in largely crotchet movement is set against the piercing timbre of the trumpet row forms at half speed (bars 116 bis), deepening the time quality.

In the organ ritornello that opens Spes (Hope) the intervals of the same RI form (now a minor 3rd higher) are arranged more widely than in Caritas, not only enlarging the musical space but adding to the movement's new sense of flexibility and momentum (Ex. 61).

EX. 61   Wider arrangement of the row to introduce Spes

The tempo of ♩ = 108 is maintained but the metre alternates between 3/8 and 5/8. The Vulgate text of Psalm 124, for solo tenor and baritone, whose wide marcato intervals and rock-like quality are repeated more or less exactly three times, is a national psalm of trust and confidence in the Lord that likens His divine protection to the unshakeability of Mount Zion. Stravinsky emphasises this quality with a single repeated dyad for male voices at the same tempo but in 3/8 metre on *confidunt* (trust), *commovebitur* (moved) and *habitat* (stand). The two melismatic responses from Psalm 129, at a faster tempo for sopranos and altos in 5/8 metre, punctuated by chords for oboes and trombone, are part of an individual penitential lament which, as in *Symphony of Psalms*, tells of the Psalmist's patient but eager waiting for forgiveness.[43] The two texts proceed antiphonally, with an answering repetition of dyads on *sustinuit* and an extended treatment of *Domino* and *a custodia* for sopranos and altos. The poetic allusion to the coming of dawn, a simple but effective figure typical of the *Songs of Ascent,* is addressed to an assembled company of worshippers.[44] The last phrase of text for solo tenor and bass at the tempo of ♪ = 108 slightly

---

43   Psalms 125, 130 in *The Book of Common Prayer*.

44   *The Songs of Ascent,* Psalms 120–134 (in the Hebrew numbering), were sung by pilgrims as they went up to Jerusalem for the festivals.

EX. 62   Continued expansion of the row to open Fides

expands the row on *habitat*, likening the Lord's encircling of his people to the hills encircling Jerusalem.[45]

The RI form that opens Fides (Faith) has the most widely-spaced intervals and a rock-like character (Ex.62).

The very space-creating row form for trombones, bassoons and double bass that follows proceeds at the original tempo of ♩ = 180 but nevertheless unfolds very slowly, with triple divisions of the pulse aspirated by rests and the elongation of repeated dyads. Momentum is further slowed at the choral entry, not only by a new slower tempo, but by the many oscillations on the word *credidi* (I believed) that begin their two phrases of text. This text from Psalm 115 (Vulgate text) expresses the thanksgiving of the individual worshipper who has been delivered from serious illness and who comes to the sanctuary to acknowledge to other worshippers what God has done. The greatest depth of time quality in this movement comes in the following six-part canonic structure (bar 219) in which the text, 'I was greatly afflicted', is set to what Stravinsky described as his barbarous counterpoint: a slow-moving construction of closely arranged serial rows and their reverse patterns for four-part choir that is juxtaposed to contrast with two instrumental forms moving at a much slower speed. Its unrelieved density finally resolves into the recall of the semitone oscillation of *credidi* for trumpets (bar 237) joined by the organ in a three-part canon. The dense heart of the work is concluded by the row form, now unison and *tranquillo*, for the softer timbres of the lower strings.

Continuing this progression to an open and flexible depth of musical time and space but at a new slower tempo, Brevis Motus Cantilenæ relates a story about the power of belief. A linear narrative tells of Jesus' response to the man who seeks a cure for his epileptic son.[46] Jesus' words develop the flexibility of the row still further with many triple divisions of the pulse and fluidly repeating dyads, and are given a resonant 'halo': the chorus shadow his words with overlapping responses, related by pitch and pulse but varied rhythmically to create striking echo effects. The contrasting density of a four-part canon for

---

45   Psalm 125.2: 'even so standeth the Lord round about his people, from this time forth for evermore'.

46   Mark 9.14–29.

the unaccompanied chorus, marked *agitato* (bar 274), slows as the father's distress becomes a free-flowing, unaccompanied recitative.[47] His wondering acknowledgement of his new-found belief is conveyed by repeating dyads and wide intervals at *Credo, Domine* (I believe, Lord). The out-of-time quality of the event is maintained in the last part of the text: *Credo, Domine, adjuva incredulitatem meam* (Lord, I believe: help thou my unbelief), as the baritone solo meditates at an even slower tempo over a pedal note D; the passage is articulated with a slightly irregular and lengthening pattern of rests. The time quality is intensified and (as with the moment of enlightenment in *Oedipus Rex*) reaches its greatest depth with the final accumulation of the row form into a softly-sustained chord.

Belief transforms the disciples' former inability to heal the sick. In the biblical story, the disciples go forth as Apostles and preach everywhere, the Lord working with them in their healing ministry. Illi autem profecti repeats the first movement in reverse, recalling the original command, completing the circular spiritual movement, and sealing the musical form. The joining of heaven and earth, the timeless and the temporal, is achieved for all time.[48]

4   Threni (1958)

Stravinsky selected verses from *The Lamentations of Jeremiah* for *Threni* although he did not have any hopes that the work would be used liturgically on Maundy Thursday.[49] *Threni's* three-part structure embodies a progression from self-examination and deep penitence, to hope and a desire for justice, and finally to faith and conversion of life. Like *Symphonies of Wind Instruments* and the Agnus Dei of his *Mass*, the shape of De Elegia Prima is that of a

---

47   The three large upward intervals of the Father's cry are reminiscent of Peter's poignant weeping in Bach's *St Matthew Passion* following his betrayal of Jesus.

48   Francis Poulenc had read *Canticum Sacrum* at Nadia Boulanger's house and found it sublime; he wrote to Stravinsky: 'What is admirable is that you are always a model of youth, faith and lucidity.' Craft, Robert. 2011, 214.

49   Stravinsky, Igor & Craft, Robert. 1979, 124. Stravinsky's title is *Lamentations*, to distinguish the work from the *Tenebrae* Service that is specifically for liturgical use in the evening of Maundy Thursday. From the late 15th to the 17th centuries, the text was often set polyphonically, usually in a simple homophonic style except for the letters, which often received a more elaborate treatment. Lamentations were last composed in the Baroque era: settings include those by Tinctoris, Tromboncino, Carpentras (used in the Papal chapel until 1587), Arcadelt, Claude Le Jeune, Palestrina (used in the Papal chapel from 1588), Morale, Tallis, Byrd, Händl, Allegri (added to Palestrina's setting in 1640 and still in use in the Papal chapel), Rosenmüller and Couperin.

litany: contrasting qualities of time and movement are interwoven into a close spiral structure whose intensity evokes a mood of deep penitence. De Elegia Tertia is largely linear, with dynamic forward movement; row forms that build on the flexibility of Fides and Brevis Motus Cantilenæ in *Canticum Sacrum* reflect the actions of the text with increasing expressivity as hope grows. De Elegia Quinta builds a monumental and resonant structure by its range of timbres, bell-strikes, and slowly oscillating dyads, and creates a large musical space for contemplative prayer.

The writings known as *The Lamentations of Jeremiah* present a vivid picture of the desolation felt by the Hebrew people following the Fall of Jerusalem and the destruction of the Temple in 586 BCE. They are to be understood as the laments or penitential liturgies of a people who saw the recent events in terms of personal and communal judgement, rather than as the heartfelt sorrow of a single prophet, Jeremiah.[50] They portray a turning point in the life of a people when, following the collapse of their religious faith and hope, they began to feel a capacity for self-criticism and the grace of penitence. Adopted into the Jewish liturgical tradition, the *Lamentations* were appointed to be read on the Fast of the 9th of Ab which commemorated the destruction of the Temple. In biblical times, this ritual dirge was performed by professionally trained women.[51]

Stravinsky's texts are taken from Chapters One, Three and Five of the *Lamentations*. Chapter One, spoken by the prophet Jeremiah to the community, describes the disasters that have befallen Jahweh's people and Jerusalem. The sin of the people and the rightness of Divine Judgement is acknowledged, and a call made for retribution to be meted out to those who have invaded them and destroyed their distinctive social and religious structures. The Covenant with Jahweh has been profaned and Jerusalem is seen, in strong imagery, as a woman taken in adultery. Chapters Three and Five are both songs of the community: Chapter Three is a lament and a confession of faith and hope, Chapter Five is a congregational prayer for restoration, both the restoration of the Temple ritual and of the Covenant relationship with God as his Chosen People. *Threni* sets only verses 19 and 21, but verses 19–22 form one of the great utterances of faith in the Bible, the climax to a prayer describing the desperate

---

50   As God's messenger and a representative of the people, Jeremiah was a mediator between God and his people. The Lamentations became associated with him because of the great love he had for his land and his people: he saw all human things as revelations of God, *sub specie aeternitatis.*

51   See 2 Samuel 1.19–27.

plight of Jerusalem with the utmost realism. The rabbis directed that verse 21 (with which *Threni* ends) should be read again in the liturgy after verse 22.

The poetic form of the original Hebrew text is that of the kinah, a 3:2 metre that, coupled with the sounds of the syllables and the repetitive tripartite form of each stanza, has a hypnotic effect. Stravinsky has preserved this hypnotic effect in his three-part musical settings and syllabic treatment of the Latin translation. The Hebrew text is acrostic in form: Chapter One has the successive letters of the Hebrew alphabet at the beginning of each stanza; Chapter Three, like Psalm 119, begins the three *stichoi* (balanced couplets) of each stanza with the proper letter, and Chapter Five has no letters but 22 verses, the number of letters in the Hebrew alphabet. These dirges, with all their hidden play of language, were used by prophets to stimulate sorrow and penitence. Stravinsky's setting of the *Lamentations* is deeply involved with his view of the 20th century as guilty of apostasy and of the 'sin of non-acknowledgement'.[52] Understood in the light of his religious beliefs, his choice of subject not only restores parts of the musical spirit in disuse but also carries a powerful message for our own times.

Stravinsky's row includes five intervals of a 3rd, three 4ths and a 5th and two semitone intervals, allowing forms of the row to combine in brief moments of tonal harmony. His deployment of the 12 notes of the row is more adventurous and more flexible than before: row forms and their transpositions are held rhythmically or timbrally distinct and overlapped or set against segments of the same or other row forms; canonic entries between row forms are contracted and expanded to vary forward momentum; row forms are paced by repeating dyads or reflecting melodic shapes through successive parts to brake or accelerate movement or vary density. Stravinsky also confounds established melodic patterns of the row with those obtained by numerical abstractions in order to brake momentum, increase density, and diminish the sense of the present. He juxtaposes row forms – including his 'own' IR form – in regular and irregular, compatible and non-compatible strata as before, increasing the complexity of pitch relationships and creating pools of consonant tonality and rest.[53]

---

52 Stravinsky, Theodor: 1953, 18 and Stravinsky, Igor. 1947, 47. Jeremiah saw the One Sin as infidelity to God, whom he conceived as wonderfully kind, but as a consuming fire.

53 Stravinsky uses the IR form often: not simply the reverse of the Inversion, but also beginning with the final note of the Prime form. Andrew Kuster observes that Stravinsky often uses the IR form to highlight moments of musical and textual-poetic significance. It is also used as a foundation row for certain sections; after moving away from it, Stravinsky returns to the IR for significant formal circumstances. See Kuster, A. 2005. 2. The IR form creates another patterned facet of the central pitch.

The work is scored for a large orchestra including sarrusaphone and flugel-horn and six soloists including a basso profundo. The opening dedication of De Elegia Prima establishes its pitch world and ontological time quality by juxta-posing P and I forms in the style of strotchny chant to more slowly unfolding instrumental transpositions of the row.

4.1   De Elegia Prima

Three contrasting qualities of movement are interwoven around a central pitch of D♯ to create a spiral form that negates the sense of forward movement in clock-time. The five initial letters Aleph to Res derive their individual timbres and harmonic character from changing instrumentation and tonal affiliations and present five different facets of a single pitch world. The deep melancholy of B minor and other fleeting harmonic areas for the final letter Res(h), for instance, are created from the juxtaposition of four row forms for sustained strings with a brief double canon in contrary motion.

The verses of the five letters Aleph to Res alternate in their construction. The choral announcements of the first, third and fifth letters, Aleph, He and Res, are followed by two rhythmic constructions of highly contrasting texture and density. The first construction (bar 23) consists of pitchless choral chanting, *sotto voce*, pierced by sustained semitone 'bell-strikes' as in the Introduction, that evoke the desolation of the city. A sudden outpouring of sorrow brings the deep time quality of the second construction (bar 42) that consists of four lines of move-ment with repeating row segments that proceed at different speeds (Ex.63): the bugle has the R form four times with small repetitions against the tenor's three more slowly repeated groups: pitches 1–5 and 1–8 of the R form. Sopranos and altos unfold the RI form twice against this with the frequent repetition of row segments, falling silent as the tenor and bugle complete their rows. The fourth layer in this juxtaposition of independent patterned lines is a tremolo ostinato in the upper strings that suggests a skeletonic form of the row. The construction creates an unfamiliar time quality, recalling Stravinsky's juxtaposed layers of reg-ular and irregular patterning in the first of the *Three Pieces for String Quartet.*

EX. 63   Juxtaposition of four lines of regular and irregular patterning: Aleph

The choral announcements of the second and fourth letters, Beth and Caph, are followed by free-flowing Diphonas for two unaccompanied solo tenors. The juxtaposition of two unbarred row forms flowing freely with repeated notes and answering rhythmic groups, serves the same structural role as the organ versets of Euntes in Mundum in *Canticum Sacrum*, of creating a great distance of musical time and space after the preceding strict construction. The stark contrasts between textural volumes, and between regular and irregular qualities of movement in De Elegia Prima, evoke great depth of sorrow at Jerusalem's fall into degradation.

4.2 *De Elegia Tertia*

The community has a new spirit as it recognises its fallen state and begins to repent. Stravinsky liberates the structure from the self-contained, hermetic atmosphere of De Elegia Prima and its central D♯, by beginning the row on the third pitch of the IR form so that juxtapositions of its segments take on a new character and new tonal colours come into prominence. The time quality of Querimonia (Complaint) gradually deepens as the unaccompanied verse settings increase from a solo line to four-part counterpoint for tenors and basses. This section also develops the unbarred free-flowing style of the Diphonas in De Elegia Prima, the solo basso profundo in Aleph having the new freedom of more widely-pitched intervals. The verses of Beth have widely-set canons for tenor and basso profundo a bar apart, their reflecting motifs used to expressive effect on *contrivit, gyro* and *circum*, where the row forms are rotated.[54] Stravinsky does not resist setting the canonic entries to the 'devilish' interval of an augmented 4th for the 'dark places' (Sheol) of line three (bar 178). In Vau, which increases to three-part counterpoint, the canonic entries and reflecting motifs gather pace in the first and third lines, but are held back at the second line for 'the removal far off'. Broken teeth and ashes are evoked with closely reflected repetitions of consonants.[55] The time quality is expanded at *spes mea* by tensionless triplets, and also at *in corde meo* and *ideo sperabo* in the dense four-part counterpoint of Zain.[56]

---

54 *Contrivit* means literally 'ground' my bones, and *gyro* and *circum* evoke circular motion.

55 The dead went to Sheol, the place of darkness: there is no concept of resurrection in early Jewish thought; the idea developed after the Maccabean revolt in the second century BCE.

56 [This I recall] to my mind, therefore have I hope.

The second section, Sensus Spei (Perceiving Hope), has sudden linear momentum that is energised by compatible rhythms and consonant contours, and checked by dissonance, wide intervals and rhythmic complexity. The large orchestra is recalled and reinstates the central pitch D♯ for the first letter, Heth, in which the orchestra joins two of the four soloists in a sustained fortepiano 'bell-strike'. Each letter from Heth to Lamed has a different character and rises a semitone, gradually heightening the sense of movement and expectation. The verses of these letters are treated antiphonally and the choral chanting radiates from the letter setting like waves from a bell. Heth has repeated dyads on *non defecerunt* and an elongation of time values on *pars mea Dominus.* The bustling, festive atmosphere suddenly recalls that of *Les Noces,* especially Lamed with its extraordinary duet for basso profundo and tenor *con voce strascicante* at the crushing underfoot of all the prisoners of the earth.

In Nun the community begins to come together, the chorus combining row forms in homogeneous rhythms and a tonal colouring of E♭ minor; the sections dwell on familiar tonic-dominant harmony as they reflect on the situation. Stravinsky's significant IR row form at the end of the third line in Nun is left incomplete, since the community is not yet pardoned. Samech varies in pace: the anger of the Lord is depicted in fast antiphonal responses that become rhythmically fluid as the sinner is compared to refuse in the city. Repeating melodic patterns trickle slowly downwards like tears through the three lines of Ain. The density increases as the waters flow overhead, the sense of the present progressively negated by two, three and four-part canons; the forward momentum finally runs to ground in a homophonic statement of *Perii* (I am cut off). Coph recalls the homophonic community song of Nun a semitone higher, accompanied by a cello obligato with the 'other-worldly' timbres of harmonics and pizzicato notes. Stravinsky treats Nun and Coph more homophonically and the community's repentance is also answered homophonically by God's quiet response set to the last four pitches of the P form: *ne timeas* (fear not).

The fluid, forward movement of Sensus Spei is checked in the third section Solacium (Compensation), in which the community recognises that however terrible the events that have befallen them, Jahweh is still the sovereign Lord of His people and His divine judgement is to be acknowledged. To embody this realisation, Stravinsky confuses all the familiar melodic shapes of the row forms by abstracting auxiliary rows derived from the basic set and concentrating the density of juxtaposed layers. He follows the ascending odd-numbered pitches of the row by the descending even-numbered pitches, divides the row into four-note segments by selecting every third pitch, and lops the row to produce a sequence as in the final letter, Thau. Density rapidly increases through

Solacium, diminishing the sense of time. In Res, the solo soprano and alto closely interweave their widely-set intervals in thanksgiving against a soft tonal wind accompaniment: in Sin, the solo tenor and bass, with alternate pitches of their IR and R forms, have many expressive repetitions accompanied by muted sustained horns. The final letter, Thau, combines three row forms for chorus and soloists in dense polyphony. The *marcato* anger of the first and third lines of text is reflected in the juxtaposition of two aspirated row forms against sustained solo lines. In the second line, that seeks recompense, all three row forms are sustained, and fluidly repeated intervals bend and flex as in sorrow.

4.3   De Elegia Quinta

The monumental temporal form of *Threni* concludes with a congregational prayer for God's help, and the sense of time diminishes as its momentum wanes. The opening time quality is established by the first line of the prayer (Ex.64). It is set for two solo unaccompanied basses, who, as 'priests', declaim the P and I forms with great rhythmic severity and authority.

EX. 64   Opening of De Elegia Quinta

After a 'bell-strike', the choral prayer responds *parlando* and *sotto voce*, against chords derived from the row. Repeating intervals flow downwards from the alto solo line to that of the basso profondo. The second verse is similarly treated, but movement is further retarded by the clarinets' repeating dyads, and closely-scored row forms that cross parts and repeat successive intervals. The most important verse, verse 21, is set extremely densely with four combined row forms accompanied simply by four horns and harp. 'Turn us unto Thee, O Lord,' sing the chorus, 'and we shall be turned' reply the four soloists, before they join together to complete the prayer: 'renew our days as of old'.

Threni, like *Apollo*, has an ascetic quality that comes from constructing its temporal nuances as economically as possible. Stravinsky's rows allow clear harmonic areas when juxtaposed to their various other forms. He treats both speech and pitched sounds antiphonally, and repeats and juxtaposes row segments of all sizes to vary movement, tonality and time quality. In Solacium, the familiar row forms are concentrated, disguised or confused by alternating pitches or shortened forms, and De Elegia Quinta vibrates with echo effects and oscillating dyads.

Although constructing time qualities as he had always done, by the end of the 1950s and the composition of *Threni* (1958) and *Movements* (1959), Stravinsky had evolved his own serial 'voice'. Every aspect of *Movements,* for example, was guided by serial forms that worked, like Webern's structures, 'as though through a crystal'.[57] *Threni,* constructed to co-ordinate the listener with a spiritual journey from despair to hope, unfolds an autonomous, multi-level web of serial relationships in ontological time that is both transparent and flexible.

57   Stravinsky, Igor & Craft, Robert. 1981, *Memories and Commentaries*, 106.

CHAPTER 15

Late Harvest

It is a measure of Stravinsky's stature as an artist that his compositional techniques and individual 'voice' continued to evolve in his last years. In the works of the 1960s, the time qualities of his spiritual subjects are constructed by increasingly refined means: his serial patterns, selected from arrays of 'family members' for their contours, are both more expressive and succinct in their representation of rhythmic manners, and chords formed from the vertical columns of hexachordal arrays are used to make dramatic contrasts of texture and moments of greater temporal depth. Stravinsky arranges the intervals of the row so that their hexachords have complementary interval content and imitative groupings, or allow transitory centres of diatonic tonality. Although the momentum of Stravinsky's serial patterning is often embellished and softened with repeating dyads and resonance, there is a new economy of expression that matches the rigorous and uncompromising spiritual standpoint of his texts. In his continuing search for 'new analogies of beauty', the qualities of time and movement that Stravinsky creates in his last works are both more fluid and concise. Stravinsky lays his religious themes bare as he refines the clarity and unity of a musical object to resonate with a spiritual quality.

1   A Sermon, A Narrative and A Prayer (1961)

Stravinsky regarded this cantata as the New Testament counterpart to *Threni*.[1] It continues three main themes of that work: hope and faith in God who is unseen, the experience of God as a consuming fire, and prophecy against the lamentable state of contemporary society.

Both works are about the virtue of hope that is found in people of great faith; Jeremiah, imprisoned but continuing to hope in the unseen God, cries out: 'I called upon thy name, O Lord ... Thou hast heard my voice ... thou saidst, Fear not.'[2] St Paul, who has been imprisoned many times on his travels but steadfastly proclaims the risen Christ, writes to the church in Rome: 'For we

---

1   A note to Paul Sacher, 7th August 1961. The texts of *A Sermon, A Narrative and a Prayer* were partly the choice of Robert Craft: Craft, Robert. 1992, 44.
2   *Threni*: text at the letter Coph.

have been saved, but only in hope. Now to see is no longer to hope: why should a man endure and wait for what he already sees?'[3]

Both works present the image of God as a consuming fire, an image that developed from the Old Testament to the New Testament. Moses encountered God in the burning bush on Mount Sinai but does not see God, he *hears* him.[4] Old Testament figures Jeremiah and Isaiah, and the New Testament Letter to Hebrews,[5] describe God as a fire that consumes those who turn away from Him and worship other gods.[6] In *A Sermon,* Stravinsky highlights the word 'fire' with a penetrating chord containing the 0–11 interval. Stravinsky returned to the image of God as Love that is a consuming fire for his unaccompanied choral setting of T. S. Eliot's poem *The Dove descending breaks the Air* (1962).[7]

Both *Threni* and *A Narrative* lament the apostasy of their respective contemporary societies. In *Threni,* Jeremiah reproaches the Jewish community in Jerusalem for the vile moral state of the city; in *A Narrative,* Stephen confronts the Sanhedrin and denounces the Jewish authorities for persecuting the prophets and murdering the 'Just One'.

The three movements of *A Sermon, A Narrative and A Prayer* build a similar temporal form to the three main sections of *Threni*: momentum that has been tightly-constrained into a spiral in the first movement is released into a dynamic linear narrative in the second movement and consolidated, in the third movement, in a monumental, timeless structure. *A Sermon* sets three texts about the hope that becomes faith by interweaving repeated sections around an Interlude in which the instrumental introduction returns in a modified form.[8] *A Narrative* tells of the stoning of Stephen, who died as the first Christian martyr for his faith in the unseen God.[9] The temporalities of this movement range from brutal action in the present to the out-of-time quality of Stephen's spiritual experience. *A Prayer* sets a poem by the 16th century writer Thomas Dekker, who prays that, should he be 'cut off' that night, he wishes his spirit to be received into the hand of God, and to be among those who sing Allelujah.[10] Stravinsky's setting of this prayer as the steady enlargement

---

3   Letter to the Romans 8.24 (New English Bible).
4   The understanding of God as a consuming fire is also found in Deuteronomy 4.24 and
      Isaiah 33.14.
5   Hebrews 11.1.
6   A Letter to Hebrews 12.29.
7   Eliot, T. S. 1968. Part IV of *Little Gidding.*
8   Letter of St Paul to the Romans 8.24–25; A Letter to Hebrews 11.1 and 12.29.
9   Acts 6.8–7.60.
10   Thomas Dekker (c.1570 – c. 1641) was a writer of plays and pamphlets and a wise
      observer of humanity, who used gentle satire to expose the daily life of the bourgeoisie

EX. 65   Related row segments: *A Sermon, A Narrative and A Prayer*

of time and space captures the spirit of biblical teaching concerning things temporal and things eternal: the unseen Kingdom of God that is hoped for in faith is unshakeable.

There is a new brevity in the texts of this work and in their settings that anticipates the extreme economy and concision of *Requiem Canticles*. After *Movements* (1959), musical events change more rapidly and their temporalities are differentiated even more clearly. There is a greater contrast between the easy linear flow of hexachordal arrays and their juxtaposition in horizontal constructions and vertical columns to create a deeper time quality.

The three contrasting temporal forms of this work are constructed with a row centred on E♭. Its four trichords, each containing a semitone, are closely patterned with reflecting contours between the interval of a 3rd, so that the pitch relationships of this musical object are particularly concentrated (Ex. 65).

1.1   *A Sermon*

Four contrasting qualities of time and movement, with one increase of tempo towards the word 'faith', alternate in a spiral litany. The repeat of the opening instrumental Section A changes in density and dynamics and the repeat of Section B (bar 45) has a more flowing quality of movement, but Sections C and D (bars 27, 31) are repeated exactly.

Section A, a light instrumental introduction in the upper register, has a fluid linear style with aspirated segments of the P form that move at ♩ = 72 towards its R form in the bass clarinet. At its repeat (bar 35) the section is fortissimo, and the bass clarinet's R form, now heard from the start of the section, gradually becomes the dominant row form.

Section B (bars 12, 45), at ♪ = 72, has six antiphonal choral lines whose intervals, in segments of the R form, are expressively widened to 7ths and 9ths as the chorus put their trust in hope. The muted timbres of trumpets and trombones soften to that of four muted horns at the repeat of 'We are saved by hope', in an instrumental statement of the whole R form (bar 17). The texture reduces to a

---

in contemporary London as profound economic and social changes took place. The language of this poem is contemporary with that of the King James version of the Bible used in the first two movements.

EX. 66   Approach to the final penetrating chord on 'faith'

spacious single line for solo tenor, who poses the final part of the question with widely-spaced intervals (bar 24). At the repeat of Section B (bar 45), the wider intervals and triplet groups create a larger musical space for 'what we see not'. It is now more lightly accompanied by strings with harmonics and pizzicato notes. The greater density of the choral parts reduces to a line shared by solo tenor and bass who affirm the virtue of patience while waiting in hope.

The faster Section C, at ♪ = 100 (bars 27–31, 64–67) answers the question posed in Section B and releases a rapid burst of energy towards the word 'faith' (Ex.66). These four brief bars contain many contrasts: the rapid *sotto voce* speech of the choir slows via a final triplet group for tenors and basses and unexpectedly acquires pitch. The timbre of choral speech is juxtaposed to instrumental tremolos, *sul ponticello,* immediately followed by an arresting change of pitch and timbre for the leap of a 10th in the soprano line. The piercing fortepiano chord on 'faith', containing the 0–11 interval in its two lower parts, signposts 'Listen'.[11]

---

11   See Chapter 6, 113 - 115: this chord is notated to imitate an untuned bell.

Section D (bars 31–34, 68–71) returns to the slower pulse of Section B but maintains a forte dynamic. The row forms (R, I) spread quickly through the choir from the upper voices, and thence to the trumpet, flute and lower strings. Fragments of the row flicker like flames. These four brief bars evoke the terror of judgement, with glistening string harmonics moving towards the final fortissimo tongue of flame. While the soprano line is a semitone higher than in the 'faith' chord heard four bars earlier, the more important symbol of transformation is that the 0–11 interval in the lower parts is now in harmonics, an octave higher. The texts of Sections C and D express the spiritual insight that even though God is a consuming fire, the Kingdom hoped for by faith will not perish at the end of time.

1.2   *A Narrative*

In contrast to the starkly abutted time qualities of *A Sermon*, this through-composed movement reflects the text with more fluidly nuanced time qualities. The Bible records that Stephen was full of faith and power and did great wonders and miracles among the people.[12] He was the most important of the first seven deacons to be appointed in the early church (the Orthodox faith regards him as an *Arch*deacon), and he was probably a Hellenistic Jew as he was chosen to lead the distribution of food and aid to the widows of the Greek community who felt marginalised. Stephen was full of inspired wisdom, but some members of the Synagogue constantly wanted to argue with him and to stir up trouble among the people. Eventually they brought Stephen before the Council accusing him of blasphemy: 'for we have heard him say this Jesus of Nazareth will destroy this place and alter the customs handed down to us by Moses'.

Stephen confronts the Council with a detailed history of the relationship between God and the Jews and of the occasions when, as at the time of the *Lamentations of Jeremiah*, they frequently turned to other gods. He refers to Moses' encounter with the unseen God on Mount Sinai, and defends Jesus' claim to destroy the Temple and raise it up again in a new form in three days.[13] Stravinsky omits these particular issues and proceeds directly to the accusation that will lead to Stephen's death: 'Was there ever a prophet your fathers

---

12   Acts 5, 6 and 8.

13   Acts 7.46–50: Stephen witnesses to the unseen God. Although Solomon had built the Temple, Stephen says: 'The Most High does not live in houses made by men; as the prophet says: "Heaven is my throne and earth my footstool. What kind of house will you build for me, says the Lord; where shall my resting-place be? Are not all these things of my own making?"'.

did not persecute? They killed those who foretold the coming of the righteous one, and now you have betrayed him and murdered him. You received the law given by God's angels and yet you have not kept it.'[14] The Council is infuriated by what they see as a further blasphemy, for Stephen speaks of seeing Jesus at the right hand of God, a vision hidden from them. They cast him out of the city and stone him.

The constant fluctuation across a wide range of time qualities in this dramatic movement belies its short performance time. The momentum changes rapidly and seamlessly between speech and pitched solos, single row forms and dense juxtapositions, sparse instrumental accompaniment and richly dramatic instrumental comment, and between a single accompanied voice and canonic constructions that mark the moments of deepest spiritual experience.

This movement begins at a slightly faster pulse than the first movement ($\flat$ = 88) with rotated hexachords in light string harmonics, wispy figures for wind instruments, and vertical columns of row forms for brass. The entry of the narrator (bar 80) is accompanied by an ingenious 'drum roll' figure for clarinets. The alto solo, with widely-spaced R and I forms, represents the disciples who are giving themselves to prayer and to the ministry of the word; she is answered by an instrumental meditation that develops great rhythmic complexity (bar 94). The narrator and the solo alto's pitched note are joined at the name of Stephen, the people's choice, 'a man full of faith and of the Holy Ghost', marking it with a special mixed timbre. The time quality increases in depth as the rapid multiplying of disciples is evoked first by rhythmic speech against two trumpets with the closely-set I form in canon (bar 102) and then by the alto's widely-pitched solo. She describes Stephen's faith and good works against a mensuration canon for three solo cellos in which it is the middle line that proceeds more rapidly. Widely-spaced angular hexachords for three then four reed instruments proliferate dramatically as the narrator recounts how Stephen's wisdom and spiritual authority is disputed at the synagogue (bar 113). The mood changes to one of menace as the people are stirred up: the alto soloist, accompanied by strings playing *sul ponticello,* recounts how Stephen's face shines before the steady gaze of the Council (bar 130) and becomes 'like the face of an angel'.[15]

Stravinsky sets the high priest's question 'Are these things so?' to the IR form that he often used at spiritually significant moments, and Stephen's indictment of the Sanhedrin is set to progressively complex juxtapositions as

---

14   Op. cit., 51–53.
15   Acts 6.14–15.

the time quality deepens. Stephen's increasingly confident manner is set to row segments for clarinets, brass and piano, and the persecution and slaying of the prophets is illustrated particularly graphically by low, rapid and percussive R forms for piano (bars 154, 158). The Council's volcanic reaction to Stephen's speech is set almost pictorially, with quadrilaterals of IR hexachords in confused order, widely-spaced intervals, strong accents and glissando effects across a register of nearly five octaves (bar 163).

Four slow chordal bars sustaining an RI hexachord (bar 168) draw back from the scene in preparation for Stephen's out-of-time experience as he sees the heavens opened. Stravinsky creates an 'other-worldly' time quality by juxtaposing two forms (P followed by R) against each other at a different pace (bar 172, (Ex. 67).

The P and R forms for tenor and harp unfold mellifluously in canon at the unison, but their contrast of pacing together with the much more widely-spaced intervals of the harp create a spacious, time-negating construction of transparent complexity. The reanimation of the Council's anger is set to two dramatic statements of the P form (the second elided) that moves from the piano (bar 179) to the brass and strings in tremolo figures, while the alto and tenor report the Council's reaction between them, sharing a line to represent the crowd's vicious actions with jerky fragments of the R form.

As witnesses lay down their clothes at a young man's feet, attention is drawn both to his name, Saul, and his future change of heart (for after his

EX. 67   Differently paced P and R forms for Stephen's out-of-time experience

conversion he will become Paul), by the rapid and seamless change from speech to the alto's pitched note, E♭, the central pitch of the work (bar 192). Stephen's name is also enhanced by this mixed timbre, the simultaneous use of speech and the central pitch (bar 194). As Stephen dies, Stravinsky marks the significance of Stephen's words (a haunting recall of Jesus' words to God his Father from the cross) by setting them to his special IR form. Slowly-evolving chords move in changing metres from IR forms for solo strings, harp and piano to a fuller mix of timbres with the I form; they deepen the time quality to one of reflection upon the significance of the scene and open a large musical space (bar 208).

1.3   *A Prayer*

The different facets of this monumental construction are centred on a related form of the row on E♭. Whereas the close spiral movement of *A Sermon* contrasted four sections, two that repeated exactly and two that were expressively modified, *A Prayer* is in four sections that gradually withdraw from the present to timelessness. The first two sections repeat the prayerful petition. In the first section, the alto solo's statement of a hexachordal rotation of the P form is lightly accompanied by I and R forms in the lower strings. In the second section, in which she is joined by the tenor solo (bar 227) and then the basses and tenors of the chorus, the time quality rapidly deepens with a four-part construction of juxtaposed I and RI forms in which the first hexachord of the I form for piano, harp and celli-basses sounds as the bass line at half the pace and with very large intervals. This four-part construction is given sudden resonance by the addition of three differently pitched tam-tams, 'high', 'middle' and 'low', each one enhancing a particular pitch of the hexachords that are slowly unfolding in the bass line.

In the third section the prayer becomes a petition to join the heavenly community (bar 240), and the alto and tenor solos lead into a second four-part construction. This begins to open out with wider intervals, particularly in the basses, and a new, more fluid triplet movement. The time quality and musical space deepen further as the triplet movement of this section begins to permeate the longer note values at the words 'Come you Blessed' (bar 247) which is underpinned by a rotation of Stravinsky's special IR form (Ex.68).

In the final section (bar 259), two layers of patterning unfold at highly contrasted speeds: the closer-patterned crotchet movement of the vocal parts moves against the slow, irregular statements of widely-spaced I and RI forms elongated by many repeating dyads, for piano, harp, basses and tam-tams. Time and movement are drawn out and stilled as the strings join the peaceful choral Allelujahs, and the syllables of the final Allelujah are aspirated. The

EX. 68   Deepening time quality: A Prayer

work is sealed by the lengthening reiterations of an instrumental chord on E♭
that is clouded by the semitones D and D♭.

2   Two Bible Stories: The Flood (1962) and Abraham and Isaac (1963)

Both of these works set stories from Genesis about righteous men with whom
God made a Covenant, but their settings stand in stark contrast. Unlike the
'resemblances' of *Petrushka*, the music of *The Flood* 'is structurally speaking,
all symbolic',[16] and in setting this mystery play in dance as well as to narration,
Stravinsky described himself as a theatre composer doing a theatre job.[17] In
contrast, his programme note to *Abraham and Isaac* does not wish the listener
any luck in discovering musical descriptions, musical symbolisms in his use
of canons, or 'expressive' rhythmic devices, for 'the notes themselves were the
end of the road'.[18] Whereas *The Flood* was written for television, with a *mélange*
of aural, visual and spatial effects as Stravinsky tried hard 'to keep *The Flood*
very simple as music',[19] the movements of *Abraham and Isaac* are spare and

---

16   Stravinsky, Igor & Craft, Robert. 1982, 72. Stravinsky compared the overt symbolism of
     The Flood to that of the upside-down pyramid of fugues in the second movement of the
     Symphony of Psalms. Ibid, 45.
17   Stravinsky, Igor & Craft, Robert. 1981, 124.
18   Stravinsky, Igor & Craft, Robert. 1966, 55–56.
19   Stravinsky, Igor & Craft, Robert. 1981: *Expositions and Developments*, 127, n.1.

concise, and its time qualities are constructed solely with the rhythmic manners of serial patterns and their juxtapositions.

3   The Flood (1962)

The text of *The Flood,* compiled by Robert Craft, joins passages from two medieval York pageants, *The Creation and the Fall of Lucifer* and *The Fall of Man,* to passages from a Chester Pageant, *Noah's Flood,* and text from the Book of Genesis.[20] Medieval mystery plays, illustrating a key story from the Old or New Testament, were performed on dressed wagons in the streets and each story was adopted by one of the city's guilds of craftsmen.[21] The adaptation of these texts for television some five hundred years later proved to be of interest to Stravinsky from the point of view of time. He thought that a more concentrated musico-dramatic form could emerge now that biblical stories could be meaningfully presented with a minimum of transitional material, and that a succession of visualisations on the television screen could be virtually instantaneous.[22]

Noah as a man, even as 'eternal man', a second Adam, or an Old Testament Christ figura like Melchizedek, was less important to Stravinsky than the symbolism of Noah's story as the Eternal Catastrophe, so Stravinsky begins *The Flood* with the entry of Sin into the fabric of Creation through Lucifer's pride and Fall, and recounts the temptation of Eve and the expulsion of Adam and Eve from Eden.[23]

Stravinsky thought it important for the audience to be able to locate Heaven, Earth and Hell as three different levels not only visually but aurally, with the music recorded at 'fixed and recognisably differentiated distances'.[24] Television, like myths, can more easily prioritise events, convey the abstract and the transcendent, and communicate meaning in scenes of unrealistic clock-time length. Writing for television allowed Stravinsky to heighten the contrast between clock-time and out-of-time qualities: Noah's speech and the dance and mime of the ark building in the here-and-now are contrasted with musical constructions for God and the praising of angels 'outside time'. Other

---

20   White, Eric W. 1979, 517. The Creation and Fall of Lucifer was performed by the barkers (tanners) and the Fall of Man by the coopers.
21   In Middle English, mystery not only meant religious rite but also trade or craft.
22   Stravinsky, Igor & Craft, Robert. 1982, 79.
23   Stravinsky, Igor & Craft, Robert. 1981, 127.
24   Stravinsky, Igor & Craft, Robert. 1982, 74.

aspects of the story are illustrated much more briefly with no overall loss of coherence.

The Flood begins and ends in a church. Movement from one 'level' to another is made via a recurring 12/4 measure that Stravinsky referred to as a 'Jacob's Ladder'. It moves from 'chaos' (bar 6), which he thought of 'as the antithesis of "serial"', to heaven.[25] The camera moves through the black velvet ceiling to the wings of Russian-style Seraphim who, framed like icons, form a triangular Byzantine altar topped by a symbol of the Cross (a *Chiasma*).[26] Stravinsky had recently represented the time quality of Stephen's vision of the heavens opening by juxtaposing two very differently-paced statements of the same row form beginning on the same pitch (*A Narrative*, fig. 170 + 2). In this 'Jacob's Ladder' (Ex. 69), the woodwind's row with repeating dyads is juxtaposed to its plain R form on the harp at a brisk speed of ♪ = 192.

EX. 69   Jacob's ladder: Prelude, *The Flood*

The 'Ladder' stretches from the C♯ below middle C to the D♭ four octaves higher, the upper woodwind repeating pitches 5–6 and 11–12 of the row. This 'misaligned' juxtaposition of the row and its reverse form is heard again as Adam and Eve are expelled from Eden (bar 179), but here it is played at the natural human pulse of ♩ = 60 by the bassoons, beginning with the contrabassoon an octave below the first 'Ladder'. It stretches across three octaves to the D♭ above middle C and leads from 'the lowest to the highest' in just fifteen seconds (Ex.70).

Stravinsky described the dramatic expansion of 'Jacob's Ladder' as 'the allegory of Eden, the curse of Original Sin', and 'the largest and most complete in itself' that he had ever composed.[27] The measure returns in its original form and pacing for woodwind and harp (bar 496) as 'a world begins to be' following the Flood, and also as the final measure of the work (but marked *meno*

---

25   Stravinsky, Igor & Craft, Robert. 1981, *Expositions and Developments*, 125.
26   Stravinsky, Igor & Craft, Robert. 1982, 72.
27   Op. cit., 75.

EX. 70   The expulsion from Eden

mosso and *rallentando*), where it suggests a continuing movement 'upward' and praise that is everlasting.

Heaven, earth and hell are differentiated as different levels of time and movement. In heaven, God's act of creating and the angels' everlasting praise are represented by juxtapositions of row forms that negate the sense of clock-time. God, who is unseen but visually represented as 'unbounded space and crystalline light' always sings in the same manner and in the same tempo, but is not unchanging in mood.[28] Perhaps inspired by George Balanchine's suggestion that God be represented by two pulsating ellipses,[29] God's words (bar 85) are sung by two bass singers, their differently-paced row forms unfolding in the same rhythm with the harsh intervals of strotchny chant and constant fluctuations of musical space. Against this static yet ever-changing construction, cellos and basses have chords derived from a third row form at a vastly slower pace, and the bass drum beats indistinctly pitched semiquavers. The differences not only of pitch and register but also of pace between the two bass soloists and the celli/basses builds a large musical space, and reflects the very wide range of time-scales in Creation itself.

As God creates Adam, 'a skilful beast', and Eve after His own 'shape and likeness', and gives them souls with which to worship Him, the movement of their two row forms is largely step-wise in character, except for the notable interval of a 9th to depict the 'spirit of life' (bars 99–100). There is a neat pun at the creation of Eve (fig. 100 + 1 – 2) as the upper R row changes to the P form and the lower IR row reverses. The calm quality of movement is even maintained as God creates Lucifer 'next after Himself', and the row forms are aptly crossed at the 'mirror of my might' (bar 120). But before God speaks with Noah, God's anger is expressed in wide-spread and angular row forms that both unfold and reverse, and change and reverse, against a shimmering halo of string tremolos,

28   Stravinsky, Igor & Craft, Robert. 1981, *Expositions and Developments*, 124.
29   Stravinsky, Igor & Craft, Robert. 1982, 73.

sul ponte (bar 180): movement back and forth along the row forms, as in *The Flood* itself, symbolises that His presence is also long-lasting. God's original quality of movement is recovered at the *Covenant of the Rainbow* (bar 458), but the slow, lightly sustained accompanying chords for flutes, harp and piano now range across a very wide register.

The angels' Te Deum, that purely by coincidence suggested to Stravinsky a 'well-known' five-note Byzantine chant,[30] begins with a canonic construction for sopranos, altos and tenors against horns and bassoons in low register (bar 8). Stravinsky wanted the sound to come from a great distance and gradually move closer to the climax (bar 46). At 'all the earth doth worship Thee' (bar 17), sopranos and altos 'chant' the first two notes of the I form five times in unison. They complete the row against pitches 7–12 of the I form at half the speed and against low horns and bassoons as before. Each phrase of the text is articulated by a chord derived from the initial 'chaos' chord until the climax at 'Holy, Holy, Holy Lord God of Sabaoth'. Here, the construction of I and RI forms is turned upside down at the midpoint of each of the two lines (bars 48, 55) against the 'celestial effulgence' of high string tremolos.

In contrast, Lucifer does not move until God names him (bar 127). He is vain, proud and ambitious, with a constantly changing 'personality'; his trumpeting tenor voice and confident statements of plain, but syncopated I, P, and IR forms are heard against very light and very widely-spaced pizzicato row forms for cellos and basses as he walks on a 'carpet of complex and sophisticated music'.[31] As Satan, he has a sibilant sweet voice, and he pants and hisses as, *sotto voce*, he confesses his envy of the human race that God has made for Love (bar 156). He is visible inside the transparent form of a serpent as he tempts Eve. As the unexpected survivor of the flood, his aria is *quasi falsetto* with an even lighter 'accompaniment', but now his personality is quieter (bar 497). As the Devil, he is inclined to take his position for granted, so that, as Stravinsky remarked, 'true Christians may overcome him'.[32]

Noah, as a terrestrial being in clock-time, does not sing. The audience is to identify with Noah at earth level as God instructs him to build an ark, and his speech is unmeasured as he looks 'up' to God in the light of the iconostasis. After the flood, when 'a world begins to be' and Noah, as the founder of the

---

30   Stravinsky, Igor & Craft, Robert, 1981, *Expositions & Developments*, 124–5.
31   Stravinsky uses the same 'mannered' motif of two rapid semiquavers with which he depicted Oedipus' pride. In March 1952, Stravinsky had revealed many of his beliefs to Robert Craft, including a belief in the physical nature of the Devil: 'The Devil wants us to believe he is only an idea, since this would make it easier for him.' Craft, Robert. 1992, 49.
32   Stravinsky, Igor & Craft, Robert. 1982, 79.

new family of humanity, relays God's commands to his sons Shem, Ham and Japheth, his speech is ordered and measured (bars 480–1).

Stravinsky described the music of the flood itself as imitating, not waves and winds, but time, in the sense of 'a time experience of something that is terrible and that lasts'.[33] He juxtaposes three layers of movement that are irregular in different ways to create a disturbingly unfamiliar time quality, recalling the first of the *Three Pieces for String Quartet*. In the top layer, hexachordal rotations in semiquavers for violins and flutes unfold in asymmetric phrases with changing metres, creating 'a skin drawn over the body of the sound'.[34] At the unclimactic midpoint (bar 427) they are reversed, forming a palindrome.[35] The second layer of patterning is composed of widely-spread hexachords of RI and I in quavers at half the pace, with the occasional irregular rhythm. The third layer, a repeating chord that acts as a drone is derived from the final pitches of Stravinsky's own IR form that introduces the movement. It articulates and cross-accents the lengthening semiquaver groupings of the violins and flutes at several points, increasing in frequency to the midpoint and decreasing on the return. The slight but constant variation of this high-pitched, tightly controlled and repetitive sound world diminishes the senses of time and space and evokes a feeling of claustrophobia.

The reversal of the opening Te Deum, beginning with 'Holy, Holy, Holy', concludes the work; like the repetition in reverse of Euntes in mundum to conclude *Canticum Sacrum,* it paradoxically frames a situation which does not end. Thanks to the medium of television, *The Flood* is remarkable for its coherent representation of a great range of time qualities from 'chaos' and the moment of Creation to the restoration of the human race, in a remarkably brief performance time.

4   Abraham and Isaac (1962–3)

Abraham and Isaac expresses Stravinsky's deep personal response to the biblical account of Abraham's call to faith. Many generations after Noah, God tested Abraham's loyalty to the point of asking him to sacrifice his own son, Isaac. Abraham obeyed God's call and as a result was promised that he would be the founder of a great nation, Israel, in land between Egypt and the great

---

33   Op. cit., 78.

34   Ibid.

35   Robert Craft suggested the music in the film sequence in *Lulu* as a model retrograde for this storm scene. Craft, Robert. 1992, 45.

river Euphrates.[36] At the time of the first performance of *Abraham and Isaac*, Stravinsky told an interviewer that in his Christian religion (speaking simply of the Old Testament), the Abrahamic sacrifice is regarded as the greatest sacrifice. Abraham's commitment to finding out God's purpose for himself and to voluntarily obeying God's call was very close to the philosophy of Kierkegaard, which Stravinsky esteemed very highly.[37]

As in *The Flood*, a brief moment of tremolo *sul ponticello* (bar 7) suggests God's presence before he appears to Abraham; God's call is again set to tremolo chords at bars 16–17 and 69–72. As in his *Mass*, the text is treated with great clarity, not only because of its spiritual importance, but also because Stravinsky had been deeply impressed by the musical quality of the Hebrew language which he had heard read by Sir Isaiah Berlin during a visit to him in 1961.[38] There is no conflict between the verbal and musical accents as in earlier works, and, like the improvisation of znamenny chant, the matching of the timbre of the syllable with the contour of the phrase is an important part of its sound world.

Abraham and Isaac takes around twelve minutes to perform, but Stravinsky's treatment of serial hexachords and row segments evokes the great length of Abraham's journey, and again differentiates between the different 'levels' of earth and heaven. He contrasts the significant details of each stage of Abraham's journey in the present with complex time-diminishing canonic constructions for Abraham's encounters with God and His angel. The six sections of the work gradually slow in pulse as God's purpose for Abraham is realised.

The Old Testament makes much of the importance of journeying to find God as both a physical and a mental activity, and the place at which the Word of God is heard becomes a particularly holy place.[39] God was only to be encountered at certain places, where he was felt to be 'nearer', and this often involved journeys of considerable length.[40] God commands Abraham to take his son

---

36   Genesis 12.2–15, 18.

37   Interview with Leroy Aarons in *American*, Dec 13th, 1964. Stravinsky, Vera & Craft, Robert. 1979, 470–471. Kierkegaard wrote of Abraham's test: 'Voluntarily to give up all is to be convinced of the glory of the good which Christianity promises. There is one thing God cannot take away from a man, namely, the voluntary – and it is precisely this which Christianity requires of man.' *Thoughts Which Wound From Behind – For Edification.* 1848, 187–8. In *Christian Discourses,* transl. Walter Lowrie 1940, 1961.

38   Stravinsky, Vera & Craft, Robert. 1979, 471.

39   Stravinsky also marks God's presence in *Babel,* with a different temporal quality (fig. 8).

40   In the Old Testament, while God is not limited to any one place, He only manifests Himself at particular places, so that worship was only offered at sacred sites such as Mount Sinai, the spring of Kadesh, or at cultic shrines such as the one Jacob established at Bethel after his dream.

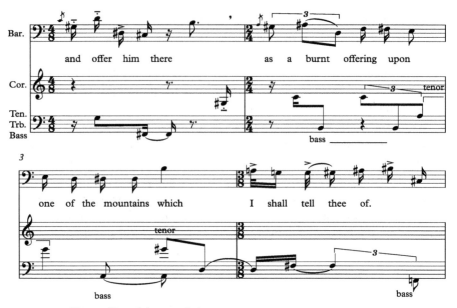

EX. 71   The marking of the sacred place

Isaac to one of the mountains in the land of Moriah, in a busy passage that has
an elaborate melisma of semitones on the name Isaac. Stravinsky increases the
depth of time quality at God's command by suddenly surrounding the baritone line with a single row form between the horn and trombones that unfolds
more slowly, with triple divisions of the pulse (Ex. 71). Widely spaced across
two octaves, with some pitches repeated (bars 41–45), the shapely contours
and slower pace mark God's words at this sacred place.

Stravinsky marks the beginning of Abraham's journey by drawing attention
to the saddling of his ass: the significance of this humble animal is marked by
a rhythmic hocket movement against the swaying of repeated dyads (bars 54–
55).[41] Abraham's journey with two of his men and his son Isaac is distinguished
by a time-diminishing construction (bars 56–69): the baritone's aspirated and
rhythmically complex patterning of rotated hexachords of the I form is accompanied by a regularly unfolding inversion canon (IR over R) between the discrete timbres of the flute and oboe, and the bass trombone and tuba some
two octaves below at a much slower pace. Their accented syncopations across
changing metres suggest the difficulty of the journey. The instrumental canon

---

41   The choice of an ass denotes humility and peace, as in Jesus' entry into Jerusalem on Palm
      Sunday.

reverses rhythmically before the instruments join in the I form (bar 66) just as Abraham approaches the place told him by God. This holy place is set to vertical columns of the P form, with the presence of God suggested by tremolo, *sul ponticello*. Abraham's view of the place afar off, 'on the third day', is suddenly set to a complex construction of syncopated semiquavers between the voice and bassoon (bars 77–78).

His onward journey with Isaac alone, by contrast, is represented by a comparatively long march-like dialogue between paired instrumental timbres (bar 91). Later, Abraham's naming of the place Jehovah-jireh (bars 197–203) is distinguished by a time-diminishing canon at the octave between the voice and tuba that is juxtaposed to a rhythmic canon for horn. The three similarly-paced lines with occasional repeated notes are held discrete by timbre, the vocal line placed in the register between the horn and tuba. The deeper time qualities of these constructions mark the significant experiences of this physical and spiritual journey.

As Abraham takes the wood and tools for the sacrifice, tension is built by repeated chords and hexachordal 'gestures' (IRa2, bars 106–112) that punctuate the vocal line. The repeated intonation of the words 'and he said' (bars 112, 116, 120, and 122–124 where Abraham's response at bar 121 is also repeated) are differently stressed to poignant effect.

The depth of Abraham's faith as he assures Isaac that God will provide (bars 129–135), is represented in a canon by inversion and augmentation of IR forms between the baritone and trumpet over a third IR form for tuba, that proceeds, after three repeated dyads, at half the pace. The time quality is deepened by three differently-paced lines held discrete in timbre and register. The close two-part patterning of the voice and strings as Abraham lays Isaac on the altar and takes his knife (from bar 151) also deepens into a three-part canonic structure for the very timely appearance of the angel of the Lord who calls to him, *cantabile* and *legato possibile* 'out of the heavens' (bar 163). In this dense construction the baritone line is surrounded by the contrasting timbre and register of the flute and tuba who pattern Stravinsky's IR form by diminution and inversion, the flute imitating the vocal movement in a rhythmic canon. The angel's direct command to stop the sacrifice (bar 171) is accompanied sparingly.

The more distanced, out-of-time quality of the angel's second appearance (bar 206, (Ex.72)) is created by the juxtaposition of two very differently-paced and differently-scored rotations of Stravinsky's IR form.

At first the horn and tuba, closer in register to the baritone patterning than before, share a slow-moving, sustained line that is softly *marcato*, before becoming part of sustained chording (bar 211). The angel brings a blessing for Abraham and his seed because he has obeyed God's call: the word-painting on

EX. 72   The angel's more distant second appearance

'multiply' and 'seed' (bars 221–222) is accompanied by rapid rotations of the IR form (9 – 10 – 11 – 12), after which, three bars of pedal point for the cello allow the rest of the prophecy to be heard clearly. To reward his faith, God promises that Abraham's descendants will be compared to the multiplying of the stars and the grains of sand on the seashore.

The work concludes with articulated chords and successive verticals of the R form in reverse (columns 11 – 10 – 9 – 8), and the significant word 'hearkened' is elaborated three times.[42] Abraham returns to settle at Beersheba, his return journey now at a much calmer walking pace in clock-time ($\flat$ = 60).

When drawing a parallel between himself and Schoenberg as common exiles to the same alien culture, Stravinsky named *Abraham and Isaac* as one of his own best works.[43]

5   Requiem Canticles (1966)

Originally planned as an instrumental work, Stravinsky's last major composition, *Requiem Canticles,* sets six texts from the traditional Roman Catholic Requiem Mass and the Libera Me from the Burial service.[44] The vocal movements are placed symmetrically like icons in a retable within the three-part instrumental frame of Prelude, Interlude and Postlude.[45] Composed for alto

---

42   For Abraham, as for Moses, the Word of God was an aural experience.

43   Stravinsky, Igor & Craft, Robert. 1982, 108.

44   Robert Craft actually chose the more 'minatory' texts from Verdi's *Requiem* rather than the consolatory ones, feeling that Stravinsky was becoming more defiant and less mellow with age. Craft, Robert. 1992, 10.

45   In April 1968 Stravinsky began to compose an extra instrumental prelude for a performance of the work in memory of Dr. Martin Luther King, 'a man of God, a man of the poor, a man of peace', but abandoned it when it could not be completed in time. White, Eric W. 1979, 542.

and bass soloists and mixed chorus, its vocal movements are stark and uncompromising in their setting of the syllabified Latin text, and their predominant attitudes of judgement and consuming fire, awe and lamentation are arranged around a central instrumental Interlude that is a 'formal lament'.[46] *Requiem Canticles* is the culmination of Stravinsky's remarkable evolution in style from that of the *Mass,* composed some twenty-two years earlier. Like the *Mass, Requiem Canticles* restores the appropriate musical spirit to each of its movements but with considerably briefer, tighter relationships between its serial forms; Stravinsky referred to this work as his 'pocket Requiem'.

Perhaps as a consequence of the work's profound subject and also of listening to much of Webern's music, this concise musical object unifies at a greater 'distance' from the listener than Stravinsky's previous works. Although its spiritual attitudes are only briefly sketched as temporal qualities, each movement acts as a patterned facet of one of two rows and as part of a spiritual spectrum concerning 'last things', so that they ultimately unify into a strong spatial-temporal form. A note that Stravinsky wrote just before the first performance of *Variations* (Aldous Huxley in memoriam, 1965) could equally apply to the style of *Requiem Canticles*: 'The density [of the 12-part variations] is the main innovation in the work. One might think of these constructions as musical mobiles, in that the patterns within them will seem to change perspective with repeated hearings. They are offset by music of a contrasting starkness ...' Although the performance time of *Requiem Canticles* is barely fifteen minutes, each movement offers a profound spiritual perspective on the human condition and the prospect of judgement. As Stravinsky remarked of *Variations,* 'The question of length (duration) is inseparable from that of depth and/or height (content) ... the musical statements [of the Variations] are concise, I prefer to think, rather than short'.[47]

As in the works from *Cantata* to *Abraham and Isaac,* points of spiritual significance and greater temporal depth are created by the juxtaposition of a variety of discrete serial layers, and momentum paced by rhythmic manners. In this work, the pacing of Stravinsky's hexachordal forms is so densely compacted that contrasts of momentum and depth shape this liturgy on a new expanded time-scale, from the Interlude's gestures of human sorrow in the here-and-now, to the Postlude's out-of-time experience of the cosmic and eternal.

---

46   Stravinsky began this work by composing a 'threnody' for wind instruments. Craft, Robert. 1967 ('Dialogues' preceding the Afterword). The inclusion of a threnody recalls the laments of *Les Noces* and the litanies of *Symphonies of Wind Instruments.*

47   White, Eric W. 1979, 537.

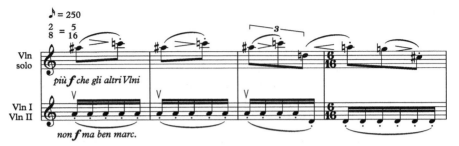

Two differently-paced layers of movement: Prelude

5.1   *Prelude*

The work is generated from two series beginning on F that have contrasting intervallic designs, the first being more tonal in character and the second being more chromatic. The Prelude for strings, composed with the more chromatic second series, juxtaposes regular and irregular rhythmic lines that are contrasted in rhythm and texture and follow their own paths of development (Ex. 73). The first line, composed of continuous staccato semiquavers for tutti strings, presents the series quickly at a brisk speed (bars 1–12) and reverses through its R form at a much slower pace (bars 12–54). The listener's attention is drawn back to this tutti semiquaver movement as an independent layer, by three breaks in its continuity. Above it, solo string instruments, beginning with a violin and increasing in number at every entry (to two solo violins, a viola, cello and bass), intermittently juxtapose rhythmically complex forms of P and I forms to bring about a massive increase in density. The first two bars of the solo violin tensions duplet and triplet quavers in 2/8 against the regular 5/8 stream of semiquavers to mark it out as a discrete line of movement.

5.2   *Exaudi*

Exaudi changes to the more tonal first series but floats away from the central pitch as God is petitioned, with contrastingly dense homophonic movement, to hear the prayer offered. Delicate, widely-spaced R forms for harp are answered by chords from vertical arrays of the P form for string harmonics and soft woodwind timbres. The soft petition is repeated with a slow, fluctuating semitone movement on *orationem* (bar 67) as if penetrating the 'distance' that the prayer has to travel. The basses join the upper voices at 'all flesh shall come before Thee' in recognition of man's universal mortality, and the extreme density of the constantly changing vertical row forms is juxtaposed to light P forms for the contrasting timbres of the horn and harp (bars 71–76). The intensity is completed by a slow presentation of successive vertical

EX. 74   Temporal-spatial depth: Dies Irae

columns from the IR grid for strings, probably Stravinsky's 'signposting' for the presence of God.

5.3   *Dies Irae*

The disruption of all things on the Day of Judgement is evoked by extreme contrasts of pace, pitch, dynamics and timbre that dislocate the sense of time and space. Dies Irae contrasts cosmic time and human time by means of two skilful constructions. Firstly, the sudden terror of this Day of Wrath is represented in two rapid rotations of the I form for piano and strings fortissimo, immediately followed by the great temporal-spatial depth created by a fortepiano declamation of 'Dies irae' (Ex.74).

The repeating bare 5th within the penetrating 0–11 frame in this chord falls away immediately to pianissimo but is sustained in an echo that evokes great distance over a long period of time. Secondly, the historic prophecy of King David and the Sybil that the world will be consumed in hot ashes (bars 88–90) is made very present by its contrasts of pace and pitch. This sudden, terrifying passage is composed of four highly contrasted timbral and textural layers: spoken syllables in duplets chanted *sotto voce* against duplets in P forms for the flutes are juxtaposed to widely-pitched triplet semiquavers for the percussive timbre of the piano and groups of five semiquavers for the resonant xylophone. But the warning of future judgement in the rest of the text is set with great clarity, the spoken semiquaver chanting simply continuing against two pitched layers at half the pace.

5.4   *Tuba Mirum*

The time qualities in this work about 'last things' are also distinguished by the pacing of repeated intervals. In the Prelude, the repeating dyads of the solo instrumental group are brisk, as befits the bright annunciatory style of an introduction. In Exaudi, the repeated dyads of *orationem meam,* personal prayer, are meditative and exploratory at a tempo of ♩ = 52. In Tuba Mirum, the repeating intervals call us to attention at a pulse of ♪ = 69: here the undulating sixths reach out across all lands to summon all before the throne. Between two martial fanfares, the bass solo and trumpets briefly share hexachordal forms, after which the bassoons' repeating dyads dissipate the tightly ordered undulations, and suggest slow, never-ending sound waves.

5.5   *Interlude*

The Interlude juxtaposes the sound worlds of the two series in a purely instrumental lament; it takes the form of Stravinsky's favoured spiral construction at the slightly slower tempo of ♪ = 52. Hexachordal variations of the two series wind around a short recurring phrase of repeated chords derived from the first vertical row form of the second series. Set for the soft timbres of pairs of flutes and horns, this repeating 'axis' chord descends in open 5ths from the central pitch F (with a single alternating pitch), and its repetition is aspirated in grief, as in *Symphonies of Wind Instruments*. It is heard four times, providing four, three, two and finally four bars of repose, its second appearance (fig. 145 – 1) followed by a single statement of Stravinsky's significant IR form in the first series for bassoons and timpani.

The first two turns of the spiral around this axis present facets of the first series. The first is a homorhythmic four-bar lament predominantly for flutes (bar 140), the second, a longer lament for alto flute and bassoons. The third spiral is an extended lament for four flutes that juxtapose the P and R of the second series to create greater depth of time (fig. 160 + 1). The repeated dyads that characterise the laments in *Les Noces* are found in this third spiral (bar 168) which concludes (bar 185) after a silent bar, with a dense concentration of rotated P forms (bar 188). The threnody concludes with Stravinsky's IR form for bassoons.

EX. 75   Penetrating staccato petitions: Rex Tremendae

5.6   *Rex Tremendae*

The dense atmosphere of mourning that has been created is suddenly swept
away by a canonic construction for the choir composed of R forms of the first
series, including grid verticals. It is underpinned by the widely-spaced intervals
of the trombones. Each choral petition for salvation directed at the heavens is
irradiated by staccato vertical chords of the I or RI form, held discrete by the
contrasting timbres of the flutes and lower strings (Ex. 75).

These repeated quaver pulsations, at ♩ = 104 – 6, emphasise the 'distance'
these petitions have to travel to the heavens after the earthly threnody. The
slow rate of change in both the choral movement and in the resonant repeating figures reinforces the sense of an enlarged time-scale.

5.7   *Lacrimosa*

The prayer for salvation in Rex Tremendae, and for mercy and rest in Lacrimosa,
both based on the first series, form the heart of the work. The stillness of the
immense sound world of Rex Tremendae is contrasted with an earthly lament
for the condition of man in the present. The solo contralto voice brings the
same expressive power of repeated pitches and dyads (even dyads *accelerando*), reflecting motifs, and widely-spaced intervals, as professional Russian
weepers and dméstvenny chanters did with traditional melodic formulæ.
Each new phrase of the text, as it spirals through a litany of IR forms, is supported and coloured by IR grid chords for the soft timbres of flutes and strings,
ending with string harmonics. Two contrasting facets of this ever-changing
sound world of successive rotations are heard in the intermittent interjections
from the brass, whose I chords are muted but marked *marcato*, and from the
separately-evolving layer of lower strings, especially double basses, and harp.

The temporal depth and monumental quality of Rex Tremendae is followed in Lacrimosa, by a kaleidoscope of independent vocal and instrumental facets distinguished by timbre.

5.8   *Libera Me*

Although Stravinsky's annotation of his score of Verdi's *Requiem* might suggest that he borrowed the effect of combining freely spoken words and pitched chanting from this source, Libera Me also evokes the Russian practice of *tuilage*, the simultaneous speaking and singing of prayers in Orthodox churches during the liturgy.[48] The bustling effect creates great temporal depth, as if the accumulated prayers of those who have gone before are reverberating with those in the present. The four soloists' slowly changing four-part chords of IR, I and R forms recall the haunting homophonic style of Stravinsky's traditional *Pater Noster* (1926), although in this movement their parts are doubled in the orchestra, and the religious concepts in the text are not cross-referenced by related motifs as in the ancient Russian chant.

5.9   *Postlude*

In the Postlude the sense of increasingly slow, revolving change that has been accumulating in Lacrimosa and Libera Me is slowed still further to 40 pulses per minute to create a reverberating sound world that recalls the conclusion of *Les Noces*. The quality of ever-changing changelessness is evoked in this movement by a chordal pattern that is repeated three times: each of three widespread bell-like chords, derived from series 1 for flutes, piano, harp and horn (bars 289, 294, 299) is followed by two bursts of 'change-ringing', groups of 4, 5, or 6 resonant chords from the P and R forms of the two rows, for celeste, campane and vibraphone. In each of these three patterns, the horn's sustained note is repeated after the first passage of change ringing to sound again as a bell's 'hum note' before the second group. The three successive 'hum' notes sound the successive pitches of an ascending F minor triad over a greatly extended period (Ex. 76): the hum notes F and G♯ (A♭) are followed by groups of 11 and 7 beats, the hum note B♯ (C♮) is followed by groups of 9 and 8 beats. In each passage of change ringing, the fluctuations of open and closed intervals at a slow pulse create the illusion of change within changelessness. The work is sealed by the juxtaposition of a very slowly-unfolding diatonic triad to this rich sound world of serial verticals, dispelling all sense of measured time.[49]

---

48   See Chapter 6.
49   See Chapter 6, Ex 20, for the composition of pitches in tuned and untuned bells.

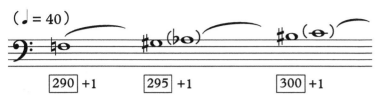

EX. 76   Repeated bell 'hum' notes between 'ring changes': Postlude

The work is concluded by three chords, the last having the added resonance of the celeste, campane and vibraphone. After a lifetime of ordering and structuring time and sound to create music with a spiritual quality, Stravinsky's last major work is an unparalleled creation of what Maritain had called 'the shining forth of some secret principle of intelligibility'.[50]

Requiem Canticles lays bare the 'distance' between the here-and-now condition of humanity and the 'other-worldly' quality of eternity with extreme and starkly-represented variations of time-scale. *Requiem Canticles* is Stravinsky's most original and advanced contribution to music as the art of time, and to musical forms as vehicles of the spiritual. Ever teasingly enigmatic, Stravinsky himself said of his legacy: 'When I die, I leave you my music ... It is music that followed rules that were not written, but I hope I have added something new to what was existing.'[51]

---

50   Maritain, Jacques. 1947, 48.
51   Interview Nov 25, 1961. Stravinsky, Vera & Craft, Robert. 1979, 363.

Epilogue

Requiem Canticles, Stravinsky's most profoundly spiritual and purely temporal work, was composed some 58 years after he had journeyed to his summer house at Ustilug to begin work on Act 1 of his opera, *Le Rossignol.* His 'speculations' in sound and time developed rapidly as he began to find ways of constructing varied time qualities to communicate spiritual meaning; the skilful juxtaposition of contrasting rhythms and resonant pitch motifs could reach beyond the emotions to ontological time. The spiritual quality of the Fisherman's Song in Act 1 of *Le Rossignol* was created by the simple juxtaposition of two contrasting layers in which the resonance of a natural scale is set against a one-bar ostinato in the key a fifth below. In *Petrushka*, gestural rhythms and the dissonant juxtaposition of keys an augmented 4th apart perfectly evoked the puppet's inner turmoil; his vivid experience after 'death' arises from the juxtaposition of two layers of movement that are greatly contrasted in rhythm, key and timbre. Set against the distant bustle of the Fair, they create a depth of time and space of which Stravinsky was justly proud. In *Zvezdoliki,* the accelerating harmonic movement of the orchestral layer against the regular chanting of the pilgrims, conveys their eager search for the 'Star-Faced One'. Their timeless encounter with Him is evoked by a particular emphasis on the resonance of the harmonic series, and a stately succession of overtone motifs expands time as they make their long journey into the desert to find salvation.

As Stravinsky began to compose *The Rite of Spring*, the creative possibilities of juxtaposing regular and irregular rhythmic layers overwhelmed him; in this work, the time qualities of an ancient ritual were laid bare in a radically new hierarchical structure of developing temporalities. In contrast to these new and powerful techniques, *Three Japanese Lyrics* explored delicate and fragmented lines of movement, to reveal how independently-evolving rhythmic layers may create remote and elusive qualities of time. They demonstrate particularly clearly how music is able to inhabit two worlds simultaneously, as the movement of sound in clock-time and as a unity of relationships outside time. In returning to native Russian techniques for the musical patterning of *Les Noces,* Stravinsky pursued this dual nature of music further. He brought together the heterophonic textures of folk singing and the many-layered sound world of the Russian Orthodox liturgy and unified their time qualities with a resonant three-note motif from the harmonic series. These musical features join earth and heaven, the world of time with the timeless, as in the wedding ritual itself, with the objective quality of an icon.

© KONINKLIJKE BRILL NV, LEIDEN, 2022 | DOI:10.1163/9789004518537_018

In composing *Three Pieces for String Quartet,* Stravinsky continued to experiment with the juxtaposition of regular and irregular layers of patterning to create an objective time world. Originally written to accompany biblical scenes from the Old Testament, the first of the *Three Pieces* combines sound patterns of various durations to create the bizarre time quality of a primitive ritual. The second of the *Three Pieces* creates the immediacy of the here-and-now with asymmetric gestural patterns. The third *Piece* alternates two sections of low-relief patterning, one low-pitched and irregular, the other high-pitched and regular. Like a litany with a regular refrain, it is reversed and lightened in a 'doxology' to create a quality of 'sacred' time. *Chant Dissident* begins in the style of dméstvenny chant and has time-deepening constructions of regular and irregular patterning at particularly spiritual moments, one of which also includes the resonant overtone motif associated with the Old Believers.

Symphonies of Wind Instruments interweaves both sections and fragments of irregular patterns. In a musical analogy of Cubist techniques, Stravinsky dismantled the movement qualities of his original chorale for *La Revue Musicale* and expanded and reassembled them in a scheme of regularly-proportioned tempi to create a monumental musical object – a memorial to Debussy aptly formed from qualities of time. Returning briefly to his Russian roots and the inspiration of Pushkin's zephyr-like movement in *The Little House at Colomna,* Stravinsky embodied the spirit of the Russian people in a particular era in a short opera, *Mavra.* In this opéra-bouffe, Stravinsky captures Pushkin's humorously objective view of life with a new type of juxtaposition: the mixing of the musical styles of East and West in inappropriate ways.

In *Symphonies of Wind Instruments* Stravinsky constructed an autonomous temporal form that ordered the irregular rhythms of life with mathematical objectivity. The concept of an art work as an object to be crafted, promoted by the neo-Thomist philosophy of Jacques Maritain and his disciple Arthur Lourié, was not only a strong influence upon Stravinsky's direction in the 1920s but resurfaced to grow stronger with the works of his later serial period. Unlike Schoenberg, Stravinsky sought new forms in which to express his spirituality; in order to co-ordinate the listener with their time qualities, his musical objects needed to be clearly mentally-imageable. *Octet* found a new form by placing the greatest weight of the musical object in the central movement: Stravinsky framed the styles of East and West and variations of various 'weights' within free-flowing outer movements that lightly recall the Baroque era. The temporal form of *Oedipus Rex* was shaped by two opposing lines of movement, those of Oedipus and the Spirit of Truth, as in Sophocles' play. In Act 1, the lines of movement proceed steadily and alternate as they approach one another; in Act 2, movement suddenly concentrates, accelerates and increases in temporal depth towards Oedipus' out-of-time enlightenment, before ending in the time-less world of the gods. *Oedipus Rex* was also shaped by a mix of styles from both East and West, but *Apollo* broke free from most of these influences: specu-lating in sound with extensive forms of a single melodic figure and poetic foot, Stravinsky patterns a musical object that is a perfect model of the variety that may arise from similarity.

For the monumental spiritual-temporal journey of *Symphony of Psalms,* Stravinsky returned to the process of temporal growth that had generated *The Rite of Spring.* The *Symphony of Psalms* reflects the spiritual journey of the Psalmist from penitence to salvation, and to joyful worship with the heavenly community. Juxtaposed lines of low-relief texture grow into a wide surface layer; the juxtaposition of melodic lines of high-relief creates two musical vol-umes that interact; interwoven sections of contrasting qualities of time and movement create facets of a heavenly hyperspace.

The musical expression of Stravinsky's spirituality changed in the 1930s and 1940s and began to diversify. Both *Perséphone* (1933) and *The Rake's Progress* (1948) are concerned primarily with the subject of time, *Perséphone* as an alle-gory of rebirth, *The Rake's Progress* as a morality tale. Perséphone sacrifices herself to ensure the coming of Spring and new life, and looks with compassion upon the lost souls in Hades who are fated to wander endlessly until the com-ing of Christ. *The Rake's Progress* is a highly moral tale demonstrating the importance of using one's time on earth wisely and avoiding the wiles of the Devil. The subject of time and its many aspects also proved to be the enduring message of Stravinsky's lectures for Harvard University on the poetics of music (1939–40). *Babel* (1944) aptly illustrated Stravinsky's skill in creating extended time qualities in a very brief performance time: it contrasts the time quality of a long migration and the subsequent rapid dispersal of many peoples, with the out-of-time presence of God.

Stravinsky returned to the Russian Orthodox Church as a communicant member of a *community.* From 1926, he introduced the Russian Orthodox musical style into Western church music with three short settings, *Pater Noster, Credo* and *Ave Maria* (1926–1934) and restored the time quality appropriate to the spirit of each part of the *Mass* (1944–8) with a memorable mix of Eastern and Western styles.

After 1952, as Stravinsky adopted Schoenberg's serial organisation of pitch, and was strongly influenced by Webern's crystalline structures, his concen-tration on the construction of clear, mentally-imageable musical objects to shine with a spiritual quality became even more apparent. The subjects of his works became explicitly religious and often apocalyptic, and in works from *Cantata* to *Requiem Canticles* he took a strong stand against what he saw as the apostasy of contemporary society. Stravinsky's venture into serial composition in *Cantata,* sets the Passion of Christ as the dense, highly expressive heart of the work, preceded by modal canons of varied momentum: the shapely movement to and from the great depth of time at the centre of the work recalls the temporal form of the *Octet,* though on a larger time-scale and with a more profound meaning. In *Canticum Sacrum* Stravinsky set the important development in spiritual insight from the Old to the New Testament, that of loving one's neighbour, in the context of the spiritual journey: at the heart of the work it leads from Love through Hope to Faith.

As in Stravinsky's *Mass,* each section of *Threni* reflects the time qualities of the spiritual journey made in the text: the first section weaves disparate qualities of time into a spiral structure, the second section builds a linear narrative, and the third section creates a timeless monolith. Stravinsky returned to this combination of shapely forms in writing *A Sermon, A Narrative and A Prayer,* which sets the story of Stephen, the first Christian martyr. The *Narrative* is preceded by the spiral form of the *Sermon,* which places Stephen's martyrdom in the context of words by St Paul on hope and faith, and on the Lord as a consuming fire. The *Narrative* is followed by an increasingly timeless prayer that expresses a wish to be part of the heavenly community and its worship. *The Flood* and *Abraham and Isaac* both deal with apocalyptic events with great brevity and create deep time qualities in a brief performance time. *The Flood* exploits the ability of television to expand or concentrate time qualities and to suggest a great variety of temporalities, from here-and-now events in clock-time, to transcendent, out-of-time qualities. *Abraham and Isaac* condenses the story of Abraham's long journey, his obedience to God's spiritual test, and his return to be the founder of a new humanity, with great economy into barely a quarter of an hour. Its brief suggestions of sudden momentum and temporal depth are constructed solely by the graduated juxtaposition of serial forms.

Requiem Canticles is a deep expression of faith and sorrow, and of the expectation of Judgement. The work constructs an apocalyptic scenario with extreme contrasts of time quality: it is a distillation of a lifetime's techniques, a challenging listening experience that is opened up rapidly in the Prelude, as in *Three Japanese Lyrics,* by two separately-evolving streams of movement: the upper layer increases in density while the lower, simpler layer advances rapidly along the row and returns slowly. The listening challenge is maintained in Exaudi, where the density of human voices on earth is contrasted with instrumental harmonics and wide intervals across several octaves, creating great depth of time and space. The Dies Irae pushes these contrasts to the limit with extremely brief extremes of texture, momentum and dynamics. Its brief flashes of sound enclose a prophecy, a central density created by three layers of movement that combine great depth of pitch with a tension between binary and triplet rhythms. After the trumpet's repeated dyads to call the nations, the Interlude recalls the interwoven time qualities of *Symphonies of Wind Instruments*: a legato litany alternates with a repeated, aspirated chord and is extended on its third hearing. This movement is articulated and concluded by two instances of the IR form that Stravinsky used at significant moments. Rex Tremendae 'reaches through' to the heavens: a dense layer of choral movement is pierced by the articulations of a repeating staccato figure, as in the third movement of *Symphony of Psalms* and Euntes in Mundum in *Canticum Sacrum*.[1] Lacrimae returns to earth with a petition to be granted mercy and rest after the Day of Judgement, and juxtaposes a rapid litany of serial forms to sustained chords and layers of slow changing movement. Libera Me evokes the multi-timbre pitch world of a Russian Orthodox service, aptly leading to the Postlude and the rich sound world of bells. Here, Stravinsky opposes complex serial 'ring changes' to the simple diatonic world of the minor tonic triad as 'hum' notes. Two pitch worlds are juxtaposed, albeit on a vaster time-scale, to evoke a 'sacred' time, just as the spiritual nature of the Fisherman in *Le Rossignol* had been created with the simple juxtaposition of two diatonic keys, many years before.

Far from wishing to initiate modernist styles of discontinuous blocks and layers moving in different spatial directions, or to construct complex rhythmic schemes to appeal to the intellect alone, Stravinsky aimed to shape and unify ontological time qualities into new temporal forms to reflect the spiritual aspects of human existence, and to restore music as a temporal art. His construction of time qualities by the layering and interaction of authentic rhythmic manners was instinctively-felt and realised in faith and trust; always open to new artistic influences, and with close friends among the famous, Stravinsky also brought new life to the classical forms of Western Europe and new directions to the development of serial composition.

In considering Stravinsky as a creative artist and as a man of deep Christian commitment, perhaps his still greater achievement is to have kept faith with himself and his gift of 'musical aptitudes' from God throughout his long life despite inevitable setbacks and unjust criticism. The strength of his inner belief in the musical and spiritual purposes of his life – to enable humankind to glimpse what he called a 'System beyond Nature' – ultimately ensured that he emerged from fallow creative periods, or periods of musical or spiritual crisis, with renewed energy and curiosity to seek new means of achieving his goal.

---

1   Stravinsky also used a repeating staccato figure to create resonance.

Although he felt, as the custodian of his talent receiving uncovenanted mercies, he had 'too often kept faith on his all-too-worldly terms', his music stands as a profound testimony not only to his legacy as a 'turning-around' point in the development of music, but also to the restoration of the balance between faith and reason. Stravinsky's true musical legacy is to have composed works that stand as a towering reaffirmation of a transcendent reality in an increasingly secular age.[2]

---

2   Horgan, Paul. 1972, 249.

Victor Ivanovitch Nesmelov: The Science of Man

Stravinsky's heavily annotated 1905 edition of this book remained part of his reading into old age as he unfailingly sought to be accountable to God for his compositions. It is likely that in earlier years, Stravinsky and his first wife Catherine discussed Victor Nesmelov's first book, *The Dogmatic System of St Gregory of Nyssa* (1897), together. Professor of Philosophy at Kazan Theological Academy, Nesmelov came to dismiss former forms of philosophy and metaphysics believing that a synthesis must be achieved between positive science and revealed religion, between empirical knowledge and faith in a transcendent reality. In *The Science of Man* Nesmelov traces the processes by which perception, thought, human free will and individuality lead to a questioning of the enigma of life and truth. Beginning with 'psychological' analysis and 'a metaphysics of life' (his terms), he argues that introspection reveals that mankind is not only part of the material world but is also, in his personal being, imperishable substance, a 'living image' of the Divine Person. He aims to present the credibility of Christian commitment from rational arguments, examining the evolution of religion and religious thinking and the critiques offered by atheism and agnosticism. He offers a true way to the perception of God based not on the moral postulates of Kant's practical reason, but on 'immediate insight' into a reality beyond phenomena.

Contents

I Consciousness and Thought
1. Consciousness as the universal form of the expression of the spirit.
2. Consciousness as the creative process of the formation of psychic phenomena.
3. Thought, as a process of linking with the gift of consciousness.
4. Thought, as the process of the formation of psychic reality.
II The Formation of Subjective Reality
1. The initial world of consciousness.
2. The process of defining this world in the sphere of sensation, localisation and objectification.
3. Idea, as the product and expression of objectification.
4. The separation of the subjective and the objective as the inevitable result of the initial thought process.
III The Organisation of the World of Ideas and Concepts

© KONINKLIJKE BRILL NV, LEIDEN, 2022 | DOI:10.1163/9789004518537_019

2. The question of the origins in man's consciousness of the idea of God. The false exposition of this question and some debatable answers to it.

3. The nature of human individuality as the real image of the true nature of God.

4. The question of the evolution of religion in man and of the essence of his religious relationship with God. The untrue exposition of this question and false solutions to it.

5. Man's consciousness of the real truth of his existence in God's being, as the fundamental content of his religious consciousness and sole foundation for any religion.

6. The truth about religious consciousness and possible falsehoods in religious thinking. The natural submission of religious thought to the principle of the joys of life and the real falsehood of any natural religion.

VIII Natural Religion and Philosophy

1. The beginnings of the critical relationship to religion and the origins of philosophy.

2. Philosophy as a scientific critique of religious faith in the name of the perception of religious truth.

3. A philosophical critique of the basic ideas of religion and the psychology of religious scepticism.

4. The striving of philosophical thought towards the elimination of religious doubt in the construction of proof of the existence of God.

5. The scientific limitations of these proofs and the logic of theoretical atheism. An explanation of the logical insubstantiality of atheism, as a deduction of knowledge based on lack of knowledge.

6. Religious agnosticism concerning the last word of philosophy. A critical appraisal of these words and a demonstration of the true way towards a perception of the truth of God.

IX The Enigma of Man

1. The unanswerable question about the ultimate purpose of mankind.

2. Wishful solutions of this question by the naturalistic religion of vain faith.

3. The experience of exchanging this question for the question of the meaning of life. Wishful concepts about this question in the sphere of the philosophy of ignorance.

4. Possible reinforcement in the philosophy of the belief in religious truths.

5. The dogmatic teaching of Christian faith as the sole solution of the enigma of mankind. The lack of understanding of the Christian solution of the enigma and the involuntary heathen quality of philosophical thought.

6. A review of the results of research and the exposition of new tasks.

Translation by Mary Worthington

Gisèle Brelet

The presence in Stravinsky's personal library of several books by one particular author affirms the crucial link between his spiritual life and his creativity. Included in a catalogue of books and music 'inscribed to and/or Autographed and Annotated by Igor Stravinsky' are seven titles by the French philosopher Gisèle Brelet (1915–1973).[1]

In 1946, Gisèle Brelet's article in *La Revue Musicale* entitled 'La Poétique d'Igor Stravinsky' drew attention to the seamless unity between Stravinsky's spiritual beliefs and his work as an artist. She compared Stravinsky's temperament with that of Debussy who had been conscious of the dynamic aspect of both music and the soul but had spoken of them as conflicting forces. Debussy himself had written of his spiritual life *vis-à-vis* music:

> Music has a rhythm whose secret force shapes the development. The rhythm of the soul, however, is quite different – more instinctive, more general, and controlled by many events. From the incompatibility of these two rhythms, a perpetual conflict arises, for the two do not move at the same speed.[2]

Gisèle Brelet was of the opinion that in Stravinsky these two rhythms were perfectly aligned with one another:

> Ainsi, chez Stravinsky l'homme explique l'artiste, comme d'ailleurs l'artiste explique l'homme, dans la mésure où l'un et l'autre se trouvent être ontologiquement identiques – comme si en lui une même verité s'expriment en deux langages – en langage artistique et en langage humain.[3]

> [Thus, with Stravinsky, the man explains the artist, as moreover the artist explains the man, to the extent that one and the other find themselves ontologically identical – as if the same truth is expressed in him in two languages – in artistic language and human language.]

---

1 Craft, Robert. In Pasler, ed. 1988, Appendix: 354–5. Craft was also amazed at the preponderance of titles concerned with Dominicans, including an 18th century volume of the *Sermons* of Massillon, and Rene Bazin's life of the hermit Charles de Foucauld. Stravinsky's funeral took place in the Dominican Church of Saint John and Saint Paul in Venice. Craft, Robert. 1992, 51.
2 Lesure, François. 1977, 36.
3 Brelet, Gisèle. 1946, 132.

The inspiration for his life and his composition flowed from the same spiritual source: his relationship with God. Stravinsky had even stated that the canons of the Church were as much a guide for musical composition as for the life of an individual, and that the more one separated oneself from the canons of the Christian Church, the further one distanced oneself from the truth.[4]

Gisèle Brelet's *Esthétique et création musicale*, published the following year (1947), continued to explore the relationship between a composer's inner life and creativity with respect to time-consciousness:

> [I]l faut nécessairement qu'en l'acte de la création s'établisse un rapport entre la forme artistique et sa vie intérieure: en l'acte de la création, la forme musicale est vécue par la conscience du musicien.[5]

> [It is necessarily in the act of creation that a rapport must be established between the artistic form and [the artist's] inner life: in the creative act, the musical form is lived through in the musician's consciousness.]

> Par ses nécessités, techniques mêmes, l'art musical réalise chez le créateur, en l'acte de la création, une information de sa vie intérieure, une reconstruction de la durée empirique selon les exigences du temps musical.[6]

> [By its necessities, even techniques, the art of music realises in the creator, in the act of creation, information about his inner life, a reconstruction of empirical time according to the requirements of musical time.]

In 1947, Stravinsky wrote to his new acquaintance, Robert Craft, recommending Gisèle Brelet's *Esthétique et création musicale* as an 'important essay'. The central proposition of the book is that music is the art of pure thinking in sound, and that the autonomy of musical creation is demonstrated most definitively where musical development follows its own laws logically, independently of the diverse psychology of its composer. Brelet proposes that pure musical thought derives from the dialogue between the experience of living as temporal and the process of analytical thinking which constructs unifying relationships:

> L'opposition Kantiènne entre l'art et le concept, entre l'imagination créatrice et la pensée théorique semble pouvoir être surmontée. La musique est l'art de penser avec des sons, et cette pensée vaut hors de l'oeuvre où elle s'exprime ... Le

---

4 Stravinsky, Vera & Craft, Robert. 1979, 295.
5 Brelet, Gisèle. 1947, 73.
6 Op. cit., 144.

compositeur ... éprouve la validité de sa pensée en la jouissance que celle-ci lui procure et où se trouve attesté son pouvoir d'embrasser une certaine région du sensible sonore.[7]

[The Kantian opposition between art and concept, between the creative imagination and theoretical thought seems to be able to be overcome. Music is the art of thinking with sounds, and this thought has a value beyond the work in which it is expressed ... The composer ... proves the validity of his thought in the joy which it gives him, and in the witness it bears to his power to embrace a certain region of sensitive sound.]

Brelet observes that a composer's inner life may either unite with a temporal form at the spiritual level, capturing ontological time by its activity, or compromise with a tendency to expressiveness in which psychological flux will ensure some human content. For a musical form to be constituted in pure time, it has to be purified of all influential states of human time emanating from a composer's psyche. Like human consciousness, music unfolds in time, both music and consciousness being organised by the same dialectic of the unchanging and the new, the play of the seen and unforeseen that produces a feeling of spontaneous organisation. Brelet sees musical form as the product of the union between the 'time' of the creator's inner life and the 'time' of the autonomous life of sounds, in whose intelligible relations we share by our quality of listening.

Brelet measures a composer's originality by the degree to which he or she brings a new form to sonority, not as endless magical effects, but as a world of sonorous relationships. She argues that a strong and autonomous musical form may only arise from the interaction between its harmonic form, its web of harmonic relationships around a central pitch, and its temporal form, that is, the measurable life of the work's movement and becoming. Without form, she suggests, pure dynamism cannot achieve a unified existence in time; without dynamism, musical form cannot achieve a real, living experience that flows with the play of the seen and unseen like our human consciousness. Liberation from the rules of an externally imposed (and therefore spatially-conceived) structure which imprisoned many works of the Classical era, allows the potential for the spontaneous organisation of sounds to grow into a temporal form at the spiritual level.

Although the experience of pure, ontological time is of a different quality to that of psychological time, Brelet describes it, not as cold and lifeless, but rather, as a real and living experience in the truest sense. Active listening and attuning to pure time as a creative force capable of bearing a logical yet freely adventurous sound-form confirms the sense we have of the *élan* of the soul towards the future and is the means

---

7   Op. cit., 31.

of bringing peace and order to it. Like Souvtchinsky, Brelet describes the experience of ontological time as having a very different quality to that of psychological time, and observes that the experience of pure time can bestow health and life-giving order upon the human psyche.

Brelet proposes that every musical form embodies its composer's unique experience of musical time and reveals his true spiritual personality; alignment with the work's *élan,* if the constructive strength of its temporal form is sufficiently robust, may transform the listener's subjective time into an experience of pure, ontological time.

Stravinsky also possessed a copy of Gisèle Brelet's second book, *Le temps musical,* published in 1949. In her Introduction, Brelet writes that in both her diploma work of 1938–9 entitled *La Musique et le Temps,* and in *Esthétique et création musicale,* 'le temps musical apparait comme le mobile profond et la source secrète de la création musicale' [*musical time appeared as the prime mover and secret source of musical creation*]. She recalls that in 1943 she had come across Pierre Souvtchinsky's essay *La Notion de Temps et la Musique* (1939) in the May/June issue of *La Revue Musicale* dedicated to Igor Stravinsky. There she found, in its principal themes, the fundamental idea that she proposes in her own book, *Le temps musical.*

Brelet begins by comparing the relationship between music and time to that of the other arts and defines music's essentially spiritual nature as uniting the concrete and the abstract:

> Si [la musique] est le plus abstrait et le plus concret de tous les arts, joignant par une soudure mystérieuse l'universel et le concret ... c'est qu'elle est l'incarnation du temps, forme de tous les processus vivants et créateurs, forme du déploiement de l'étre biologique et de l'être spirituel ... c'est l'essence de notre aventure temporelle, c'est aussi l'incarnation de ce temps que la pensée se construit pour elle seule et afin de se construire elle-même.[8]

> [If music is the most abstract and most concrete of all the arts, mysteriously welding together the universal and the concrete ... it is because it is the incarnation of time, a form of all the living and creative processes, a form which displays biological and spiritual being ... it is the essence of our temporal experience, it is also the incarnation of the time that thought constructs for music alone in order for it to be constructed.]

Brelet offers a perceptive analysis of Debussy's unique role in liberating music to realise its temporal function:

---

8   Brelet, Gisele. 1949, 33.

Chez Debussy, l'amour de la matière sonore en elle-même détruit la durée psychologique au bénéfice du temps musical ... la sonorité, chassant la durée psychologique et comblant le temps, éveille en nous l'apaisement d'une contemplation qui nous empêche de nous laisser divertir par le passé et par l'avenir en nous repliant sur l'achèvement du présent ...[9]

[With Debussy, the love of sonorous matter itself destroys psychological time to the benefit of musical time ... sonority, driving out psychological time and filling up time, awakens in us a pacifying quality of contemplation that prevents us from being distracted by the past and the future, in drawing us back to complete the present ...]

Brelet suggests that a musical form embodies the temporal experience of the composer and achieves form and stability to the degree that it achieves the 'space' of pure, ontological time. This temporal experience is realised in patterns of sound that vary like human consciousness, and she suggests three specific categories for measuring the constitutive elements of musical form.[10] The first category is tempo: tempo in a musical form is expressed in constancy of metre, while tempo in consciousness is the means whereby the soul experiences its mode of being in time. The second category is living movement: in a musical form, rates of harmonic and rhythmic change are expressed in constantly changing relationships in the same way as our experience of life as temporal fluctuates according to the amount of mental work needed to make sense of information and events. The third category is rhythm: rhythm in a musical form orders time, and variations within rhythms express three aspects of forward movement: the struggle to become, the nature of the process, and changing identity. In human consciousness, rhythmic play recalling the patterns of language and gesture, both with the metre and counter to it, appeals to both the senses and the intellect. She concludes that it is a skilful balance between the senses and the intellect that overcomes the tyranny of psychological flux and frees consciousness to experience the flow of pure, ontological time.[11]

Brelet suggests that these three categories, tempo, living movement and rhythm, are those most easily synthesised by the memory systems to create a sound-object. Only by their synthesis can music express nothing but itself, unite every level of our being, and be a vehicle for our deepest spiritual experiences.

Brelet continues by noting the importance of rhythm in ordering human consciousness:

---

9   Brelet, Gisèle. 1949, 692–5.

10   Op. cit., 473.

11   Ibid.

Nous vivons nécessairement le temps sous la forme du rythme: nous nous soumettons aux rythmes du monde et à ceux du corps, et c'est par rapport à eux que s'organise notre vie même, que déjà ils contraignent à une certaine sagesse: mais trop souvent nous nous désintéressons du rythme de notre âme, rythme ... qui, si nous voulons, nous accordera au temps ... en faisant l'exact reflet de nous-même.[12]

[We live time necessarily in the form of rhythm: we submit to the rhythms of the world and those of the body, and it is by relating to those that organise our very life, that they already compel us to a certain wisdom: but too often we are not interested in the rhythm of our soul, rhythm ... that, if we wish, will tune us to time ... in making an exact reflection of ourselves.]

When asked to comment on W. H. Auden's view of music as 'a virtual image of our experience of living as temporal, with its double aspect of recurrence and becoming', Stravinsky, always the practical artisan, replied:

If music is to me an 'image of our experience of living as temporal' (and however unverifiable, I suppose it is), my saying so is the result of a reflection, and as such is independent of music itself. But ... I cannot do anything with it as a truth, and my mind is a doing one ... Jazz improvisation is the dissipation of the time image and, if I understand 'recurrence' and 'becoming', their aspect is greatly diminished in serial music. Auden's 'image of our experience of living as temporal' (which is also an image), is above music, perhaps, but it does not obstruct or contradict the purely musical experience.[13]

Brelet addresses the temporal-spatial nature of music and proposes that musical space is built by a network of harmonic relations, whereas an arrangement of simultaneous sounds [as a chord] abolishes three-dimensional space in two ways. Firstly, simultaneous sounds are not separate units juxtaposed as in visual space, but a new entity

---

12   It is interesting to note that in the latter half of the 1940s, within ten years of articles and books by Souvtchinsky, Brelet and Stravinsky on music and time, and as Stravinsky and Auden were writing *The Rake's Progress*, psychoanalysis was beginning to recognise that all sterile and pathological states of consciousness stem from a refusal or evasion of time. Research into the human psyche began to explore how the human spirit may choose to abandon itself to the destructive powers of its pathological states, or may come to recognise and work with the temporal aspects of life, and identify its intrinsic forward '*élan*' in order to liberate and nourish its creative powers. See Rappaport, Herbert. 1990. The author, a psychoanalyst, considers how our personalities, our problems, and their treatment are shaped by temporal dysfunction and anxiety.

13   Stravinsky, Igor & Craft, Robert. 1979, 18–19.

unified within the single dimension of time. Secondly, it is through harmonic relationships that intelligible thought is expressed in time without becoming a solid object in visual space. The most important aspect of harmonic relations lies not in the 'distances' with which they would deceive us, but in the patterns of change and recurrence in the volumes they create. The coherence of these patterns is greatly dependent upon the audibility of a central pitch to which other pitches are attracted and against which they interact, and upon articulations which mark out organic patterns of growth.[14] Brelet concludes that sound organised in this way provides a medium in which the conflict between thought (as harmonic relationships) and life experience (as rhythm and melody) is resolved in the dimension of time.

Brelet observes that music is like dance and the art of gesture in being based in the time of living experience, and that music creates time which is 'lived through' by both performer and listener. With obvious relevance to Stravinsky's background in ballet and keen sensitivity to the rhythmic manners of being and becoming, she observes that although dancing is performed in visual space, it is, nevertheless, the temporal dimension of the art that predominates because it is 'lived through', by the spectator, with the dancer:

> La danse, art du geste vécu, temporalise l'espace en lui communiquant cette durée concrète que le geste déploie en se déployant ...[15]

> [Dance, the art of living gesture, temporalises space in imparting to it the real time of the gesture as it unfolds ...]

She observes that both the ballerina and the instrumentalist reveal the *élan* of their soul by their physical movements:

> Un organisme au travail est présent devant nous, qui ressert et qui traduit: un dynamisme intérieur exprimé dans un mécanisme, et, par de semblables moyens, la traduction d'états semblables. La ballerine et l'instrumentaliste sont tous deux au service de cette présence: tous deux coulent l'élan de leur âme dans cette précision des muscles.[16]

> [A working organism is present before us, that compresses and translates: an inner dynamism expressed in a mechanism, and by similar means, the translation

---

14   Stravinsky liberates harmony from concepts of 'consonance' and 'dissonance' that have obtained in the past and affirms pitch axes as poles of attraction, as an 'eternal necessity'. Stravinsky, Igor. 1947, 35.

15   Brelet, Gisèle. 1949, 23.

16   Bayer, Raymond. *L'Esthétique de la Grace.* 212–213. In Brelet, Gisèle. 1949, 23.

of similar states. The ballerina and the instrumentalist are both at the service of this presence: in both, the momentum of their soul flows out into this precision of the muscles.]

Stravinsky had a horror of listening to music with his eyes shut: he thought the sight of the gestures and movements of the various parts of the body were fundamentally necessary if music was to be grasped in all its fullness.[17] Brelet remarks on the unity of sound and gesture and its ability to draw us into its being and becoming:

> Le mouvement du geste ne conserve sa réalité et son actualité que parce-que l'accompagne sa sonorité propre, hors de laquelle il reste purement imaginaire. Le geste muet que nous bornons à voir n'est que pure image extérieure à nous-même, tandis qu' un geste que nous entendons est immediatement interiorisé et refait par nous: et la musique qui accompagne la danse a pour essentielle mission de nous faire sympathiser avec les gestes de la danseuse.[18]

> [The movement of a gesture only retains its reality and presence because its own sound accompanies it, otherwise it remains purely imaginary. The silent gesture that we are content to look at is only a pure image outside ourselves, while a gesture that we hear is immediately interiorised and restored by us: music that accompanies dance has for its essential mission, to draw us into the gestures of the dancer.]

Stravinsky's awareness of movement in time as well as space had surely been nurtured in his early years by his frequent attendance at the ballet and opera at the Mariinsky Theatre in St Petersburg. Where rhythmic gestures had already found perfect expression in the music of the past, Stravinsky did not hesitate to 'borrow' them and make them his own. As early as 1914, Boris Asaf'yev had remarked upon Stravinsky's 'ability to grasp with an intuitive perspicacity the spirit and sense of any preceding epoch and to stylise it by means of the most ingenious techniques at his disposal today'.[19]

---

17 Stravinsky, Igor. 1975, 72.
18 Brelet, Gisèle. 1949, 24. Diaghilev wrote to Stravinsky, March 8th, 1915: 'After having thirty-two rehearsals of the Liturgie, we have concluded that absolute silence is death ... and that aerial space is not absolute silence and can't be ... Therefore, dance action must be supported ... by filling the ear harmonically.' Stravinsky, Igor & Craft, Robert. 1981: *Memories and Commentaries*, 101–2.
19 Asaf'yev, Boris. *Muzyka,* December 27th 1914 (Old Style). Brown, Malcolm H. In Pasler, ed. 1988, 44.

Bibliography

Adorno, Theodor W. *Philosophy of Modern Music*, trans. Anne G. Mitchell & Wesley V. Blomster, London: Salisbury Press, 1973.

Adorno, Theodor W. 'Stravinsky: A dialectical portrait'. In *Negative Dialectics*, trans. E.B. Ashton. London: Routledge Press, 1973.

Allen, Edwin. 'The Genius and the Goddess'. In *Confronting Stravinsky*, ed. Pasler, 1986, 327–331.

Ansermet, Ernest. 'The Crisis of Contemporary Music, II: the Stravinsky Case'. *Recorded Sound*, April 1964.

Ansermet, Ernest. *Les Fondements de Musique dans la Conscience Humaine*. La Baconnière,1961.

Apel, Willi, ed. *Harvard Dictionary of Music*. London: Heinemann Educational Books Ltd., 1970.

Aquinas, St Thomas. *Summa Theologica*. trans.The Fathers of the Dominican Province. Benziger Bros. 1947.

Aquinas, St Thomas. *Theological Texts*. Selected & trans. Robert Gilby. Oxford University Press, 2006.

Aristotle. *Poetics*. Loeb Classical Library. London: Heinemann., 1932.

Asaf'yev, Boris. (Igor Glebov). *A Book about Stravinsky*. trans. Richard F. French. Leningrad: 1929.

Babbitt, Milton. 'Order, Symmetry, and Centricity in Late Stravinsky'. In *Confronting Stravinsky*, ed. Pasler, University of California Press, 1986. 247–261.

Babbitt, Milton. 'Stravinsky's Verticals and Schoenberg's Diagonals: A Twist of Fate'. In *Stravinsky Retrospectives*, ed. Haimo & Johnson. University of Nebraska Press, 1987. 15–35.

Bamberger, Jeanne. 'What develops in musical development?'. In *The Child as Musician: A Handbook of Musical Development*, ed. McPherson, 2003. 69–92.

Barton, John. *A History of the Bible*. Penguin Books, 2020.

Bergson, Henri. *Time and Free Will*. Dover Publications, 2001.

Bergson, Henri. *Matter and Memory*. trans. N. Margaret Paul & W. Scott Palmer. Dover Publications, 2004.

Bergson, Henri. 'La Perception du changement': conférences faites à l'université d'Oxford, 26/27 Mai, 1911. Oxford Clarendon Press, 1911.

Bergson, Henri. *Creative Evolution*. trans. Arthur Mitchell. New York: Dover, 1998.

Bergson, Henri. *An Introduction to Metaphysics*. trans. T. E. Hulme. Macmillan and Co. Ltd., 1913.

Black, Matthew & Rowley, H. H., eds. *Peake's Commentary on the Bible*. London: Thomas Nelson and Sons, Ltd., 1967.

Boretz, Benjamin & Cone, Edward T., eds. *Perspectives on Schoenberg and Stravinsky*. Oxford University Press, 1969.

Boucourechliev, André. *Stravinsky*. trans. Martin Cooper. Gollancz, 1987.

Boulez, Pierre. 'Schoenberg is Dead'. The Score. May 1952.

Boulez, Pierre & Thévenin, Paule. *Stocktakings from an Apprenticeship*. Knopf, 1968.

Boulez, Pierre. *Introduction: Webern Op.1–31*. CBS records, 1978.

Brajnikov, Maxim. 'Russian church singing in XII-XVIII centuries'. In *Russian Music and its Sources in Chant and Folksong*. Alfred, J. Swan. London: John Baker, 1973.

Brelet, Gisèle. 'La Poétique d'Igor Stravinsky', *La Revue Musicale*, May, 1946.

Brelet, Gisèle. *Le temps musical*. Paris: Presses Universitaires de France, 1949.

Brelet, Gisèle. *Esthétique et création musicale*. Paris: Presses Universitaires de France, 1947.

Brooks, Jeanice. *The Musical Work of Nadia Boulanger: Performing Past and Future between the Wars*. Cambridge University Press, 1947.

Brothers, L., Shaw, G.L., Wright, Eric L. 'Durations of extended mental rehearsals are remarkably reproducible in higher level human performances'. *Neurological Research* 15, 413–416.

Brown, Malcolm H. 'Stravinsky and Prokofiev: Sizing up the Competition'. In *Confronting Stravinsky*, ed. Pasler. University of California Press, 1986.

Carter, Rita. *Mapping the Mind*. London: Weidenfeld and Nicolson, 1998.

Cassirer, Ernst. *The Philosophy of Symbolic Forms*. Yale University Press, 1953.

Clark, Suzannah & Rehding, Alexander, eds. *Music in Time: Phenomenology, Perception, Performance*. Harvard Publications in Music, 2016.

Clifton, Thomas. 'Music as constituted object'. In *Music and Man*. ed. Smith & White. Gordon and Breach, 1976. 2, 1/2.

Clifton, Thomas. *Music as Heard*. Yale University Press, 1983.

Cone, Edward T. 'Stravinsky: The Progress of a Method'. In *Perspectives of New Music*, 1962. 1/1, a 18–26.

Corle, Edwin, ed. *Igor Stravinsky: Articles and Essays*. New York: Duell, Sloane and Pearce. 1949.

Corle, Edwin, ed. *Igor Stravinsky*. New York: Books for Libraries Press, 1969.

Craft, Robert. 'A personal Preface'. *The Score*, June 1957.

Craft, Robert. *Dix Ans avec Stravinsky*. Monaco, 1958.

Craft, Robert. *Dialogues and a Diary*. London: Faber and Faber, 1968.

Craft, Robert, ed. *Dearest Bubushkin. Selected Letters and Diaries of Vera and Igor Stravinsky*. trans. Lucia Davidova. Thames & Hudson, 1985.

Craft, Robert. *Bravo Stravinsky*. World Publishing Co., 1967.

Craft, Robert. *Stravinsky: Chronicle of a Friendship*. Victor Gollancz, 1972.

Craft, Robert, ed. Igor Stravinsky: *Selected Correspondence. Vol.1*. London: Faber and Faber, 1982.

Craft, Robert, ed. Igor Stravinsky: *Selected Correspondence. Vol.II*. London: Faber and Faber, 1984.

Craft, Robert, ed. Igor Stravinsky: *Selected Correspondence. Vol.III*. London: Faber and Faber, 1985.

Craft, Robert. *Glimpses of a Life*. London: Octopus Publishing Group, 1992.

Craft, Robert. *Down a Path of Wonder*. Naxos Books, 2006.

Cross, Ian. 'Music, cognition, culture, and evolution'. In *The Cognitive Neuroscience of Music*, ed. Peretz, & Zatorre. 2003, 42–56.

Cross, Jonathan. *The Stravinsky Legacy*. Cambridge University Press, 1998.

Daley, Mary F. *Natural Knowledge of God in the Philosophy of Jacques Maritain*. Catholic Book Agency, 1966.

Davies, Paul. *About Time: Einstein's unfinished Revolution*. Penguin Books, 1995.

Debussy, Claude. 'Why I wrote Pelléas'. (April 1902). In *Debussy on Music*, coll. by François Lesure. London: Secker and Warburg, 1977.

Drake, Carolyn & Bertrand, Daisy. 'The quest for universals in temporal processing in music'. In The Cognitive Neuroscience of Music, eds. Peretz & Zatorre. 2003, 21–31.

Druskin, Mikhail. *Igor Stravinsky: His personality, works and views*. trans. Martin Cooper. Cambridge University Press, 1983.

Dushkin, Samuel. 'Working with Stravinsky'. In *Stravinsky*. ed. Corle. Merle Armitage, 1949.

Eliade, Mircea. *Cosmos and History. The Myth of the Eternal Return*. New York: Harper and Row, 1959.

Eliade, Mircea. *Myth and Reality*. George Allen and Unwin, 1964.

Eliot, Thomas S. *Four Quartets*. London: Folio Society, 1968.

Ehrenzweig, Anton. *Psycholanalysis of Artistic Vision and Hearing*. Routledge and Kegan Paul Ltd., 1953.

Ewen, David. *The World of Twentieth Century Music*. London: Prentice-Hall, 1968.

Farah, Martha J. 'The Neural Basis of Mental Imagery'. *Cognition*. 1984. Vol.18.

Forte, Allen. *The Harmonic Organisation of The Rite of Spring*. New Haven and London: Yale University Press, 1978.

Fraser, Julius T. *Time, Conflict and Human Values*. University of Illinois Press, 1999.

Funayama, Takashi. 'Three Japanese Lyrics and Japonisme'. I. ed. Pasler. University of California Press, 1986. 273–283.

Grainger, Roger. *The Language of the Rite*. London: Darton, Longman and Todd, 1974.

Gregory, Richard L., ed. *The Oxford Companion to the Mind*. Oxford University Press, 1987.

Haimo, Ethan. 'Problems of Hierarchy in Stravinsky's Octet'. In *Stravinsky Retrospectives*. ed. Haimo & Johnson. University of Nebraska Press, 1987, 36–54.

Haimo, Ethan & Johnson, Paul, eds. *Stravinsky Retrospectives*. Lincoln: University of Nebraska Press, 1997.

Hanson, Anthony T. 'Time and Eternity'. *A Dictionary of Christian Theology*. SCM Press, 1969.

Hampson, P.J., Marks, D.F. & Richardson, J. T. E., eds. *Imagery: Current Developments*. London: Routledge, 1990.

Handschin, Jacques. 'Le Chant Eccléstiastique Russe'. *Acta Musicologica* XXIV, (3) 1952.

Hawking, Stephen. *A Brief History of Time*. Bantam Press, 1988.

Heidegger, Martin. *Being and Time*. Oxford: Basil Blackwell, 1978.

Heim, Karl. *Christian Faith and Natural Science*. trans. Neville Horton Smith. London: SCM Press, 1953.

Henson, R.A. & Critchley, MacDonald, eds. *Music and the Brain*. Heinemann, 1977.

Hindemith, Paul. *The Craft of Musical Composition. vol.1: Theory*. trans. Arthur Mendel. Associated Music Publishers, 1945.

Hodson, Millicent. *Stravinsky and the Ballets Russes*. Interview on DVD, Bel Air Media, 2008.

Horgan, Paul. *Encounters with Stravinsky*. A Personal Record. London: Bodley Head, 1972.

Ihde, Don & Slaughter, Thomas F. *Studies in the Phenomenology of Sound*. International Philosophical Quarterly 10.2. (June 1970), 232–251.

James, William. *The Principles of Psychology*. New York: Dover Publications, Inc., 1950.

James, William. *The Varieties of Religious Experience*. Penguin Classics, 1985.

Järvinen, Hanna. 'They Never Dance: The Choreography of Le Sacre du Printemps'. In *A Laboratory of Spring*. ed.Wachowski. Avant: Warsaw Centre for Philosophical Research. 2013, IV/ 3.

Kamens, Edward. *Utamakura, Allusion, and Intertextuality in Traditional Japanese Poetry*. Yale University Press, 1997.

Karsavina, Tamara. 'A Recollection of Stravinsky'. *Tempo*, Summer 1948.

Kirstein, Lincoln. 'Working with Stravinsky'. Modern Music. 1937, xiv/ 3.

Kramer, Jonathan D. 'Discontinuity and Proportion in the music of Stravinsky'. In Confronting Stravinsky. ed. Pasler. University of California Press, 1988, 194.

Kramer, Jonathan D. *Time in Music: New Meanings, New Temporalities, New Listening Strategies*. Schirmer Books, 1988.

Kuster, Andrew. *Stravinsky's Topology*. 2005 Lulu.com.

Langer, Suzanne K. *Philosophy in a New Key*. Harvard Press, 1960.

Leng, Xiaodan & Shaw, Gordon. 'Toward a neural theory of higher brain function using music as a window'. *Concepts in Neuroscience*: World Scientific Publishing Company. 1991, 2/2, 229–258.

Leng, Xiaodan, Shaw, Gordon, & Wright, Eric L. 'Coding of Musical Structure and the Trion model of Cortex'. *Music Perception*. University of California Press. 1990, 8/ 1, 49–62.

le Poidevin, Robin & MacBeath, Murray, eds. *The Philosophy of Time*. Oxford University Press, 1993.

Lesure, François. *Debussy on Music*. London: Secker and Warburg, 1977.

Lesure, François. *Igor Stravinsky: Le Sacre du Printemps. Dossier de Presse. Anthologie de la critique musicale*. Paris: Editions Minkoff, 1980.

Lévi-Strauss, Claude. *Structural Anthropology. vol.1*. Allen Lane: The Penguin Press, 1968.

Lévi-Strauss, Claude. *Myth and Meaning*. Routledge & Kegan Paul, 1978.

Lewis, Penelope A. 'Finding the Timer'. *Trends in Cognitive Sciences*, 2002, 6/5, 195.

Lineff, Eugènie. *The Peasant Songs of Great Russia, Vol. 1*. St Petersburg, 1905.

Lineff, Eugènie. *The Peasant Songs of Great Russia, Vol. 2*. Moscow, 1911.

Lochhead, Judy. 'Temporal Structure in Recent Music'. In *Understanding the Musical Experience*. ed. Smith. Gordon and Breach, 1989.

Lourié, Arthur. 'La Sonate pour Piano de Stravinsky', *La Revue Musicale*, 1925, 6/10 (1st August).

Lourié, Arthur. 'The Music of Stravinsky'. *Versty*. Paris 1926, vol.1.

Lourié, Arthur. 'A propos de l'Apollon d'Igor Stravinsky', *Musique*: Revue Mensuelle 1927, 1/3.

Lourié, Arthur. 'Neogothic and Neoclassic'. *Modern Music*, 1928, 5/3.

Lourié, Arthur. 'Oedipus Rex'. *La Revue Musicale*, 1929/10.

Lourié, Arthur. 'An Inquiry into Melody'. *Modern Music*. 1929–30, 7/1, 3–4.

Macquarrie, John. *Principles of Christian Theology*. New York: Charles Scribner's Sons, 1977.

Mann, Thomas. *The Magic Mountain*. trans. John E. Woods. Vintage International Edition, 1996.

Maritain, Jacques. *La Philosophie Bergsonienne*. Paris: Marcel Rivière, 1914.

Maritain, Jacques. *Art et Scolastique*. Librairie de l'Art Catholique, 1920.

Maritain, Jacques. *Frontières de la Poésie*. Paris: Louis Rouart et Fils, 1935.

Maritain, Jacques. *Art and Poetry*. London: Poetry Editions, 1945.

Maritain, Jacques. *Art and Poetry*. trans. E.P. Matthews. New York: Philosophical Library, 1943.

Maritain, Jacques. *Creative Intuition in Art and Poetry*. London: Harvill Press, 1954.

Maritain, Jacques. *Approaches to God*. London: Allen and Unwin, 1955.

Maritain, Raissa. 'A Handful of Musicians'. *The Commonweal*: 29th Oct. 1943.

Marsh, Kathryn & Young, Susan. 'Musical Play'. In *The Child as Musician: A Handbook of Musical Development*, ed. McPherson. 2006, 289–310.

Martin, A. et al. 'Observation of static pictures of dynamic actions enhances the activity of movement-related brain areas'. *PLoS One*, 2009. 4(5): e5389.

Martin, A. et al. 'Discrete cortical regions associated with knowledge of color and knowledge of action'. *Science*, 1995. 270, 102–105.

Meck, Warren. 'Internal Clocks in the Striatum', *GEO*, *Neurobiologie* (German edition) 1996, Sept./Oct.

McAngus Todd, Neil P. 'Motion in Music: a Neurological Perspective'. *Music Perception*, 1999, 17/1, 115–126.

McDermott, Vincent. 1972. (Summer). 'A Conceptual Musical Space'. *The Journal of Aesthetics and Art Criticis* 489–94.

McGilchrist, Iain. *The Master and his Emissary.* New Haven and London: Yale University Press, 2009.

McLaughlin, Terence. *Music and Communication.* London: Faber and Faber, 1970.

McPherson, Gary E. ed. *The Child as Musician: A Handbook of Musical Development.* Oxford University Press, 2006.

Merleau-Ponty, Maurice. *Phenomenology of Perception.* trans. Colin Smith. London: Routledge and Kegan Paul, 1966.

Messiaen, Olivier. 'Le rythme chez Igor Strawinsky', *Revue Musicale*, 1939, 191.

Messiaen, Olivier. *Technique de mon langage musical.* 1944. trans. John Satterfield. Paris: LeDuc, 1957.

Miller, Arthur. *Einstein, Picasso: Space, Time and the Beauty that Causes Havoc.* Basic Books, 2001.

Mind and Brain: Readings from Scientific American. New York Freeman and Company, 1993.

Monighetti, T. B. 'Stravinsky's Russian Library'. In *Stravinsky and his World.* ed. Tamara Levitz. Princeton University Press. 2013, 61–78.

Monter, Barbara H. *Koz'ma Prutkov: The Art of Parody.* The Hague: Mouton, 1972.

Mountcastle, V. B. 'An organising principle for cerebral function: the unit module and the distributed system' in G. M. Edelman & V. B. Mountcastle, eds., *The mindful brain.* Cambridge: MIT, 1978.

Nesmelov, Viktor I. *The Science of Man.* England: Gregg International Publishers, 1971.

Olkhovsky, Yuri. *Vladimir Stasov and Russian National Culture.* Ann Arbor, Michigan: UMI Research Press. 1983.

Orlov, Henry F. 'The Temporal Dimensions of Musical Experience'. *Musical Quarterly*, 1979, 65/368.

Ornstein, Robert. *The Psychology of Consciousness.* London: Pelican Books, 1986.

Osaka, Naoyuki et al. 'Implied motion because of instability in Hokusai Manga activates the human motion-sensitive extrastriate visual cortex: an fMRI study of the impact of visual art'. *Behavioural, integrative and clinical neuroscience.* 2010, 264–7.

Osaka, Nauoyuki. 'Walk-related mimic word activates the extrastriate visual cortex in the human brain: an fMRI study'. *Behavioural Brain Research*, 2009.

Parncutt, Richard. 'Prenatal Development'. In *The Child as Musician: A Handbook of Musical Development*, ed. McPherson, 2006, 1–32.

Pasler, Jann. 'Stravinsky and The Apaches'. *The Musical Times*, 1982/123.

Pasler, Jann, ed. *Confronting Stravinsky: Man, Musician and Modernist*, University of California Press, 1986.

Peake's Commentary on the Bible. Thomas Nelson & Sons Ltd. 1962.

Peretz, Isabelle & Zatorre, Robert eds. *The Cognitive Neuroscience of Music*. Oxford University Press, 2003.

Perrin, M. 'Stravinsky in a Composition Class'. *The Score*, June 1957.

Petsche, Helmut. et al. 'The EEG: An Adequate Method to Concretize Brain Processes Elicited by Music'. *Music Perception*, 6/2, 133–160. University of California Press, 1988.

Petsche, Helmut, Richter, P. et al. 'EEG Coherence and Musical Thinking'. *Music Perception*, 11/2, 117–151. University of California Press, 1993.

Pope Paul VI. *Unitatis redintegratio*. December Discourse: 1975.

Price, Percival. 'Bell': *The New Grove Dictionary of Music and Musicians*. ed. Sadie. London: Oxford University Press, 1980, 426–7.

Purves, Dale, & Augustine, George. J. et al., eds. *Neuroscience*. (3rd Edition). Massachusetts, USA: Sinauer Associates, Inc., 2004.

Ramachandran, Vilayanur. *The Emerging Mind*: BBC Reith Lectures. London: Profile Books, 2003.

Ramuz, Charles F. *Souvenirs sur Igor Stravinsky*. Editions Mermod. Paris: Nouvelle Revue Francaise, 1929.

Rappaport Herbert. *Marking Time*. Simon and Schuster, 1990.

Rauscher, Frances H., Shaw, G.L. & Ky, K.N. 'Listening to Mozart enhances spatial-temporal reasoning: towards a neurophysiological basis'. *Neuroscience Letters* 1995 (185).

Rayment-Pickard, Hugh. *The Myths of Time: from St Augustine to American Beauty*. London: Darton, Longman and Todd, 2004.

Read, Herbert. *The Meaning of Art*. Penguin Books, 1949.

Reich, Willi. *Schoenberg: A Critical Biography*. Longman, 1971.

Reisberg, Daniel, ed. *Auditory Imagery*. Lawrence Erlbaum Associates, 1992.

Richardson, Alan, ed. *A Dictionary of Christian Theology*. London: SCM Press, 1969.

Rosen, Charles. *The Classical Style*. London: Faber and Faber, 1972.

Rosen, Charles. *Schoenberg*. Fontana/Collins, 1976.

Rover, Thomas. *The Poetics of Maritain*. Washington: Thomist Press, 1965.

Saffran, Jenny R. 'Mechanisms of musical memory in infancy'. In *The Cognitive Neuroscience of Music*. eds. Peretz & Zatorre. 2003, 32–41.

Sarnthein, Johannes, von Stein, Astrid, et al. 'Persistent patterns of brain acivity: An EEG coherence study of the positive effect of music on spatial-temporal reasoning'. *Neurological Research*, 1997/19 (April), 107–116.

Schatz, Carla. 'The Developing Brain': *Mind and Brain: Readings from Scientific American*. New York: W.H. Freeman and Company, 1993, 15–26.

Schouvaloff, Alexander & Borovsky, Victor. *Stravinsky on Stage*. London: Stainer and Bell, 1982.

Schoenberg, Arnold. *Style and Idea*. Faber and Faber, 1975.

Schubert, Emery & McPherson, Gary E. 'The perception of emotion in music'. In *The Child as Musician: A Handbook of Musical Development*. ed. McPherson. Oxford University Press, 2006, 193–212.

Sellick, Phyllis. 'Cyril Smith Remembered'. *Hi-fi News and Record Review* February, 1999.

Shattuck, Roger. 'Making Time: A Study of Stravinsky, Proust and Sartre'. *Kenyon Review*, 1963. 25/257.

Shaw, Gordon L. *Keeping Mozart in Mind*. California: Academic Press, 2000.

Shaw, Gordon & Brothers, L. 'The Role of Accurate Timing in Human Performance'. In *Models of Brain Function*. ed. Cotterill. Cambridge University Press, 1990.

Sills, Helen. 'Some temporal implications of the patterning of Mozart and Stravinsky in the light of recent neurological research into spatial-temporal reasoning'. *Time: Perspectives at the Millennium*. ed. Marlene P. Soulsby and J.T. Fraser. Greenwood Publishing, 2001.

Sills, Peter. *Light in the Darkness*. Sacristy Press, 2020.

Smith, E.J. and White, J.D, eds. *Music and Man*. Gordon and Breach, 1976.

Smith, F. Joseph. *The Experiencing of Musical Sound*. Gordon and Breach, 1979.

Sokolov, Yuriy M. *Russian Folklore*. Folklore Associates, 1966.

Souvtchinsky, Pierre. 'La Notion du Temps et la Musique'. *La Revue Musicale*, Mai-Juin, 1939, 70–80 (310–320).

Souvtchinsky, Pierre. 'Igor Stravinsky'. *Contrepoints*, 1946/2. (February).

Souvtchinsky, Pierre. 'Sur la Genèse de la Musique Russe'. *Contrepoints*, 1949/6, 79–101.

Souvtchinsky, Pierre. 'Stravinsky au loin'. *Stravinsky, Etudes et Temoignages*. ed. F. Lesure, Paris: Lattès, 1982.

Stambaugh, Joan. 'Expressive Autonomy in Music'. In *Understanding the Musical Experience*, F. Joseph Smith. Gordon and Breach, 1989.

Stambaugh, Joan. 'Music as a Temporal Form'. *Journal of Philosophy*, April 1964.

Stein, Erwin, ed. *Arnold Schoenberg: Letters*. London: Faber and Faber, 1987.

Stein, Leonard. 'Schoenberg and Kleine Modernsky'. In *Confronting Stravinsky*. ed. Pasler, 1986.

Storr, Anthony. *Music and the Mind*. London: HarperCollins, 1993.

Stravinsky, Igor. 'Ce que j'ai voulu exprimer dans Le Sacre du Printemps'. In *Igor Stravinsky: Le Sacre du Printemps*, Dossier de Presse. ed. F. Lesure. Paris: Éditions Minkoff, 1980.

Stravinsky, Igor. *Poetics of Music*. trans. Arthur Knodel and Ingolf Dahl. London: Oxford University Press, 1947.

Stravinsky, Igor. 'An interview with Igor Stravinsky' ed. Robert Craft. *The National Broadcasting Company of America*, 1957.

Stravinsky, Igor. Interview in Mainichi Shimbun, April 8th, 1959. In programme notes for the Naxos recording of Histoire du Soldat/Renard: Robert Craft. Stravinsky Vol. 7. 2007.

Stravinsky, Igor. *An Autobiography*. London: Calder and Boyars, 1975.

Stravinsky in Conversation with Robert Craft. London: Pelican Books, 1962.

Stravinsky, Igor & Craft, Robert. *Themes and Episodes*. A.A. Knopf, 1966.

Stravinsky, Igor & Craft, Robert. *Dialogues and a Diary*. London, Faber and Faber, 1968.

Stravinsky, Igor & Craft, Robert. *Themes and Conclusions*. Faber and Faber, 1972.

Stravinsky, Igor & Craft, Robert. *Conversations with Igor Stravinsky*. London: Faber Music Ltd, 1979.

Stravinsky, Igor & Craft, Robert. *Expositions and Developments*. London: Faber Music Ltd., 1981.

Stravinsky, Igor & Craft, Robert. *Memories and Commentaries*. London: Faber Music Ltd., 1981.

Stravinsky, Igor & Craft, Robert. *Dialogues*. London: Faber Music Ltd., 1982.

Stravinsky, Theodor. *The Message of Igor Stravinsky*, trans. Robert Craft & André Marion. London: Boosey & Hawkes, 1953.

Stravinsky, Theodor. *Catherine and Igor Stravinsky: A Family Album*. London: Boosey & Hawkes, 1975.

Stravinsky, Vera & Craft, Robert. *Stravinsky in Pictures and Documents*. London: Hutchinson, 1979.

Swan, Alfred J. 'The Znamenny Chant of the Russian Church', Part I. The Musical Quarterly, 1940. XXVI/ 2 (April), 232.

Swan, Alfred J. 'The Znamenny Chant of the Russian Church', Part II. *The Musical Quarterly*, 1940. XXVI, 365.

Swan, Alfred J. 'The Nature of the Russian Folk song'. *The Musical Quarterly*, 1943. IV, (October).

Swan, Alfred J. *Russian Music and its Sources in Chant and Folksong*. London: John Baker, 1973.

Taruskin, Richard. 'Russian Folksong Melodies in The Rite of Spring'. *Journal of the American Musicological society*. 1980/ 33. (Fall).

Taruskin, Richard. 'Stravinsky's Rejoicing Discovery'. In Stravinsky Retrospectives, ed. Haimo & Johnson. University of Nebraska Press, 1987.

Taruskin, Richard. *Stravinsky and the Russian Traditions: a Biography of the works through Mavra*. University of California Press, 1996, vols 1 & 2.

The Cloud of Unknowing and Other Works, trans. Clifton Wolters. Penguin 1961, 1978.

Turner, Frederick & Pöppel, Ernst. 'The Neural Lyre: Poetic Metre, the Brain and Time'. *Poetry*, 1983, 142/5.

Turner, Victor W. *The Ritual Process*. Penguin Books, 1974.

Trehub, Sandra. 'Musical predispositions in infancy: an update'. In *The Cognitive Neuroscience of Music*. eds. Peretz & Zatorre. Oxford University Press, 2003. 3–20.

van den Toorn, Pieter C. *The Music of Igor Stravinsky*. Yale University Press, 1983.

van den Toorn, Pieter C. 'Octatonic Pitch Structure in Stravinsky'. In *Confronting Stravinsky* ed. Pasler. University of California Press, 1986.

Vanstone, William H. *The Stature of Waiting*. London: Darton, Longmann and Todd, 1983.

Vernadsky, N. 'The Russian Folksong'. *The Russian Review*, 1944. 3/2. 94–99.

von Rad, Gerhard. *Genesis*. London: SCM Press, 1981.

Vlad, Roman. *Stravinsky*. Oxford University Press, 1960.

Wachowski, Witold, ed. *A Laboratory of Spring*. Poland: Avant, 2013.

Walsh, Stephen. *Stravinsky: A Creative Spring, Vol. 1*. London: Pimlico edition, 2002.

Walsh, Stephen. *Stravinsky: The Second Exile, Vol. 2*. London: Pimlico edition, 2007.

Ware, Timothy. *The Orthodox Church*. London: Penguin Books, 1983.

Watkins, Glen. *Pyramids at the Louvre*. Belknap Press, Harvard University, 1994.

Weiser, Artur. *The Psalms*. London: SCM Press, 1979.

Westermann, Claus. *What does the Old Testament Say about God?* London: SPCK, 1979.

White, Eric W. *Stravinsky's Sacrifice to Apollo*. Hogarth Press, 1930.

White, Eric W. *Stravinsky: The Composer and his Works*. London: Faber and Faber, 1966.

White, Eric W. *Stravinsky: The Composer and his Works*. London: Faber and Faber, 1979.

White, Eric W. Stravinsky: Interview in Excelsior, 29 April and 1 May, 1934. In *Stravinsky: The Composer and his Works*, Appendix A, 581. University of California Press, 1985.

White, Pamela C. *Schoenberg and the God-Idea: Music and Text in the works of A. Schoenberg*. UMI Research Press, Michigan, 1983.

Whitrow, Gerald J. *What is Time?* Oxford University Press, 2003.

Writings from the Philokalia on Prayer of the Heart. trans. E. Kadbouvlosky & G.E.H. Palmer. London: Faber and Faber, 1951.

Zguta, Russell. *Russian Minstrels*. Oxford: Clarendon Press, 1978.

Zundel, Maurice. *The Splendour of the Liturgy*. London: Sheed and Ward, 1943.

Index